How To Prepare For College Board Achievement Tests

ENGLISH

Third Revised Edition

ENGLISH COMPOSITION TEST
with Essay/without Essay

LITERATURE TEST

by

Jerome Shostak

Former Supervisor of Guidance,
District 27, New York City

Barron's Educational Series, Inc., Woodbury, New York

© Copyright 1977 by Barron's Education Series, Inc.

Prior editions © Copyright 1974, 1969, 1964 by Barron's Educational Series, Inc.

All rights reserved.
No part of this book may be reproduced
in any form, by photostat, microfilm, xerography,
or any other means, or incorporated into any
information retrieval system, electronic or
mechanical, without the written permission
of the copyright owner.

All inquiries should be addressed to:
Barron's Educational Series, Inc.
113 Crossways Park Drive
Woodbury, New York 11797

Library of Congress Catalog Card No. 77-21378

International Standard Book No. 0-8120-0932-0

Library of Congress Cataloging in Publication Data
Shostak, Jerome.
   How to prepare for college board achievement tests,
English.
   1. English philology — Examinations, questions, etc.
2. English language — Idioms, corrections, errors.
I. Title.
PE1114.S55 1977   808'.042'076   77-21378
ISBN 0-8120-0932-0

PRINTED IN THE UNITED STATES OF AMERICA

7 8 9 10 11

CONTENTS

INTRODUCTION ... iv

THE ENGLISH COMPOSITION TEST

SECTION One: **Correctness and Effectiveness of Expression** ... 1

    What Is Being Measured ... 1
    Problems in Grammar and Usage ... 2
    Sentence Variety and Styling Problems ... 26
    Diction ... 29
    Problems in Proper Punctuation and Capitalization ... 54
    Spelling Check Tests ... 63
    Review Tests of Mastery ... 69

SECTION Two: **Practice Examinations for the English Composition Test** ... 81

    Typical Questions ... 82
    Ten Practice Examinations ... 84
    Answers to Practice Examinations with Analyses of Answers ... 127

SECTION Three: **Writing the Essay** ... 149

    A Closer Look ... 149
    Improving Prose Style and Organization ... 150
    Steps in Planning Your Essay ... 166
    Practice Essay Assignments ... 170

THE LITERATURE TEST

SECTION Four: **Improving Your Ability to Read Critically** ... 172

    The Nature of the Achievement Test in Literature ... 172
    Taste and Sensitivity in Poetry ... 173
    Terms of Literary Analysis ... 183

SECTION Five: **Practice Examinations in Literature** ... 196

    Ten Practice Examinations ... 196
    Answers to Practice Examinations ... 228

Introduction

THE COLLEGE ENTRANCE EXAMINATION BOARD provides standardized tests for admission to most colleges. Over 850 colleges require applicants to take the College Board's Scholastic Aptitude Test (SAT). About one-third of the colleges requiring the SAT also require two or three of its Achievement Tests.

Scholastic Aptitude Test and the Achievement Tests

The SAT is a three-hour examination designed to measure ability to do general college work. It consists of three sections, one evaluating verbal skills, another evaluating general number concepts; and the newest section, the Test of Standard Written English, evaluating basic grammar and usage skills.

The Achievement Tests are one-hour tests designed to evaluate a candidate's level of achievement in particular subjects. These tests are offered in 15 subjects. The results are used to help the colleges not only reach admission decisions but also decide which applicants can be exempted from courses covering material they already know, especially in English, mathematics, and foreign language.

The College Board provides two different Achievement Tests for measuring student ability in the general field of English. One of the examinations is the English Composition Test. The other is the Literature Test.

The English Composition Test consists of two forms. The form for December includes 40 minutes of multiple-choice questions and a 20-minute essay question. The forms for January and May contain 1 hour of multiple-choice questions only.

Which Test Should You Take?

Usually the colleges make the decision about whether a candidate should take the SAT or not. However, the situation with the Achievement Tests is much more complex. Some admissions offices stipulate the specific test or tests that must be taken.

Some, for example, may require the English Composition Test With Essay; some may require the English Composition Test, without the essay, or the Literature Test only or in combination with one of the forms of the English Composition Test. Still others leave it to the applicant as to which Achievement Tests to take. The last option only requires that the student take a definite number of achievement examinations.

If the college leaves the choice to you, then the material that follows will prove invaluable in helping you decide whether you will take the English Composition With Essay or without the Essay, or the Literature Test. By taking the practice examinations in the book, you will be able to determine what the areas include and assess your strengths in each.

If You Are Taking the ENGLISH COMPOSITION TEST

To register for this test, pick up a registration form and *Student Bulletin* in the college office of your school or write to

College Entrance Examination Board
Box 592
Princeton, New Jersey 08540

or

Box 1025
Berkeley, California 94701

The English Composition Test is given on the College Board test dates in December, January, and May. It measures two major aspects of writing ability:

correctness and effectiveness of expression
taste and sensitivity in the use of language.

Determine which form of the English Composition Test you are going to take. The English Composition Test in December includes an essay topic for you to write on. The tests for January and May consist of multiple-choice questions only.

English Composition Test With Essay

This is a one-hour test with an additional fifteen minutes for initial instruction. The December form has 40 minutes of multiple-choice questions and one essay question requiring 20 minutes.

INTRODUCTION

English Composition Test — Without Essay

The January and May forms are one-hour tests with an additional fifteen minutes for initial instruction. They contain three sections of multiple-choice questions.

How This Book Can Help You

How to Prepare for College Board Achievement Tests in English contains a review of the background information upon which your skill in Standard Written English must be based. Once you have this material under control, then you should try the ten practice examinations that follow. These practice examinations will enable you to evaluate the extent of your knowledge and ability; they will familiarize you with the techniques that will lead to your doing your best on the coming examination.

If you are planning to take the form that includes the writing of an essay, the review and practice assignments will help you to sharpen your skill in writing themes in a brief period of time.

If You Are Taking the LITERATURE TEST

To register for this test, pick up a registration form and *Student Bulletin* in the college office of your school or write to:

College Entrance Examination Board
Box 592
Princeton, New Jersey 08540

or

Box 1025
Berkeley, California 94701

The Literature Test is given on the test dates in December, January, and May—the same ones on which the English Composition Test is given.

The Literature Test is a one-hour examination with an additional fifteen minutes for initial instructions. It attempts to measure how well you can read and interpret literary material. The test consists of questions based on several reading passages selected from English and American literature; the selections may be either prose or poetry. The questions may be on content or on elements of form and style.

How This Book Can Help You

Of course, there is no published reading list that can prepare you for this test. However, *How to Prepare for College Board Tests in English* contains descriptions of the basic literary forms, the stylistic terms and concepts, and the tools of poetry that you need to critically analyze literature. Mastery exercises will sharpen your control of this basic information and help you develop the ability to apply it to your reading. The Practice Tests that follow will familiarize you with the techniques that help you do your best on the examination. They will give you essential control over types of questions; they will familiarize you with the types of passages that lend themselves to such testing.

The basic purpose is to help you do your best on the Achievement Tests in English. Since the emphasis, question-types, and techniques stressed are so different, none of the sections are valid preparation for the Verbal part of the SAT. For specific preparation for the Scholastic Aptitude Test, you should find *Barron's How To Prepare for College Entrance Examinations (SAT)* most useful.

The English Composition Test

Section ONE : Correctness and Effectiveness of Expression

1. What Is Being Measured

2. Problems in Grammar and Usage

3. Sentence Variety and Style Problems

4. Diction

5. Problems in Proper Punctuation and Capitalization

6. Spelling Check Tests

7. Review Tests of Mastery

1. What is Being Measured

The English Composition Test does not measure writing ability directly. The most valid test in this area would require the actual writing of themes, essays, reports, narratives, and so forth. However, there is no way in which the written material could be so rated that the results could be compared objectively with those achieved by other candidates. To obtain objective results, the items in the College Entrance Examination Board's English Composition Test were developed as indirect methods of measurement. Studies have shown that the scores achieved on this test correlate very highly with the ability to write clearly and forcefully—as shown in subsequent college work.

The items on the English Composition Test stress the mechanics of writing ranging from the simpler to the more subtle. The recognition of errors and the ability to eradicate them are emphasized much more than control of literary forms or creative and imaginative approaches.

The English Composition Test evaluates ability in one of the dialects of the language—Standard Written English. This is the language system of oral and written communication used on the college level. The test is a measurement of potential college success. College success depends heavily upon the student's ability to function in an atmosphere almost wholly dominated by Standard Written English; however, there is no underlying assumption of superiority of one dialect over another.

In the College Board publications, the terms *correct* and *incorrect* are used interchangeably with *acceptable* and *not acceptable*, respectively, when referring to specific forms in usage, diction, and spelling. Thus, items labeled here as acceptable in current Standard Written English may be labeled as either *acceptable* or *correct* in directions and in test items on the exam.

FORMAT OF THE TEST

The question format is similar to that found on the verbal portion of the SAT, given in the morning. To answer each of the multiple-choice questions, you will be required to blacken a rectangle on your scoring sheet.

The test consists of three groups of multiple-choice questions. These will test your ability to express ideas in correct Standard Written English, to recognize the most effective expression, to use language with awareness of appropriateness of tone, and to avoid confusion in meaning.

The items on the test deal with problems in grammatical relationships, current usage, diction, English idioms, sentence construction, modern punctuation, word discrimination, clichés, comparisons, and style.

HOW TO MAKE THE BEST USE OF YOUR STUDY TIME: STEPS TO A HIGH SCORE

1. Take the first Practice Examination on page 84 to discover how you react to typical questions. Assess your strengths and weaknesses and plan a schedule for using the review digests in this section.

2. Study the digest approach to the testing material. Scan through each group in each section and check the items that you have to review. Do not spend time in going over items you have already mastered. Space your learning. Frequent short study sessions are more productive than long cram sessions; the more frequent the periods of learning, the greater your mastery.

3. After your study sessions, take another Practice Examination. Simulate the actual examination in time and privacy and evaluate your progress and discover the areas needing additional review. Gain confidence by familiarizing yourself with the style and question types to be found on the exam. Improve your speed and control through continued practice with examination-type questions. Compare your level of achievement on the Practice Examinations with that of other candidates.

2. Problems in Grammar and Usage

In Standard Written English, the range of what is considered unacceptable runs the gamut from those that would be inexcusable when committed by a high school freshman to those that involve subtleties of style and tone. You must know how to recognize unacceptable forms and how to correct them.

How Much Grammar? Grammar is the systematic description of how a language works. Usage is concerned with alternative choices—the differences between standard and nonstandard expressions. You are not required to know the grammatical reason why a form is unacceptable nor will you be required to correct it. At the most you may be required to indicate whether the error is one of tone, of grammatical usage or of word usage (diction); common sense will usually help you to classify unacceptable expressions into one of these general areas.

However, returning to the initial question, how much grammar should you know? Of course, if you can explain the error in grammatical terms, you will have a definite advantage over the one who knows no grammar. You will be able to generalize the error and be able to spot it much more quickly. Therefore, if you can understand the grammatical reasons, take the few extra minutes and gain this advantageous mastery.

If you and grammar are separated by miles of misunderstanding and fear-filled uneasiness, then you would be wasting too much time trying to master the approach outlined above. If you and grammar are not on friendly terms, then you must learn to identify the error by being able to associate it with one of the examples that follow. Study the explanations. They are, in the main, not grammatical in form. Memorize the name of the error, the example and the correct form. This method will not give you as firm a mastery of grammatical abusage, but it will enable you to function more than satisfactorily on these examinations and in college writing assignments.

NOTE: In College Board publications, the terms *correct* and *incorrect* are used interchangeably with *acceptable* and *not acceptable*, respectively, when referring to specific forms in usage, diction, and spelling. Thus, items labeled here as acceptable in current Standard Written English may be labeled as either *acceptable* or *correct* in directions and in test items of the English Composition Test; items labeled here as *not acceptable* may be identified as either *not acceptable* or *incorrect* in the explanatory material and directions of the English Composition Test.

CORRECTNESS AND EFFECTIVENESS OF EXPRESSION

THE MOST FREQUENT AND THE COSTLIEST ERRORS

The errors in this group are considered the most serious ones that can be made by college students. Of course, there are errors labeled as illiterate that are just as serious on the high school level. However, by the time a student reaches his senior year in high school or the freshman year in college, he has eliminated *ain't, ain't got no, he don't, haven't no*. Not that all people have eliminated these errors, but all who plan to enter college or plan to pursue their education successfully into the senior year in high school have learned to avoid such errors. Therefore, in this section we are concentrating on those errors that would label college themes as failing regardless of the level of their content.

The Run-on Sentence

DEFINITION: A *run-on sentence is one in which two or more sentences are punctuated as though they were one.*

Typical Examples

1. Those caused by the use of a comma in place of a period (These are sometimes called *comma-splice* or *comma sentences*.)

The error was unavoidable, it just could not be prevented at that time.

EXPLANATION: This unit consists of two complete ideas. They could have been separated by a period. A comma cannot be used to separate two complete ideas. A comma cannot take the place of a period.

METHODS OF CORRECTION: There are three basic methods of correction:

Add a coordinating conjunction (*and, but, or, for, nor, and so*)

The error was unavoidable, *and* it could not be prevented at that time.

Divide into two sentences, using period and capital letter

The error was unavoidable. It could not be prevented at that time

Subordinate one of the ideas, using one of the subordinating conjunctions (*after, although, because, if, since, unless, until, when, while, as if, where, whereas, though, so that*)

The error was unavoidable *because* it could not be prevented at that time.

NOTE: There is a fourth possible way of combining two complete ideas. This method involves the use of a semicolon. This method must not be overused. It is appropriate when the two ideas are very close to each other.

The room was filled with smoke; I could hardly breathe.

2. Those caused by conjunctive adverbs

Harold had lost his temper, nevertheless he was held responsible for his subsequent actions.

EXPLANATION: This unit consists of two complete ideas. Such ideas may be joined together by coordinating conjunction *and, but, or, for, nor*. (Some authorities will include *so*, and *yet* in this group. However, for this examination, it is better to avoid *so* as a conjunction and to consider *yet* as a conjunctive adverb.) Conjunctive adverbs do *not* have the privilege of being able to join two ideas together when they are preceded by a comma. The following conjunctive adverbs cannot do the work of a coordinating conjunction:

nevertheless hence also besides therefore then otherwise moreover consequently however meanwhile on the other hand in the meantime in fact accordingly indeed

METHODS OF CORRECTION:

Sentences containing conjunctive adverbs may be treated correctly in the following manner:

Add a conjunction:	Harold lost his temper, but nevertheless he....
Use semicolon:	Harold lost his temper; nevertheless, he....
Divide into two sentences:	Harold lost his temper. Nevertheless, he....
Subordinate one of the ideas:	Since Harold had lost his temper, he was held....

3. Those caused by close ideas that are treated as one

Paul had one last desperate hope he could reach safety if his numbed mind could recall the combination of the safety factor.

EXPLANATION: Although these ideas flow into each other, only one of the three basic ideas has been subordinated. The one beginning with *if* has been treated correctly. The first two ideas, however, have been run-together without a grammatical connection. *Paul had one last desperate hope* is one complete idea. *He could reach safety* is a second complete idea.

METHODS OF CORRECTION:

Separate with a period:	Paul had one last desperate hope. He could....
Join with a conjunction:	Paul had one last desperate hope, and he could....
Subordinate one of the ideas:	Paul had one last desperate hope that he could....
Use the semicolon:	Paul had one last desperate hope; he could....
Use semicolon and conjunctive adverb:	Paul had one last desperate hope; in fact, he could reach safety....

The Sentence Fragment

DEFINITION: A *sentence fragment is a portion of a sentence treated as though it were complete.*

In practice, since the sentence fragment is a portion of a sentence, in order to correct this error, all that we have to do, in most cases, is not to add additional material, but to change the punctuation. The sentence fragment should be joined to the group of ideas from which it has been incorrectly separated. In each of the following examples, the italicized sentence is the sentence fragment. The method of correction is to join it to the preceding or following sentence to which it grammatically belongs.

Typical Examples

(In each of the following examples, the italicized sentence is the sentence fragment.)

1. Dependent clauses treated as independent

Adverb Clauses: The conditions are the same. *Although he thinks they have improved.*
If you listen to him. His arguments begin to seem logical.
The entire performance took on a vital liveliness. *Because Philip suddenly awakened to the requirements of his role.*

Relative Clause: Milton is the man. *Who claims to know the solution.*

ACCEPTED FORM:
The conditions are the same *although he thinks they have improved.*
If you listen to him, his arguments begin to seem logical.
The entire performance took on a vital liveliness *because Philip suddenly awakened to the requirements of his role.*
Milton is the man *who claims to know the solution.*

2. Verbal phrases treated as independent ideas

Infinitive: There was one thing he wanted above all. *To clear his name of this stigma.*
Participle: *Coming to the end of the road.* The old man sat down to rest.
Gerund: We intensified our understanding of the island culture. *By our learning much of its folklore.*

ACCEPTED FORM:
There was one thing he wanted above all, *to clear his name of this stigma.*
Coming to the end of the road, the old man sat down to rest.
We intensified our understanding of the island culture *by our learning much of its folklore.*

3. Prepositional phrases

They placed the formula in the safe. *On the morning of the third day.*
From every nook and cranny of the old house. Came groans and shrieks of despair.

ACCEPTED FORM:
They placed the formula in the safe *on the morning of the third day.*
From every nook and cranny of the old house came groans and shrieks of despair.

4. Appositives

I was proud to be introduced to Ben Edwards. *The champion chess player.*
There are certain things that I consider most necessary for successful living. *Such as adequate income, satisfying goals, and social approval.*

ACCEPTED FORM:
I was proud to be introduced to Ben Edwards, *the champion chess player.*
There are certain things that I consider most necessary for successful living—*such as, adequate income . . .*

5. Coordinating Conjunctions

We tried every combination that came to our minds. *But we were unable to stumble on the correct one.*

EXPLANATION: The coordinating conjunctions, *and, but, or* logically *join* ideas; they do not separate ideas. Therefore, they should not be used to begin sentences—as a rule. However, many modern writers use them to introduce sentences when an unusual effect is desired. For examination purposes, such sentences are to be considered errors and are to be avoided.

ACCEPTED FORM:
We tried every combination that came to our minds, *but we were . . .*

Principal Parts of Verbs

The different forms of the verb are all derived from its principal parts. By knowing the principal parts, you can avoid some of the most costly errors, the ones that are usually labeled as *illiterate.*

Example: He had (chose, chosen) the latter.
EXPLANATION: Since there is an auxiliary verb (had) already present, the past participle must be used.
ACCEPTED FORM: He *had chosen* the latter.

Example: Yesterday I (drank, drunk) three glasses of well water.
EXPLANATION: Since there is no auxiliary verb present, the simple past tense is required.
ACCEPTED FORM: Yesterday I *drank* three glasses of well water.

Study the following list of troublesome verbs. Do not spend time on those that give you no trouble. Memorize the principle parts of those that you are not certain.

Principal Parts of 53 Troublesome Verbs

PRESENT (Now I . . .)	PRESENT PARTICIPLE	PAST (Yesterday I . . .)	PAST PARTICIPLE (I have, or I had . . .)
arise	arising	arose	arisen
awake	awaking	awoke (awaked)	awoke (awaked)
bear	bearing	bore	borne
beat	beating	beat	beaten (or beat)
bid	bidding	bade	bidden
bid (at cards)	bid	bid	bid
bind	binding	bound	bound
bite	biting	bit	bitten
break	breaking	broke	broken
choose	choosing	chose	chosen
cling	clinging	clung	clung
drink	drinking	drank	drunk
drive	driving	drove	driven
eat	eating	ate	eaten
fall	falling	fell	fallen
fight	fighting	fought	fought
fly	flying	flew	flown
forbid	forbidding	forbade	forbidden
forget	forgetting	forgot	forgotten
freeze	freezing	froze	frozen
get	getting	got	gotten
go	going	went	gone
grow	growing	grew	grown
hang	hanging	hung	hung
hang (execute)	hanging	hanged	hanged
hide	hiding	hid	hidden
know	knowing	knew	known
lay	laying	laid	laid
lie	lying	lay	lain
ring	ringing	rang	rung
see	seeing	saw	seen
shoot	shooting	shot	shot
shrink	shrinking	shrank (or shrunk)	shrunk
sing	singing	sang	sung
sit	sitting	sat	sat
slay	slaying	slew	slain
slide	sliding	slid	slid
spin	spinning	spun	spun
spring	springing	sprang	sprung
steal	stealing	stole	stolen
sting	stinging	stung	stung
stride	striding	strode	stridden
strive	striving	strode	striven
swear	swearing	swore	sworn
swim	swimming	swam	swum
swing	swinging	swung	swung
take	taking	took	taken
tear	tearing	tore	torn
throw	throwing	threw	thrown
wake	waking	woke (or waked)	waked (woke or woken)
wear	wearing	wore	worn
wring	wringing	wrung	wrung
write	writing	wrote	written

Confusion of Adjectives and Adverbs

1. Similarity in Forms

Example: Drive (slow, slowly).

EXPLANATION: There are several older words in the language that have the same form for both the adjective and the adverb. Among these are

well far late early fast just right hard deep slow

Some of the adverbs have two parallel forms that convey exactly the same meaning. Among these are *slow-slowly, deep-deeply, quick-quickly.* Therefore you can say, "Go quick" or "Go quickly." In the example above, both forms are correct!

ACCEPTED FORM: Drive slow.
or
Drive slowly.

2. Good, well

Example: Ever since her operation, she has not felt (good, well).

EXPLANATION: When *well* refers to health, it is an adjective. Otherwise, it is used as the adverb form. Since in the example, health is implied, the correct form is not the adjective form *good*, but the adjective form *well*.

ACCEPTED FORM: Ever since her operation, she has not felt *well*.

Example: The driver operates that machine (good, well).

EXPLANATION: The adjective form is *good*. The adverb form is always *well*. Since in this case what is being described is *how* the machine ran rather than the driver, we need the adverb to modify the verb *operates*.

ACCEPTED FORM: The driver operates the machine *well*.

Example: The cake tastes (good, well).

EXPLANATION: The verbs *seem, appear, look, smell, taste* and *feel* can be used as linking verbs, verbs that do not describe the action of the subject, but act as equal signs. In the example, the cake is not tasting. The cake = (good, well). What is being described is the cake, not the tasting. Therefore we need an adjective to modify cake (as a predicate adjective) and not an adverb to modify the verb.

ACCEPTED FORM: The cake tastes good.

ACCEPTED FORM: The *patient* appeared *quieter* today.

ACCEPTED FORM: The police *appeared quietly* on the scene.

ACCEPTED FORM: The experimenter *smelled* the solution very *carefully*.

ACCEPTED FORM: The *flowers* smelled *sweet* to the ailing child.

TEST OF MASTERY

Each of the following units contains two apparent sentences. If there are no errors in either unit, then write C in the space provided to the left. If there is an error, then write the necessary changes in the space to the left.

Example:

,we   1. If you ever go there. we should like to accompany you.

. . . . 1. The situation was hopeless Henry would have to admit defeat. There was nothing else he could do.

. . . . 2. Although the day seemed endless. When I finally became interested in what I was doing, the situation became more bearable.

. . . . 3. The waiter was well trained; he was completely unobtrusive. We were scarcely aware of his presence.

. . . . 4. I don't know how well he can sew on that machine, you will just have to let him try.

. . . . 5. It was so good of you to come. Before any of the others so that you could help in the arrangements.

. . . . 6. Let me know the answer. I have to know whether the lake has really froze over.

. . . . 7. This cake tastes deliciously. What recipe did you use for it?

. . . . 8. Go slow. Especially when you travel over the ice slick.

. . . . 9. The horse seems gentle enough, however I still refuse to take a chance.

. . . . 10. Because of this, I felt I had born the burden long enough. Someone else could now carry it for a while.

. . . . 11. I was driven to a startling realization. Phil had growed so tall during the last few months!

. . . . 12. When it was all over, we realized that another and more serious problem had arose. We had bid more for the vase than it was worth.

. . . . 13. I haven't felt so good in months; nevertheless, I shall continue to take the pills until the doctor tells me to discontinue.

. . . . 14. The well-disciplined students walked quietly to the nearest exits; there was no evidence of panic in their actions.

. . . . 15. The old car was running as smooth as ever. Our fears of mechanical failure had been laid to rest.

. . . . 16. Our friends sprung to our assistance; each one quickly came to our defense.

. . . . 17. Therefore we drank the last of the water, they even seemed happy to have us do so.

. . . . 18. Delve deep into this or not at all. So that we clear his good name now or never.

. . . . 19. The group had gotten beyond my control, nevertheless I was much too proud to call for help.

. . . . 20. He has clung to one hope all these months. Helen could have forgot to write as she had promised.

. . . . 21. You should have seen him! That style had went out with Noah's flood.

. . . . 22. He tried his best and strove to train us properly. Our ingratitude, therefore, had not sprang from anything that he had caused.

. . . . 23. This dress must be worn proper or not at all. Unless you follow directions, we shall not take it from the closet where it has hung all these months.

. . . . 24. This hot chocolate tastes too sweetly. I could have sworn that he put three spoonfuls of sugar into it.

. . . . 25. The bolt had slid silent into the lock. Otherwise, we would have heard the trap being sprung, and we would not have been caught so easily.

. . . . 26. That angry mob in a crescendo of fury and violence finally hanged Ben Edwards. The poor farmhand accused of setting the barn on fire.

. . . . 27. I could never have stridden across the stage with the self-assurance he possessed at that moment. However much I tried.

. . . . 28. Because he had forbad us sternly to disobey their bidding, we could not have chosen any other path of resistance.

. . . . 29. Our big guns swung quickly into action, the entire island quivered under the impact of their fury.

. . . . 30. The police looked thoroughly into every one of his statements. Hoping to prove that he had lied to avoid suspicion.

. . . . 31. I have swam in that pool every day this summer; in fact, I had even helped to build it.

. . . . 32. When Charlie Chan pointed to the butler and accused him of being the killer, I was not the least bit surprised. I knewed it all the time.

. . . . 33. Far from the turmoil and strife that are basic to city life. Allan settled in the small valley and found quiet and peace.

. . . . 34. That jacket looks good on you, I would not return it.

. . . . 35. We struggled late into the night; the solution seemed further away than ever. When suddenly Edna shrieked and shouted that she had the answer.

CORRECTNESS AND EFFECTIVENESS OF EXPRESSION

ANSWER KEY: TEST OF MASTERY

1. . Henry
2. , when
3. Correct
4. . You
5. before
6. frozen
7. delicious
8. , especially
9. . However,
   (; however,)
10. borne
11. grown
12. arisen
13. well
14. Correct
15. smoothly
16. sprang
17. . They
18. , so
19. . Nevertheless
    (; nevertheless,)
20. forgotten
21. gone
22. sprung
23. properly
24. sweet
25. silently
26. , the
27. , however
28. forbidden
29. . The
30. , hoping
31. swum
32. knew
    (had known)
33. , Allan
34. you;
35. , when

ADDITIONAL PROBLEMS FOUND FREQUENTLY ON EXAMINATIONS

Space your study of the following errors in grammatical usage. Discover quickly the ones that you have already mastered. Do not waste your time in drilling yourself on these. Concentrate your efforts on finding out just which ones cause you loss of credit. Review this group until you have them under complete control.

Agreement of Subject and Verb

DEFINITION: *If the subject is singular, the verb that follows must be singular. If the subject is plural, then the verb that follows must be plural.*

The difficulty that faces the students lies not in the statement of the rule, but in familiarizing themselves with the following constructions that offer problems.

1. Intervening elements: When a singular subject is separated from its verb by an intervening clause or phrase, the student often tends to make the verb agree with the nearest noun even though it is not the subject of the sentence.

Example: Margery, as well as her three friends, (was, were) invited to try out for the part of Helen in the varsity play.

EXPLANATION: The subject of the sentence is Margery. When the subject is followed by a group of words introduced by *with, together with, as well as* these words are not part of the subject. Therefore, *friends* is not the subject.

ACCEPTED FORM: *Margery*, as well as her three friends, *was* invited to try out for the part of Helen in the varsity play.

Example: A basket of apples (is are) in the car for you.

EXPLANATION: The subject of the sentence is *basket*. When the subject is followed by a group of words introduced by a preposition, this group is called a prepositional phrase and it modifies the subject. Therefore *apples* cannot be the subject.

ACCEPTED FORM: A *basket* of apples *is* in the car for you.

Example: A group of soldiers (has have) been detailed to guard the munitions dump.

EXPLANATION: The subject is *group*. Since it is *one* group (*a* group), *group* is singular.

ACCEPTED FORM: A *group* of soldiers *has* been detailed to guard the. . . .

Example: A set of four thousand books (lies, lie) on the shelves, waiting for you to catalogue them.

EXPLANATION: It is not *books* that is waiting but *a set*. Since *set* is singular, the verb form must be singular.

ACCEPTED FORM: A *set* of books *lies* on the shelves. . . .

2. Indefinite pronouns: Although the sentence may seem to carry a plural sense when certain indefinite pronouns are used, the reader must know which of these pronouns are singular and have them followed by singular verbs.

Example: Every one of the four thousand pens (doesn't, don't) work. Everybody (know, knows) that.

EXPLANATION: When *body* and *one* are compounded (*somebody, anybody, nobody, everybody, someone, anyone,* and *everyone*) they are still singular and should be followed by a singular verb. *Either, neither,* and *each* are also singular.

ACCEPTED FORM: *Every one* of the four thousand pens *doesn't* work. Everybody *knows* that.

Example: Some of the men (was, were) ready to leave before noon.

EXPLANATION: Since *some, few, several* are plural in form, they should be followed by plural verbs.

ACCEPTED FORM: *Some* of the men *were* ready to leave before noon.

3. Compound subjects: When *and* is used, the rule is simple.

Example: Edna and Bea (is, are) waiting in the anteroom for the doctor.

EXPLANATION: When *and* joins the elements of the subject, the subject is plural, and the verb must be plural.

ACCEPTED FORM: *Edna and Bea are* waiting in the anteroom for the doctor.

Example: Neither Henry nor his brothers (was were) present at the meeting.

EXPLANATION: When a compound subject is connected by the correlative conjunctions (*neither . . . nor, either . . . or, not only . . . but also*), the verb is determined by the subject word closest to it. If that word is plural, then the verb must be plural; if that word is singular, then the verb must be singular.

ACCEPTED FORM: Neither Henry nor his brothers were present at the meeting.

Example: Either Paula or I (is, am, are) scheduled to lead the discussion.

EXPLANATION: Since the last subject word is *I*, the verb must agree with *I*.

ACCEPTED FORM: Either Paula or I am scheduled to lead the discussion.

4. After relative pronoun: In ordinary cases, there is very little difficulty in discovering which is the correct form to follow a relative pronoun.

Example: Tom is the one who (was, were) to judge the contest.

EXPLANATION: The antecedent of *who* is *one*. Since *one* is singular, the verb form must be singular.

ACCEPTED FORM: *Tom is the one who was* to judge the contest.

Example: It is I who (is, are, am) to make the final decision.

EXPLANATION: Since *I* is the antecedent of *who*, the form that follows *who* must be the form that would follow *I*.

ACCEPTED FORM: *It is I who am* to make the final decision.

Example: I saw him pass the note to one of the men who (has, have) been standing outside the windows.

EXPLANATION: The antecedent of *who* is *men* (the noun closest to it). Therefore the verb must agree with *men*, a plural noun.

ACCEPTED FORM: I saw him pass the note to one of the *men who have* been standing outside the windows.

5. After *there* and *here*: When *there* and, much less frequently, *here* are used to introduce sentences, the subject word *follows* the verb rather than *precedes* it.

Example: There (is, are) several plausible explanations for this phenomenon.

EXPLANATION: The subject is *explanations*, a plural noun, and therefore the verb must be plural.

ACCEPTED FORM: There *are* several plausible *explanations* for this phenomenon.

Example: Here (lie, lies) the heroes fallen in the defense of their country.

EXPLANATION: The subject is *heroes*, plural in form; the verb must be plural.

ACCEPTED FORM: Here *lie* the *heroes* fallen in the defense of their country.

6. Compound subjects as a unit: The elements of a compound subject lose their individuality when they become a single entity in the mind of the speaker.

Example: Ham and eggs (is, are) my favorite cold weather breakfast.

EXPLANATION: Since *ham and eggs* is treated as a unit the verb should be singular.

ACCEPTED FORM: *Ham and eggs is* my favorite cold weather breakfast.

Example: Ham and eggs (is, are) the ingredients of an American meal.

EXPLANATION: Here each of the parts of the compound subject is being treated separately, and therefore the compound subject requires a plural verb.

ACCEPTED FORM: *Ham and eggs are* the ingredients of an American meal.

Example: Twenty dollars (was, were) too much to pay for that article.

EXPLANATION: The sum of money is a unit; therefore, the verb should be singular.

ACCEPTED FORM: *Twenty dollars was* too much to pay for that article.

NOTE: Even collective nouns like *group, army, set, jury*, etc. are affected by the meaning in the mind of the user. Normally these words govern a singular verb, but when the speaker or writer is considering the individuals of the group as separate entities, the verb should be plural.

Example: The jury (is, are) unable to agree on the amount of the settlement.

EXPLANATION: The members of the jury cannot agree. More than one person must be involved in such an action; the speaker actually means the individual members. Therefore, the verb should be plural.

ACCEPTED FORM: The jury are unable to agree on the amount of the settlement.

7. Nouns plural in form, singular in meaning

Example: Measles (is, are) dangerous when contacted by adults.

EXPLANATION: Nouns like *billiards, mumps, news, economics, mathematics, civics, molasses, tactics, statistics, physics, comics, aeronautics* while they end in *s* are singular in meaning.

ACCEPTED FORM: Measles is dangerous when contracted by adults.

8. With fractions and percentages

Example: Seven percent of the dollar bills (is, are) badly frayed.

EXPLANATION: Since individual items (*dollar bills*) are being represented, the verb should be plural. If the noun following *of* is plural, the verb is plural.
ACCEPTED FORM: Seven percent of the dollar bills *are* badly frayed.

Example: Three-fourths of the dam (is, are) gone!
EXPLANATION: Since only *one* dam is involved, the verb should be singular. If the noun following *of* is singular (*dam*), the verb is singular.
ACCEPTED FORM: Three-fourths of the dam *is* gone!

9. Commonly mistaken plurals
Example: No thanks (is, are) due to you for this!
EXPLANATION: The following group of nouns while plural in form and requiring a plural form of the verb are often mistaken as singular

ashes   clothes   goods   links   nuptials   oats
pliers proceeds remains riches spectacles
suds   thongs   victuals vitals wages

Therefore, in the example above the plural form of the verb should be used.
ACCEPTED FORM: No thanks *are* due to you for this!
NOT ACCEPTED: The wages of sin *is* death!
ACCEPTED FORM: The wages of sin *are* death!

10. Double subject
Example: (Paul and I, we) (Paul and I) will attend the lecture.
EXPLANATION: *Paul and I* form the subject. The word *we* is completely unnecessary and the addition of a second subject is an error.
ACCEPTED FORM: Paul and I will attend the lecture.
NOT ACCEPTED: The Puerto Ricans, they are citizens of the United States.
ACCEPTED FORM: The *Puerto Ricans are* citizens of the United States.
NOT ACCEPTED: The radio, it is not playing well tonight.
ACCEPTED FORM: The *radio is not* playing well tonight.

11. Subjects joined by *or*
Example: Paul or you (has, have) the right to choose the route.
EXPLANATION: When the conjunction joining a compound subject is *or*, the noun or pronoun *after* the *or* determines the form of the verb. Since *you* is after the *or*, the *form* of the verb must be second person.
ACCEPTED FORM: Paul or *you have* the right to choose the route.
NOT ACCEPTED: Henry or I *are* mentioned in the dispatch.
ACCEPTED FORM: Henry or *I am* mentioned in the dispatch.

12. *All, none, any, some* as pronouns
Example: (Is, Are) any of the money still in the desk drawer?
EXPLANATION: The pronouns *all, any, none, some* may be singular or plural depending upon their meaning in the sentence. In the example, any refers to a single quantity (*money*) and therefore *any* is singular.
ACCEPTED FORM: *Is any of the money* still in the desk drawer?
Example: (Is, Are) any of the teachers still in the building?
EXPLANATION: In this example, *any* refers to individual units, and therefore it is plural in nature.
ACCEPTED FORM: Are any of the teachers still in the building?
NOT ACCEPTED: All that is left *are* one piece of crumb cake.
ACCEPTED FORM: All that is left *is* one piece of crumb cake.
NOT ACCEPTED: All of the books *has* now been returned.
ACCEPTED FORM: All of the books *have* now been returned.

13. Subjects and predicate nominatives
Example: The major obstacle (is, are) pedestrians crossing at other than intersections.
EXPLANATION: The verb agrees with the subject (*obstacle*) and not with the noun (*pedestrians*) used as predicate nominative.
ACCEPTED FORM: The major *obstacle is* pedestrians crossing at other than intersections.
ACCEPTED FORM: *Pedestrians are* the major obstacle. . . .

14. Title
Example: My Most Interesting Cases (is, are) compulsory reading for all would-be surgeons.
EXPLANATION: The title of a book is treated as a singular subject even when the title contains a plural idea.
ACCEPTED FORM: *My Most Interesting Cases is* compulsory reading for all would-be surgeons.

Agreement of Pronoun and Its Antecedent

DEFINITION: *A pronoun is a word that refers to a noun or another pronoun. The pronoun must agree with that noun or pronoun (its antecedent) in both person and number. A singular noun demands a singular pronoun. A plural noun requires a plural pronoun (number). A masculine noun is the antecedent of a masculine pronoun, and a feminine noun must be followed by a feminine pronoun (person).*

The problems usually arise with having to choose *them* or *him, her; their* or *his, here, its; they* or *he,* or *she*.

1. With indefinite pronouns: The error most frequently involves the indefinite pronouns—*each, everyone, everybody, someone, nobody, anyone, anybody, either, neither.*

Example: Each of the actors made (his, their) entrance on time.

EXPLANATION: Since *each* is singular, and since the pronoun *his-their* must refer back to *each* and not to *actors* which is not the subject, the singular possessive pronoun *his* must be used.

ACCEPTED FORM: *Each* of the actors made *his* entrance on time.

Example: Everyone in the group should be given an opportunity to state (his, their) views in this matter.

EXPLANATION: Since the subject is *everyone* and *everyone* is singular, the pronoun referring to it should be singular.

ACCEPTED FORM: *Everyone* in the group should be given an opportunity to state *his* views on this matter.

Example: I thought any one could have taken it for (himself, themselves).

EXPLANATION: Since *anyone* is singular, the pronoun referring to it must be singular.

ACCEPTED FORM: I thought *anyone* could have taken it for *himself*.

2. Mixed gender: Many speakers allow themselves to become involved in an awkward sentence pattern when they attempt to refer to both men and women in a previously mentioned group.

Example: Every student in this audience must do (his, their, his or her) own homework each day.

EXPLANATION: Even though the speaker is referring to a mixed group, when such a group is involved, the speaker should use the masculine singular form to refer to both.

ACCEPTED FORM: *Every student* in the audience must do *his* own homework each day.

3. Pronouns used impersonally: When *you, one* and sometimes *he* are used impersonally, they must be followed by their corresponding pronouns.

Example: One must never jump to conclusions hastily. (One, You) must train (one's self yourself) to see the complete problem before reaching a decision.

EXPLANATION: Since the speaker had begun with *one*, he should not have changed to the *you* form. You must be consistent. If you begin with *you*, then the forms of *you* must be continued. If you begin with *one*, then the forms of *one* must be continued. Usage allows *his, him* to follow *one*, but not *you*.

ACCEPTED FORM: *One* must never jump to conclusions hastily. *One* must train *one's self* to see the complete problem before reaching a decision.

or

You must never jump to conclusions hastily. *You* must train *yourself* to see the complete problem before reaching a decision.

The Case of Pronouns

DEFINITION: *The troublesome pronouns are the ones that change their forms, depending upon their use in the sentence. If the pronoun is the subject of the verb or is used as an appositive to the subject, or as a predicate nominative, then it is in the subjective case.*

Subjective Case: *I, he, she, we, they*

If the pronoun is used to show possession, then we must use the possessive case.

Possessive Case: *my, mine, your, yours, his, her, hers, its, our, ours, their, theirs, everyone's, somebody's*

If the pronoun is used as object of the verb, participle, gerund, infinitive or preposition or as appositive to an object then it must be in the objective case.

Objective Case: *me, him, her, us, them*

The problems dealing with case that arise and that are found on examinations, range from those dealing with some of the crudest errors to some of the more subtle ones.

1. Problems involving the subjective case

Example: Lucy and (I, me) were chosen to be members of the varsity team.

EXPLANATION: Whether the pronoun is used alone or as part of a compound subject, when it is used as subject, it must be in the subjective case. The pronoun in this example is part of a compound subject.

ACCEPTED FORM: *Lucy and I were chosen* to be members of the varsity team.

Example: (We, Us) seniors must assume the role of leadership.

EXPLANATION: The pronoun in this case is in apposition with the noun it is in close association with. It must be in the same case as that noun. The word, *seniors* is subject in this sentence. Therefore the pronoun must be in the subjective form.

ACCEPTED FORM: *We seniors* must assume the role of leadership.

Example: They assumed that the culprit was (she, her).

EXPLANATION: A pronoun standing for the same person or thing as the subject and placed after a copulative verb is a predicate pronoun. The copulative verbs are principally *to be* and the following verbs when they are used to be synonymous with *to be: to seem, to grow, to appear, to become.* The pronoun in these cases renames the subject and is also in the subjective case.

ACCEPTED FORM: They assumed that the culprit *was she*.

NOTE: In colloquial usage, *It is me* had become an accepted form. However *It is I* is still the accepted form in Standard Written English. In both colloquial and standard usage, you must use the subjective form for the other pronouns: It is (*she, he, we, they*).

Example: Helen knows more about that field than (we, us).

EXPLANATION: In sentences containing comparisons introduced by *than* or *as* the correct form of the pronoun can be determined by the simple device of adding the missing words.

EXPANDED SENTENCE: Helen knows more about that field than (we, us) do. Obviously, we need a subject for the missing verb *do*.

ACCEPTED FORM: Helen knows more about that field *than we do*.

Example: The note was intended for the person (who, whom) is to address the meeting.

EXPLANATION: Many of the difficulties involved in deciding whether to use *who* or *whom* can be overcome if you test to see whether *he* or *him* can be fitted into the sentence without changing its meaning. If *he* fits, then we need the subjective form, *who*; if *him* fits, then we should use the objective form, *whom*. In the above example, the key clause becomes *he is to address the meeting*. The pronoun then is the subject of the verb *is*.

ACCEPTED FORM: The note is intended for the person who is to address the meeting.

Example: Give the note to (whoever, whomever) is in the office.

EXPLANATION: The pronouns *whoever, whosoever, whomever, whomsoever* depend for their case on their use in the clause to which they belong. In the above example *whoever, whomever* are part of the clause . . . *is in the office*. The clause can be completed by *he* (*He is in the office*). Therefore *whoever* is correct.

ACCEPTED FORM: Give the note to *whoever* is in the office.

ACCEPTED FORM: Give the note to *whomever* you meet.

2. Problems involving the possessive case

Example: The manager announced that (your, you're) entry had won first place.

EXPLANATION: Personal pronouns have special forms for the possessive case. None of these forms therefore require an apostrophe: *mine, my, its, their, theirs, your, yours, his, her, hers, our, ours*. When personal pronouns contain an apostrophe, they stand for a contraction of a verb form plus the pronoun: *it's* (it is), *they're* (they are), *you're* (you are).

ACCEPTED FORM: The manager announced that your entry had won first place.

Example: We objected to (him, his) taking all of the credit.

EXPLANATION: The objection was not to the person, *him*, but to what he did, to the taking of all of the credit, to *his* taking all of the credit.

ACCEPTED FORM: We objected to *his taking* all of the credit.

3. Problems involving the objective case

Example: The bridge could never be built without (he, him).

EXPLANATION: The object of a preposition is in the objective case. Some of the prepositions causing difficulty are

except   with   but (meaning *except*)   between
among

ACCEPTED FORM: The bridge could never be built *without him*.

Example: They had notified everyone except Margie and (she, her)

EXPLANATION: When the object of a preposition is compound, both parts of that object are in the objective case.

ACCEPTED FORM: They had notified everyone except Margie *and her*.

TROUBLESOME FORM: Between you and (I, me) he's the one at fault.

ACCEPTED FORM: *Between you and me*, he's the one at fault.

TROUBLESOME FORM: No one but Henry or (we, us) could handle the machine.

ACCEPTED FORM: No one but Henry *or us* could handle the machine.

Example: The defeat did not hurt him as much as (they, them).

EXPLANATION: Since the sentence contains *as* in a comparison, it should be expanded:
The defeat did not hurt him as much as it hurt (they, them).
The pronoun in doubt is object of the verb *hurt*, and it should be in the objective case.

ACCEPTED FORM: The defeat did not hurt him as much as it hurt *them*.

Example: The victim of the practical joke turned out to be (I, me).

EXPLANATION: Both the subject and the object of an infinitive are in the objective case.

ACCEPTED FORM: The victim of the practical joke turned out *to be me*.

Example: For (who, whom) was the gift intended?

EXPLANATION: Since the statement is in question form, it should be turned into a declarative sentence for the analysis.

The gift was intended for (who, whom)
Now, using the substitution method, we test *he, him* in place of the *who-whom* and discover that *him* is the correct form since we need an object of the prepo-

sition *for*. Therefore we must use the objective form, *whom*.

ACCEPTED FORM: For *whom* was the gift intended?

Example: The dean suspended Alex and (she, her) this afternoon.

EXPLANATION: Each element in a compound object of a verb must be in the objective case.

The dean suspended *Alex*.
The dean suspended *her*.

ACCEPTED FORM: The dean *suspended* Alex and *her* this afternoon.

The Subjunctive in English

Although the subjunctive form of the verb is common in most languages, English has very few instances of it.

Example: If he (were, was) my brother, I would never allow him to waste his talents on such trivia.

EXPLANATION: In a statement that is not true, contrary to the facts, in a clause beginning with if (a conditional statement contrary to the facts), the subjunctive form of the verb is used. Since the verb *to be* is the one most frequently involved, you must know that *were* is the present subjunctive form and *had been* the past subjunctive form. In the above example, therefore, since *he* is *not* my *brother*, the subjunctive verb form must be used.

ACCEPTED FORM: If he *were* my brother, I would never allow him. . . .

Example: If they (would have been, had been) there on time, this complication would never have arisen.

EXPLANATION: They had *not* been there on time. Therefore, this is a conditional statement contrary to the facts, and since it is in the past tense, the past of the subjunctive must be used.

ACCEPTED FORM: If they *had been* there on time, this complication would never have arisen.

Example: If he (would have listened, had listened) to me, the car would still be running.

EXPLANATION: Since he *had not* listened, the past subjunctive should be used. (*Had* is the sign of the past subjunctive.)

ACCEPTED FORM: If he *had listened* to me, the car would still be running.

Example: I wish he (was, were) here.

EXPLANATION: In a wish that is contrary to the facts, the subjunctive form is still used.

ACCEPTED FORM: I *wish* he *were* here.

Pronominal Reference

The specific noun or pronoun that a pronoun has as its antecedent must be clear to the reader. Two common types of errors in usage arise in this area.

1. **Vague reference**

Example: He said that I had not even read the book, which angered me very much.

EXPLANATION: The relative pronoun *which* in the above sentence should refer to a specific noun or pronoun. Instead it refers back to the entire idea in the preceding clause. The sentence must be recast so that the error is eliminated.

ACCEPTED FORM: He said that I had not even read the book, a statement which angered me very much.

or

His statement that I had not even read the book angered me very much.

2. **Ambiguous reference**

Example: Bess told Blanche that she did not understand the assignment.

EXPLANATION: The culprit in this case is the pronoun *she*. Does *she* refer to Bess or to Blanche? In this sentence as it stands the reader cannot tell. The sentence must be recast to eliminate this ambiguity.

ACCEPTED FORM: Bess told Blanche, "You do not understand the assignment."

or

Bess told Blanche, "I do not understand the assignment."

Indefinite Reference

Example: In New York City they are very considerate of visitors who ask questions.

EXPLANATION: The pronoun *they* is used without a definite antecedent. The sentence can be recast so that this indefinite reference can be eliminated.

ACCEPTED FORM: New Yorkers are very considerate of visitors who ask questions.

Example: In this book it states that the price of food is a prime concern of all good governments.

ACCEPTED FORM: The author of this book states that the price of food. . . .

Implied Reference

Example: Although Harold has read much poetry, he has never attempted to write one himself.

EXPLANATION: Obviously, the writer meant by *one* a single poem, but there is no *poem* in this sentence for the word to refer to.

ACCEPTED FORM: Although Harold has read much poetry, he has never attempted to write a poem of his own.

Example: He hopes to become a famous surgeon some day even though the study of *it* will require long years of apprenticeship.

CORRECTNESS AND EFFECTIVENESS OF EXPRESSION

ACCEPTED FORM: He hopes to become a famous surgeon some day even though the study of surgery will require long years of apprenticeship.

Dangling Elements

DEFINITION: *Adjectives and adverbs, whether they are single words or phrases, must have a word in the sentence that they logically modify. Very often, especially with adjective phrases, the writer or speaker in a hurry to make a point implies this specific word, but omits it from the sentence. The result can be humorous or misleading, but it is always wrong.*

1. Dangling participial phrases

Example: Realizing how richly he deserved to win, my feelings of jealousy turned into feelings of admiration.

EXPLANATION: Obviously, *Realizing how richly he deserved to win* is a participial phrase modifying the pronoun *I*; but the speaker omitted *I*. As the sentence stands, (*my*) *feelings* is the only word that the phrase can modify, and *feelings* just *cannot* realize anything. Therefore the phrase dangles without a true noun for it to modify.

ACCEPTED FORM: Realizing how richly he deserved to win, *I* discovered that my feelings of jealousy were turning into feelings of admiration.

2. Dangling gerund phrases

Example: Upon entering the room, the missing ring was soon found on the floor.

EXPLANATION: The gerund phrase, *Upon entering the room,* has no word in the sentence for it to modify. The missing *ring* could not enter the room! A noun or pronoun must be added to the sentence for the phrase to modify.

ACCEPTED FORM: When *I* entered the room, I soon found the missing ring on the floor.

or

Upon entering the room, *I* soon found the missing ring on the floor.

3. Dangling infinitive phrases

Example: To plan carefully in case of fire, doors must not be kept locked when the auditorium is in use.

EXPLANATION: As the sentence stands, the only known word that *To plan carefully* can modify is *doors*. However, *doors* cannot *plan*. Therefore *To plan* dangles. A satisfying noun or pronoun must be added and the sentence recast if necessary.

ACCEPTED FORM: To plan carefully in case of fire, you must make certain that the doors of the auditorium are not locked when it is in use.

4. Dangling elliptical clauses and phrases

Example: When four years old, Paul's father died.

EXPLANATION: As the sentence stands, the father died at the age of four! The sentence must be expanded or recast to make clear just who is being referred to.

ACCEPTED FORM: When Paul was four, his father died.

Example: On reaching his fifth birthday, his uncle bought him a tricycle.

EXPLANATION: As the sentence stands, the uncle was five years old.

ACCEPTED FORM: When Allan reached his fifth birthday, his uncle. . . .

Misplaced Modifiers

Modifiers may be single words, phrases or clauses. A modifying word, phrase, or clause must be placed close to the word being modified and not near another word that it could mistakenly seem to modify.

1. Misplaced relative clauses

Example: The dealer finally agreed to sell me the picture of the horses which hung from the ceiling.

EXPLANATION: As the sentence stands, the relative clause, *which hung from the ceiling,* is closest to *horses,* and therefore it appears to modify that word. However, the sentence then becomes one containing an absurd idea.

ACCEPTED FORM: The dealer finally agreed to sell me the picture of the horses. *This* is the *one which* hung from the ceiling.

Example: The teacher had the pamphlet on his desk which I had borrowed from the library.

ACCEPTED FORM: The teacher had on his desk the pamphlet which I had borrowed from the library.

2. Misplaced phrases

Example: We learned that no one had been injured by the next morning.

EXPLANATION: The phrase *by the next morning* seems to modify *had been injured*. The sense of the sentence is that it should modify *learned*. Therefore, the phrase must be put closer to the verb it really modifies.

ACCEPTED FORM: *By the next morning we learned* that no one had been injured.

or

We *learned by the next morning* that no one had been injured.

Example: They solemnly promised that they would be here the last time we saw them.

EXPLANATION: The phrase, *the last time we saw them,* belongs with *promised* and not with *would be*.

ACCEPTED FORM: The last time we saw them, they solemnly promised that. . . .

3. Misplaced adverbs

Example: I almost saw the entire film.

ACCEPTED FORM: The adverb almost does not modify the verb; it does modify the adjective *entire*; therefore, it should be placed closer to the word it modifies. In this sentence *almost saw* would make no sense.

ACCEPTED FORM: I saw *almost* the entire film.

Example: He *only* sold two books during the entire week.

ACCEPTED FORM: He sold *only two* books during the entire week.

NOTE: There are seven adverbs that must be watched to prevent their being placed too close to a word that they do not modify. Such an incorrect placement could either change the meaning of the sentence or make the sentence meaningless. These seven adverbs are

almost   ever   even   just   merely   only   scarcely

4. Squinting modifiers

Example: He shouted that if we did not leave in five minutes we would be forcibly ejected.

EXPLANATION: The meaning intended by the speaker does not come through clearly. Did he mean that we had to leave in five minutes? Or did he mean that we would be thrown out in five minutes? The phrase, *in five minutes*, is a squinting modifier since it could modify either of the two subordinate verb forms. It must be relocated to make unambiguous the meaning intended.

ACCEPTED FORM: He shouted that if we did not leave we would be forcibly ejected *within five minutes*.

or

He shouted that if, *within five minutes*, we had not left, we would be forcibly ejected.

Errors in Comparisons

DEFINITION: Most adjectives and adverbs have three forms.

The positive form is the original adjective:

beautiful   young   quiet   harmful

The comparative form of the adjective is that form ending in er or preceded by more:

more beautiful   younger   quieter   more harmful

The superlative form of the adjective is that form ending in est or preceded by most:

most beautiful   youngest   quietest   most harmful

Example: Reenie is the (politer, politest) of the three.

EXPLANATION: The comparative form of the adjective is used when two are being compared. When three or more are in the comparison, then the superlative form of the adjective or adverb is used.

ACCEPTED FORM: Reenie is the *politest* of the *three*.

Example: This vase is much more (lovelier, lovely) than the other one.

EXPLANATION: Since there are two ways of indicating the comparative and superlative degrees, when *one* method is used, the other should not be.

ACCEPTED FORM: This vase is much *more lovely* than the other one.

or

This vase is much *lovelier* than the other one.

Example: Alice is faster than (any typist, any other typist) in her class.

EXPLANATION: Since Alice is herself one of the members of the class, she cannot be faster than all of the girls in her class which includes herself. Therefore the word *other* must be included.

ACCEPTED FORM: Alice is faster than any *other* girl in her class.

Example: She is definitely as (capable, capable as) or more capable than her sister.

EXPLANATION: The two forms for comparison are as . . . as and more . . . than. Each of these compounds must be completed correctly If the second *as* is not included in the example above, then the word *than* would go with as and more, an incorrect assumption

ACCEPTED FORM: She is definitely *as* capable *as* or *more* capable *than* her sister.

Example: It was the most *unique* experience I ever had.

EXPLANATION: Certain adjectives and adverbs cannot have comparative or superlative forms. The adjective unique, for example, means *of one of a kind*. The noun therefore is either *unique* or *not unique*.

ACCEPTED FORM: The experience I just had was *unique*.

NOTE: Other adjectives that should be used in the positive degree only are *dead, everlasting, final, last, round*.

Example: He not only enjoys playing Mozart but also listening to that master's symphonies.

EXPLANATION: The pairs of correlatives, not only . . . but also, neither . . . nor, either . . . or, must be placed immediately before the parallel terms.

ACCEPTED FORM: He enjoys *not only playing* Mozart *but also listening* to that master's symphonies.

CORRECTNESS AND EFFECTIVENESS OF EXPRESSION

Parallel Structure

DEFINITION: *Elements in a sentence that are equal in importance should be expressed by parallel grammatical constructions.*

Example: He spoke forcefully and with clarity.

EXPLANATION: *Forcefully* and *with clarity* explain how he spoke; therefore, they should be in the same grammatical construction. They should both be adverbs or prepositional phrases, not a mixture.

ACCEPTED FORM: He spoke *with force* and *with clarity*.
or
He spoke *forcefully* and *clearly*.

Example: The men were ordered to see the film, to write a report on its effectiveness and that they should discuss it afterwards.

EXPLANATION: Two of the commands are in infinitive form (*to see, to write*). The third command is a clause, *that they should discuss it afterwards*. Since all three are commands, they should be in the same construction.

ACCEPTED FORM: The men were ordered *to see* the film, *to write* a report, and *to discuss* it afterwards.

Example: The children told us that they enjoy going to the beach, watching the surf board riders perform and to eat lunch near the water's edge.

EXPLANATION: Two of the activities enjoyed are gerunds (*going, watching*). The third is an infinitive—*to eat*. Since all three are equal in importance, they should be in the same construction.

ACCEPTED FORM: The children told us that they enjoy *going* to the beach, *watching* the surfboard riders perform, and *eating* lunch near the water's edge.

Example: During the afternoon lesson, he learned the importance of hand signals, the main purpose of the rear-view mirror and how to set the hand brake in times of emergencies.

EXPLANATION: Two of the items learned are nouns (*importance, purpose*). The third is in an infinitive form and should be converted to agree in form with the other two.

ACCEPTED FORM: During the afternoon lesson, he learned *the importance of* hand signals, *the main purpose* of the rear-view mirror, and *the function* of the hand brake in emergencies.

Example: Jack was flighty, extravagant, and liked to let his emotions lead him.

ACCEPTED FORM: Jack was *flighty, extravagant,* and *emotional*.

Confusion in Tense

DEFINITION: *Tense is used to define the built-in time factor found in verbs. The verb bears the main responsibility of establishing time relationships. Sometimes this relationship is fairly simple and definite. When the sentence contains a single action, then the verb may be in the present, future or past. However, when the sentence contains two clauses, then the complications arise when the action in one clause relates to a time different from that found in the other clause.*

The examples that follow cover the areas usually stressed in examinations.

1. Past and present

Example: When I finally entered the building, he (walks, walked) up to me.

EXPLANATION: When the action is in the past and occurs at the same or nearly the same time in both clauses, the both verbs should be in the past tense. In this example, there is no need for shifting to the present in the main verb.

ACCEPTED FORM: When I finally *entered* the building, he *walked* up to me.

Example: The main thing that Columbus proved was that the world (is, was) round.

EXPLANATION: When an action occurred in the past, the verb should be in the past tense. That rule would explain why the form *proved* is correct. The second verb is governed by a completely different principle since it does not describe a past action but a general truth. A general truth must be in the present tense, regardless of the tense used for the action verb in the sentence.

ACCEPTED FORM: The main thing that Columbus proved was that the world *is* round.

Example: The minister preached a sermon last week on the thesis that without hope and faith man was unable to function as a social being.

ACCEPTED FORM: The minister preached a sermon last week on the thesis that without hope and faith man *is* unable to function as a social being.

2. Present perfect and the past

Example: We (lived, have lived) in our present apartment for ten years.

EXPLANATION: The past (*lived*) is used to represent action completed. The present perfect (*have* or *has* plus a past participle—*have lived*) represents an action which took place in the past but has consequences extending right into the present. The present perfect is also used to represent action which began in the past and continues through the present. Since in the example above, the people lived in the house in the past and are still living in it, the present perfect should be used.

ACCEPTED FORM: We have lived in our present apartment for ten years.

ACCEPTED FORM: I saw it! (definite action completed at a definite time in the past)

ACCEPTED FORM: I have seen it! (The action is *now* completed.)

3. **Past perfect and the past**

Example: When he saw us, he (already notified, had already notified) the authorities.

EXPLANATION: The subject had done two things in the past. One of these actions (the notification) had occurred before the other (the seeing). The action completed before another in the past must be expressed in the past perfect.

ACCEPTED FORM: When he saw us, he had already notified the authorities.

CONSISTENCY OF POINT OF VIEW

1. **From active to passive (voice)**

DEFINITION: *In the active voice, the subject is the doer of the action. In the passive, the subject is the receiver of the action. Active:* The angler caught the fish. *Passive:* The fish was caught by the angler.

Example: We saw what was wrong, and the carburetor was soon fixed.

EXPLANATION: The first clause has the subject doing the action (active); the second clause has the subject receiving the action (passive). There is a needless shift from the active to the passive voice; whichever voice is used, it should be used consistently throughout the sentence.

ACCEPTED FORM: We saw what was wrong and soon had the carburetor fixed.

2. **From person to person**

Example: When one wants to work most efficiently, you must plan each step in advance.

EXPLANATION: *One* is an impersonal pronoun; *you* is personal. Decide in advance whether a piece of writing is to be personal or impersonal and do not change the point of view.

ACCEPTED FORM: When *you* . . . , *you* must . . .
or
When *one* . . . , *one* must . . .

3. **From imperative to indicative (mood)**

DEFINITION: *The indicative mood is used to make an assertion or to ask questions. Most writing is in the indicative mood. The imperative mood is used for commands, directions, or requests. Indicative:* We can leave now. *Imperative:* Go!

Example: Walk away quickly, and you should not look back.

EXPLANATION: The first verb *walk* is in the imperative mood; the second verb *should look* is in the indicative mood. There is no apparent reason for the shift.

ACCEPTED FORM: Walk away quickly, and do not look back.
or
You should walk away quickly and not look back.

TEST OF MASTERY

If the sentence contains no unacceptable form, then write *Accepted* in the space provided to the left. If the sentence contains an unacceptable form, then put a line through the unaccepted form, and write the accepted form in the space to the left.

GROUP ONE

. . . . 1. The set of answers which everyone was given were carefully checked by the supervisor.

. . . . 2. There is, as far as I can tell at the present time, only two possible solutions that he could offer.

. . . . 3. Either he likes them better than me or prefers their products to ours.

. . . . 4. Everyone of the salesmen who are waiting hopes that their products will be the ones selected.

. . . . 5. Between you and me, except for Sal and she, there is no one here who can really be critical.

. . . . 6. No one but him knew that the winner was to be me.

. . . . 7. If I were her, you would never hear me complaining about preferential treatment.

. . . . 8. If you would have treated Paul and me as equals, this unhappy situation would never have arisen.

. . . . 9. Harriet told Bess that Phyllis and she would be consulted.

. . . . 10. In this book the author states definitely that anyone that wanted to could sell their shares to the officers of the company at any time.

. . . . 11. This article is as good or even better than the one which is to be published in our next issue.

. . . . 12. Upon entering the room, horror filled us

when we saw the destruction wrought by their homemade bomb.

.... 13. Everyone will be entitled to know the results of the morning test by evening.

.... 14. Nobody claimed that the others almost have enough points to be declared the winners.

.... 15. No one, including Ira and I, has a greater right than she to being chosen counselor for the defense.

.... 16. One of the students who is waiting for us stated definitely that Mac is brighter than any boy in his own official class.

.... 17. To speak distinctly is just as important as being polite.

.... 18. My father bought this house before my sister was married.

.... 19. No one except we questioned his statement that man is too self-centered to be able to work for the welfare of all.

.... 20. Thomas and I lived in this house for the past five years.

.... 21. Evelyn as well as the girls who live next door have borrowed the new guitar to see whether its tone is as mellow as we have claimed.

.... 22. We object to your claiming that the set of papers were corrected without our help.

.... 23. Bread and butter has always been the staple food in our family.

.... 24. Neither Henry nor I am ready to leave without Wilma and she.

.... 25. They not only sold the boat to our neighbors and us but also all of the additional equipment that they had bought.

.... 26. Those of us who knows the score are truly sympathetic and wish the coach more luck than he has had so far.

.... 27. Every one of the members of the family that has been evicted have tried in vain to borrow the necessary rent money.

.... 28. News of the type that Mildred and I have been reading in the local papers are better left unprinted and unrevealed.

.... 29. The wages he pays us are low enough without him deducting fees for breakage that had never occurred.

.... 30. The Alaskans, they are as much concerned over this new tax law as any New Yorker, or as you or I.

.... 31. Has any of my friends given their opinion on this matter?

.... 32. Each of us, including you and she, must submit his statement within the next forty-five minutes.

.... 33. The dean told we seniors that the time had come for us to assume the responsibilities of maturity.

.... 34. Under such circumstances there cannot be a more perfect solution than the one that you have suggested.

.... 35. I am positive that he said that you are to give the package to whomever in your opinion can make best use of it.

GROUP TWO

.... 1. Nobody but her objected to you signing the petition as our representative.

.... 2. The only ones who were injured by her callousness seemed to be we.

.... 3. Finding the room empty of all of our precious possessions, panic filled us with a gnawing fear.

.... 4. Of course they could have done all of the homework without you helping if they had listened to the instructor's explanations.

.... 5. Anybody who thinks that your going to solve the world's problems is much more gullible than I had ever imagined a human being to be.

.... 6. I wish he was my brother just for a few minutes this morning.

.... 7. Frances entered the room with you and him, which surprised me very much.

.... 8. Alex told his best friend that he could borrow the car any time he had a definite need for it.

.... 9. In this article they state emphatically that cigaret smoking is injurious to all, but more so to some.

.... 10. To reach the city with a minimum of delay, the new toll road should be used by all who know how to drive carefully.

.... 11. When she was four, her mother taught dancing to the children of the neighborhood in order to pay the mounting doctor bills.

.... 12. I had placed the article on the desk which I had planned to have you read.

.... 13. I even have sold copies of his book to members of the faculty that had objected to its publication.

.... 14. The dean told us that if we agreed by nine we could leave together.

.... 15. Everyone in our class knows that Bill is stronger than any boy in his group.

.... 16. They left it for we to say that there could be no lovelier vase than this one.

.... 17. I thought that I lived long enough when I heard Alice admit that she had made a serious error.

.... 18. We soon realized that Arthur was overemotional, unstable, and liked to be flighty.

.... 19. Salk proved beyond a reasonable doubt that man was capable of curing all of his ills once he put all of his efforts into the task at hand.

.... 20. Pauline together with Phil and we was present during the entire discussion.

.... 21. Any one of the apples that are now rotting away in the cold bin are better than this one that he just selected for us.

.... 22. I am certain that all are not lost; some of the men must have escaped through the emergency hatch installed by Jerry and I.

.... 23. Not only Joan but her sisters as well knows the combination to the safe which contains the list of the family securities.

.... 24. Knowing that its been a long evening, I

suggest that all of us bid each other a curt goodnight and leave quickly and quietly.

.... 25. I did not believe them when they told me that it was I who is to be driven this afternoon.

.... 26. Has there ever been any more willing than they to misdirect our youthful energies?

.... 27. Ten percent of the men lies on the field of battle, calling for medical assistance that just is not available at the present time.

.... 28. Seven-eighths of the box of crackers were eaten before any of our group even knew that Helen was planning to offer us a special treat.

.... 29. My book, it is on the teacher's desk along with the ones that belong to Cecily and her.

.... 30. Phyllis told me when she came in I was to leave immediately.

.... 31. I think she was right when she said that she resented everyones trying to interfere with her personal plans.

.... 32. It was clear to we spectators that no one in that group was capable of assuming leadership.

.... 33. Mr. Taft is the man whom I think can best teach the group the unit on navigational instruments.

.... 34. Everyone of us knows that we would never be where we are without the encouragement we received from you and she.

.... 35. If they would have gone home on time, this tragic incident could never have resulted.

ANSWER KEY: TEST OF MASTERY

GROUP ONE / Page 16

1. *was* carefully checked
2. There *are*
3. He *either* likes
4. *his* products
5. Sal and *her*
6. correct
7. If I were *she*
8. If you *had treated*
9. Harriet told Bess, "You and Phyllis.
10. sell *his* shares
11. as good *as*
12. Upon entering the room, we were filled with horror
13. By evening, everyone
14. *almost enough*
15. Ira and *me*
16. any *other* boy
17. *Speaking distinctly* is emphatically
18. *had* bought
19. except *us*
20. *have* lived
21. *has* borrowed
22. *was* corrected
23. correct
24. and *her*
25. sold *not only* the boat
26. us who *know*
27. *has* tried
28. *is* better left
29. without *his* deducting
30. (omit) *they* Alaskans are
31. *Have* any
32. including you and *her*
33. told *us* seniors
34. a *better* solution
35. to *whoever* in your opinion can make

GROUP TWO / Page 17

1. to *your* signing
2. to be *us*
3. possessions, *we* were filled with
4. without *your* helping
5. *you're* going
6. he *were*
7. . This act surprised me ...
8. friend, "You may borrow ...
9. *the author* states
10. delay, you must take the new ... toll road if you know how to ...
11. When *Alice* was four
12. I had placed on the desk the article which
13. *even* to members
14. leave together by nine
15. any *other* boy
16. for us
17. I *had* lived long enough
18. unstable, and *flighty*
19. man *is* capable
20. and *us*
21. *is* better
22. Jerry and *me*
23. correct
24. it's been
25. who *am*
26. have
27. *lie* on the field
28. *was* eaten
29. My book is on the ...
30. told me, "When I come in, you are to ...
31. everyone's trying
32. us spectators
33. *who* I think *can teach*
34. from you and her
35. If they had gone

GLOSSARY OF THE TERMS OF GRAMMAR AND USAGE

The student who claims that he knows the standard form but does not know why it is so is definitely on safe ground. In usage the main purpose of instruction is to make certain that the student is habituated to the accepted forms. Whether you can explain the difference between the standard and the nonstandard in grammatical terminology is of secondary importance. However, there is much more assurance in the answer of the student who knows *why* one answer is preferred over the other. The secret of being able to explain *why* is based on vocabulary. If you know the terms of grammar and usage, you can understand and remember why certain forms are acceptable.

If your background is sparse, do not try to absorb the following definitions and applications in one or two sittings. You will reap the greatest benefit if you concentrate on a few a day.

If you have a fairly good understanding of usage, then run quickly through the following terms to discover which ones you do not know and therefore should devote time to in studying.

Words may be labeled as parts of speech (noun, verb, etc.) according to their

grammatical function: *modifier, connective*
grammatical form: s = sign of the plural of nouns
    ed = past tense of verbs
meaning: *noun* = name of a person, place, thing
    verb = statement of action.

Because of the necessity for brevity in the following list, most of the terms are defined according to their meaning.

abstract noun (See **concrete noun**.) A name which refers to a quality or idea that cannot be identified by one of the five senses.

>*distaste kindness sympathy*

active voice (See **passive voice**.) A form of the verb which indicates that the subject acts.

>The police *captured* the escaped criminal.

adjective A word which modifies (limits or describes) a noun or pronoun.

>Limiting: *sixteen* men, *an* exercise, *some* people
>Describing: *cold* weather, *tan* trousers, *noisy* neighbor

adjective clause (See **clause**.) A dependent (subordinate) clause which modifies a noun or pronoun. We visited Stella, *who has worked in the theater for years.*

adjective phrase A group of words which, as a unit, modifies a noun or pronoun.

>The end *of the road* was in sight.

adverb A word which modifies a verb, an adjective, or another adverb. Adverbs are used to indicate time (when), place (where), manner (how), and degree (to what extent).

>We shall go *later*. (time)
>Bring it *here*. (place)
>Come *quickly*. (manner)
>He is *too* careful. (degree)
>He left *early*. (modifies verb *left*)
>He is *very* happy. (modifies adjective *happy*)
>It appeared *very* slowly. (modifies adverb *slowly*)

adverbial clause (See **clause**.) A dependent (subordinate) clause which modifies a verb, an adjective, or an adverb.

>Jill left *after we had spoken to her*. (modifies verb *left*)
>He was happy *because Helen had spoken to him*. (modifies adjective *happy*)
>She left so quickly *that she forgot her hat*. (modifies adverb *so*)

affix An affix is either a prefix added at the beginning of a word base or a suffix added at the end of a word base.

>*pre*tend *mis*judge (prefix)
>pretend*er* tall*est* (suffix)

agreement The correspondence of one word with another in gender, number, case, or person.

>In gender: Phil left *his* pen on the desk.
>In number: Everyone *is* here.
>In case: Paul and *I* could easily do the work.
>In person: *I am* willing to listen.

antecedent The noun or pronoun to which a pronoun refers.

>The man *who* entered is my brother.
>(The antecedent of *who* is *man*.)

appositive A noun or pronoun used to explain another noun or pronoun.

>John Henry, the *hero* of folk literature, lived not so long ago.
>(The appositive *hero* explains who John Henry is.)

article Three adjectives are given the special title of *article*. The *definite* article is *the*; the *indefinite* articles are *a* and *an*.

attributive (See **predicate adjective**.) An adjectival word or phrase that stands directly before or immediately after the noun it modifies.

>The *light* ball was carried by the wind.
>The pancakes, *light* and *tasty*, were most enjoyable.

auxiliary The helping verb used in the formation of verb phrases.

>*should have* gone   *will* follow   *had been* seen

bound form A language unit that is never spoken alone (*ation, fer, re*). Most prefixes and suffixes and many word bases are bound forms. A **free form** is a language unit that can stand alone (*form, stand, can*).

A bound form may be added to a free form to make another free form:

>*ation + form = formation*

A bound form may be added to another bound form to make a free form:

>*re + fer = refer*

case The form of a noun or pronoun that indicates its relationship to the rest of the sentence. Nominative case shows subject; objective case shows object; possessive case shows ownership. The case of a noun as a subject or as an object is determined by its use in the sentence.

>Nominative: *I* have to leave. The *girl* has to leave.
>Objective: He forced *me* to leave. He forced the *girl* to leave.
>Possessive: This is *my* book. This is the *girl's* book.

clause A group of words containing a subject and predicate. The main (independent) clause can stand alone. The subordinate (dependent) clause must be joined to a main clause to make a complete thought or sentence; dependent clauses may be adjective, adverbial, or noun clauses.

>Independent: I shall see you later.
>Dependent: When you are willing to discuss the issue.

cognate *Cognate* means *related through the same origin*. Cognate languages have a common source. French, Spanish, and Italian are cognate languages since they are all derived from Latin. Cognate words are words in different languages with the same origin in another language.

Mater in Latin and *mother* in English are cognates since they come from the same Indo-European word. Cognate objects are similar in meaning to the verb they follow.

live a *life*, run a *race*

colloquialism A word or expression acceptable in informal speaking and writing, but not acceptable in Standard Written English.

We have a *date* in the *lab* with the *prof*.

comparative degree (See **positive** and **superlative degree**.) The *more, less* or *er* form of adjectives and adverbs.

more slowly   better   less wild

complement A word that completes the predicate of a sentence. Four kinds of complements are predicate adjective, predicate nominative, direct object, and indirect object.

Indirect object and direct object: She taught *him* a *lesson*.
Predicate nominative: It is *I*.
Predicate adjective: The airport was *noisy*.

complex sentence A sentence containing one independent clause and at least one dependent clause. Dependent clauses may be adjective, adverbial, or noun clauses.

With adjective clause: I saw the bat *which had been broken*.
With adverbial clause: *If you want me to*, I shall go with him.
With noun clause: He said *that I could not prove anything*.

compound sentence A sentence containing two or more independent clauses joined by a coordinate conjunction.

The time had come, and there was nothing else for us to do.

compound-complex sentence A sentence containing one or more independent clauses and one or more dependent clauses.

concrete noun (See **abstract noun**.) A noun which refers to something that can be identified by one of the five senses.

book   thunder   ice

conjugation The inflection of a verb, showing all of the forms of the verb and its uses.

conjunction (See **coordinate, correlative,** and **subordinate conjunctions**.) A word that connects words, phrases, and clauses.

conjunctive adverb An adverb that has the force of a conjunction since it links main clauses. A conjunctive adverb may not function as a coordinating conjunction since different punctuation is required. Some of the more common conjunctive adverbs are: *however, moreover, therefore, nevertheless, hence, then, consequently*.

Conjunction: The soup was delicious, and Alice asked for the recipe.
Conjunctive adverb: The soup was delicious; therefore, Alice asked for the recipe.

connective Connectives are used to join parts of a sentence and show relation. Coordinate conjunctions, correlative conjunctions, and conjunctive adverbs connect elements of equal rank. Subordinate conjunctions, relative pronouns, and relative adverbs (*how, where, when, while*) join elements of unequal rank. A preposition shows the relationship of its object to another word.

consonants Sounds made by interrupting a breath group. Letters representing these sounds are: *b, c, d, f, g, h, j, k, l, m, n, p, q, r, s, t, v, w, x, z,* and sometimes *y*.

consumer (See **transformation grammar**.) In transformational grammar the *consumer* is the sentence to which a word, phrase, or clause is added. The new combination is called the *output*. The sentence that is condensed into the word, phrase, or clause is called the *input* sentence.

Consumer: The girl was upset.
Input: She left early.
Output: The girl *who left early* was upset.

contact clause A relative clause in which the relative pronoun (*who, whom, whose, which, that*) has been omitted.

The boy *I saw* wore a green hat.

coordinate conjunction A conjunction that joins words, phrases or clauses of equal rank. The coordinating conjunctions are: *and, but, or, nor, for, whereas, yet*.

Paul *and* I   Harriet *or* Mary   poor *but* honest

copulative verb A verb which does not take an object and serves as a link between the subject and the complement. The complement may be a noun or an adjective. The more common linking verbs are: *be, feel, appear, seem, become, taste, smell, look*.

Adjective complement: The tone is *magnificent* now.
Noun complement: The speaker was their *leader*.

correlative conjunctions Words that work in pairs to connect parallel elements. The correlative conjunctions are: *both . . . and, either . . . or, neither . . . nor, not only . . . but also*.

dangling modifier A modifying word, phrase, or clause *dangles* if there is no word in the sentence for it to modify.
Dangling: *Looking out my window,* a fire truck raced by.
Correct form: *Looking out my window,* I saw a fire truck race by.
Dangling: *To be a good skier,* lessons are necessary.
Correct form: *To be a good skier,* you must take lessons.

declension The changes in the form of nouns and pronouns to show such relationships as person, number, case, and gender.

demonstrative adjective or pronoun A word used as an adjective or as a pronoun to point out the item referred to. The demonstrative adjectives or pronouns are: *this, these, that, those.*

derivation Derivation can refer to the etymology of a word, the process of tracking its growth in the language, or the process of forming words from bases by the addition of prefixes and suffixes, or by phonetic change. In linguistic studies, derivation describes the formation of a word from another word or word base (root) by the addition of an affix (a prefix or suffix). A derivational suffix changes the meaning or the part of speech of a word: confer-confer*ence*. A derivational prefix changes the meaning of a word: write-*re*write.
recounting: from the Old French *reconter*—*re-* (again), *conter* (to tell), *-ing* (suffix denoting present participle)

descriptive grammar (See **prescriptive grammar**.) In descriptive grammar, language usage and principles are listed and explained. Practices are described, but they are not labeled correct, incorrect, or preferred.

determiner A term used in modern grammar to identify a word that signals that a noun is coming. In traditional grammar these words are classified as types of adjectives. Determiners traditionally called articles: *the, a, an.* Determiners traditionally called possessive pronouns: *my, our, your, his, her, its, their.* Determiners traditionally called demonstrative adjectives: *this, these, that, those.*

direct quotation The exact words that were spoken.
She repeated, "I have nothing to do with this incident."

ellipsis The omission of grammatically important words from a sentence.
He runs faster than I (do).

etymology The study of word derivations, in which words and word parts are traced to the language of origin.

expletive A word that helps to round out the sentence, has no grammatical part in the sentence, and is not a part of speech. *It* and *there* are commonly used as expletives.
It is cloudy; *there* will be a storm.

figurative The opposite of *literal. Literal* language takes words at face value: *rose petals* do come from a rose. *Figurative* language, on the other hand, expresses an idea through an expressed or implied comparison; *pearly teeth* must be taken figuratively. Figurative language involves *figures of speech* in which one object is identified with another one more familiar to the reader. Some typical figures of speech are *similes* and *metaphors*. A simile is a comparison in which *like* or *as* appears: He roared *like a lion*. A metaphor is an implied comparison: I found myself *in hot water*.

form class Modern grammarians classify as form classes those words that traditional grammar calls nouns and pronouns, verbs, adjectives, and adverbs. The words in the four form classes have dictionary definitions. They are contrasted to structure (function) words (like *or, and, but, if, on, of, a, the*), which can be defined only in terms of the function they perform in a phrase or sentence.

formed word A word made by adding a prefix or a suffix to a word base. *Re* in front of *form* creates *reform*.

free form A language unit that can stand alone (*form, stand, can*).

functional shift A functional shift takes place when a word that is classified as one part of speech is used as another: *Monday* is normally a noun; however, in *Monday wash* it has been used as an adjective in a functional shift.

gender The grammatical expression of sex. The three genders in English are *masculine, feminine,* and *neuter*.

genitive (See **possessive case**.) A word that means the same as *possessive* when referring to case.

gerund The *-ing* form of a verb used as a noun. (It is a present participle which is used as a noun.) *Painting* is my favorite hobby.

grammar (See **morphology** and **syntax**.) A system of classification or description of the words of a language. *Linguistics* is the broader term that refers to the science of language.

headword (head) In modern grammar, a word that is modified. A noun headword is found in a noun cluster.
Noun cluster: the lovely child
Noun headword: child
Adjective headword: very *tall*
Verb headword: *answer* quickly
Adverb headword: very *often*

homograph A word which has the same spelling as another word but a different meaning. *Port* may mean harbor or a type of wine.

homonym Words which sound alike but are spelled differently and have different meanings.
bear—bare wholly—holy break—brake

Homophones are words which sound alike but differ in meaning. Practically all homonyms are homophones!

idiom An expression peculiar to a language.
He has been *walking on thin ice* for too long.

immediate constituent analysis Many linguists use immediate constituent analysis instead of diagraming to study the structure of the sentence and to reveal the relationship between its parts. The sentence is divided into two parts (binary fission), subject and predicate. Then each of these is divided in turn into other binary structures, through clauses, phrases, words, and finally morphemes and phonemes. The parts revealed by the analysis are the immediate constituents.
The braves fought to save their village.
Subject: The braves
Predicate: fought to save their village

The subject and the predicate are the immediate constituents.
Noun cluster: The braves

The determiner *the* and the noun *braves* are the immediate constituents of the noun cluster.

indefinite pronoun A pronoun that does not refer to a specific person. Some examples of indefinite pronouns are: *anyone, someone, somebody, anything, anybody, few, some, either, neither.*

indirect quotation A restatement of the speaker's words, usually introduced by *that* and containing a shift in person.
Direct: Helen said, "I could not do that."
Indirect: Helen said that she could not do that.

infinitive The verb form that is preceded by *to*. The *to* is sometimes omitted but understood. Infinitives may be used as nouns, adjectives, or adverbs.
As a noun: I plan *to leave* early. (object of the verb *plan*)
As an adjective: This is truly a house *to see*. (modifies the noun *house*)
As an adverb: We were unhappy *to go*. (modifies the adjective *unhappy*)

inflection The form of a word which indicates certain grammatical relationships such as case, number, gender, and tense.

intensifiers Words such as *more, most, quite, somewhat, too,* and *very* are classified as adverbs in traditional grammar. They are called *intensifiers*—in that they show degree—by modern grammarians, whether they modify adjectives or adverbs.

intensive pronoun (See **reflexive pronoun**.) A pronoun used in an appositive position to emphasize its antecedent. Examples of intensive pronouns are: *myself, himself, yourself, ourselves,* etc.
I *myself* saw the accident.

interjection A word expressing emotion and having no grammatical relationship to the other words of the sentence. Examples of interjections are: *Oh, no, well, alas, goodness.*

interrogative pronoun *Who, whom, whose, which,* and *what* when used to form a question.
Who is responsible for this?

intransitive verb A verb expressing action but taking no object.
He *was walking* toward us.

irregular verb (a strong verb) A verb that forms its past by changing a vowel in its base.
ring (rang) bring (brought) fling (flung)

linguistics The broad term for the scientific study of language. It includes usage, grammatical systems, word derivation, history of languages, comparative language studies, vocabulary, dialects.

main (independent) clause A group of words containing a subject and a verb and capable of being a complete sentence.
Because the storm was so severe, *we did not leave the house.*

modifier A word, phrase, or clause that limits or explains another word, phrase, or clause (usually either adjectival or adverbial).

mood (mode) The three moods of a verb (indicative, imperative, and subjunctive), used to indicate the attitude of a speaker toward his own statement.
Indicative: I *go* to the store.
Imperative: *Go* to the store.
Subjunctive: I wish I *were going* to the store.

morpheme In linguistics, a morpheme is the smallest meaningful unit of language. A *free morpheme* is a single syllable that can be uttered alone with meaning: *bird, their, want.* A *bound morpheme* is one that is always joined to one or more morphemes to form a word. Prefixes or suffixes are bound morphemes: *de, ry, re.*

morphology (See **syntax**.) The branch of grammar concerned with the structure and form of words. It concentrates on the analysis of sentences through the parts of speech of the words involved and the analysis of words by prefix, word base, and suffix.

nominative absolute A phrase consisting of a noun or pronoun and a participle which modifies the

whole sentence but is grammatically independent of the rest of the sentence.
Victory assured, the army was disbanded.

nominative case The form of the noun or pronoun when it is used as a subject or predicate nominative.
It is *she*.

nonrestrictive A modifier which supplies additional information about the word it modifies but does not limit its meaning. It is usually set off by commas.
Nonrestrictive: My uncle, *who is a postal clerk*, lives with us.
Restrictive: The animal *that fails to escape its clutches* dies quickly.

noun (See **abstract noun** and **concrete noun**.) A word that names a person, place, thing, condition, or quality. A proper noun is the name of a particular person, place, or thing. A common noun is a noun that is not a proper noun. A collective noun refers to a group.
Proper nouns: *Mr. Molendyk Europe Empire State Building*
Common nouns: *man country building*
Collective nouns: *flock army team herd*

noun clause (See **clause**.) A subordinate clause used as a noun.
He said *that I was right*. (object of the verb *said*)
Whoever is chosen shall be satisfactory to me. (subject to *shall be*)

noun cluster In modern grammar a noun and its modifiers are called a noun cluster. In traditional grammar this combination is called a *noun phrase*.

number The change in nouns, pronouns, and verbs to show singular or plural form.

object A noun or pronoun which answers the question *whom?* or *what?* after a verb or preposition. The object may be *direct* (object of a verb), *indirect* (object of the understood preposition *to* or *for*), or the *object of a preposition*. An indirect object is regularly followed by a direct object.
Direct object: He caught the *ball*.
Indirect object: He gave *me* a watch.
Object of preposition: The dean spoke to *the assembled students*.

objective case The form of a noun or pronoun when it is used as the object of a verb or preposition.
Between *you and me*, I like *her* very much.

parenthetic expression A word or phrase added to a sentence, usually set off by punctuation. Examples of parenthetic expressions are: *however, by the way, for example, of course*.
Parenthetic Expression: Many colleges, *however*, still require a core curriculum.
Not a Parenthetic Expression: *However* angry you become, do not let your emotions show. (Here, *however* modifies angry.)

participle The *-ing* form of the verb (present participle) used as an adjective, or the *-d, -ed, -t,* or *-n* form of the verb (the past participle) used as an adjective.
the *laughing* boy   the *overlooked* principle
the *chosen* leader

particles In traditional grammar, articles, conjunctions, interjections, and prepositions, four of the eight parts of speech, are called particles because they are short and never change in form.

parts of speech Theoretically, the eight different functions of words, which are: *adjective, adverb, conjunction, interjection, noun, preposition, verb.*

passive transformation In transformational grammar, passive transformation occurs when the subject of a sentence changes place with the object, with the subject changing from the doer to the one acted upon.
Kernel sentence: The *batter* hit the *ball*.
Transform: The *ball* was hit by the *batter*.

passive voice (See **active voice**.) The form of a verb which has no object, whose action is directed toward the subject.
Active: The boy *shot* the deer.
Passive: The deer *was shot* by the boy.

past participle The *-d, -ed, -t,* or *-n* form of the verb, acting as an adjective. It may be used as:
Part of a verb: They had *intended* to leave promptly.
An adjective: The *browned* turkey smelled delicious.

person A form of the pronoun or verb which designates involvement.
First person: I, we (the person speaking)
Second person: you (the person spoken to)
Third person: he, she, it, they (the person spoken about)

personal pronoun A pronoun that shows which person is the subject. These pronouns are: *I, me, my, mine, you, your, yours, he, she, it, him, her, its, his, hers, we, us, our, ours, they, them, their, theirs.*

phoneme In linguistics, the smallest unit of speech that can be called a distinctive sound. The *segmentals* are the vowel and consonant phonemes: s, t, o, u, etc. The *suprasegmentals* are the phonemes that represent accent, pause, and pitch in the actual sounding of words and sentences.

phrase A group of words that does not contain a subject and verb. The five principal kinds of phrases are: prepositional, participial, infinitive, gerund, and verb.

Participial phrase: *Coming into the room,* I saw the entire incident.

Prepositional phrase: He is the last *of the autocrats.*

positive degree The form of the adjective or adverb which makes no comparison. The *comparative degree* (*more, less,* or *-er*) compares two. The *superlative degree* (*most, least,* or *-est*) compares three or more.

POSITIVE	COMPARATIVE	SUPERLATIVE
quiet	quieter	quietest
lonesome	more lonesome	most lonesome
quickly	less quickly	least quickly

possessive (genitive) case The form of the noun or pronoun indicating possession.

Pronouns: *my, mine, your, yours, his, her, hers, its, our, ours, their, theirs, whose*

Nouns: *Jerry's, ladies', men's*

predicate What is said about the subject. The predicate contains the verb, its modifiers, and sometimes an object and its modifiers.

Alice *called for us much earlier than usual.*

predicate adjective An adjective modifying the subject word, but used *after* a linking (copulative) verb.

They seem *willing.* Lucy is *excited.*

predicate nominative (predicate noun) A noun or pronoun that identifies the subject and is used after a copulative verb.

Our neighbor is *Concetta Bonom.*

prefix An addition to the beginning of a word to alter its meaning.

*ex*pend   *in*tend   *re*ply

preposition A word which shows a relationship between its object and some other word in the sentence. Some of the more frequently used prepositions are: *in, of, by, off, from, to, over, under, by, into, onto, beneath, between, except.*

The solution *to* the problem is right there.

prescriptive grammar The study and analysis that leads to the rules of language that are to be followed. Usage is labeled right or wrong. *Prescriptive grammar* is opposed to *descriptive grammar,* which records but does not judge.

present participle The *-ing* form of the verb. It generally functions as an adjective; when it functions as a noun, it is considered a gerund. It may be used as

Part of a verb: They will be *going* soon.

An adjective: The *shining* car disappeared around the corner.

A noun (gerund): *Selling* beer to minors is prohibited.

principal parts The four forms of the verb upon which all other forms are based:

PRESENT	PRESENT PARTICIPLE	PAST	PAST PARTICIPLE
wish	wishing	wished	wished
sing	singing	sang	sung

pronoun A word that takes the place of a noun or another pronoun. The classes of pronouns are *personal, relative, interrogative, demonstrative, indefinite, intensive,* and *reflexive.* Examples would include: *I, me, my, you, him, she, anyone, who, that, which, myself, these.*

proper adjective An adjective formed from a proper noun.

Wilsonian   American   Shakespearean

proper noun A word that names a specific person, place, or thing.

Arthur   Luzerne   Lake George
St. Marks Cathedral

qualifiers In some modern grammar systems the adverbs that modify adjectives or adverbs are called qualifiers. As nouns are signaled by noun determiners, and verbs by auxiliaries, so adjectives and adverbs are signaled by qualifiers such as: *very, much, less, so, mighty, more, most.* A qualifier is a member of a structure class, identifiable by position.

reflexive pronoun (See **intensive pronoun**.) A pronoun that renames the subject and is the object of a verb or preposition.

He cut *himself.*
He went by *himself.*

regular verb (a weak verb) A verb that forms the past tense by the addition of *d, t,* or *ed.*

want (wanted)   live (lived)

relative pronoun A pronoun that introduces a dependent adjective clause and has its case determined by its function in the subordinate clause.

Relative pronouns are: *who, whom, whose, which, that.*

restrictive A modifier that restricts or limits the meaning of the word it modifies and is not set off by punctuation marks.

The snake *that they caught* had bitten me.

semantics Semantics is the study of the meaning of words and the changes that take place in their meaning.

sentence A group of words containing a subject and verb and expressing a complete thought. There are several different types of sentences:

Simple sentence: A sentence containing one independent clause.

Jerry worked hard to reach success.

Compound sentence: A sentence containing two or more independent clauses.

I stood by the fireplace, and Bea sat in the chair.
Complex sentence: A sentence containing an independent clause and one or more dependent clauses.
I shall go wherever you wish us to go.
Compound-complex sentence: A sentence containing two or more independent clauses and one or more dependent clauses.
Because he had spoken to me, I could not take sides; but I did tell Mr. Lurie, his adviser, that I felt that the other side was right.

Split infinitive An infinitive with a modifier between the *to* and the verb form. Formal usage considers it not acceptable.
to actually go   to seriously consider

squinting or misplaced modifiers (See **dangling modifier**.) These unacceptable forms result from misplacing the modifier. Squinting modifiers point in two directions at the same time.
Misplaced: I saw a bluejay *looking out my window*.
Accepted form: *Looking out my window*, I saw a bluejay.
Squinting: I thought of joining the Peace Corps *several times* after reading articles about it.
Accepted form: *Several times* after reading articles about it, I thought of joining the Peace Corps.

structural linguistics The branch of linguistics which describes language forms and patterns is called structural linguistics; the stress is on form, not on meaning, and on oral, rather than on written, language.

structure words In modern grammar, articles (*the, an, a*), conjunctions (*and, or, but*), prepositions (*of, in, on*), and auxiliary (helping) verbs are called *structure words*; their primary function is to signal a part of speech or show grammatical structure. They are also called *function words*.

subject The person, place, or thing in a clause or sentence about which an assertion is made.
The *boy* was delighted with the toy.

subjunctive mood A class of verb forms used to express desire, hope, concession, promise. The main use of the subjunctive mood today is to indicate conditions that are contrary to the accepted facts.
If I *were* his sister, I would not go.
If I *had been* there, things would have been different.
I wish he *were* home.

subordinate (dependent) clause A group of words containing a subject and a predicate and grammatically dependent upon some other element in the sentence. The subordinate clause cannot stand alone.
I shall gladly assist *when they ask me to*.

subordinate conjunction A word that joins a dependent clause to the main clause. Subordinate conjunctions, unlike relative pronouns, have no grammatical function in the clause they subordinate. Subordinate conjunctions include: *after, since, although, because, unless, until.*
He came to our conference *although* he had not been invited.

substantive A term used to denote a word, phrase, or clause used as a noun.

suffix An addition at the end of a word to change the meaning or part of speech.
confine   confine*ment*

superlative degree (See **positive** and **comparative degree**.) The form of an adjective or adverb that is preceded by *most* or *least* or contains the suffix *-est*.
loveliest   least advisable   most beautiful

syntax The grammatical relationships between words in sentences. To give the syntax, you must explain how a word is used in a particular sentence. Syntax deals with phrase and clause patterns, while *morphology*, the other major component of grammatical study, concentrates on the forms and structure of words.

tense The time element built into verb forms.
Present tense (now): I follow.
Future tense (tomorrow): I shall follow.
Past tense (yesterday): I followed.
Present perfect tense (now): I have followed. He has followed.
Future perfect tense (tomorrow): I will have followed.
Past perfect tense (yesterday): I had followed.

transformational grammar The study of all possible grammatical patterns which occur in a language. The English sentence, for example, can be condensed to its most basic form, a kernel sentence: *Men ran. Girls laugh.* The term *transformation* applies to the rules for the changing of a kernel sentence into a more complex type. A *transform* (transformed sentence) is a kernel sentence transformed through the addition of new elements or the rearrangement of grammatical elements.
Kernel sentence: Men ran.
Transform: The men who had seen the crash ran to aid the victims.

transitive verb An action verb that has a direct object.
The car *hit* the tree.

verb The word expressing action or a state of being. A verb may be transitive, intransitive, or copulative.
His hat *flew* off.   I *sensed* danger.
She *appears* bright.

verbal A verb form that is used as some other part of speech. The three verbals in English are the gerund, the infinitive, and the participle.

voice A verb form indicating whether the subject is the doer or is being acted upon. The verb is in the *active voice* if the subject is the doer. The verb is in the *passive voice* if the subject is the receiver of the action.
Active voice: I *carried* the victim out of danger.
Passive voice: The victim *was carried* to safety.

vowels The sounds represented by *a, e, i, o, u*; the sounds formed by not interrupting the breath group with the tongue, teeth, lips, etc.

3. Sentence Variety and Styling Problems

The College Board Achievement Test in English Composition attempts to evaluate more than the student's ability to avoid errors in usage, diction, and sentence structure. Sensitivity to elements of style is included as a measurable item on the tests through questions involving sentence pattern variety and variety in sentence beginnings. The material that follows will familiarize you with those elements of style that are tested. The *Mastery Tests* will allow you to determine the extent of your command of these items.

SENTENCE VARIETY

The mature writer varies the type and organization of the sentences he uses so that the reader will not be distracted by *how* he states his position; the reader's complete attention will be focused on *what* he has to say. The necessary sentence variety can be gained in three main ways.

1. Sentence types

Simple Sentence: Lucy borrowed the dictionary.

Simple Sentence with Compound Subject: *Lucy and Margie* borrowed the book.

Simple Sentence with Compound Verb: Lucy *borrowed* the book and *read* it.

Simple Sentence with Compound Object: Lucy borrowed the *dictionary* and the *novel*.

Compound Sentence: Lucy borrowed the dictionary, and Margie took the novel.

Complex Sentence: When Lucy borrowed the dictionary, Margie took the novel.

Compound-Complex Sentence: If Lucy borrows the dictionary, Margie may take the novel; but I don't think that she should.

2. Variety through sentence types: A theme that is based on simple sentences only will sound immature. A theme that contains only compound sentences will also sound as though it is lacking in depth. A theme that contains only complex sentences tends to sound pompous. The experienced writer soon learns to combine simple sentences into compound or complex ones. He can also convert complex sentences into simple ones when necessary or change compound sentences into complex or simple when variety is required.

Examples
Simple into complex
Simple: Harold played the cello. The cello belongs to Bess.
Complex: Harold played the cello which belongs to Bess.

Compound into complex
Compound: Arthur watched us play the game of Scrabble, and he munched contentedly on his apple.
Complex: As he watched us play the game of Scrabble, Arthur munched contentedly on his apple.

Compound into simple
Compound: Phyllis is reading *The Catcher in the Rye*, and Dave is reading the same book.
Simple (with Compound Subject): Phyllis and Dave are both reading *The Catcher in the Rye*.

Complex into simple
Complex: The story which he had told us is truly astounding.
Simple: He told us a truly astounding story.

TEST OF MASTERY

Convert each of the following sets of sentences into one complex sentence for each group.

1. The letter was just written. It is addressed to Mr. Shapiro. He is my father's best friend.
2. The dog is in the backyard. It howled for an hour. We called the police. The owner seems to have disappeared.
3. Columbia University is located on Morningside Heights. This is in Manhattan. Brooklyn College is in Flatbush.

CORRECTNESS AND EFFECTIVENESS OF EXPRESSION

4. I really wanted to listen to that program. Our radio went silent suddenly. I rushed into my neighbors' house to hear the end of the play.

5. The game had ended. I realized that John was in a state of collapse. John had been the star of the evening.

Convert each of the following sentences into one simple sentence for each group.

6. David told the entire story to Helen, and then he told the entire story to me.

7. Harriet saw the accident. Mike also saw the accident.

8. I have a great need. I need an assistant. He must be reliable.

9. The store is located on the corner. It is owned by Mr. Kulkin. He is our neighbor.

10. Alan is tired, but he claims that he is also happy.

ANSWER KEY: TEST OF MASTERY
(*Answers may vary.*)

1. This letter, which was just written, is addressed to Mr. Shapiro, who is my father's best friend.

2. Because the dog misses its owner and howled for an hour, we called the police since the owner seems to have disappeared.

3. While Columbia University, which is located on Morningside Heights, is in Manhattan, Brooklyn College is in Flatbush.

4. Since I really wanted to listen to that program, when our radio set went silent suddenly, I rushed into my neighbors' house to hear the end of the play.

5. When the game had ended, I realized that John, who had been the star of the evening, was in a state of collapse.

6. David told the entire story to Helen and then to me.

7. Both Harriet and Mike saw the accident.

8. I have a great need for a reliable assistant.

9. The corner store is owned by our neighbor, Mr. Kulkin.

10. Alan is tired but happy.

VARIETY THROUGH VARYING SENTENCE BEGINNING

A simple effective way to gain emphasis and to vary the sentence pattern is to place part of the sentence out of its normal order. Usually a sentence begins with the subject followed by the predicate; however, below are some of the accepted ways to vary the pattern.

Introductory Adverb: *Suddenly* the doorbell rang.

Introductory Prepositional Phrase: *By the next morning*, the swelling had subsided.

Introductory Participial Phrase: *Depressed by the scene*, I left quickly.

Wishing to help us, he arrived early the next morning.

Introductory Adverbial Clause: *When the curtain went down*, the applause told us that we had succeeded.

If you wish to work with us, you will have to arrive much earlier.

TEST OF MASTERY

Wherever possible, vary the order of the following sentences by putting one of the sentence elements first. In the space provided to the left, write the name of the element that you had placed first.

1. I was as expert as the others by the end of the day.
.... 1. ....

2. She opened the blind when she saw that he was examining the cloth with a magnifying glass.
.... 2. ....

3. The owner, hoping to please his regular customers, installed an expensive set of audio equipment in the studio.
.... 3. ....

4. The investigator quietly gathered the evidence that would prove his client innocent of the charges.
.... 4. ....

5. The tree would have been destroyed by the storm if we had not protected it from the blasts of the hurricane-force wind.
.... 5. ....

6. The enemy troops had slipped silently away during the early hours of the morning.
.... 6. ....

7. He would ask me to help him occasionally with his homework.
.... 7. ....

8. The team of horses bolted across the lawn, frightened by the flames that were enveloping the carriage.
.... 8. ....

9. He was right, moreover, in deciding to let us choose our own parts.
.... 9. ....
....
....

10. Bob left the house early, knowing how much work he had ahead of him.
.... 10. ....
....

ANSWER KEY: TEST OF MASTERY

(*Answers may vary.*)

1. Introductory prepositional phrase   By the end of the day I was as expert as the others.
2. Introductory adverbial clause   When she saw that he was examining the cloth with a magnifying glass, she opened the blind.
3. Introductory participial phrase   Hoping to please his regular customers, the owner installed an expensive set of audio equipment in the studio.
4. Introductory adverb   Quietly, the investigator gathered the evidence that would prove his client innocent of the charges.
5. Introductory adverbial clause   If we had not protected the tree from the blasts of the hurricane-force wind, it would have been destroyed by the storm.
6. Introductory prepositional phrase   During the early hours of the morning, the enemy troops had slipped silently away.
7. Introductory adverb   Occasionally he would ask me to help him with his homework.
8. Introductory participial phrase   Frightened by the flames that were enveloping the carriage, the team of horses bolted across the lawn.
9. Introductory adverb   Moreover, he was right in deciding to let us choose our own parts.
10. Introductory participial phrase   Knowing how much work he had ahead of him, Bob left the house early.

VARIETY THROUGH COMBINING SENTENCE ELEMENTS

By combining sentence elements to gain sentence variety and complexity, the writer achieves additional values. He is enabled to subordinate secondary ideas and give increased emphasis to the more important ideas. Superfluous words are eliminated, and his written expression gains in maturity of tone.

1. **Combining Through the Use of the Present Participle**
   Original: Alice hoped to gain our confidence. She brought us little gifts.
   Combined: *Hoping to gain our confidence,* Alice brought us little gifts.

2. **Combining Through the Use of the Past Participle**
   Original: The boat was tied to the dock. It had little chance to ride out the storm.
   Combined: *Tied to the dock,* the boat had little chance to ride out the storm.

3. **Combining Through the Use of a Relative Clause**
   Original: One of the leaders of our community is Harold Carlin. He is the arbiter in all our disputes.
   Combined: One of the leaders of our community is Harold Carlin *who is the arbiter in all of our disputes.*

4. **Combining Through the Use of an Adverbial Clause**
   Original: He knew just when I would leave the house. He was on the corner to greet me.
   Combined: *Because he knew just when I would leave the house,* he was on the corner to greet me.

5. **Combining Through the Use of an Appositive**
   Original: Philip Groisser is chairman of the Social Studies Department. He is a noted authority on the Revolutionary Period in America.
   Combined: Philip Groisser, *chairman of the Social Studies Department,* is a noted authority on the Revolutionary Period in America.

6. **Combining Through the Use of a Compound Subject**
   Original: Alicia left early in order to see her favorite television program. Tom also left early for a similar reason.
   Combined: Both *Alicia and Tom* left early in order to see their favorite television programs.

7. **Combining Through the Use of a Compound Verb**
   Original: Arthur knew the danger he faced. He realized fully what his chances for survival were.
   Combined: Arthur *knew* the danger he faced and *realized* what his chances for survival were.

CORRECTNESS AND EFFECTIVENESS OF EXPRESSION

TEST OF MASTERY

Combine the units found in each of the following into a single sentence. Use the device suggested.

1. I was paralyzed with terror. I sensed that Arthur could not rely on luck this time.
   1. PRESENT PARTICIPLE ....
   ....

2. The vases were wrapped in cotton. They were placed very carefully into the packing crate.
   2. RELATIVE CLAUSE ....
   ....

3. Poseidon was the Greek god of the sea. He supposedly decided the fate of all who embarked in ships destined for faraway shores.
   3. APPOSITIVE ....
   ....

4. Edna was horrified by the sight. She tried in vain to scream for help.
   4. PAST PARTICIPLE ....
   ....

5. City University serves the five boroughs of New York City. It has an enrollment of more than 200,000 students.
   5. COMPOUND VERB ....
   ....

6. Richard Benton has signed the contract. He must be held liable for any damage done to the equipment.
   6. ADVERBIAL CLAUSE ....
   ....

7. England was our ally in World War II. France was also our ally in that war.
   7. COMPOUND SUBJECT ....
   ....

8. Edwin Arlington Robinson, who was a poet of the 1920's, worked as a civil servant for many years.
   8. APPOSITIVE ....
   ....

9. The Crosstown Expressway, which was closed for repairs for several months, was completely resurfaced.
   9. PAST PARTICIPLE ....
   ....

10. He was careless for just one moment after years of prudent caution, and therefore he lost all that he had gained.
    10. ADVERBIAL CLAUSE ....
    ....

ANSWER KEY: TEST OF MASTERY

1. Sensing that Arthur could not rely on luck this time, I was paralyzed with terror.
2. The vases which had been wrapped in cotton were placed very carefully into the packing crates.
3. Poseidon, the Greek god of the sea, supposedly decided the fate of all who embarked in ships destined for faraway shores.
4. Horrified by the sight, Edna tried in vain to scream for help.
5. City University serves the five boroughs of New York City and has an enrollment of more than 200,000 students.
6. Since Richard Benton signed the contract, he must be held liable for any damage done to the equipment.
7. Both England and France were our allies in World War II.
8. Edwin Arlington Robinson, a poet of the 1920's, worked as a civil servant for many years.
9. Closed for repairs for several months, the Crosstown Expressway was completely resurfaced.
10. Because he was careless for just one moment after years of prudent caution, he lost all that he had gained.

4. Diction

The English language is a composite of many systems of communication both in usage and in diction (choice of words). When different systems of communications (dialects) are being used by the writer and reader, or by the speakers and listeners, only confusion and misunderstanding result.

BASIC SYSTEMS OF DICTION

STANDARD: Words that are used to convey the thoughts of one person to another on the widest communication band. This is the system of our best speakers and writers.

NONSTANDARD: Words that are used by social, geographical, occupational, ethnic, and religious groups to convey thoughts to a restricted number of people.

WORD	STANDARD DEFINITION	DEFINITION NONSTANDARD
scream	loud sound revealing fright: hear a *scream*.	funny, amusing: It's a *scream*!
smashed	broken to pieces; destroyed: *smashed* the vase.	drunk: He's *smashed*.
hip	part of body: carry the child on her *hip*.	aware: He's *hip*.
square	even: a geometrical figure: draw a *square*.	old-fashioned, conservative: be a *square*.

Both Standard and Nonstandard words are subdivided into five overlapping groups.

Formal: Words that are used when dignity is the primary requirement. This is the level of sermons, the language of ceremony, the wording of treaties and binding agreements.

Written: Words that are used in written communications for precision and clarity to tell an entire story, to convey a complete idea, or give a full description.

Colloquial (Oral): Spoken words that are in everyday use when formality and presentation of a complete unit of thought is not being stressed.

Technical: Words that have very specific meaning for those in certain occupations, calling for a precision of identification not needed by the public.

　macron (pronunciation)
　octave (prosody)
　anhydrous (chemistry)

Foreign: Words and phrases that are taken along with their pronunciation, directly from another language. Very often they parallel good, acceptable English words.

　en passant (in passing)
　entre nous (between us)
　gaucheries (awkwardness)

Into this group fall Briticisms—words that are acceptable in England but for which we have American substitutes that are preferred here.

　braces (suspenders)
　lift (elevator)

Examples of standard words:

FORMAL	WRITTEN	COLLOQUIAL
acquire	obtain	get
inter	bury	bury
scrutinize	examine	look over
irate, enraged	angry	mad
secrete	hide	put away
possess	own	have
inquired	questioned	asked
relate	describe	tell
complete	finish	end

Nonstandard words are also included in the following classifications:

Archaic: Words that were once in standard usage but are no longer current; words associated with pre-Elizabethan English.

　quoth　prithee　perchance　kine　mayhap

Obsolete: Words that were in standard usage in post-Elizabethan English but are no longer in current usage.

　moil (trouble)　*assoil*

Poetic: Words that are or were once in standard use in poetry but which are no longer acceptable in standard speech, prose, or poetry.

　o'er　ope　oft　e'en

Jargon: Words that are occupational in nature, the occupational slang of those working in specific fields; a mixture of two or more existing languages. Pidgin English and Chinook are jargons.

Contractions and Clipped Words: Words that have been abbreviated for everyday oral and written communication.

　phone (telephone)　*can't* (can not)
　chem (chemistry)

Slang: A loose term for words that are not accepted as part of the Standard English vocabulary. It includes newly coined words and phrases and terms that have been arbitrarily termed unacceptable.

　flip a lid　cool it man　in a fix

Localism: Words that are used with specific meanings only in certain areas of the country and which do not have countrywide acceptance.

　tote (carry)　*poke* (paper bag)　*reckon* (think)

No longer used are such judgmental terms as *illiterate, vulgarism,* or *barbarism* for words in limited dialects. *Dialectal* has become a neutral term referring to any system of language, instead of referring to localisms only.

The examination that you are going to take tests your command of Standard Written English. Therefore make certain that when you have completed going over the following list, you are in full command of Standard Written English forms.

CORRECTNESS AND EFFECTIVENESS OF EXPRESSION

TROUBLESOME PHRASES

accidently — nonstandard for *accidentally*
NONSTANDARD: He slipped accidently and almost fractured his forearm.
STANDARD: He slipped accidentally and almost fractured his forearm.

ad — colloquial form for *advertisement*
COLLOQUIAL: He plans to have the *ad* inserted in the afternoon edition.
WRITTEN: He plans to have the *advertisement* inserted in the afternoon edition.

agree — agree *with* a person, agree *to* a plan, agree *in* an opinion
NONSTANDARD: I agree *with* his suggestion that we investigate further.
STANDARD: I agree *to* his suggestion that we investigate further.

aim — colloquial when used to mean *intend*
COLLOQUIAL: I *aim* to spend the next four hours in the library.
WRITTEN: I *intend* to spend the next four hours in the library.

ain't — to be avoided as a symbol of nonstandard English
NONSTANDARD: There *ain't* anything wrong.
STANDARD: There *isn't* anything wrong.

alibi — colloquial when used as a synonym of *excuse*
COLLOQUIAL: What is your *alibi* this time for coming late?
WRITTEN: What is your *excuse* for coming late this time?

all the farther — localism when used to mean *as close as* or *as far as*
LOCALISM: This is *all the farther* I am willing to follow.
STANDARD: This is *as far as* I am willing to follow.

allow — localism when used to mean *think* or *say*
LOCALISM: I *allow* that your plan is the best one suggested so far.
STANDARD: I *think* that your plan is the best one suggested so far.

alright — nonstandard for all right
NONSTANDARD: Everything will be *alright*.
STANDARD: Everything will be *all right*.

altho — simplified spelling that was never accepted in general use
NONSTANDARD: I will really try *altho* I don't see how we can succeed.
STANDARD: I will really try *although* I do not see how we can succeed.

alumnus — is the singular and *alumni* is the plural used to refer to men. A girl is an *alumna*. The plural of *alumna* is *alumnae*.
NOT ACCEPTED: The note was sent to the president of the *alumni* association of the girls' college.
ACCEPTED FORM: The note was sent to the president of the *alumnae* association of the girls' college.

and etc. — omit *and* since *etc.* means *and other things*
NOT ACCEPTED: I shall repeat each letter of the alphabet, a, b, c, *and etc.*
ACCEPTED FORM: I shall repeat each letter of the alphabet, a, b, c, *etc.*

anent — archaic for *concerning*
ARCHAIC: Harold will speak to you *anent* your new responsibilities.
STANDARD: Harold will speak to you *concerning* your new responsibilities.

angle — colloquial when used to mean *point of view*
COLLOQUIAL: You must learn to see things from your superior's *angle*.
WRITTEN: You must learn to view matters from your superior's *point of view*.

angry — angry *with* people, angry *at* things or animals, angry *about* events or situations
COLLOQUIAL: Edna was very angry *at* her daughter for disobeying her.
WRITTEN: Edna was very angry *with* her daughter for disobeying her.

any — colloquial when used to mean *at all*
COLLOQUIAL: She hasn't spoken *any* to us for almost an hour.
WRITTEN: She has not spoken to us *at all* for almost an hour.

any more — colloquial when used to mean *no longer*
COLLOQUIAL: Annie doesn't live here *any more*.
WRITTEN: Annie does not live here *any longer*.

anyways — localism for *anyway*
LOCALISM: She would not have helped us *anyways*.
STANDARD: She would not have helped us *anyway*.

anywheres — nonstandard for *anywhere*
NONSTANDARD: You will not find another one like this *anywheres*.
STANDARD: You will not find another one like this *anywhere*.

around — colloquial when used to mean *about*
COLLOQUIAL: They shall arrive around ten o'clock.
WRITTEN: They shall arrive about ten o'clock.

as . . . so — In Standard Written English use *as . . . as* when the sentence is affirmative; use *so . . . as* when the sense is negative.
- WRITTEN: He is *as* skillful *as* anyone in our group.
- COLLOQUIAL: He is *not as* skillful *as* the ones in our group.
- WRITTEN: He is *not so* skillful *as* the ones in our group.

at about — repetitious (redundant); *at* is unnecessary
- COLLOQUIAL: The train will be here *at about* six o'clock.
- WRITTEN: The train will arrive *about* six o'clock.

awful, awfully — colloquial when used to mean *very much, very*
- COLLOQUIAL: She was *awfully* pleased with your gift.
- WRITTEN: She was *very much* pleased with your gift.

badly — colloquial when used as a synonym for *very much*
- COLLOQUIAL: Alice said that she wanted to see Milton *badly*.
- WRITTEN: Alice said that she *very much* wanted to see Milton.

balance — colloquial when used to mean *rest* or *remainder*
- COLLOQUIAL: Spend the balance of your time in the library preparing for the test.
- WRITTEN: Spend the remainder of your time in the library in preparation for the test.

bank on — colloquial for *depend on, rely on*
- COLLOQUIAL: Can you *bank on* him when the going becomes rough?
- WRITTEN: Can you *depend on* him when the going becomes rough?

being as — localism for *since* or *because*
- LOCALISM: *Being as* you are a friend of mine, I'll lend the pen to you.
- WRITTEN: *Since* you are a friend of mine, I shall lend the pen to you.

being that — nonstandard when used in place of *since* or *because*
- NONSTANDARD: *Being that* you are here, we can rehearse now.
- STANDARD: *Since* you are here, we can rehearse now.

blame on — colloquial for *blame*
- COLLOQUIAL: Don't *blame* everything *on* me!
- WRITTEN: Don't *blame* me for everything!

both alike — repetitious (redundant)—omit *both*
- COLLOQUIAL: Shirley said that she found them *both alike*.
- WRITTEN: Shirley said that she found them *alike*.

bunch — colloquial when used as a synonym for *group*
- COLLOQUIAL: Alec warned me that a *bunch* of the men was waiting for me.
- WRITTEN: Alec warned me that a group of the men was waiting for me.

bust, busted — nonstandard for *burst*
- NONSTANDARD: The pipe must have *busted* during the cold weather.
- STANDARD: The pipe must have *burst* during the cold weather.

but — when *but* means *only* it conveys a negative sense and therefore no other negative should be used with it.
- NONSTANDARD: He didn't come to see us *but* once.
- STANDARD: He came to see us but once.

but what — nonstandard for *but that*
- NONSTANDARD: I have no doubt *but what* you are absolutely correct.
- STANDARD: I have no doubt *but that* you are absolutely correct.

calculate — localism (New England and Southern areas) when used for *suppose*
- LOCALISM: I *calculate* that he should be here any minute.
- STANDARD: I suppose that he will arrive any minute.

cannot seem — colloquial for *seem unable to*
- COLLOQUIAL: For the past few days, Don *cannot seem* to do the work.
- WRITTEN: For the past few days, Don *seems unable* to do the work.

can't hardly — nonstandard for *can hardly* since *hardly* contains negative force
- NONSTANDARD: I can't hardly wait until the term ends.
- STANDARD: I can hardly wait for the term to end.

can't help but — colloquial for *can't help* or *can but*
- COLLOQUIAL: We *can't help but* do the paper the way we think best.
- WRITTEN: We *can't help* doing the paper the way we think best.
  or We *can but* do the paper the way we think best.

case — jargon borrowed from legalisms and to be avoided
- JARGON: We were advised exactly what the procedure should be in this *case*.
- STANDARD: We were advised exactly what the procedure should be in this *situation*.

combine — colloquial when used as a noun-substitute for *combination*

CORRECTNESS AND EFFECTIVENESS OF EXPRESSION

COLLOQUIAL:	They joined in a profitable business *combine*.		**could of**	nonstandard for *could have*
WRITTEN:	They organized a profitable business *combination*.		NONSTANDARD:	They could *of* left an hour ago.
			STANDARD:	They could *have* left an hour ago.
company	colloquial when used as a synonym for *guests*		**couple**	use *couple* to refer to two; *several* should be used when referring to more than two
COLLOQUIAL:	Who will be our company for dinner this evening?		NONSTANDARD:	A *couple of* the members may be present.
WRITTEN:	Who will be our guests for dinner this evening?		STANDARD:	*Several* of the members may be present.
compare *to*	use to designate *likenesses* between objects and persons		**criticize**	used to refer to favorable and unfavorable criticism
compare *with*	use to refer to both *likenesses* and *differences*		STANDARD:	When you *criticize*, mention the good points first.
NONSTANDARD:	Her playing does not compare *to* his.		**crowd**	colloquial when used to mean *group, set*
STANDARD:	Her playing does not compare *with* his.		COLLOQUIAL:	Our *crowd* decided to attend the evening performance.
STANDARD:	This violin compares favorably *with* that one.		WRITTEN:	Our *group* decided to attend the evening performance.
STANDARD:	This violin compares favorably *to* that one.		**cute**	colloquial, trite, overworked, has too many meanings
complected	localism for complexioned		COLLOQUIAL:	He is a *cute* man. You have a *cute* idea there.
LOCALISM:	Did you meet the dark-*complected* stranger?		WRITTEN:	He is a *handsome* man. You have a *clever* idea there.
STANDARD:	Did you meet the dark-complexioned stranger?		**data**	*datum* is the singular form; *data* is plural
concur	use *concur in* for opinions, *concur with* for persons		COLLOQUIAL:	*This is* the data that I have just checked.
NONSTANDARD:	I *concur with* this interpretation of the facts.		WRITTEN:	*These are* the data that I have just checked.
STANDARD:	I *concur in* this interpretation of the facts.		**date**	colloquial when used as a noun-substitute for *appointment*
consensus of opinion	redundant, omit *of opinion*		COLLOQUIAL:	I have *a date* with the family doctor tonight.
NONSTANDARD:	The *consensus of opinion* is that there will be no more world wars.		WRITTEN:	I have *an appointment* with the family doctor tonight.
STANDARD:	The *consensus* is that there will be no more world wars.		**deal**	colloquial when used to mean *transaction*
considerable	nonstandard when used to mean *very, very much* as an adverb		COLLOQUIAL:	I expect to realize no profit from this *deal*.
NONSTANDARD:	He was *considerable* upset when he learned the results.		WRITTEN:	I expect to realize no profit from this *transaction*.
STANDARD:	He was *very much* upset when he learned the results.		**differ**	use differ *with a person* and differ *from a thing*
STANDARD:	He owns a *considerable* amount of property in the downtown area.		NONSTANDARD:	His case differs greatly *with* the one I am buying.
contact	colloquial when used as a verb to mean *get in touch with,* call		STANDARD:	His case differs greatly *from* the one that I am buying.
COLLOQUIAL:	We shall *contact* you when the package arrives.		STANDARD:	I differ with you in this matter.
WRITTEN:	We shall *call* you when the package arrives.		**different than**	colloquial for *different from*
cool	nonstandard when used as a generalized substitute for *appropriate* or *excellent*		COLLOQUIAL:	Helen's outlook is different *than* mine.
NONSTANDARD:	That was a *cool* performance.		WRITTEN:	Helen's outlook is different *from* mine.
STANDARD:	That was an *excellent* performance.			

disremember	localism for *forget* or unable to recall		
LOCALISM:	I *disremember* whether she had been here or not that evening.		
STANDARD:	I cannot recall whether she had been here that evening.		
doctor	colloquial when used to mean *repair, mend, adulterate*		
COLLOQUIAL:	Phyllis *doctored* the broken key in the piano.		
WRITTEN:	Phyllis mended the broken key in the piano.		
dove	colloquial for *dived*		
COLLOQUIAL:	The lifesaver dove into the water in a vain attempt to rescue the spent swimmer.		
WRITTEN:	The lifesaver dived into the water in a vain attempt to rescue the spent swimmer.		
drownded	nonstandard for *drowned*		
NONSTANDARD:	The mother feared that all of the children had been *drownded*.		
STANDARD:	The mother feared that all of the children had been *drowned*.		
drug	nonstandard for *dragged*		
NONSTANDARD:	The tow car *drug* the abandoned car from the ditch.		
STANDARD:	The tow car *dragged* the abandoned car from the ditch.		
due to	colloquial when used to modify a verb; standard when used as an adjective		
COLLOQUIAL:	*Due to* his illness, the opening night was postponed.		
WRITTEN:	The opening night was postponed because of his illness.		
STANDARD:	The accident was *due to* carelessness.		
each other	use *each other* to refer to two; *one another* is used to refer to more than two		
COLLOQUIAL:	The four men discussed the problem with *each other*.		
WRITTEN:	The four men discussed the problem with *one another*.		
eats	nonstandard when *used* as a substitute for *food*		
NONSTANDARD:	Lucy is in charge of the preparation of the *eats* for the party.		
STANDARD:	Lucy is in charge of the preparation of the food for the party.		
elegant	colloquial when used as synonym for *delicious* or *good*		
COLLOQUIAL:	That was a most *elegant* meal.		
WRITTEN:	That was a most *delicious* meal.		
else	redundant when used with *no one*		
COLLOQUIAL:	She will speak to *no one else* but you.		
WRITTEN:	She will speak to *no one* but you.		
endorse on the back of	*endorse* means on the back of, and therefore *on the back of* is unnecessary		
COLLOQUIAL:	Please *endorse* the check *on the back*.		
WRITTEN:	Please *endorse* the check.		
enthused	colloquial, clipped form for *enthusiastic*		
COLLOQUIAL:	I just didn't feel too *enthused*.		
WRITTEN:	I just did not feel very *enthusiastic*.		
equally as	omit *as* as unnecessary		
COLLOQUIAL:	Of course, your work is *equally as* good.		
WRITTEN:	Of course, your work is *equally* good.		
etc.	other than for an obvious series, *etc.* is to be avoided in Standard Written English		
NOT ACCEPTED:	We finally had an interview with Mr. Smith, *etc.*		
ACCEPTED FORM:	We finally had an interview with Mr. Smith and the other members of the firm.		
every so often **every now and then** **every once in a while**	colloquial when used to mean occasionally; in formal writing and speaking prefer *occasionally*		
COLLOQUIAL:	We do meet at regional conferences *every now and then*.		
WRITTEN:	We do meet at regional conferences *occasionally*.		
everyone, everybody	as pronouns, these should be written as one-word units		
NOT ACCEPTED:	Will *every one* please be seated.		
ACCEPTED FORM:	Will *everyone* please be seated.		
everywheres	nonstandard for *everywhere*		
NONSTANDARD:	You can see Jack Frost's handiwork *everywheres* you go.		
STANDARD:	You can see Jack Frost's handiwork *everywhere* you go.		
except	localism when used as substitute for *unless*		
LOCALISM:	You will be fired *except* you do exactly as you are told.		
STANDARD:	You will be fired *unless* you do exactly as you are told.		
expect	localism when used as synonym for *suspect* or *suppose*		
LOCALISM:	We *expect* he will be home much later.		
STANDARD:	We *suppose* that he will be home much later.		
STANDARD:	I *expect* to receive his reply in the return mail.		
extra	nonstandard when used as adverb to mean *unusually* or *extremely*		
NONSTANDARD:	Please be *extra* cautious as you walk

CORRECTNESS AND EFFECTIVENESS OF EXPRESSION

	down the slope tonight.
STANDARD:	Please be *extremely* cautious as you walk down the slope tonight.
STANDARD:	They hired three *extra* packers during the sale period.
faze	colloquial for *affect adversely*
COLLOQUIAL:	Harold was *fazed* by the vague wording of the assignment.
WRITTEN:	Harold was *puzzled* by the vague wording of the assignment.
fellow	colloquial and general for *one, man, boy, person,* etc.
COLLOQUIAL:	Do you know the *fellow* who just came in?
WRITTEN:	Do you know the *man* who just came in?
fine	colloquial and overworked; in Standard Written English prefer more precise word
COLLOQUIAL:	It is such a *fine* day!
WRITTEN:	It is such a bright, sunny day!
fix	colloquial for *repair*
COLLOQUIAL:	I plan to have the damage *fixed*.
WRITTEN:	I plan to have the damage *repaired*.
flunk	colloquial for *fail*
COLLOQUIAL:	I have the distinction of being the only one to *flunk* that test.
WRITTEN:	I have the distinction of being the only one to *fail* that test.
folks	colloquial when used as noun-substitute for family, relatives
COLLOQUIAL:	Tom plans to spend the evening with his *folks*.
WRITTEN:	Tom plans to spend the evening with his *parents*.
STANDARD:	How many *folk* songs can you teach us tonight?
former, latter	refer to two only
COLLOQUIAL:	Of the three, I prefer the *latter* (*former*).
WRITTEN:	Of the three, I prefer the *last* (*first*).
funny	colloquial when used to mean *strange, peculiar*
COLLOQUIAL:	That was a *funny* thing for you to say at a time like this!
WRITTEN:	That was a *strange* thing for you to say at a time like this!
gent	nonstandard for *man* or *gentleman*
NONSTANDARD:	Who is the *gent* standing there?
STANDARD:	Who is the *man* standing there?
get	overworked colloquial term to be avoided in Standard Written English
COLLOQUIAL:	I am *getting* tired just standing here.
WRITTEN:	I am *becoming* tired from just standing here.
good	nonstandard when used as an adverb
NONSTANDARD:	He plays *good*.
STANDARD:	He plays *well*.
got to	colloquial when used as a synonym for *must*
COLLOQUIAL:	You *got to* listen to me.
WRITTEN:	You *must* listen to me.
graduate	colloquial when used as a substitute for *graduate from* or *be graduated from*
COLLOQUIAL:	I hope *to graduate* high school this June.
WRITTEN:	I hope *to be graduated* from high school this June.
guess	colloquial when used to mean *think* or *suppose*.
COLLOQUIAL:	I *guess* I should not have left so early.
WRITTEN:	I *suppose* that I should not have left so early.
had ought, hadn't ought	nonstandard for *ought* or *should not*
NONSTANDARD:	I *had ought* to do my homework earlier.
STANDARD:	I *ought* to do my homework earlier or I *should have done* my homework earlier.
hardly	must not be used with negative since *hardly* has negative value
COLLOQUIAL:	I *hadn't hardly* sufficient time to read the book.
WRITTEN:	I had *hardly* sufficient time to read the book.
a heap of	colloquial when used as substitute for *many*
COLLOQUIAL:	Stan has *a heap of* things to do when he comes home.
WRITTEN:	Stan has *many* things to do when he comes home.
help	colloquial when used to mean employees
COLLOQUIAL:	The owner told his help of the difficulty.
WRITTEN:	The owner told his employees of the difficulty.
hisself	nonstandard for *himself*
NONSTANDARD:	He will have to complete the entire translation *hisself*.
STANDARD:	He will have to complete the entire translation *himself*.
humans	colloquial when used as substitute for *human beings*
COLLOQUIAL:	He treats the animals as though they were *humans*.
WRITTEN:	He treats the animals as though they were *human beings*.
in back of	colloquial for *behind*

COLLOQUIAL:	You will have to stand *in back of* the others.	
WRITTEN:	You will have to stand *behind* the others.	
in regards to	colloquial for *in regard to*	
COLLOQUIAL:	I plan to see him *in regards to* a possible summer position for me.	
WRITTEN:	I plan to see him *in regard to* a possible summer position for me.	
inside of	colloquial for *within* (for time)	
COLLOQUIAL:	The doctor will be here *inside of* an hour.	
WRITTEN:	The doctor will be here *within* the hour.	
invite	nonstandard when used as substitute for *invitation*	
NONSTANDARD:	When do they plan to mail the *invites*?	
STANDARD:	When do they plan to mail the *invitations*?	
irregardless	nonstandard for *regardless*	
NONSTANDARD:	Ira plans to leave *irregardless* of what we do.	
STANDARD:	Ira plans to leave *regardless* of what we do.	
is when, is where	colloquial for *is a place where, occurs when*	
COLLOQUIAL:	The most exciting scene *is when* the dam finally bursts.	
WRITTEN:	The most exciting scene *occurs when* the dam finally bursts.	
just	inexact, colloquial when used to mean *simply* or *quite*	
COLLOQUIAL:	This is *just* beautiful.	
WRITTEN:	This is *simply* beautiful.	
just exactly	*exactly* is unnecessary	
COLLOQUIAL:	It was *just exactly* what we were waiting to hear.	
WRITTEN:	It was just what we had been waiting to hear.	
kick	nonstandard when used to mean *complain*	
NONSTANDARD:	What is the use of *kicking*?	
STANDARD:	What is the use of *complaining*?	
kind of, sort of	colloquial for *rather* or *somewhat*	
COLLOQUIAL:	She does look *kind of* tired.	
WRITTEN:	She does look *rather* tired.	
kind of a	colloquial substitute for *kind of*	
COLLOQUIAL:	That was the *kind of a* peach that I really enjoy eating.	
WRITTEN:	That was the *kind of* apple that I really enjoy eating.	
later on	colloquial for *later*	
COLLOQUIAL:	May we see you *later on* in the evening?	
WRITTEN:	May we see you *later* in the evening?
leave	mainly colloquial when used for *let* to mean *permit* or *allow*
COLLOQUIAL:	*Leave* me go. *Leave* her have her own way.
WRITTEN:	*Let* me go. *Let* her have her own way.
leave go of	nonstandard for *let go*
NONSTANDARD:	*Leave go of* my hand, please.
STANDARD:	*Let go of* my hand, please.
let on	colloquial when used to mean *pretend* or *admit*
COLLOQUIAL:	My father will never *let on* that he had been fooled.
WRITTEN:	My father will never *admit* that he had been fooled.
line	colloquial when used as a substitute for *kind, business*
COLLOQUIAL:	What *line* will they invest the money in?
WRITTEN:	In what *business* will they invest the money?
locate	colloquial when used to mean *settle*
COLLOQUIAL:	They intend to *locate* in Brooklyn.
WRITTEN:	They intend to *settle* in Brooklyn.
lose out, win out	colloquial for *lose, win*
COLLOQUIAL:	I am certain that they will *win out* in the end.
WRITTEN:	I am certain that they will *win* in the end.
lots, lots of	colloquial when used as synonyms for *many* or *much*
COLLOQUIAL:	We have *lots of* time.
WRITTEN:	We have *much* time.
math	colloquial clipped form of *mathematics*
COLLOQUIAL:	He plans to do graduate work in *math*.
WRITTEN:	He plans to do graduate work in *mathematics*.
may of	nonstandard for *may have*
NONSTANDARD:	I *may of* lost every copy of the letter.
STANDARD:	I *may have* lost every copy of the letter.
mean	colloquial when used as a synonym of *cruel, malicious, ill-tempered*
COLLOQUIAL:	Scrooge was for a long time just a *mean* old man.
WRITTEN:	Scrooge was for a long time just an *ill-tempered* old man.
might of	nonstandard for *might have*
NONSTANDARD:	The results *might of* been very different.

CORRECTNESS AND EFFECTIVENESS OF EXPRESSION

STANDARD: The results *might have* been very much different.

mighty — colloquial when used to mean *very* or *exceedingly*
COLLOQUIAL: It was a *mighty* interesting film.
WRITTEN: It was a *very* interesting film.
STANDARD: The *mighty* battleship was doomed when torpedoes were perfected.

more preferable — nonstandard for *preferable*
NONSTANDARD: Anything would be *more preferable* to this torture.
STANDARD: Anything would be *preferable* to this torture.

most — colloquial when used as an adverb in place of *almost* or *nearly*
COLLOQUIAL: We visit our grandparents *most* every Sunday.
WRITTEN: We visit our grandparents *almost* every Sunday.

muchly — nonstandard for *much, very much*
NONSTANDARD: I enjoy this type of program *muchly*.
STANDARD: I enjoy this type of program *very much*.

myself — nonstandard when used as a substitute for *I* or *me*
NONSTANDARD: Frances and *myself* are going to head the group.
STANDARD: Frances and *I* are going to head the group.

near — nonstandard when used in place of *nearly*
NONSTANDARD: The steak is *near* done.
STANDARD: The steak is *nearly* done.

nice — generalized, colloquial; avoid as substitute for *pleasant, agreeable, delightful*
COLLOQUIAL: We had a very *nice* time this evening.
WRITTEN: We had a very *pleasant* time this evening.

no account — colloquial when used to mean *worthless*
COLLOQUIAL: Where is that *no account* nephew of mine!
WRITTEN: Where is that *worthless* nephew of mine!

nohow — nonstandard for anyhow
NONSTANDARD: I would not have done it *nohow*.
STANDARD: I would not have done it *anyhow*.

no place — nonstandard for *nowhere*
NONSTANDARD: The boy was *no place* to be found.
STANDARD: The boy was to be found *nowhere*.

nowheres — localism for nowhere
LOCALISM: The pen was *nowheres* near where you had said it would be.
STANDARD: The pen was *nowhere* near where you had said it would be.

oft — archaic for *often*
ARCHAIC: How *oft* have I thought of those most pleasant days long past.
STANDARD: How *often* have I thought of those most pleasant days long past.

off of — colloquial for *off*
COLLOQUIAL: Take the pot *off of* the table.
WRITTEN: Take the pot *off* the table.

ok — colloquial term to be avoided in Standard Written English
COLLOQUIAL: He said that everything would be *ok*.
WRITTEN: He said that everything would *turn out well*.

out loud — colloquial for *aloud*
COLLOQUIAL: The sentry called my name *out loud*.
WRITTEN: The sentry called my name *aloud*.

outside of — colloquial when used to mean *except*
COLLOQUIAL: I spoke to no one *outside of* Bill.
WRITTEN: I spoke to no one *except* Bill.

over — colloquial when used to mean *more than*
COLLOQUIAL: He wants *over* two thousand dollars for the skiff.
WRITTEN: He wants *more than* two thousand dollars for the skiff.

over with — colloquial for *over*
COLLOQUIAL: The game will soon be *over with*.
WRITTEN: The game will soon be *over*.

owing to — colloquial when used as a prepositional phrase
COLLOQUIAL: *Owing to* conditions beyond our control, we are forced to suspend operations.
WRITTEN: *Because of* conditions beyond our control, we are forced to suspend operations.

party — nonstandard when used to mean *person*; legal jargon when used in the phrase *party of the first part*
NONSTANDARD: He is one *party* I really want to meet.
STANDARD: He is one *person* I really want to meet.

per — jargon when used instead of *each*
COLLOQUIAL: The driver is paid one dollar *per* passenger.
WRITTEN: The driver is paid one dollar *for each* passenger.

percent, per cent — colloquial when used to mean percentage; per cent (percent) should follow numbers only
COLLOQUIAL: There is a high *percent* of waste in this process.
WRITTEN: There is a high *percentage* of waste in this process.
STANDARD: We pay the agent ten *percent* of our gross income.

photo	colloquial, clipped form of *photograph*
COLLOQUIAL:	Milton carries Betty's *photo* in his wallet.
WRITTEN:	Milton carries Betty's *photograph* in his wallet.
piece	localism for *a short distance*
LOCALISM:	Walk with me a *piece*.
STANDARD:	Walk with me a *short distance*.
plan on	colloquial when used as a synonym of *plan to*
COLLOQUIAL:	Are you *planning on* leaving early?
WRITTEN:	Are you *planning to* leave early?
plenty	colloquial when used as an adjective or adverb to mean *very, quite, much, very much*
COLLOQUIAL:	You would be *plenty* annoyed too if you had been so mistreated.
WRITTEN:	You would be *very much* annoyed too if you had been so mistreated.
poorly	localism when used to mean *not well*
LOCALISM:	I feel *poorly* today.
STANDARD:	I do *not* feel *well* today.
posted	colloquial when used to mean *informed*
COLLOQUIAL:	Keep us *posted* of your progress.
WRITTEN:	Keep us *informed* of your progress.
prof	nonstandard clipped form of *professor*
NONSTANDARD:	I have an interview with the *prof* this morning.
STANDARD:	I have an interview with the *professor* this morning.
proven	colloquial for *proved*
COLLOQUIAL:	These data would have *proven* him wrong!
WRITTEN:	These data would have *proved* him wrong!
put up with	colloquial when used to mean *endure*
COLLOQUIAL:	How will we be able to *put up with* his sense of humor for two weeks?
WRITTEN:	How will we be able to *endure* his sense of humor for two weeks?
quite a few	colloquial for *many*
COLLOQUIAL:	There were *quite a few* errors in spelling that I had to correct.
WRITTEN:	There were *many* errors that I had to correct in spelling.
quite some time	colloquial for *a long time*
COLLOQUIAL:	He has been doing well in his studies for *quite some time*.
WRITTEN:	He has been doing well in his studies for *a long time*.
rather unique	colloquial for *unique* (It is either *unique* or *not unique*; there can be no in between.)
COLLOQUIAL:	He has a *rather unique* method for gaining his customer's confidence.
WRITTEN:	He has a *unique* method for gaining his customer's confidence.
real	dialectal when used as an adverb in place of *really* or *very*
COLLOQUIAL:	I did *real well* on the final examination.
WRITTEN:	I did *very well* on the final examination.
reason is because	colloquial for *reason is that*
COLLOQUIAL:	The *reason* for his success *is because* he listens.
WRITTEN:	The *reason* for his success *is that* he listens.
reckon	localism when used to mean *think* or *suppose*
LOCALISM:	Do you *reckon* that he did not hear what we had said to him?
STANDARD:	Do you *think* that he had not heard what we had said to him?
refer back	colloquial for refer (*back* is repetitious)
COLLOQUIAL:	May I *refer back* to my notes?
WRITTEN:	May I *refer* to my notes?
repeat again	colloquial for *repeat* (*again* is repetitious)
COLLOQUIAL:	Will you please *repeat* that statement *again*?
WRITTEN:	Will you please *repeat* that statement!
right	localism and archaic when used to mean *very*
LOCALISM:	We were *right* sorry to hear of your misfortune.
STANDARD:	We were *very* sorry to hear of your misfortune.
right away	colloquial when used to mean *immediately*
COLLOQUIAL:	We shall prepare the meal *right away*.
WRITTEN:	We shall prepare the meal *immediately*.
run	colloquial when used to mean *manage, control, conduct*
COLLOQUIAL:	Does Sally think that she can *run* the business by herself?
WRITTEN:	Does Sally think that she can *manage* the business by herself?
said	legal jargon in the phrase *said person*
NONSTANDARD:	The *said* person was present during the entire incident.

CORRECTNESS AND EFFECTIVENESS OF EXPRESSION

STANDARD:	*This* person was present during the entire incident.
seldom ever	colloquial for *seldom if ever*
COLLOQUIAL:	She is *seldom ever* at home alone.
WRITTEN:	She is *seldom if ever* at home alone.
should of	nonstandard for *should have*
NONSTANDARD:	You *should of* seen the look on his face!
STANDARD:	You *should have* seen the look on his face!
show up	colloquial when used to mean *expose, appear, arrive*
COLLOQUIAL:	How many members *showed up* at the meeting?
WRITTEN:	How many members *arrived for* the meeting?
sign up	colloquial when used to mean *enlist*
COLLOQUIAL:	Do you plan to *sign up* or wait until you are drafted?
WRITTEN:	Do you plan to *enlist* or wait until you are drafted?
simply	colloquial when used in place of *really*
COLLOQUIAL:	This is *simply* the best performance I have ever seen.
WRITTEN:	This is *really* the best performance I have ever seen.
someplace	nonstandard for *somewhere*
NONSTANDARD:	They live *someplace* near the school.
STANDARD:	They live *somewhere* near the school.
somewheres	localism for *somewhere*
NONSTANDARD:	You will find the money *somewheres* near the desk.
STANDARD:	You will find the money *somewhere* near the desk.
sort of a	nonstandard for *sort of*
NONSTANDARD:	It was the *sort of a* compliment that makes me feel uncomfortable.
STANDARD:	It was the *sort of* compliment that makes me feel uncomfortable.
start in	colloquial when used instead of *begin to*
COLLOQUIAL:	Don't *start in* asking questions now.
WRITTEN:	Don't *begin to* ask questions now.
sure	colloquial when used in place of *surely*
COLLOQUIAL:	He is *sure* wrong.
WRITTEN:	He is *surely* wrong.
sure and	barbarism for *sure to*
COLLOQUIAL:	Be *sure and* sign your name to the note.
WRITTEN:	Be *sure to* sign your name to the note.
suspicion	localism when used as a verb, in place of *suspect*
NONSTANDARD:	I *suspicioned* that he was not at home.
STANDARD:	I *suspected* that he was not at home.
swell	general, over-used colloquial term when used in place of *excellent, pleasant, congenial, likable*
COLLOQUIAL:	We had a *swell* time at the party.
WRITTEN:	We had a *pleasant* time at the party.
terribly	colloquial when used as substitute for *very much*
COLLOQUIAL:	We were *terribly* annoyed by his self-centered disregard of others.
WRITTEN:	We were *very much* annoyed by his self-centered disregard of others.
theirselves	nonstandard for *themselves*
NONSTANDARD:	They will have to do all of the work *theirselves*.
STANDARD:	They will have to do all of the work *themselves*.
these kind, those kind	nonstandard for *this kind, that kind,*
these sort, those sort	nonstandard for *this sort, that sort*
NONSTANDARD:	He will eat only *these kind* of candy.
STANDARD:	He will eat only *this* kind of candy.
thisaway, thataway	nonstandard for *this way, that way*
NONSTANDARD:	You must learn how to do it *thisaway*.
STANDARD:	You must learn how to do it *this way*.
this here, that there	nonstandard for *this, that*
NONSTANDARD:	*That there* is the one I want.
STANDARD:	*That* is the one I want.
thru	nonstandard spelling for *through*
NONSTANDARD:	Go *thru* that door.
STANDARD:	Go *through* that door.
try and	colloquial for *try to*
COLLOQUIAL:	Please *try and* do it as soon as possible.
WRITTEN:	Please *try to* do it as soon as possible.
up	colloquial when used as a unit with *divide, fold, settle, end* (*divide up, fold up, settle up, end up*)
COLLOQUIAL:	I don't know just where this will *end up*.
WRITTEN:	I don't know just where this will *end*.
up until	colloquial for *until*
COLLOQUIAL:	You could have paid at this office *up until* yesterday.
WRITTEN:	You could have paid at this office *until yesterday*.
U.S.	colloquial for the *United States*

COLLOQUIAL:	He plans to visit the *U.S.* in the near future.	**ways**	colloquial when used as a substitute for *way*
WRITTEN:	He plans to visit the *United States* in the near future.	COLLOQUIAL:	He has a long *ways* to go.
		WRITTEN:	He has a long *way* to go.
used to could	localism for *used to be able to*	**where**	colloquial when used for *that*
NONSTANDARD:	Several years ago, I *used to could* pick up that entire bundle by myself.	COLLOQUIAL:	I see in the book *where* the authors state that women live longer than men.
STANDARD:	Several years ago, I *used to be able to* pick up that entire bundle by myself.	WRITTEN:	I see in the book *that* the authors state *that* women live longer than men.
very	colloquial when used to modify a past participle without *much*	**where at**	colloquial for *where*
COLLOQUIAL:	He was *very* excited when he heard the good news.	COLLOQUIAL:	*Where* did he find the book *at*?
WRITTEN:	He was *very much* excited when he heard the good news.	WRITTEN:	*Where* did he find the book?
wait on	colloquial when used as a substitute for *wait for*	**which**	nonstandard when used as pronoun to refer to people
COLLOQUIAL:	I just can't *wait on* his answer a minute longer.	NONSTANDARD:	Is that the woman *which you* saw?
WRITTEN:	I just cannot *wait for* his answer a minute longer.	STANDARD:	Is that the woman *whom you* saw?
want	colloquial when followed by a clause used as its object	**without**	nonstandard when used as a substitute for *unless*
COLLOQUIAL:	I want *that you should listen to what I have to say*.	NONSTANDARD:	She refuses to go *without* you go first.
WRITTEN:	I want *you to listen to what I have to say*.	STANDARD:	She refuses to go *unless* you go first.
want for	localism for *want*	**would have**	nonstandard when used in *if* clause instead of *had*
LOCALISM:	They *want for you* to wait until the telephone rings.	NONSTANDARD:	If you *would have* watched, you would not have made this mistake.
STANDARD:	They *want you* to wait until the telephone rings.	STANDARD:	If you *had* watched, you would not have made this mistake.
		would of	nonstandard for *would have*
		NONSTANDARD:	I *would of* gone there myself.
		STANDARD:	I *would have* gone there myself.

TEST OF MASTERY

In the space provided to the left in each of the following sentences write:
  acceptable if it contains no error in diction
  the word to be omitted if it can be made acceptable by an omission
  the word or phrase that must be substituted if one of the expressions must be eliminated

GROUP ONE

.... 1. Being that he is still my best friend, he may give me a copy of the note.
.... 2. She can't help but complain about her working conditions.
.... 3. This record cannot compare with the one you bought me.
.... 4. The consensus of opinion is that considerable sums of money must still be spent on this project.
.... 5. They could of tried to cool off the mixture by placing it into the refrigerator.
.... 6. An endorsement on the back of the check is acceptable.
.... 7. We expect them to vote an extra sum of money as a bonus for every one who was in the performance.
.... 8. He is one fellow that I never expected to see here.
.... 9. There aren't hardly enough days left to the week when we complete the projects he plans for Monday alone.
.... 10. You had ought to know that he would have had some such idea in the back of his mind.
.... 11. This is the kind of situation that you must leave exactly as is irregardless of how you feel about it.
.... 12. Later on in the evening, she said that she would leave earlier than we had planned.

... 13. Most of the proofreading was done by Arnold and myself.
... 14. There is no account that I would be more willing to plan on giving up.
... 15. I would have put up with all this nonsense if she could have proved that we were accomplishing something worthwhile.
... 16. Herb had not reckoned the costs when he repeated the same mistakes again.
... 17. This unique specimen of sports car has been mine for quite some time.
... 18. The reason that it was placed to the right away from the others is because Helen was afraid that it would be broken easily.
... 19. Would it be right for him to refer back to his notes?
... 20. Someone must know the address since I am certain that they do live someplace in this neighborhood.
... 21. Margie warned us to be sure and see the film currently shown in the local movie house.
... 22. You have waited too long to settle up this old account.
... 23. Edna is certainly a long ways from the end of the road.
... 24. If you would have done without all of this fanfare, the crew could have been dismissed hours ago.
... 25. If we are allowed to leave soon, you can spend some time preparing the ad.
... 26. The Alumni Association was accidently omitted from the published list of school organizations.
... 27. The ending would have been alright if only he had not allowed her to lose the formula.
... 28. How can you allow yourself the luxury of becoming angry with so many people!
... 29. The plot is not so good as he tried to tell us anyways.
... 30. The inspector placed the time of the awful train wreck at around seven in the evening.
... 31. Don't bank on their both looking alike.
... 32. Being as he is able to do the work, I do not think that you should complain.
... 33. I can't hardly wait until I read all of the testimony in the negligence case.
... 34. There is considerable evidence to prove that we should concur with the opinions expressed by the prosecuting attorney.

GROUP TWO

... 1. These data are so different than the ones I had anticipated.
... 2. The crowd outside the station was due to leave within three minutes.
... 3. The five men on the raft shouted words of encouragement to each other.
... 4. This package is for Henry and for no one else but Henry.
... 5. Every now and then Sarah becomes enthused about our chances.
... 6. Please be extra careful since we expect the inspector to arrive shortly.
... 7. The conclusion has got to make the audience laugh.
... 8. When given a choice of folk singing, folk dancing, or square dancing, I prefer the latter.
... 9. When the chemist analyzed the heap of bones, he concluded that the former inhabitant of the cave was not opposed to eating humans.
... 10. If all goes well, Helen will be graduated from high school inside of two terms.
... 11. There is just exactly twelve cents remaining in the treasury.
... 12. It should be the kind of a scene that Mrs. Mackey always enjoyed seeing.
... 13. Now, in regard to your request for additional funds, leave me speak to the director on Thursday to see what he would suggest.
... 14. They may of forgotten that the valve is located midway between the two entrances.
... 15. My weakest subjects this term are math and English.
... 16. He most always is ready long before the buzzer is sounded.
... 17. It was nice of you to invite us to lunch so near the end of the term.
... 18. Owing to the lateness of the hour, we posted all of the notices on two of the bulletin boards.
... 19. I agree with Milton when he says that we should look for a solution and not for an alibi.
... 20. She allowed that we could go no further with our plans until we had seen his totals.
... 21. The department head was very much annoyed anent the new regulations.
... 22. Altho I had grown to love Burl Ives' joyful tones, I think that Ed McCurdy is a more authentic folk singer.
... 23. I promise that you will not have to pay any more here than you would pay anywheres else.
... 24. The police notified us at about ten o'clock that Allen had been badly injured in that awful train wreck.
... 25. You will spend the balance of the afternoon sorting the bunches of bananas.
... 26. Frances vowed that she wouldn't try but once again.
... 27. The detective tried to calculate the time it would take the combine to reach the hideout.
... 28. Compared to her brother, she is the model of deportment.

.... 29. The messenger went through considerable trouble to contact the owner of the stray dog.

.... 30. Arthur could not help but differ with Paul when he persisted in a vain effort to disprove a statement without definite proof.

.... 31. I just disremember at which moment he achieved sufficient courage and dived into the water after the retreating ferryboat.

.... 32. Due to his acts of kindness, we are now able to offer hope to these unfortunate homeless waifs.

.... 33. Do not endorse the check on the back unless you really want to cash it at that very moment.

.... 34. Even the prospect of being confined to his room for a week did not faze him.

.... 35. Everywhere I went, I noted that the police were being extra cautious as they directed the tense groups of people away from the center of town.

GROUP THREE

.... 1. I am certain that you would of done the same thing had you been in my place.

.... 2. The teacher wants for all of us to come to the gymnasium immediately.

.... 3. The exciting scene is where the door of the cage is opened accidentally.

.... 4. She is one of the girls which were chosen to wait on the tables during the Freshman Rush.

.... 5. Without your cooperation, we could never have brought him around to agreeing with our plan to raise student morale.

.... 6. When I worked for that company, I just didn't seem to do satisfactory analyses.

.... 7. The three cases of mumps that the doctor reported all came from the group of men which had attended the rally.

.... 8. She allowed that I was by far the best student in the three classes.

.... 9. Everytime I hear her use the word *ain't*, I become mad and see red.

.... 10. As an alumna of the school, Helen can buy many products at a discount—medallions, bookends, notebooks, and etc.

.... 11. I just cannot see his angle when he pretends to be angered by everything that the seniors try to do.

.... 12. Phyllis wanted to see the picture so badly that she persuaded her father to buy tickets for the preview evening.

.... 13. Place the blame on those who claimed that the two cheeses were both alike.

.... 14. We do not doubt but what his theories are based on too much imagination and too little experimentation.

.... 15. During the cool hours toward dawn, we were considerable annoyed by the swarms of midges.

.... 16. I differ with you when you suggested that someone in our crowd could have done much better than Helen did under these circumstances.

.... 17. A couple of my friends were sufficiently annoyed by his rudeness to write a letter of criticism to his superior in the company.

.... 18. When it comes to doctoring the punch to make it palatable to both dieters and those who enjoy their sweets, there is no one comparable to Allen.

.... 19. He did not seem so enthused about the elections as we had hoped.

.... 20. Except they come earlier than usual, they will definitely not have time to consult with their lawyers.

.... 21. In the back of the car was a statue of the king hisself.

.... 22. The noisiest part of the play was when the airplanes took off.

.... 23. In regard to your recent request, I have enclosed the sort of a bulletin you should be publishing.

.... 24. You just cannot leave go of a bird in the hand for one in the bush.

.... 25. Where the building lots of the corporation are now located, we will definitely lose out if we build at the wrong time.

.... 26. A mighty army prepared to fight famine is more preferable to an army poised for conquest.

.... 27. No house in the group is off of the lake front property.

.... 28. The policeman near lost his life when he entered the bank while the hold-up was in progress.

.... 29. Outside of his three closest friends, he has told no one of his unusual opportunity.

.... 30. He is seldom ever seen without a book under his arm.

.... 31. When I was much younger I used to could pick up one of these bales by myself.

.... 32. Please try and do what you can to lessen the fears that fill her mind.

.... 33. Where did you say the keys were at?

CORRECTNESS AND EFFECTIVENESS OF EXPRESSION

ANSWER KEY: TEST OF MASTERY

GROUP ONE / Page 40

1. Since
2. help complaining
3. correct
4. of opinion
5. have
6. on the back
7. correct
8. person
9. are hardly
10. ought to have known
11. regardless
12. on
13. me
14. to give
15. endured
16. again
17. quite
18. that
19. back
20. somewhere
21. to
22. up
23. way
24. had
25. advertisement
26. accidentally
27. all right
28. correct
29. anyway
30. about
31. depend
32. Since
33. can hardly
34. concur in

GROUP TWO / Page 41

1. from
2. correct
3. one another
4. else
5. enthusiastic
6. very
7. must
8. last
9. human beings
10. within
11. exactly
12. a
13. let
14. have
15. mathematics
16. almost
17. considerate
18. Because of
19. excuse
20. thought
21. by
22. Although
23. anywhere
24. at
25. remainder
26. n't
27. group
28. with
29. correct
30. help differing
31. can not recall
32. Because of
33. on the back
34. discourage
35. very

GROUP THREE / Page 42

1. have
2. for
3. occurs when
4. who
5. to
6. correct
7. who
8. granted
9. angry
10. and
11. point of view
12. much
13. both
14. that
15. considerably
16. group
17. complaint
18. mixing
19. enthusiastic
20. unless
21. himself
22. occurred
23. a
24. let
25. out
26. more
27. of
28. nearly
29. Except for
30. if ever
31. could
32. to
33. at

ADDITIONAL PROBLEMS WITH WORDS

This unit contains another series of problems to which attention is given on the examination. Once you have learned how to identify the trouble spots and have become familiar with typical examples, you will be able to approach the examination items with the confidence that leads to highest scores.

Wordiness

DEFINITION: *Wordiness (verbosity) is the use of repetitious elements that add nothing to the meaning of the sentence and are not justified by any need for special emphasis.*

There are several other terms associated with wordiness:

Circumlocution (deadwood) involves using two or more words for the one exact word.

> loud and annoying for *noisy*
> quiet and peaceful for *subdued*

Redundancy (tautology) describes the use of words that needlessly repeat the meaning of other words.

> stoop *with lowered shoulders*
> at 3 p.m. *in the afternoon*

The pitfalls of verbosity include the following:

1. **Definition used instead of word itself**
   WORDY: cause to go faster
   CONCISE: accelerate

2. **Relative clause in place of adjective**
   WORDY: a child *who is idle*
   CONCISE: an *idle* child

3. **Redundant phrase in place of briefer term or word**
   WORDY: smaller in size
   CONCISE: smaller

4. Longer words used for shorter ones
carefulness for *care*

5. Unnecessary preposition added to verb

write *up*   descend *down*
write *down*   ascend *up*
repeat *again*   redo *again*
lose *out*   win *out*

Become familiar with the following list of frequently used verbose phrases; they find their way into examination items.

VERBOSE PHRASES	CONCISE PHRASES
cooperate together	cooperate
expert in the field of	expert
seen by the eyes	seen
means to imply	implies
because of the fact	because
green in color	green
few in number	few
same identical	identical
advance notice	notice
of an indefinite nature	indefinite
in order to	to
by means of	by
isolated by himself	isolated
close to the point of	close to
the modern world of today	the world of today
different in a number of ways	different
novelist writes in his novels	novelist writes
New Year's party celebration	New Year's celebration
connected up with	connected with
fundamental principles	principles
attractive in appearance	attractive
at about	about
both alike	alike
consensus of opinion	consensus
endorse on the back	endorse
have need for	need
give instruction to	teach
give encouragement to	encourage
for the purpose of	for
with respect to	about
despite the fact that	though
with a view to	to
come into conflict	conflict
in view of the fact that	because, since
make an adjustment in	adjust
give consideration to	consider
of a confidential nature	confidential
is of the opinion	believes
along the lines of	like
in the amount of	for
in accordance with	by
make inquiry regarding	inquire
on the occasion of	when
for the reason that	since
in the case that	if
have under consideration	is considering

Use of Idiomatic Phrases

DEFINITION: *An idiomatic phrase is an expression peculiar to a language and not explainable through rules of logic or grammar. Custom, not principles of grammar, establishes its form and meaning.*
so long as = while

When used in an idiomatic phrase, a word loses its individual meaning; the expression or phrase takes on a meaning different from the literal meaning of the words involved.

1. Idiomatic phrases in compounds

If two idiomatic phrases are used in a compound construction, each phrase must be completed.

Example: He is *as good* if not better than the others.
ACCEPTED FORM: He is as good as . . . .
Example: He was fully aware but not disturbed by the noise.
ACCEPTED FORM: He was fully aware *of* but not disturbed by the noise.

2. Fixed prepositions in idiomatic phrases

The preposition that an idiom ends with is usually set by custom and should not be varied. Below are some of the accepted combinations.

agree *to* a proposal
    on a procedure
    with a person
argue *with* a person
    for, *against* or *about* a measure
compare *to* a thing with a definite resemblance
    with something on the basis of similarities or dissimilarities
comply *with*
differ *with* a person in an opinion
    from in appearance
different *from*
identical *with*
independent *of*
in search *of*
show interest *in*
listen *to*
necessary *to*
plan *to*

CORRECTNESS AND EFFECTIVENESS OF EXPRESSION

required *of*
stay *at* home
superior *to*

3. Synonymous pairs of idiomatic phrases

Custom often labels one of a pair of synonymous idioms standard and the other nonstandard. Below is a list of such pairs that you should have under complete control.

STANDARD	NONSTANDARD
as far as	all the farther
among all three	between the three
cannot help	cannot help but
blame us for it	blame it on us
doubt that	doubt if
in search of	in search for
within an hour	inside of an hour
kind of	kind of a
type of	type of a
try and see	try to see

4. With Gerunds and Infinitives

Certain words in idiomatic use are followed by gerunds and others by infinitives.

ACCEPTABLE	NOT ACCEPTABLE
like to go	like going
cannot help seeing	cannot help to see
hesitate to look	hesitate looking
enjoy seeing	enjoy to see
capable of doing	capable to do
intend to do	intend on doing

Avoidance of clichés

DEFINITION: *A cliché is an expression that once may have been striking but has been used so often that it has lost its effectiveness.*

quick as a flash   tired but happy

The major aspect of this problem is in realizing that the term or phrase has been overused. Clichés, like jokes, are novel and new—if you have not heard them often. Examine the following list of tried and true clichés so that you can sharpen your sensitivity to them.

in a bad way	as luck would have it
dead as a doornail	slow but sure
make a beeline	untiring efforts
making hay while the sun shines	fought like tigers
true blue	snake in the grass
sigh of relief	the worse for wear
do justice to	come down to earth
a silver lining	method in his madness
all work and no play	in on the ground floor
make a long story short	clear the air
blow off steam	time marches on
be that as it may	straight from the shoulder
give the Devil his due	in my considered judgment
a tower of strength	hold no brief for
calm before the storm	bolt from the blue

Identifying mixed metaphors

DEFINITION: *Metaphors and similes are comparisons between two things which are unlike except in one particular. A simile is a comparison in which the comparison between two different things is indicated explicitly by terms such as* like *or as. In a metaphor, the comparison is made without* like *or* as.

Simile: The quiet in the room was like the silence in a birdless woods at twilight.
Metaphor: A twilight silence filled the room.

A mixed metaphor is one in which the literal meaning of the words used causes an apparent contradiction or absurdity.

Example: Caught in the tide of misfortune, he walked on, a penniless man.

EXPLANATION: Caught in a tide, one can be swept away or drowned; one should not be walking amid the flood.

TEST OF MASTERY

Read each of the following sentences carefully. In the space to the left write

A if the sentence contains a phrase or expression that is not idiomatic
B if the sentence contains a cliché
C if the sentence contains a mixed metaphor
D if the sentence is verbose (wordy) or contains a redundant phrase (unjustifiable repetition)
E if the sentence contains none of the above

.... 1. If you do not comply to this request within four hours, I shall notify the authorities to act.
.... 2. The doctor found that her pulse was just as rapid if not more rapid than it had been a week earlier.
.... 3. Rosy-fingered dawn brought color back into the surrounding landscape.
.... 4. Because of his carelessness, I shall have to redo again the cement work around the patio.
.... 5. I would wear my fingers to the bone working for you if only you were to show some gratitude.

.... 6. An avalanche of doubt slithered through his mind.
.... 7. Did you say that this is identical to the one you had bought?
.... 8. True to his word, Henry completed the project by the next evening.
.... 9. This package is so attractive in appearance that I am willing to overpay for it.
.... 10. The results were so different than we had anticipated.
.... 11. The fury of the gale terrorized the stranded tourists.
.... 12. Her iron will was our wall of strength as we flew in the face of his anger.
.... 13. In view of the fact that he was not present when the incident occurred, he should be allowed to see the unpublished minutes.
.... 14. He planted the seeds of distrust in the minds of his television listeners and gave them the power to break the shackles of ignorance.
.... 15. The supervisor will have to make an adjustment in our schedule if we are to attend the annual game.
.... 16. This vase is identical to the one I had bought.
.... 17. I just do not have the heart to break the news to them.
.... 18. Straight as arrows, his words, backed by irrefutable facts, flew to the heart of the problem.
.... 19. Downcast by the disquieting news, I had no patience for the chattering of the children.
.... 20. If you were to stay to home more often, you would get more of your own work done on time.
.... 21. He is as happy as a lark even though he does not have a penny to his name.
.... 22. You must seize every opportunity; take the plunge while the iron is hot.
.... 23. They are both so alike that even their parents have difficulty in telling them apart.
.... 24. I am certain that you will enjoy to see how far she has progressed in her studies.
.... 25. Going full-steam ahead, we plunged into problems confronting us and soon sailed into the sea of success.
.... 26. Because of the fact that the contract will be signed tomorrow, we must be most patient today.
.... 27. Ignorance may not be bliss, but wisdom often turns out to be less than heavenly.
.... 28. We advanced forward slowly and patiently, aware that the initiative was in the hands of the opposition.
.... 29. Since we are all friends of long standing, we should be able to settle this tempestuous uproar without making waves.
.... 30. Do not let black despair force you to cross your bridges before you come to them.
.... 31. If you are willing to ascend up the stairs to the third floor, there you will find a much larger selection.
.... 32. I am in search for an answer to this dilemma, and I shall not rest until I find it.

ANSWER KEY: TEST OF MASTERY

1. (A) If you do not comply *with* . . .
2. (A) . . . just as rapid *as* . . .
3. (B) The cliché is *rosy-fingered dawn*.
4. (D) The term *again* is unnecessary.
5. (B) The cliché is *wear my fingers to the bone*.
6. (C) An avalanche cannot slither like a snake.
7. (A) . . . identical *with* . . .
8. (B) The cliché is *true to his word*.
9. (D) The phrase *in appearance* is unnecessary.
10. (A) . . . different *from* . . .
11. (E) no error
12. (C) A wall of strength mixes badly with flying.
13. (D) The wordiness is in *In view of the fact that*.
14. (C) Seeds of distrust are too fragile to break chains.
15. (D) The single word *adjust* should be used in place of *make an adjustment*.
16. (A) . . . identical *with* . . .
17. (B) The clichés are *not have the heart* and *break the news*.
18. (B) The clichés are *straight as arrows, irrefutable facts, heart of the matter*.
19. (E) no error
20. (A) . . . stay *at* . . .
21. (B) The clichés are *happy as a lark, penny to his name*.
22. (E) no error
23. (D) The word *both* is unnecessary.
24. (A) . . . enjoying *seeing* . . .
25. (C) Sailing, going full steam ahead, and plunging mix metaphors.
26. (D) The phrase *of the fact that* is unnecessary.
27. (E) no error
28. (D) The word *forward* is not necessary.
29. (C) Calming a tempest of noise by not making waves is mixing metaphors.
30. (B) The clichés are *black despair* and *cross your bridges before*. . . .
31. (D) The word *up* is unnecessary.
32. (A) . . . in search *of* . . .

CORRECTNESS AND EFFECTIVENESS OF EXPRESSION

WORD PAIRS FREQUENTLY CONFUSED

The words in this section cause difficulty because they are either so close in meaning that the student tends to confuse them; or they are so close in spelling that they cause the careless to intermix them. Run through this list quickly. Those pairs that do not cause you any difficulty can be disregarded. Check those that you have had trouble with or you have not been aware of as troubling twins. Concentrate your efforts on these. Memorize the definitions or helpful hints. Study the nonstandard and standard forms. You should achieve 100% mastery of these words.

Group One: The Fourteen Most Frequent

1. A—An
a	used before a consonant sound	*a* man, *a* unit, *a* hotel
an	used before a vowel sound	*an* apple, *an* honest man

NONSTANDARD: I spoke to him for *a* hour.
STANDARD: I spoke to him for *an* hour.

2. Don't—Doesn't
doesn't	used with third person singular	he *doesn't*; she *doesn't*; it *doesn't*
don't	used with all other persons	I *don't*; they *don't*; we *don't*

NONSTANDARD: *Don't* he know any better!
STANDARD: *Doesn't* he know any better!

3. In—Into
in	refers to place or position	It is *in* the book.
into	refers to the action toward	Put it *into* the book.

NONSTANDARD: Go *in* the house as quickly as you can.
STANDARD: Go *into* the house as quickly as you can.

4. Lets—Let's
let's	contraction for *let us*	*Let's* do it together.
lets	third person singular of *let*	He *lets* us work in his room.

NONSTANDARD: *Lets* go to the matinee this afternoon.
STANDARD: *Let's* go to the matinee this afternoon.

5. Lie—Lay
lay	means *to place* or *put* and it takes an object	Today I *lay* the book down. I am *laying* it down. I *laid* it down yesterday. I have *laid* it down.
lie	means *to rest* or *recline*, and it does not take an object	Now I *lie* down. I am *lying* down. Yesterday I *lay* down. I have *lain* down.

NONSTANDARD: The ring *laid* in the mud all night.
STANDARD: The ring *lay* in the mud all night.

6. Loose—Lose
loose	not fastened, not tight	The collar is too *loose*.
lose	misplace; be defeated	We shall not *lose* this time.

NONSTANDARD: We cannot afford to *loose* time.
STANDARD: We cannot afford to *lose* time.

7. Quiet—Quite
quiet	noiseless	The nurse walked through the *quiet* corridor.
quite	completely	He is *quite* right in his statement.

NOT ACCEPTED: You must keep *quite* if you want to remain in this room.
ACCEPTED: You must keep *quiet* if you want to remain in this room.

8. Than—Then
than	used in comparisons	He is faster *than* we had imagined.
then	at that time	It was *then* that I realized my error.

NOT ACCEPTED: It is better *then* ever now that you fixed it.
ACCEPTED: It is better *than* ever now that you fixed it.

9. Their—There
their	belonging to them	It is *their* turn now.
there	in that place;	Harold placed the package over *there*.
there	used before a verb when the subject follows	*There* are three pens here. *There* once was a wicked king.

NOT ACCEPTED: We will play the game on *there* home field.
ACCEPTED: We will play the game on *their* home field.

10. To—Too
to	introductory word in an infinitive	*to* do *to* go *to* speak
to	used as a preposition	*to* the store
too	also	Helen went *too*.
too	more than enough; over	He spoke *too* quickly.

NOT ACCEPTED: The truck arrived *to* soon.
ACCEPTED: The truck arrived *too* soon.

11. Your—You're
your	possessive form of *you*	It is *your* turn.
you're	contraction for *you are*	*You're* next.

WRONG: I wonder whether *your* going to be called upon to speak.

NONSTANDARD: I wonder whether *your* going to be called upon to speak.
STANDARD: I wonder whether *you're* going to be called upon to speak.

12. Were—Where

| were | plural form of *was* | They *were* ready. |
| where | at what place | *Where* did you put the ribbon? |

NOT ACCEPTED: Place it *were* it will be most useful.
ACCEPTED: Place it *where* it will be most useful.

13. Were—We're

| were | plural form of *was* | The men *were* here. |
| we're | contraction of *we are* | *We're* ready if you are. |

NONSTANDARD: I don't know where *were* going.
STANDARD: I don't know where *we're* going.

14. Whose—Who's

| whose | possessive form of *who* | *Whose* hat did she borrow? |
| who's | contraction of *who is* | *Who's* going to run the meeting? |

NONSTANDARD: She is the girl *who's* book I am using.
STANDARD: She is the girl *whose* book I am using.

Group Two: Basic List of Words Frequently Confused

accept	to receive	Helen *accepted* my apology.
except	excluding	Everyone *except* Paul was present.
except	to exclude	Al was *excepted* from the list of players.

NOT ACCEPTED: The men *excepted* the supplies we sent them.
ACCEPTED: The men *accepted* the supplies we sent them.

| advice | counsel | She will listen to your *advice* now. |
| advise | to give counsel | I cannot *advise* you in this matter. |

NOT ACCEPTED: He was known for his sound *advise*.
ACCEPTED: He was known for his sound *advice*.

affect	to influence	The smoke *affected* his breathing.
effect	result	What is the *effect* of smoke on him?
effect	to accomplish	He *effected* a change in my schedule.

NOT ACCEPTED: What is the *affect* of the iodine on the open wound?
ACCEPTED: What is the *effect* of the iodine on the open wound?

| aggravate | to make worse | The cold draft *aggravated* his coughing. |
| irritate | to annoy | Your meaningless smile *irritated* him. |

COLLOQUIAL: Stop *aggravating* me!
WRITTEN: Stop *irritating* me!
(A condition is *aggravated*; a person is *irritated*.)

| all together | in a group | The books are *all together* on that shelf. |
| altogether | entirely, completely | You are *altogether* wrong this time. |

NOT ACCEPTED: Now, let us say it *altogether*.
ACCEPTED: Now, let us say it *all together*.

| already | at a previous time | I had *already* seen the photograph. |
| all ready | all prepared | They are *all ready* to enter the room. |

NOT ACCEPTED: Edna has *all ready* eaten.
ACCEPTED: Edna has *already* eaten.

| allusion | reference | I resent your *allusion* to my forgetfulness. |
| illusion | error in vision | The mirage gave the *illusion* of a lake on the road. |

NOT ACCEPTED: Happiness is an *allusion* that fools mankind!
ACCEPTED: Happiness is an *illusion* that fools mankind!

| among | connects more than two | Divide the prize *among* the three brothers. |
| between | connects only two | Divide the cake *between* Lucy and Margery. |

COLLOQUIAL: This matter must be settled *between* the members of the club.
WRITTEN: This matter must be settled *among* the members of the club.

| angel | supernatural being | Her thoughts are among the *angels*. |
| angle | corner | Use the square to make a right *angle*. |

NOT ACCEPTED: She has the sweet voice of an *angle*.
ACCEPTED: She has the sweet voice of an *angel*.

| ascent | upward movement | The guide led the *ascent* to the top of the mountain. |
| assent | agreement; to agree | The coach *assented* to my plan. |

NOT ACCEPTED: I shall never give my *ascent* to such a suggestion.

ACCEPTED: I shall never give my *assent* to such a suggestion.

as	*as* introduced a clause	Tastes good *as* a cigar really should.
like	*like* is used as a preposition	He looks *like* a good player.

COLLOQUIAL: Do just *like* I tell you to.
WRITTEN: Do just *as* I tell you to.

base	vile	That was a *base* thing for you to do.
base	bottom	The package is at the *base* of the stairs.
bass	lowest part in music	Jerry will sing the *bass* part in our number.

NOT ACCEPTED: Do you think that he will be able to reach the *base* notes?
ACCEPTED: Do you think that he will be able to reach the *bass* notes?

beside	by the side of	She will sit *beside* me in the theater.
besides	in addition	I left early, and *besides*, I had heard enough.

COLLOQUIAL: Place the trunk *besides* the bed.
WRITTEN: Place the trunk *beside* the bed.

born	given birth to	The calf was *born* early this morning.
borne	carried	The balloon was *borne* aloft by the breeze.
borne	endured	I have *borne* this burden long enough.

NOT ACCEPTED: How many presidents were *borne* in log cabins?
ACCEPTED: How many presidents were *born* in log cabins?

borrow	take from	May I *borrow* your pen for a moment?
lend	give to	I shall *lend* it to you in a minute.
loan	the item involved	I shall return the *loan* by this evening.

COLLOQUIAL: May I have a *loan* of the book?
NONSTANDARD: May I *lend* your book *from you* for a while?
ACCEPTED: May I *borrow* your book?

breath	respiration	Onions linger on one's *breath*.
breathe	to respire	She *breathes* as though she has a cold.

NOT ACCEPTED: I went out for a *breathe* of fresh air.
ACCEPTED: I went out for a *breath* of fresh air.

bring	carry to the speaker	*Bring* the package to me right now.
take	carry to any other direction	*Take* your books with you.

NONSTANDARD: *Bring* the machine to the office.
STANDARD: *Take* the machine to the office.

can	implies ability	He *can* speak French fluently.
may	implies permission	*May* I help you sort the mail?

COLLOQUIAL: The teacher said that you *can* enter the room now.
WRITTEN: The teacher said that you *may* enter the room now.

canvas	coarse cloth	The canoe was covered with *canvas*.
canvass	examine; solicit	*Canvass* the neighborhood for orders.

NOT ACCEPTED: The salesman *canvased* from door to door without making a sale.
ACCEPTED: The salesman *canvassed* from door to door without making a sale.

capital	excellent	That is a *capital* idea.
capital	chief town	Washington is the *capital* of the United States.
capital	money	How much *capital* do you have invested?
capitol	state house	The *Capitol* is located in Albany.

NOT ACCEPTED: Albany is the *capitol* of New York State.
ACCEPTED: Albany is the *capital* of New York State.

carat	unit of weight twenty-fourth part	The diamond weighed one *carat*. He bought a 10 *carat* gold ring.
caret	mark of omission	The printer placed a *caret* where the author had omitted a word.
carrot	vegetable	Rabbits love raw *carrots*.

NOT ACCEPTED: Ten-*caret* gold is harder than 18-*caret* gold.
ACCEPTED: Ten-*carat* gold is harder than 18-*carat* gold.

cite	to refer to	I shall *cite* several instances.
sight	ability to see	This instrument will test your *sight*.
sight	that which is seen	He is a *sight* for all to see.
site	location	This is the *site* of the new school building.

NOT ACCEPTED: I tried to forget the awful *cite*.
ACCEPTED: I tried to forget the awful *sight*.

click	a slight, sharp sound	The *click* of the key in the lock awakened us.
clique	group of persons; a set	He is a member of the leading *clique*.

NOT ACCEPTED: I refused to join the snobbish *click* ruling our school.
ACCEPTED: I refused to join the snobbish *clique* ruling our school.

coarse	rough; gross; not refined	His *coarse* remarks hurt his chances.
course	progress	What *course* will the disease follow?
course	career	I plan to take the college *course*.

NOT ACCEPTED: He has a *course* sense of humor.
ACCEPTED: He has a *coarse* sense of humor.

complement	that which completes	This hat will *complement* her costume.
compliment	praise	I *compliment* you on your choice of friends.

NOT ACCEPTED: Her remarks were anything but *complementary*.
ACCEPTED: Her remarks were anything but *complimentary*.

consul	diplomatic representative	He is the American *Consul* assigned to Rome.
council	group of advisers	I spoke to the *council* of elders.
counsel	advice	I need your *counsel* in my present difficulty.
counselor	camp assistant	I applied for a summer job as general *counselor*.

NOT ACCEPTED: If you do not follow my *council*, I can be of no help to you.
ACCEPTED: If you do not follow my *counsel*, I can be of no help to you.

contemptible	worthy of scorn	That was a *contemptible* trick.
contemptuous	full of scorn	His *contemptuous* smirk infuriated the manager.

NOT ACCEPTED: How can you be so *contemptible* of another's best efforts!
ACCEPTED: How can you be so *contemptuous* of another's best efforts!

continual	occurring in steady, rapid, but not unbroken order	His bitter comments were a *continual* source of irritation to me.
continuous	occurring without interruption	The men formed a human chain that was *continuous* for 100 feet.

NOT ACCEPTED: Her *continuous* interruptions finally befuddled me completely.
ACCEPTED: Her *continual* interruptions finally befuddled me completely.

costume	dress; apparel	What was the *costume* worn by the zoot-suiter?
custom	usage	It is a *custom* that I have learned to dislike.

NOT ACCEPTED: When did the *costume* of kissing originate?
ACCEPTED: When did the *custom* of kissing originate?

deceased	dead	Who are the kin of the *deceased*?
diseased	infected	The dentist treated the *diseased* tooth.

NOT ACCEPTED: This reaction can only be the output of a *deceased* mind.
ACCEPTED: This reaction can only be the output of a *diseased* mind.

disinterested	fair; without prejudice	Get the opinion of a *disinterested* outsider
uninterested	not concerned	I am completely *uninterested* in his affairs.

NONSTANDARD: To judge fairly you must take an *uninterested* attitude.
STANDARD: To judge fairly you must take a *disinterested* attitude.

desert	barren region	Death Valley is part of the American *desert*.
desert	reward	You will receive your just *deserts* in time.
dessert	last course	Shall we have pie for *dessert* tonight?

NOT ACCEPTED: Ice cream is my favorite *desert*.
ACCEPTED: Ice cream is my favorite *dessert*.

emigrate	to leave a country	They plan to *emigrate* from Australia.
immigrate	to enter a country	They plan to *immigrate* to America.

NOT ACCEPTED: They *immigrated* from the Old World.
ACCEPTED: They *emigrated* from the Old World.

eminent	high in rank	He is an *eminent* authority in his field.
imminent	threatening; at hand	He is in *imminent* danger of failing.

NOT ACCEPTED: I met the *imminent* professor of nuclear physics, Dr. Schub.
ACCEPTED: I met the *eminent* professor of nuclear physics, Dr. Schub.

envelop	to enclose	The night *envelops* us.
envelope	surrounding cover	Place the note in a sealed *envelope*.

NOT ACCEPTED: Did you find his pay *envelop*?
ACCEPTED: Did you find his pay *envelope*?

fewer	refers to individual units	He made *fewer* mistakes this time.

CORRECTNESS AND EFFECTIVENESS OF EXPRESSION

less	refers to quantity	He has *less* money than I do.

NOT ACCEPTED: There are *less* people here today than yesterday.
ACCEPTED: There are *fewer* people here today than yesterday.

formally	in a formal manner	I was *formally* introduced to the principal.
formerly	at a previous time	It was *formerly* a luxury hotel.

NOT ACCEPTED: He was *formally* my best friend.
ACCEPTED: He was *formerly* my best friend.

gorilla	large ape	We watched the *gorilla* in its cage.
guerrilla	irregular soldier	The *guerrillas* destroyed the airfield.

NOT ACCEPTED: The French *gorillas* harassed the Germans behind their own lines.
ACCEPTED: The French *guerrillas* harassed the Germans behind their own lines.

hail	to call; originate	*Hail* a taxi for me, please.
hail	frozen pellets	We were caught in a summer *hail* storm.
hale	strong, healthy	He was *hale* and hearty at eighty.

NOT ACCEPTED: Where do you *hale* from?
ACCEPTED: Where do you *hail* from?

hanged	reserved for people	The traitor was *hanged* at dawn.
hung	for all other objects	The picture was *hung* on the kitchen wall.

COLLOQUIAL: The artist and not the picture should have been *hung*.
WRITTEN: The picture was *hung* where the artist should have been *hanged*.

healthy	possessing health	He has a *healthy* look.
healthful	bringing about health	The clear air seemed so *healthful*.

COLLOQUIAL: He wisely chose only *healthy* foods.
WRITTEN: He wisely chose only *healthful* foods.

hoarse	rough voiced	He called out in *hoarse* tones.
horse	animal	My kingdom for a *horse*!

NOT ACCEPTED: He shouted himself *horse*.
ACCEPTED: He shouted himself *hoarse*.

idle	inactive	*Idle* hands lose their skill.
idol	image for worship	He bowed before the stone *idol*.

NOT ACCEPTED: He never has an *idol* hour.
ACCEPTED: He never has an *idle* hour.

imply	indicate or suggest	He *implied* that I could never pass the course.
infer	draw a conclusion from	He *inferred* consent from my silence.

NONSTANDARD: He *inferred* in his statement that we would win the case.
STANDARD: He *implied* in his statement that we would win the case.

incredible	unbelievable	He told us an *incredible* tale of struggle.
incredulous	unbelieving	He had an *incredulous* look on his face.

NOT ACCEPTED: His *incredible* smile told us that he did not believe our story.
ACCEPTED: His *incredulous* smile told us that he did not believe our story.

ingenious	clever	His *ingenious* trap finally caught the fox.
ingenuous	naive; frank	His *ingenuous* question made us smile.

NOT ACCEPTED: The *ingenious* youngster did not realize his lack of social graces.
ACCEPTED: The *ingenuous* youngster did not realize his lack of social graces.

later	more late	Better *later* than never.
latter	more recent	I prefer the *latter* to the former.

NOT ACCEPTED: If I had my own way, I would chose the *later* of the two.
ACCEPTED: If I had my own way, I would choose the *latter* of the two.

learn	to gather knowledge	I *learned* my lesson from that experience.
teach	to give knowledge	I *taught* them how to drive.

NONSTANDARD: He *learned* us how to speak well.
STANDARD: He *taught* us how to speak well.
(teach *to*, learn *from*)

mad	out of one's mind	The *mad* man was declared insane by the judge.
angry	very much annoyed	I am *angry*, and I want you to know it.

COLLOQUIAL: His actions made me very *mad*.
WRITTEN: His actions made me very *angry*.

moral	virtuous, ethical	It was a *moral* tale told well.
moral	ethical point	The *moral* of the tale was clear to all of us.

moral	virtue	I do not question the *morals* of this group.
morale	group spirit, confidence	His words raised our *morale* to a new high.

NOT ACCEPTED: The *moral* of the troop is very low at this moment.
ACCEPTED: The *morale* of the troop is very low at this moment.

passed	did pass	The feeling of weakness *passed* quickly.
past	gone by; former time; beyond	He is *past* all hope.

NOT ACCEPTED: I could have *past* that subject easily.
ACCEPTED: I could have *passed* that subject easily.

practical	sensible, useful	His suggestions made our machine *practical*.
practicable	timely; capable of being accomplished	His ideas are not *practicable* right now.

NOT ACCEPTED: He is a *practicable* person who would not spend time foolishly.
ACCEPTED: He is a *practical* person who would not spend time foolishly.

principal	main	This is my *principal* reason.
principal	head of school	Mr. Bellafiore is our *principal*.
principal	sum of money	We shall receive interest on the *principal*.
principle	fundamental truth	I believe in the *principles* of democracy.
principle	moral standard	My religious *principles* guide my actions.

NONSTANDARD: My *principle* suggestion is that he be allowed to work independently.
STANDARD: My *principal* suggestion is that he be allowed to work independently.

prophecy	prediction	I hope his *prophecies* of doom prove false.
prophesy	to predict	I *prophesy* a great future for their team.

NOT ACCEPTED: All of my *prophesies* shall come true.
ACCEPTED: All of my *prophecies* shall come true.

provided	on condition that	He can leave *provided* he has the train fare.
providing	furnishing, giving	They will be *providing* all of the food.

COLLOQUIAL: *Providing* you listen, I shall play the record once again.
WRITTEN: *Provided* you listen, I shall play the record once again.

raise	increase	I shall be given a *raise* next week.
raise	to lift up	I *raised* my hand at the right moment.
rise	to come up	The sun will *rise* at 6 o'clock.

NONSTANDARD: The stream *raised* three inches during the storm.
STANDARD: The stream *rose* three inches during the storm.

(*raise, raising, raised* always take an object; *rise, rising, risen* describes the subject and do not take an object.)

respectfully	with respect	He bowed *respectfully* in our direction.
respectively	in the order already suggested	Paul and Helen gave a dollar and two dollars *respectively*.

NONSTANDARD: He signed the note, "Respectively yours,"
STANDARD: He signed the note, "Respectfully yours,"

spill	accidental action	The car *spilled* over the top of the runway.
pour	intentional action	May I *pour* the coffee for you?

NONSTANDARD: He *spilled* the water calmly over my head.
STANDARD: He *poured* the water calmly over my head.

statue	piece of sculpture	I saw the new *statue* that had been placed in the village square.
stature	height	He gained in *stature* as a result of his honest stand on the matter.

NOT ACCEPTED: Did you see the *stature* of Washington in the museum?
ACCEPTED: Did you see the *statue* of Washington in the museum?

TEST OF MASTERY

In the space provided to the left in each of the following sentences, write *correct* if it contains no error in word confusion. If a word form is misused, then put a line through the error and write the correct word in the space provided to the left.

CORRECTNESS AND EFFECTIVENESS OF EXPRESSION

GROUP ONE

.... 1. I could feel the breathe of the monster on my hand!
.... 2. How much will the loan be this time?
.... 3. No one beside me knows what his plans are.
.... 4. In which city is the capitol located?
.... 5. The diamond weighs at least three carets.
.... 6. His remarks were not complimentary to us.
.... 7. He was so disinterested in what I was doing that he just sat there with a faraway look on his face.
.... 8. All hale, to thee, conquering hero!
.... 9. This had formerly been an army barracks.
.... 10. The eraser was laying on the desk all that time.
.... 11. To be a giant, you must have the mental stature of a giant.
.... 12. Let's not make a error this time.
.... 13. May I put the cake in the oven now?
.... 14. He don't want us to lose the advantage we now have.
.... 15. They said their goodbyes during the quite hours of the early morning.
.... 16. Helen too knows were the locket has been hidden.
.... 17. Whose been so careless to anger him again?
.... 18. Your interfering will only aggravate the situation.
.... 19. If we work altogether, the counselor will have a pleasant summer.
.... 20. You will have to learn how to except advice when it is offered to you by those who sincerely want to help you.
.... 21. What will the affect of this change be on their plans?
.... 22. You will have to reach a decision between the three of you.
.... 23. Do like I tell you and you will receive your just desserts.
.... 24. I have borne as much of his criticism as I can.
.... 25. There base of operations is beside the stream.
.... 26. You may bring this chair to your room now.
.... 27. The police plan to canvas the neighborhood for a site that would be ideal for the new playground.
.... 28. I do not know what coarse this council plans to follow, but I know the one that I must take.
.... 29. They dressed the diseased in the costume that he had worn when he had made his debut forty years ago.
.... 30. The line formed an unbroken, continual chain of people completely around the square.
.... 31. The warmth of her welcome envelopes us with an incredible air of security.
.... 32. The climate here is so healthy that even the horses live to receive their social security payments on retirement.
.... 33. For the past four days, I have been trying to learn him how to decode the messages as they come over the secret radio channel.
.... 34. The later is an ingenious device for doing homework automatically.
.... 35. I prophecy that you will win provided you follow your exact plans.

GROUP TWO

.... 1. Who is going to be the principle speaker this evening?
.... 2. Provided his plan is practicable, I shall lend him my full support.
.... 3. I poured my tale of woe into their respective ears.
.... 4. Don't he realize that it is a real honor for us to be present?
.... 5. Let's let it lay just where it is lying now.
.... 6. Their game is better then it ever was.
.... 7. I hope we're not to late to enter the contest.
.... 8. Whose going to judge whether your being fair or not?
.... 9. My advice to you is to think twice before you except his gift.
.... 10. They are already for the ascent the moment the weather clears.
.... 11. His illusion to my habit of being punctual did not amuse me.
.... 12. None but an angle could have borne so much for so long with so few complaints.
.... 13. And besides, he sings bass, not tenor!
.... 14. May I have a loan of some capital to tide me over this busy weekend?
.... 15. This ring of ten-carat gold is a cite to behold.
.... 16. I am contemptuous of all who must join clicks in order to assert their individualities.
.... 17. They plan to dessert their comrades and emigrate to America.
.... 18. The imminent professor will deliver no fewer than seven lectures in this fortunate city.
.... 19. The gorrila fighters blew up three bridges to slow down the advance of the enemy.
.... 20. From the remarks of the judge, I inferred that the killer will be hanged before another day dawns.
.... 21. The idol was hanged on a silver chain in front of the altar.
.... 22. The moral of the story is that you must not allow yourself to become so mad that you lose control of your tongue.
.... 23. Joe thinks he may have past the test that he took.
.... 24. The deadly gas raised from the floor of the valley and floated toward the principal city.

.... 25. You just put your money back in your pocket, and let's forget the entire incident.
.... 26. A hungry dog was laying on the path in front of us, and we didn't dare pass him with our basket of frankfurters.
.... 27. I would rather loose than have them think that I did not even try.
.... 28. We're just expecting to much from so inexperienced a coach.
.... 29. You are altogether wrong in your prediction of the effect of smoke on the finish given to this furniture.
.... 30. The colors of this wheel so complement those of the car that they appear as though they were really planned to be used as an unit.
.... 31. The counselor-at-law counciled us to avoid speaking to members of the panel.
.... 32. Only a disinterested outsider would be fully aware of how his continual criticism enraged us.
.... 33. The summer season was formally ushered in by a furious hail storm.
.... 34. If less people had been present, he would have learned how to whisper.
.... 35. They all advised me to except his generous offer.

ANSWER KEY: TEST OF MASTERY

GROUP ONE / *Page 53*

1. breath
2. correct
3. besides
4. correct
5. carats
6. correct
7. uninterested
8. hail
9. correct
10. lying
11. correct
12. an
13. into
14. doesn't
15. quiet
16. where
17. Who's
18. correct
19. all together
20. accept
21. effect
22. among
23. as
24. correct
25. Their
26. take
27. canvass
28. course
29. deceased
30. continuous
31. envelops
32. healthful
33. teach
34. latter
35. prophesy

GROUP TWO / *Page 53*

1. principal
2. correct
3. correct
4. Doesn't
5. lie
6. than
7. too
8. Who's
9. accept
10. all ready
11. allusion
12. angel
13. correct
14. borrow
15. sight
16. cliques
17. desert
18. eminent
19. guerrilla
20. correct
21. hung
22. angry
23. passed
24. rose
25. into
26. lying
27. lose
28. too
29. correct
30. a
31. counseled
32. correct
33. correct
34. fewer
35. accept

5. Problems in Proper Punctuation and Capitalization

Modern writing tends to follow specific rules for the use of punctuation marks. The day when a student could be either generous or stingy in sprinkling commas or periods through his written themes is part of a past era.

This section is not an attempt to summarize all of the rules governing marks of punctuation. Rather it treats of the common errors found in student writing. The problems faced are those that students make in writing the essay and those that are usually used to test student ability in the objective questions.

USING THE APOSTROPHE

Most of the errors that occur in the use of the apostrophe occur because of carelessness. Since this is the mark of punctuation most frequently misused by high school seniors and college freshmen, the penalties for its misuse are severe and the apostrophe becomes a predictable item on examination papers.

With Pronouns

Example: The book is now (yours, your's).

EXPLANATION: The possessive pronouns are *my, mine, your, yours, his, its, her, hers, our, ours, their, theirs, whose*. These pronouns show possession in their own right. Therefore, they are *not* used with apostrophes.

ACCEPTED FORM: The book is now *yours*.

Example: (Its, It's) time for us to leave.

EXPLANATION: When one of the personal pronouns contains an apostrophe, the apostrophe stands for a missing letter or letters, usually missing from a verb form. The personal pronoun containing an apostrophe is always a contracted form. The test to discover whether such a pronoun belongs in the given sentence is to supply the missing letter or letters.

ACCEPTED FORM: *It is* time for us to leave. *It's* time for us to leave.

ACCEPTED FORM: Who's (Who is) to write the notice for the bulletin board?

CORRECTNESS AND EFFECTIVENESS OF EXPRESSION

ACCEPTED FORM: Whose (*Who is* does not fit) coat did he borrow?

With Nouns

Example: The president plans to speak to all of the (students, students', student's).

EXPLANATION: The apostrophe with nouns is usually used to indicate possession. It is not used as a sign of the plural. In the above example, *students* shows no ownership. Therefore there should be no apostrophe in this plural form.

ACCEPTED FORM: The president plans to speak to all of the *students*.

Example: The teacher showed the completed project to the (childrens', children's) parents.

EXPLANATION: The rule is simple. If the noun showing possession ends in other than *s*, add 's; if the noun showing possession ends in *s*, then just add '. The application of the rule is just as simple, IF mentally you change the possessive phrase into the *of* form. For example, the above possessive phrase becomes parents *of the children*. We thus discover that the noun *children* ends in *n*; therefore, the correct form is 's.

ACCEPTED FORM: The teacher showed the completed project to the *children's* parents.

Example: The mothers were wheeling their (baby's, babies', babie's) carriages.

EXPLANATION: By changing the possessive phrase into the *of* form we discover *carriages of the babies*. Therefore the possessive noun ends in *s* and all we need add is the apostrophe. The word is written as is and the apostrophe is then added.

ACCEPTED FORM: The mothers were wheeling their *babies'* carriages.

Example: There was not a single (lady's, ladies', ladie's) voice raised in protest.

EXPLANATION: The *of* form is *voice of a single lady*. The possessive noun does not end in *s*, therefore the word is written as is and 's is added.

ACCEPTED FORM: There was not a single *lady's* voice raised in protest.

With Proper Names Ending in s

Example: May I introduce you to (Charles', Charles's) brother?

EXPLANATION: With names like *Harris, Thomas, Jones, Phyllis,* names ending in *s*, you may write *s'* or *s's*. The preferred American form at the present time is the *s's*.

ACCEPTED FORM: May I introduce you to *Charles's* (or *Charles'*) brother?

With Hyphenated Nouns

Example: Did Mr. Smith help build his (son's-in-law's, son-in-law's) new house?

EXPLANATION: While the sign of the plural will be placed usually on the important word in the compound (son-in-law), the sign of the possessive is always placed at the *end* of the compound word.

ACCEPTED FORM: Did Mr. Smith help build his *son-in-law's* new house?

USING THE COMMA

With Dependent Phrases and Clauses

Example: He did not see the error (,) ( ) until I pointed it out to him.

EXPLANATION: When a dependent phrase or clause is in its natural order in the sentence, it is *not* separated from the rest of the sentence by a comma. Only when the phrase or clause is placed at the beginning of the sentence, before the main idea, is a separating comma needed.

ACCEPTED FORM: He did not see the error until I pointed it out to him.

Example: When Margie saw the extent of the damage (,) ( ) she burst into tears.

EXPLANATION: The main clause is *she burst into tears*. This independent clause follows the dependent clause, *When Margie saw the extent of the damage*. Therefore the reader must be alerted to this inverted order.

ACCEPTED FORM: When Margie saw the extent of the damage, she burst . . .

Example: Far from the center of town (,) ( ) our cabin is hidden from view by a grove of towering pine trees.

EXPLANATION: The phrase *far from the center of town* is out of its natural order. To indicate that it is not the main idea, the writer must insert a comma.

ACCEPTED FORM: Far from the center of town, our cabin is . . .

ACCEPTED FORM: Our cabin is hidden from view by a grove of towering pine trees far from the center of town.

With Appositives

Example: Abel plans to spend the summer at Lake Luzerne (,) (.) (One) (one) of the quaint towns that stud the Adirondack region.

EXPLANATION: The group of words, *one of the quaint towns that stud the Adirondack region*, is not a complete thought. This group of words help to explain what Lake Luzerne is. Therefore they constitute an appositive phrase. Appositive phrases are set off by commas, not by periods.

ACCEPTED FORM: Abel plans to spend the summer at Lake Luzerne, *one of* . . .

With Words or Phrases in Series

Example: We followed the circus to the railroad station (,) ( ) to the center of town (,) ( ) to the suburbs (,) ( ) and finally to the Exhibition Field.

EXPLANATION: When two or more words or phrases of the same construction are joined by conjunctions, then no commas are needed. However, when the conjunctions are omitted, then commas are placed wherever the conjunction has been omitted. In the example above there are four parallel phrases and the conjunction has been omitted between the first and second and the second and third. Therefore commas are needed at these points.

ACCEPTED FORM: We followed the circus to the railroad station, *to the center of town,* *to the suburbs* and finally to the Exhibition Field.

ACCEPTED FORM: I ordered peas and carrots and tomatoes and green beans.

ACCEPTED FORM: I ordered peas, carrots, tomatoes and green beans.

ACCEPTED FORM: Max, Dan, and I left for the trip to the ball field.

NOTE: The comma before the expressed conjunction (*and* in the above example) is an optional one. This means that it may or may not be used; however, modern usage prefers that it be used.

With Two Adjectives Modifying the Same Noun

Example: Tom has always been a cautious (,) ( ) accurate worker.

EXPLANATION: When both adjectives are of equal value and *and* can be inserted without changing the meaning, then a comma should be employed.

ACCEPTED FORM: Tom has always been a cautious, accurate worker.

ACCEPTED FORM: We learned to avoid the house guarded by that vicious barking dog.

EXPLANATION: The adjective *vicious* is not equal to *barking*. It is a *barking dog* that is vicious. Therefore no comma is used.

Restrictive and Non-Restrictive Modifiers

Example: Men (,) ( ) who have breathed free air (,) ( ) will never accept slavery.

EXPLANATION: A restrictive clause is one that so limits the meaning of the word it modifies that the entire meaning of the sentence is changed if the clause is removed. If the clause is removed in the above example, the sentence then becomes *Men will never accept slavery*. When a restrictive clause is used, then no commas must be employed to set that clause off from the rest of the sentence.

ACCEPTED FORM: Men who have breathed free air will never accept slavery.

Example: Edgar Zwilling (,) ( ) who had been my father's best friend (,) ( ) is professor of zoology in an Eastern college.

EXPLANATION: A non-restrictive clause does not limit or restrict; it gives additional information. As with an appositive, it may be removed without destroying the original sense of the sentence. Such clauses are set off from the rest of the sentence by commas.

ACCEPTED FORM: Edgar Zwilling, *who had been my father's best friend,* is . . .

Example: All buildings (,) ( ) not mentioned specifically in the agreement (,) ( ) will be out of bounds for all soldiers.

EXPLANATION: With phrases too the test to decide whether they are restrictive or non-restrictive rests on whether the meaning of the sentence is changed by their omission. If we omit the phrase in the example, then the rest of the sentence becomes *All buildings will be out of bounds for all soldiers*, a statement contrary to the intent of the original sentence. Therefore the phrase is restrictive; therefore, no commas should be used.

ACCEPTED FORM: All buildings not mentioned specifically in the agreement will be . . .

Example: The old house (,) ( ) filled with memories of days long since past (,) ( ) was a friendly refuge for the retired general.

EXPLANATION: The phrase *filled with memories of days long since past* merely adds additional information, and its omission does not alter the meaning of the sentence. Therefore commas should be used since the phrase is non-restrictive.

ACCEPTED FORM: The old house, filled with memories of days long since past, was . . .

Between Verbs and Their Objects

Example: The leader of the group stated very emphatically (,) ( ) that he would not be responsible for our actions.

EXPLANATION: The object of the sentence is *that he would not be responsible for our actions*. Since it is introduced by *that*, too many students confuse *that* with *and, but, or*. This object should not be separated from its verb by a comma.

USING THE SEMICOLON

After Salutations

Example: Dear Alice (;) (:) (,)

EXPLANATION: After the salutation in a friendly letter, the comma is the correct mark of punctuation. In a formal letter, the colon (:) or the comma may be used. In neither instance may you use the semicolon.

ACCEPTED FORM: Dear Alice,

ACCEPTED FORM: Dear Mr. Smith: (*or* Dear Mr. Smith,)

In Compound Sentences

Example: I really did not want to purchase that lamp (,) (:) (;) but I had no other choice.

EXPLANATION: The semicolon is used to separate two complete ideas when they are closely related and when the conjunction is omitted. When the conjunction is present and the two independent clauses contain no other commas, they should be separated by a comma. The colon cannot take the place of the comma.

ACCEPTED FORM: I really did not want to purchase that lamp, *but* I had no other choice.

ACCEPTED FORM: I really did not want to purchase that lamp; I had no other choice.

Example: Because the decision had to be made by Jack Rosenthal, our family lawyer, Pearl did not allow us to discuss the issue (,) (:) (;) and we waited impatiently until he had gathered all of the facts.

EXPLANATION: When a compound sentence contains ideas that require commas, then the conjunction that joins the two main thoughts is preceded by a semicolon and not by a comma. In the example

ACCEPTED FORM: The leader of the group stated very emphatically that he . . .

Example: The course is a grueling one; however (,) (;) ( ) I expect to complete it!

EXPLANATION: With conjunctive adverbs used to join two independent ideas, a comma follows the conjunctive adverb when a semi-colon precedes it.

The principal conjunctive adverbs are

*therefore, hence   moreover, consequently
            however*

ACCEPTED FORM: The course is a grueling one; however, . . .

above, the first independent idea contains necessary commas.

ACCEPTED FORM: Because the decision had to be made by Jack Rosenthal, our family lawyer, Pearl did not allow us to discuss the issue; and we waited . . .

Example: Denise followed my explanation (,) (;) ( ) and was able to do all of the practice problems.

EXPLANATION: The example does not contain two independent ideas (*was able to do all of the practice problems is not a complete idea*). This sentence contains a compound verb, two sentence elements joined by *and*. In this case, there should be no intervening mark of punctuation.

ACCEPTED FORM: Denise followed my explanation and was able to do . . .

With Conjunctive Adverbs

Example: Alexia had refused to see our side of the controversy (,) (;) (:) therefore, we saw no point in asking for her opinion.

EXPLANATION: The principal conjunctive adverbs are

*therefore   hence   moreover   consequently
            however*

When these are used without a conjunction such as *and, but* or *or*, they may *not* be preceded by a comma. They can begin a new sentence or be preceded by a semicolon and followed by a comma.

ACCEPTED FORM: Alexia had refused to see our side of the controversy; therefore, . . .

ACCEPTED FORM: Alexia had refused to see our side of the controversy. Therefore we . . .

ACCEPTED FORM: Alexia had refused to see our side of the controversy, and therefore we . . .

USING THE COLON

With Quotations

Example: Paul said (,) (:) (;) "Right should make might. Let me illustrate. . . ."

EXPLANATION: The quotation may be preceded by a comma or a colon. However modern usage prefers the comma.

ACCEPTED FORM: Paul said, "Right should make might. Let me . . ."

ACCEPTED FORM: Paul said: "Right should make might. Let me . . ."

In a Listing

Example: I have four reasons for considering this question. My reasons are (,) ( ) (:)

EXPLANATION: Even though an enumeration will follow, the preference of modern usage is to have *no* mark of punctuation follow *are* or *were*.

ACCEPTED FORM: My reasons are that he . . . and that he . . .

Example: We shall speak of three different types of drivers (,) (:) (;) namely (,) ( ) (:) . . .

EXPLANATION: When the series is introduced by expressions like

such as, namely, that is,

it is preceded by a colon and the introductory phrase is followed by a comma.

ACCEPTED FORM: We shall speak of three different types of drivers: namely, . . .

Example: The valise contained four items (;) (:) (,) the old gun, the note, a cuff-link, and a blood-stained handkerchief.

EXPLANATION: When a formal listing is not introduced by a form of *to be*, then it should be introduced by a colon.

ACCEPTED FORM: The valise contained four items: the old gun, . . .

USING QUOTATION MARKS

Setting off Titles

Example: She sang a selection from ("Lakme," *Lakme*, 'Lakme').

EXPLANATION: The preferred modern method of identifying titles is very definite. Main titles are underlined in themes (italicized in printed matter). Short compositions or parts of a larger work are set off by quotation marks.

ACCEPTED FORM: She sang a selection from *Lakme*.

ACCEPTED FORM: I have just finished reading the short story "My Old Man."

ACCEPTED FORM: I learned to respect Silas Marner in the novel *Silas Marner*.

NOTE: The name of the author is not set off. It requires neither underlining nor quotation marks.

ACCEPTED FORM: Our class is reading *The Return of the Native* by Thomas Hardy.

Accompanying Punctuation

Study the following examples. They illustrate the correct method of handling the various problems that arise in using quotations in themes.

ACCEPTED FORM: Helen asked, "Should we really accept his conclusions?"

ACCEPTED FORM: "Should we," Helen asked, "really accept his conclusions? I find him too self-seeking to be respected!"

ACCEPTED FORM: "I had left at twelve," she said. "When did you?"

ACCEPTED FORM: Did Helen say, "I find him too self-seeking to be respected"?

NOTE: In handling sustained dialogue, a new paragraph is required for each change of speaker, regardless of the number of words each one says.

ACCEPTED FORM: "What did you say?"
"Nothing!"
"Nothing?"
"Yes, nothing."

Position of Quotation Marks

Example: I have memorized the first stanza of "Song of Myself (.") (".)

EXPLANATION: The period and comma are always placed within the quotation marks.

ACCEPTED FORM: I have memorized the first stanza of "Song of Myself."

Example: I just did not understand Poe's "Bells(;") (";) then Jerry read it aloud to me.

EXPLANATION: The colon and the semi-colon are placed outside the quotation marks.

ACCEPTED FORM: I just did not understand Poe's "Bells"; then . . .

Example: What is the meaning of "as slick as a skinned herring("?) (?")

EXPLANATION: The question mark and the exclamation point are placed *within* the quoted material when the reference is to the quoted matter only. These marks are placed outside when they refer to the whole sentence.

ACCEPTED FORM: What is the meaning of "as slick as a skinned herring"?

ACCEPTED FORM: "When will the test be given?" Edna asked.

Indirect Quotations

Example: Milton said (, "That) (that) he would not visit the museum at all (.") (.)

EXPLANATION: Only the exact words of the speaker are set off in quotation marks. When the words are changed so that the quotation is not directly what had been said, no quotation marks must be used. In the example above, Milton had actually said, "I shall not visit the museum at all." Since the above example does not contain his exact words, quotation marks should not be used. When *that* is a necessary introductory word, the statement that follows is usually not a direct quotation.

ACCEPTED FORM: Milton said that he would not visit the museum at all.

USING THE HYPHEN

With Numbers

Example: I saw twenty(-) ( ) one applicants in one hour!

EXPLANATION: The hyphen is used with compound numbers from twenty-one to ninety-nine.

ACCEPTED FORM: I saw *twenty-one* applicants in one hour!

With Fractions

Example: They gave us one (-) ( ) third of the winnings.

EXPLANATION: The hyphen is used to separate the numerator from the denominator in fractions that are spelled out.

ACCEPTED FORM: They gave us *one-third* of the winnings.

With Prefixes

Example: He solemnly swore that he would re(-) ( ) establish order.

EXPLANATION: Usually when the prefix will cause confusion because two vowels are placed next to each other, a hyphen is used unless the word has become part of long-established usage.

ACCEPTED FORM: He solemnly swore that he would re-establish order.

ACCEPTED FORM: We shall need all the *cooperation* we can get.

Example: I spoke to the ex (-) ( ) president of the local bank.

EXPLANATION: A hyphen is generally used with the prefixes *self-, post-, all-, ex-, anti-* when they are added to complete words.

   self-centered   anti-war   all-American
       post-season   ex-husband

ACCEPTED FORM: I spoke to the ex-president of the local bank.

ACCEPTED FORM: He is a most *selfless* leader.

With Compound Modifiers

Example: He is an all (-) ( ) weather pilot.

EXPLANATION: A hyphen is used to join two or more words used as a single adjective preceding the noun.

ACCEPTED FORM: He is an all-weather pilot.

Example: The answer is well (-) ( ) known.

EXPLANATION: Since the compound modifier does *not* precede the noun, no hyphen is used.

ACCEPTED FORM: The answer is *well known*.

ACCEPTED FORM: Alex is a *well-known* referee.

Example: He insists that it is not an overly(-) ( ) complicated case.

EXPLANATION: If the first of the compound modifiers ends in *ly*, then *no* hyphen is used.

ACCEPTED FORM: He insists that it is not an overly complicated case.

USING ABBREVIATIONS

Example: 1416 East 26 (th) ( ) Street

EXPLANATION: Following the preference of the postal authorities, present usage requires the omission of *rd, st, th* after numbers.

ACCEPTED FORM: 1416 East 26 Street

Example: 1416 East 26 Street
        B'klyn., 10, N.Y.

EXPLANATION: The preferred form is to spell the word out rather than to abbreviate it. However, if in the abbreviation an apostrophe is used, then no period should be used. Therefore, if you must use the abbreviated form, use either *B'klyn* or *Bklyn.* and not both forms combined. The zone or zip code number is an integral part of the name. It is *not* an additional item. It is inseparable from the name.

ACCEPTED FORM: 1416 East 26 Street
        Brooklyn, N.Y. 21210

Example: ( ) (Dr.) Milton F. Gitlin, M.D.

EXPLANATION: The title can be given only once. Therefore if we use *Dr.*, we should not use M.D. If we use M.D., we should not use Dr.

ACCEPTED FORM: Milton F. Gitlin, M.D. *or* Dr. Milton F. Gitlin

ACCEPTED FORM: Mr. George Getnick *or* George Getnick, Esq.

Example: I plan to visit the (U.N. UN) Building this Wednesday.

EXPLANATION: Most abbreviations are identified by terminal periods. However the names of many governmental bureaus and agencies omit the periods.

ACCEPTED FORM: I plan to visit the UN Building this Wednesday.

ACCEPTED FORM: My father was able to obtain an FHA loan when he bought our house.

USING NUMERALS

Example: I spoke to all (five, 5) of my cousins.

EXPLANATION: Most textbooks agree that if the number is long, you can use the arabic form. They also agree that numbers from one to thirteen and the multiples of ten up to one hundred should be spelled out.

ACCEPTED FORM: I spoke to all *five* of my cousins.

ACCEPTED FORM: There were *115* candidates who showed up at practice.

Example: We shall meet promptly at (six-thirty P.M., 6:30 P.M.).

EXPLANATION: When time is expressed with A.M. or P.M., numbers are preferred.

ACCEPTED FORM: We shall meet promptly at 6:30 P.M.

Example: I finally sold 317 pens, 243 desks and (forty, 40) pads.

EXPLANATION: In a series of numbers, consistency should be the guide.

ACCEPTED FORM: I finally sold 317 pens, 243 desks and 40 pads.

Example: (Thirty-six, 36 seniors) were appointed to the staff.

EXPLANATION: When numbers must be used at the beginning of a sentence, they should be written out. If the number is very large, the sentence should be recast so that it does not appear first in the sentence.

ACCEPTED FORM: *Thirty-six* seniors were appointed to the staff.

ACCEPTED FORM: We finally had accumulated 3,452 pennies.

USING SPECIAL TERMS

Example: We were able to avoid the mountain range by traveling due (North, north).

EXPLANATION: Points of the compass are not capitalized. However when *north, south, east, west* are used to refer to specific regions in our country, they are capitalized.

ACCEPTED FORM: We were able to avoid the mountain range by traveling due *north*.

ACCEPTED FORM: We plan to live in the *East* for the next few years.

Example: In order to be chosen for the honor course I shall have to achieve 90% in (english, English) and (mathematics, Mathematics).

EXPLANATION: School subjects per se are *not* capitalized. However, we do capitalize the titles of those subjects whose names are derived from the names of languages.

ACCEPTED FORM: In order to be chosen for the honor course, I shall have to achieve 90% in English and mathematics.

Example: There are several groups of (jewish, Jewish) people who have lived among the (Chinese, chinese) for centuries.

EXPLANATION: Adjectives derived from the names of religions and countries are capitalized. Therefore *Protestant, Catholicism, Nigerian* should be capitalized.

ACCEPTED FORM: There are several groups of *Jewish* people who have lived among the *Chinese* for centuries.

Example: Ralph Bunche was one of the great (negro, Negro) leaders of the Twentieth Century.

EXPLANATION: Words that refer to race are capitalized. Therefore *Negro, Caucassian* (white) are capitalized. The words black and white are not.

ACCEPTED FORM: Ralph Bunche was one of the great Negro leaders . . .

Example: I had to telephone my (uncle, Uncle) three times today.

EXPLANATION: Names that denote close relationship unless they are used with a proper noun or stand alone are usually *not* capitalized.

ACCEPTED FORM: I had to telephone my uncle three times today.

ACCEPTED FORM: I had to telephone Uncle Harold three times today.

ACCEPTED FORM: Did you telephone Mother today?

ACCEPTED FORM: I had a long conversation with Uncle tonight.

CORRECTNESS AND EFFECTIVENESS OF EXPRESSION

TEST OF MASTERY

In each of the following groups, no sentence, one sentence, two, three or all four of the sentences may be punctuated in an acceptable form. In the space provided to the left, write *accepted* if the punctuation is acceptable in that sentence.

.... 1. (a) Its time for the men and women to pack the gear.
.... (b) What is mine is mine, and what is yours is yours.
.... (c) They had left early; consequently, they cannot be accused.
.... (d) We all tried to start the engine, before the mechanic arrived.
.... 2. (a) There were thirty three-inch boxes on the top shelf.
.... (b) There were thirty-three inch boxes on the top shelf.
.... (c) He is a fair minded leader.
.... (d) Their leader was very fair-minded.
.... 3. (a) They introduced us to lox and bagels, pizza and beer, and cream cheese and black bread.
.... (b) The Navajo worked behind the counter, and displayed the jewelry to the tourists.
.... (c) They had wanted me to see the exhibition; it was their first.
.... (d) The new land stretched out for endless miles; filling the pioneers with the thrill of expectancy.
.... 4. (a) We have three main tasks; feeding the animals, paying the bills, and waiting for the next set of orders.
.... (b) "What did he say?" questioned the old doctor.
.... (c) "If you listen carefully", replied the salesman, "you too will hear the difference."
.... (d) Did Phil say, "I need one too"?
.... 5. (a) The old house is falling apart, therefore, you will really have to see that it is repaired.
.... (b) Lucy wants to talk with you; therefore you had better listen.
.... (c) Margie is on the porch. Therefore, you will have to go out there if you want to see her.
.... (d) The price has gone up; therefore, we will either have to pay more or not get a copy for ourselves.
.... 6. (a) I have just completed reading, *Treasure Island*.
.... (b) How will we ever be able to hold him to his preelection promises!
.... (c) Men who want to assume authority must be prepared to be criticized.
.... (d) Men, who know Mr. Coleman well, all say that he never looked better.
.... 7. (a) If you want to see him you had better enter now.
.... (b) We were unaware that he had gone, until the roll was called.
.... (c) You had better smile when you say that to me!
.... (d) Because he failed the test, he will have to attend the help class.
.... 8. (a) Olaf said: "Once we fix the amplifier, our reception will be much improved."
.... (b) George Edwards, who is our Chemistry teacher, lives in that apartment house.
.... (c) The coach turned to the team and said, "That they should do the best that they could, and no one would expect more of them."
.... (d) The article compared four presidents: Washington, Lincoln, F.D.R. and Kennedy.
.... 9. (a) Alice, who normally helps us on Friday, reported ill today and went home directly; and our stalwart, Mr. Bonom, had an accident at home and didn't even come in.
.... (b) When Vic tried to take command; the others quickly put him in his place.
.... (c) We had traveled ten miles along the dangerous, old road.
.... (d) Two fourth termers led the parade, but they were overshadowed by freshmen twirlers.
.... 10. (a) The three men were: Henry, Allan, and Jack.
.... (b) The wall finally collapsed, then we saw where the money had been hid.
.... (c) The wall finally collapsed; then we saw where the money had been hid.
.... (d) The wall finally collapsed. Then we saw where the money had been hid.
.... 11. (a) The storekeepers son's were rude to many of the customers.
.... (b) It's about time that Harris' demands were met.
.... (c) My father-in-law's car, an old four-door sedan was still running ten years after he had bought it.
.... (d) Your 5's have begun to resemble 2's.
.... 12. (a) "I cannot do it now," exclaimed Helen. "Let's wait until tomorrow, please."
.... (b) "We must decide now," replied my brother, "Otherwise time will make the decision for us."
.... (c) Of course, the book he is referring to is "Of Human Bondage."
.... (d) Does anybody know who wrote, "Trees."
.... 13. (a) We shall go on a trip to Idlewild Airport on Columbus day.
.... (b) May I introduce you to Reverend Smith.
.... (c) We bought 5 tubes, 3 transformers and 81 assorted connectors.
.... (d) The plant finally climbed the six-foot wall after ten years.
.... 14. (a) The victory will be ours, and not theirs.

.... (b) But me no *but's*.
.... (c) The babies toys were strewn all over the road, a mute testimony to the tragic accident.
.... (d) Far out on the island, is the house where the plants are being grown.
.... 15. (a) The bright, sunny day dazzled the old man.
.... (b) He is a strange young man.
.... (c) They are sick, disappointed people.
.... (d) It was a clear, blue sky when we started out.
.... 16. (a) Singing at the top of his lungs was his sole exercise for hours.
.... (b) Singing the latest songs, Alice attempted to appear chic.
.... (c) I shall never forgive him if he leaves early.
.... (d) If he really wants to do it I shall not stand in his way.
.... 17. (a) His brother, Milton, arrived before all the others.
.... (b) Alfred Kennedy, who is unmarried, lives in the attic apartment.
.... (c) "How often," she shouted, "Must I tell you this!"
.... (d) Tell me, Jerry, did he really react so favorably?
.... 18. (a) She is the teacher, who raised my mark.
.... (b) The boy groaned; his body was wracked by pain.
.... (c) He is willing to listen, isn't he?
.... (d) The three stars are: Sirius, Polaris, and Cepheus.
.... 19. (a) He plans to complete his in-service training in two months.
.... (b) I saw several of our neighbors there; namely, Mrs. Tesso, Mr. Lurie and Mrs. Schiff.
.... (c) Alex Frey enjoys modern plays, especially those that are truly realistic in tone.
.... (d) I never said that; and I cannot be forced to admit that I did.
.... 20. (a) It was the end of the line, we all had to leave.
.... (b) When we came to the end of the line, we all had to leave.
.... (c) It was the end of the line. We all had to leave.
.... (d) It was the end of the line: we all had to leave.
.... 21. (a) "It was some experience!" exclaimed Edna. "I shall never forget it."
.... (b) My brothers-in-law's business has been in their family for generations.
.... (c) There were two-third termers waiting in the room for the instructor.
.... (d) One of the most self-ish people that I know is my cousin Alfred.
.... 22. (a) We shall live in the Northern part of the state.
.... (b) I find that I do best in English and Mathematics.
.... (c) The Chinese and the Negroes contributed to the settling of our West.
.... (d) We visited my Uncle when he arrived at Idlewild Airport.
.... 23. (a) Tom and Jerry, Paula and Mac, and Harry and Martha will be the participants in the dance contest finals.
.... (b) The message was from Stella Lasker; an old friend of the family.
.... (c) The men, moreover, were unwilling to take part in the plans.
.... (d) Lucy was prepared to take the test: hence, she was upset when it was postponed.
.... 24. (a) The meeting did begin on time; in fact it was even over before it was scheduled to end.
.... (b) Did Philip say, "Go to Third Avenue"?
.... (c) They tried to say that the book was their's, but we challenged their statement, and they retracted.
.... (d) The babies dresses were starched and ironed by Mrs. Stanley, our neighbor.
.... 25. (a) They were given a dollar's worth of candy when they asked for contributions to their party.
.... (b) They're going to be all right; consequently, we should not interfere.
.... (c) Stan was given a Cadillac roadster for his birthday; at least that's what he told us.
.... (d) During the summer, I plan to visit our great American West.

ANSWER KEY: TEST OF MASTERY / *Page 61*

1. (b), (c)	6. (c)	11. (d)	15. (c)	19. (a), (c)	23. (a), (c)
2. (a), (b)	7. (c), (d)	12. (a)	16. (a), (b), (c)	20. (b), (c)	24. (b)
3. (a), (c)	8. (a), (d)	13. (c), (d)	17. (b), (d)	21. (a), (b)	25. (a), (b), (c)
4. (b), (d)	9. (a), (d)	14. (a), (b)	18. (b), (c)	22. (c)	
5. (c), (d)	10. (c), (d)				

6. Spelling Check Tests

Spelling can be a major problem for those taking the English Composition Test. The objective questions do not test spelling ability, but the student who is prone to misspellings of this kind will normally reveal such weakness by not doing well in other areas of English compositional skills.

The words that follow are the favorites for misspellings in essays and in freshman college courses.

These are the spelling words that cause the costliest deductions. Run through the tests as quickly as possible. Make a list of those that you missed, and then make certain that you have them under control when you take the Achievement Test. By gaining control of these words, you can make certain that you will have command over those words that are most frequently misspelled on college themes.

TEST OF MASTERY

Rewrite in the space provided to the left the accepted spelling of each word containing dashes in the following list. Each dash may represent no letter, one letter, or two or more letters.

Group One

.... 1. His mother signed his note of ab–se–n–e.

.... 2. He ac–dent–ly overlooked the third problem.

.... 3. This 100% in sociology is the great ach–v–ment of his school career.

.... 4. He has played a–mat–u–r basketball for years.

.... 5. I refused to accept his half-hearted attempt at an a–po–l–gy.

.... 6. His shabby a–pe–r–nce made the jury most sympathetic.

.... 7. He was so cross that no one dared to a–pro–ch him.

.... 8. What was the a–r–gu–m–nt all about?

.... 9. The a–t–nd–nce was largest when the Limelighters were featured.

.... 10. When must we pay the ba–l–nce?

.... 11. This task is be–g–n–ing to become difficult.

.... 12. We shall visit Great Bri–t–i–n this summer.

.... 13. Each day's passage meant just another check on the ca–l–n–d–r for her.

.... 14. The old man was ca–r–ing three packages when he slipped and fell.

.... 15. I am bored when the exercises contain no cha–l–n–ge for me.

.... 16. The faculty com–i–t–e will judge his case.

.... 17. The car will be com–ple–t–ly overhauled before delivery.

.... 18. I refuse to con–d–m– them before hearing their side of the issue.

.... 19. Paula is most cons–nt–ous when handling the accounts belonging to others.

.... 20. The robot can be contr–l–ed by a computer.

.... 21. His cri–t–ism was most unjust when he found fault with our data.

.... 22. C–ur–i–sity may have killed a cat, but it is most proper in a detective.

.... 23. What could you have gained by dec–ving us?

.... 24. The lawyer for the de–fend–nt will cross examine the next witness.

.... 25. She is a de–s–nd–nt of one of the first to settle in our area.

.... 26. We gave a d–scr–tion of the robber to the police when they arrived.

.... 27. He must have felt very de–s–p–r–ate when he resorted to violence.

.... 28. You will have to keep us posted on the latest dev–l–p–ments.

.... 29. I felt that I just could not dis–a–p–oint them again.

.... 30. It was the most dis–ast–rous defeat of his long career.

.... 31. You must learn not to di–s–i–pate your energies in so many directions.

.... 32. Alex will be in charge of the construction of the new d–rm–t–ries.

.... 33. He will never know the joy, the e–c–ta–y of doing a task perfectly.

.... 34. I was so em–ba–r–as–ed that I was speechless for the first time in my life!

.... 35. She has a tendency to exa–g–r–ate when retelling an anecdote.

.... 36. This is an exc–l–nt copy of *Mona Lisa*.

.... 37. Only a f–e–nd from the fires of the damned could have conceived of such exquisite torture for a fellow human being.

.... 38. Carl calmly announced that he is the ge–n–i–s of our generation.

.... 39. I did not think that that story was very hu–m–r–us.

40. His handwriting is such a scrawl that his messages are almost i–l–g–ble.
41. She speaks daily to an i–m–g–n–ry sister who never existed.
42. I would advise your seeing the doctor im–ed–t–ly.
43. Ivan asked us to speak only when in our considered ju–g–ment what we had to say warranted the expenditure of time.
44. Tom applied for a part-time job in the biology la–b–r–t–ry.
45. The bold strokes of light–n–ing were followed by rolling peals of thunder.
46. A surge of lo–n–l–ness swept through Alice's mind and brought back the realization of her great loss.
47. The cost of ma–nt–n–nce will exceed the initial price of the car.
48. The ma–r–g–e ceremony will take place at ten in the morning.
49. Her reaction was so si–m–l–r to mine!
50. And I had thought that I really could su–pr–se you!

Group Two

1. I have never heard a more abs–rd excuse!
2. The files will be much more a–c–e–s–ble now that they have been moved.
3. The apartment cannot a–c–om–date more than three people at a time.
4. He is no mere a–qu–a–nt–nce of mine.
5. Of course I do not believe everything I read in the adv–rti–s–ments.
6. You may not exceed the a–lot–ed time by more than ten seconds.
7. You will not find his name am–ng the missing.
8. When it comes to killing a joke, I am a professional a–s–a–sin.
9. I think that this dress is the one that is most bec–om–ing.
10. When the com–p–t–tion becomes keen, Fred just wilts.
11. The faculty group con–fe–red for two hours.
12. What salve can he use to soothe his troubled cons–c–nce?
13. The chairman seemed unable to handle the debate that raged during the cont–r–v–rsy over the recent suggestion that rates be increased.
14. Who would dare say that Harold is d–f–nit–ly at fault!
15. He will not be pleased until he has d–stro–ed all who oppose him.
16. What is the di–f–r–nce between the two suggestions?
17. Watch how quickly I can make a dollar di–sa–p–e–r.
18. They are now in the midst of a fight for their very ex–st–nce as an independent nation.
19. How fa–mil–ar are you with his method of handling dangerous isotopes?
20. Paul specializes in collecting for–n stamps.
21. He can gen–r–ly be found sitting in the local park on sunny days.
22. Lucy plans to become a gu–d–nce counselor after graduation.
23. I promise that this shall prove a minor hind–r–nce rather than a major handicap to our plans.
24. Joel plans to become an ind–p–nd–nt rather than a fraternity man.
25. Don't let his look of complete in–o–cen–e fool you!
26. You can find me in the local lib–r–r–y working on my report.
27. That such lov–l–ness should be spoiled by a foul temper!
28. My favorite subject has always been math–m–tic–s.
29. You mi–s–pel–ed *all right* five times in your composition!
30. Mr. Aarons has been our next-door n–ghb–r for more than ten years.
31. Helen has always been my favorite n–ce.
32. Peter had done so much studying for that quiz that he was dismayed when he found that he had received only a ni–n–ty on it.
33. Even so eminent a scholar as Dr. Schub can make a mistake o–cas–ion–ly.
34. When shall we win pe–rm–n–nt control over the property?
35. How can one person pos–e–s so much charm and still lack scruples!
36. The settling of the pra–r–e was the Great American Adventure.
37. I am convinced that he has allowed blind pre–ju–dice to distort all of his values.
38. May we have the pri–v–le–ge of being the first to congratulate you!
39. The instructor re–c–o–mends that we begin with the books in the school library.
40. The kind priest did all that he humanly could to rel–ve the child's anxieties.
41. She offered a most r–d–cu–l–ous reason for not being able to come to the meeting on time.
42. The school sec–re–t–ry told me that I had an appointment with the dean.

CORRECTNESS AND EFFECTIVENESS OF EXPRESSION

.... 43. You must learn to se–p–r–te the trivial from the unimportant.
.... 44. Do you really think that she is sinc–r–ly interested in our welfare?
.... 45. I hope that you will be su–ce–s–fu–l in your endeavors.
.... 46. Francie must realize that she has a tend–ncy to be pessimistic.
.... 47. I have often wondered how Othello could have averted the tra–g–dy that destroyed all of his well-deserved happiness.
.... 48. I do not agree that undo–tedly you are right.
.... 49. I have us–u–ly found him more than willing to listen to a logical defense.
.... 50. Poverty and ignorance were the vi–l–ns that twisted the strands of her life and brought unhappiness to all that knew her.

Group Three

.... 1. The children seemed to have an abund–nce of energy.
.... 2. How many months did it take you to a–cum–late all these items?
.... 3. I shall never become a–c–st–med to her rude manners.
.... 4. Oscar will assemble the a–p–r–at–s for the experiment.
.... 5. The chairman will make the a–pr–pr–ate remarks when the time comes.
.... 6. The reception committee will be in charge of all a–r–ang–ments.
.... 7. Fill the ba–l–on slowly with the oxygen.
.... 8. Have you ever visited the National Cem–t–ry at Arlington, Virginia?
.... 9. She just did not feel very comf–rt–ble in our presence.
.... 10. Fred felt compe–led to apologize for our actions during the game.
.... 11. How can you stand before me and deny so coo–ly something that I saw with my own eyes!
.... 12. The bank teller easily spotted the co–nterf–t ten-dollar bill.
.... 13. She borrowed a cup–f–u–l of flour.
.... 14. The judge promised to reach a de–c–sion within three or four days.
.... 15. She had become too dep–nd–nt upon mental crutches.
.... 16. There seemed to be no way out of this most annoying d–le–ma.
.... 17. The dean did not di–sa–prove completely of the plan.
.... 18. This is the best equi–ped operating room in the hospital.
.... 19. He has a memory so extr–rdin–ry that he can recall verbatim every conversation he ever had with us.
.... 20. Alec made a fund–m–nt–l mistake when he disregarded Grace's suggestions.
.... 21. I spent many hours relearning my French gra–m–r.
.... 22. The insects ha–ra–sed us so during our trip through the swamplands that I did not enjoy it at all.
.... 23. We shall remain hop–ful–l until our last breath.
.... 24. The speaker glanced hu–r–edly at his notes during the outburst of applause.
.... 25. They have been inse–p–r–ble companions during the entire voyage.
.... 26. Some day I hope to have sufficient l–e–sur– time so that I will not feel guilty whenever we devote an hour to bridge playing.
.... 27. Without a trade, how does he expect to earn a liv–l–h–od?
.... 28. Why must Helena feel that she must mo–n–p–lize the conversation?
.... 29. Because you disagree, he need not ne–ce–s–r–ly be wrong.
.... 30. His inability to control his temper became more and more no–t–c–ble.
.... 31. They should never have o–mi–ted his name from the announcement.
.... 32. This is one o–p–rtu–nity that I would not miss for the world.
.... 33. Will you be able to prove that the two lines are pa–r–a–l–l?
.... 34. In which year did the Giants win the National League Pe–n–nt?
.... 35. He who has learned the lesson of pe–se–v–r–nce has learned a way of life.
.... 36. The bullet p–e–rced the fleshy part of his arm, but it did not hit the bone.
.... 37. How much more ple–s–nt is the day when she is agreeable!
.... 38. There are three po–s–ble solutions to this problem.
.... 39. You will have to give this matter p–r–ce–d–nce over all others.
.... 40. We were in the midst of our pre–p–r–tions for the annual dinner.
.... 41. I dare not offer that as the excuse for my not keeping my appointment with the chemistry pro–fe–s–r.
.... 42. What is the correct p–ro–n–uncia-tion of *women*?
.... 43. We must learn that pr–p–g–nda can be harmful or beneficial.
.... 44. I wish you would not p–rsu– that topic any farther.
.... 45. Mary is accustomed to doing well on all of the qui–z–es.
.... 46. You will find the book on the re–f–r–nce shelf.

.... 47. I scarc–ly knew him!
.... 48. I have spent all of my spare time in stu–d–ing for the literature test.
.... 49. The chairman tried in vain to su–pre–s the smoldering antagonisms in the group attending the meeting.
.... 50. He who seeks ve–ng–nce allows fire to consume his own spirit.

Group Four

.... 1. You will be admitted if you are a–comp–n–ed by the captain of the team.
.... 2. How was he able to ac–om–plish so much in so little time!
.... 3. After five hours of deliberation, the jury finally a–qu–i–t–ed him of the murder charge.
.... 4. You must set aside an a–d–qu–te amount of time if you ever expect to study properly.
.... 5. Who ever said that the period of a–dole–s–en–e lacks adult responsibilities!
.... 6. The walk in the rain merely a–gr–v–ted the conditions that were leading to the rupture in our plans.
.... 7. They hope to make this picnic an a–nu–l affair.
.... 8. They have been a–pl–ing the wrong principles in attempting to analyze this difficulty.
.... 9. Someday you will a–pre–c–te what I have been trying to do for you.
.... 10. Who is the auth–r of *To Kill a Mockingbird*?
.... 11. To what extent will this decision be ben–fi–c–l to the American people.
.... 12. A commission was created to settle the bo–nd–r–es between the two new countries.
.... 13. The cas–l–ties resulting from the airplane crash overtaxed the emergency facilities in the local hospital.
.... 14. Into which ca–t–g–ry does this specimen belong?
.... 15. Only the president of the Student Council was invited to attend the ground breaking ce–r–mon–es.
.... 16. Allen will act as cha–f–e–r, driving the group of children from their homes to the party and then back again.
.... 17. The local utility com–p–n–es banded together and hired one lawyer to protect their claims in the libel case.
.... 18. Will attendance be comp–l–ry at all meetings?
.... 19. We just could not conc–ve of her attempting to hurt innocent bystanders.
.... 20. He was confid–nt that the outcome would be favorable to his side.
.... 21. What monument shall be erected to the memory of the man who will be labeled "Conqu–r–r of Fear"?
.... 22. Even in his refusal to assist you, he was con–s–st–nt in his antagonistic rejection of all of his former friends.
.... 23. She has been interrupting me continu–ly all morning.
.... 24. I shall be very much pleased to meet you at your earliest conv–en–nce.
.... 25. We have been able to obtain all of the letters that were part of their cor–e–sp–nd–nce during those important three years.
.... 26. Unless you appear courag–us when you meet them, you will be unable to negotiate on equal terms.
.... 27. His induction was def–r–ed for three weeks to allow him to arrange his business affairs.
.... 28. Do not d–sp–r; we shall help you as much as we can.
.... 29. I hope to be able to d–velo–p– a perfected model within a few months.
.... 30. Helen and I will be din–ing out tonight.
.... 31. From di–s–atisfaction can come improvement.
.... 32. You will have to e–l–m–nate the background noise before I can accept the set.
.... 33. Lucy did ex–eption–ly well on the Core III test.
.... 34. The road is extrem–ly slippery and should not be used now.
.... 35. The sight of the young children fa–s–nated the stranger.
.... 36. May we tell you how feas–ble we think this plan is!
.... 37. After long months of negotiation, we fin–ly were able to buy the property.
.... 38. The test proved that this is a ge–nu–n– diamond.
.... 39. Who is the present gov–rn–r of the Empire State?
.... 40. The missile zoomed upward to a h–ght of ten miles.
.... 41. Only one of the he–r–o–s of old could have withstood such hardship.
.... 42. Without the slightest he–s–t–ncy, I recommend Pete for the position.
.... 43. The entire matter was delayed until some in–d–f–n–te time.
.... 44. I have found the dictionary an ind–s–pens–ble aid to my studies.
.... 45. Leora is one of the most lov–ble characters in modern American fiction.
.... 46. The dean warned me that I must ma–nta–n– a B average in order to remain.
.... 47. She has n–ther humility nor pride.
.... 48. Which is the most pois–n–us of all snakes?

CORRECTNESS AND EFFECTIVENESS OF EXPRESSION

.... 49. The town fell after only a brief period of re–s–st–nce.

.... 50. He will need more self-confidence if he is ever to su–c–ed–.

Group Five

.... 1. Please accept this as a–kno–le–g–ment of the package you sent me.
.... 2. Do you know the a–dre–s of the State Capitol?
.... 3. Place the ruler aga–nst the wall.
.... 4. I shall be a–l– right by morning.
.... 5. What is the total a–m–nt of the bill?
.... 6. You must learn how to a–n–l–ze the results yourself.
.... 7. We had never an–t–c–p–ted such difficulties.
.... 8. Her tensions and an–i–t–es drove her to the verge of madness.
.... 9. You will never be able to as–nd the stairs with that heavy valise.
.... 10. How long will he remain in the a–kw–rd stage, breaking everything that he stumbles into!
.... 11. I just do not bel–ve that story one bit.
.... 12. All of his instructors consider him a bri–l–nt student.
.... 13. I still do not know why they should know all of our bu–s–ne–s.
.... 14. We can hide kind thoughts, but jealousy is difficult to ca–m–o–fla–g–e.
.... 15. Does that instructor place a c–ling on the marks he will hand out?
.... 16. How quickly he added up those three co–l–u–m–s of figures!
.... 17. Will she be co–m–ng along with us?
.... 18. How could he have com–i–ted the crime when his lawyer has proof that he had never been near the scene?
.... 19. Of course the quality of this one is co–mp–r–ble to that of yours.
.... 20. The solution is comp–r–t–iv–ly simple.
.... 21. I shall not cond–s–end to name-calling as he has!
.... 22. His selfishness was more co–ntem–t–ble than her forgetfulness.
.... 23. How much further the c–urt–us reply can get you than the curt brush-off ever will.
.... 24. I would have forgiven anything but this act of deliberate dec–t!
.... 25. How quickly can fear dev–st–te and destroy humanity.
.... 26. Yellow will be the dom–n–nt color in the kitchen.
.... 27. Who is the most e–f–c–e–nt worker in the factory?
.... 28. We shall ende–v–r to prove that ours is the more logical stand.
.... 29. This record shall never be equ–l–ed by another!
.... 30. He held that e–r–on–us assumption because he had failed to gather all of the data.
.... 31. The fin–nc–l page contains quotations on the most important stocks.
.... 32. It must ever be a gov–r–m–nt *of*, *for* and *by* the people.
.... 33. Who can say that his gr–v–nces are greater or more valid than mine!
.... 34. Tie a han–k–rch–f around your face to protect yourself from the fumes.
.... 35. Stop trying to i–mit–at– him!
.... 36. Only an incr–d–ble series of blunders could have accomplished this!
.... 37. Disaster is i–nevit–ble once reason is disregarded.
.... 38. Her parents felt that they had always been too le–n–nt in disciplining her.
.... 39. I do not know how ma–nag–ble he will be after this bitter defeat.
.... 40. We had saved enough to pay the monthly sum due on the mor–g–g–e.
.... 41. We placed the money in the nin–th bin.
.... 42. How obst–n–te can a spoiled child be!
.... 43. This outra–g–us attack on law-abiding citizens must cease.
.... 44. I am pa–ticul–rly interested in seeing who will buy the small colt.
.... 45. He has a most pec–ul–r idea of what cooperation means.
.... 46. You must let me know what your pre–f–e–r–nce is.
.... 47. The court will decide just what the proce–d–re will be in this instance.
.... 48. The insect repe–l–nt gave us long hours of relief from their attacks.
.... 49. Her paintings are on display on the local rest–r–nt.
.... 50. What signific–nce did you attach to his last remark?

ANSWER KEY / SPELLING CHECK TESTS

GROUP ONE / *Page 63*

1. absence
2. accidentally
3. achievement
4. amateur
5. apology
6. appearance
7. approach
8. argument
9. attendance
10. balance
11. beginning
12. Britain
13. calendar
14. carrying
15. challenge
16. committee
17. completely
18. condemn
19. conscientious
20. controlled
21. criticism
22. Curiosity
23. deceiving
24. defendant
25. descendant
26. description
27. desperate
28. developments
29. disappoint
30. disastrous
31. dissipate
32. dormitories
33. ecstasy
34. embarrassed
35. exaggerate
36. excellent
37. fiend
38. genius
39. humorous
40. illegible
41. imaginary
42. immediately
43. judgment
44. laboratory
45. lightning
46. loneliness
47. maintenance
48. marriage
49. similar
50. surprise

GROUP TWO / *Page 64*

1. absurd
2. accessible
3. accommodate
4. acquaintance
5. advertisements
6. allotted
7. among
8. assassin
9. becoming
10. competition
11. conferred
12. conscience
13. controversy
14. definitely
15. destroyed
16. difference
17. disappear
18. existence
19. familiar
20. foreign
21. generally
22. guidance
23. hindrance
24. independent
25. innocence
26. library
27. loveliness
28. mathematics
29. misspelled
30. neighbor
31. niece
32. ninety
33. occasionally
34. permanent
35. possess
36. prairie
37. prejudice
38. privilege
39. recommends
40. relieve
41. ridiculous
42. secretary
43. separate
44. sincerely
45. successful
46. tendency
47. tragedy
48. undoubtedly
49. usually
50. villains

GROUP THREE / *Page 65*

1. abundance
2. accumulate
3. accustomed
4. apparatus
5. appropriate
6. arrangements
7. balloon
8. Cemetery
9. comfortable
10. compelled
11. coolly
12. counterfeit
13. cupful
14. decision
15. dependent
16. dilemma
17. disapprove
18. equipped
19. extraordinary
20. fundamental
21. grammar
22. harassed
23. hopeful
24. hurriedly
25. inseparable
26. leisure
27. livelihood
28. monopolize
29. necessarily
30. noticeable
31. omitted
32. opportunity
33. parallel
34. Pennant
35. perseverance
36. pierced
37. pleasant
38. possible
39. precedence
40. preparations
41. professor
42. pronunciation
43. propaganda
44. pursue
45. quizzes
46. reference
47. scarcely
48. studying
49. suppress
50. vengeance

GROUP FOUR / *Page 66*

1. accompanied
2. accomplish
3. acquitted
4. adequate
5. adolescence
6. aggravated
7. annual
8. applying
9. appreciate
10. author
11. beneficial
12. boundaries
13. casualties
14. category
15. ceremonies
16. chauffeur
17. companies
18. compulsory
19. conceive
20. confident
21. Conqueror
22. consistent
23. continually
24. convenience
25. correspondence
26. courageous
27. deferred
28. despair
29. develop
30. dining
31. dissatisfaction
32. eliminate
33. exceptionally
34. extremely
35. fascinated
36. feasible
37. finally
38. genuine
39. governor
40. height
41. heroes
42. hesitancy
43. indefinite
44. indispensable
45. lovable
46. maintain
47. neither
48. poisonous
49. resistance
50. succeed

GROUP FIVE / *Page 67*

1. acknowledgment
2. address
3. against
4. all right
5. amount
6. analyze
7. anticipated
8. anxieties
9. ascend
10. awkward
11. believe
12. brilliant
13. business
14. camouflage
15. ceiling
16. columns
17. coming
18. committed
19. comparable
20. comparatively
21. condescend
22. contemptible
23. courteous
24. deceit
25. devastate
26. dominant
27. efficient
28. endeavor
29. equaled
30. erroneous
31. financial
32. government
33. grievances
34. handkerchief
35. imitate
36. incredible
37. inevitable
38. lenient
39. manageable
40. mortgage
41. ninth
42. obstinate
43. outrageous
44. particularly
45. peculiar
46. preference
47. procedure
48. repellent
49. restaurant
50. significance

CORRECTNESS AND EFFECTIVENESS OF EXPRESSION   69

7. Review Tests of Mastery

TEST 1

DIRECTIONS: On the left below are sentences containing words or phrases that are underlined and numbered. On the right you will find a series of ways in which the underlined words or phrases may be made acceptable if they are not acceptable. You are to choose the best correction or improvement of the indicated word or phrase. If none of the methods suggested can correct or improve the word or phrase, then circle (1) *No Change*; otherwise, circle the number of the change that you think is best.

Everyone of the students
(1)
who was present handed in
     (2)
their assignments on time.
(3)
It was time for we student
                 (4)
to leave them know who
   (5)   (6)
they were hurting.

Between you and me I
                 (7)
think that no one but he
                      (8)
knew the combination to that safe.
I shall try and bring the
         (9)
copy of the picture to the art room.
When fifteen years old his
     (10)
uncle decided to teach him a trade.
The student who they
            (11)
finally chose for the lead role could so easily have been her!
              (12)
The fury of the mob would be sated, regardless of who-
                (13)   (14)
ever they hung
           (15)
If I would have tried to
   (16)
handle the heavy case without Paul and he, I could
                    (17)
never have moved it.
The gift was intended for Harold and myself.
            (18)

He has proven to be a man
       (19)
who's word cannot be
(20)
trusted.
You must admit that this coin is shinier then that
                       (21)
one of yours.
        (22)
Since his paper contains less mistakes than ours, his
     (23)   (24)
will be entered in the contest.
Every now and then one of
(25)
the scouts who has just
             (26)
achieved another badge becomes too enthused and
        (27)
decides to issue a challenge
(28)
to Paul or me.
          (29)

We planned to study the
   (30)
affects of radiation only as
(31)
a afterthought because we
(32)
found so many of our ani-
(33)
mals maimed by the rays.
The one to suffer most will be her if everyone in the
       (34)
class but she is forced to
        (35)(36)
come early.
We have had scarcely no
                    (37)
news from them since around ten o'clock.
(38)
I want one of the rings so badly that I am willing to
(39)
go anywhere to buy it.
   (40)
While sitting on the porch,
(41)
an ambulance raced by.

1. (1) *No Change* (2) every one
2. (1) *No Change* (2) were
3. (1) *No Change* (2) his
4. (1) *No Change* (2) us
5. (1) *No Change* (2) let (3) allow
6. (1) *No Change* (2) whom
7. (1) *No Change* (2) I
8. (1) *No Change* (2) him
9. (1) *No Change* (2) try and take (3) try to bring (4) try to take
10. (1) *No Change* (2) When fifteen, (3) When Peter was fifteen, (4) At fifteen,
11. (1) *No Change* (2) whom
12. (1) *No Change* (2) she
13. (1) *No Change* (2) irregardless
14. (1) *No Change* (2) whomever
15. (1) *No Change* (2) hanged (3) had hung (4) could have hung
16. (1) *No Change* (2) should have (3) had
17. (1) *No Change* (2) him
18. (1) *No Change* (2) myself and Harold (3) Harold and I (4) Harold and me.

19. (1) *No Change* (2) been proven (3) proved
20. (1) *No Change* (2) whose
21. (1) *No Change* (2) shinier than (3) more shiny then (4) more shinier than
22. (1) *No Change* (2) your's (3) yours'
23. (1) *No Change* (2) fewer
24. (1) *No Change* (2) our's (3) ours'
25. (1) *No Change* (2) Every so often (3) Occasionally (4) Every once in a while
26. (1) *No Change* (2) have
27. (1) *No Change* (2) becomes too enthusiastic (3) become too enthusiastic (4) become too enthused
28. (1) *No Change* (2) decide
29. (1) *No Change* (2) I
30. (1) *No Change* (2) were planning (3) had planned
31. (1) *No Change* (2) effects
32. (1) *No Change* (2) an
33. (1) *No Change* (2) find (3) had found
34. (1) *No Change* (2) she
35. (1) *No Change* (2) her
36. (1) *No Change* (2) are

37. (1) *No Change* (2) any
38. (1) *No Change* (2) about

39. (1) *No Change* (2) much (3) bad
40. (1) *No Change* (2) anywheres

41. (1) *No Change* (2) When (3) After (4) While I was

"She feels good now," said
         (42)
the doctor. "She will be
         (43)
alright from now on."
 (44)

If I were you, I would
      (45)

42. (1) No Change (2) well
43. (1) No Change (2) , "she (3) ; "She (4) , "She
44. (1) No Change (2) all-right (3) al-right (4) all right
45. (1) No Change (2) was (3) had been (4) would have been

never question him leaving
              (46)
so early!", exclaimed De-
   (47)
nise.
He writes like he just
              (48)
doesn't know when to stop.

46. (1) No Change (2) his
47. (1) No Change (2) early"! (3) early", (4) early!"
48. (1) No Change (2) as (3) as if

TEST 2

DIRECTIONS: On the left below are sentences containing words or phrases that are underlined and numbered. On the right you will find a series of ways in which the underlined words or phrases may be made acceptable if they are not acceptable. You are to choose the best correction or improvement of the indicated word or phrase. If none of the methods suggested can correct or improve the word or phrase, then circle (1) *No Change*; otherwise, circle the number of the change that you think is best.

In that case you should be ready by twelve, I shall be
                         (1)
back then.
No sooner had I lay down
          (2)   (3)
when the telephone began to ring endlessly.
I was surprised to be greeted by a man whom I
                                  (4)
knew less well than her.
                 (5)
After the gun was fired,
         (6)
Thomas' windshield was
 (7)
found shattered.
When addressing a large
     (8)
group, your tone of voice should be clear and loud.
Helen as well as her four friends are in the engineers
                   (9)   (10)
cabin.
Owing to previous difficul-
 (11)
ties, Alex was tense, lacking in humor, and a person
                              (12)
who was distrustful of others.

The men in the group did not speak to Lucy or I be-
    (13)   (14)
fore Phyllis had entered
              (15)
the room.

1. (1) No Change (2) :I (3), since I (4) ; I
2. (1) No Change (2) would (3) were (4) should
3. (1) No Change (2) lie (3) laid (4) lain
4. (1) No Change (2) who
5. (1) No Change (2) she
6. (1) No Change (2) is (3) had been (4) would be
7. (1) No Change (2) Thomas's (3) Thomas (4) Thomases
8. (1) No Change (2) While addressing (3) When you address (4) Upon addressing
9. (1) No Change (2) is
10. (1) No Change (2) engineers'
11. (1) No Change (2) due to (3) On account of (4) Because of
12. (1) No Change (2) a man who was (3) one who was (4) (omit)
13. (1) No Change (2) were not speaking (3) had not spoken (4) spoke not
14. (1) No Change (2) me
15. (1) No Change (2) entered (3) enters (4) was entering

For who did you write
   (16)
down this address for?
  (17)   (18)

May I loan your pen , since
       (19)   (20)
neither Edna or I am able
              (21)(22)
to find ours.

Attempting to find the most unique shells, his dive
                  (23)   (24)
took him into the deepest water in the area.

We showed him the picture, and gave him your
        (25)
note.
Each story in this collection of modern tales were
                               chosen by the editors stu-
                                (26)   (27)
dents.
At the age of ten, his par-
     (28)
ents moved to Tennessee.

I can't hardly find any-
  (29)
thing in their statements
         (30)
to dispute.
Because he had been in a bad accident; his parents
                           (31)
make certain that he don't
                    ever exhaust himself.
                    (32)
I only have eaten three of
  (33)

16. (1) No Change (2) whom
17. (1) No Change (2) write up (3) write (4) enscribe
18. (1) No Change (2) for. (3) [omit] (4) for!
19. (1) No Change (2) lend (3) borrow (4) have a loan of
20. (1) No Change (2) ; since (3) since (4) . Since
21. (1) No Change (2) nor
22. (1) No Change (2) are (3) is
23. (1) No Change (2) more unique (3) unique
24. (1) No Change (2) .His dive took him (3) ;his dive took him (4) ,he dove
25. (1) No Change (2) ; and (3) and (4) : and,
26. (1) No Change (2) were chose (3) was chosen (4) was chose
27. (1) No Change (2) editor's
28. (1) No Change (2) When ten years of age (3) When he was ten, (4) When ten years old,
29. (1) No Change (2) cannot hardly (3) can hardly (4) cant' hardly
30. (1) No Change (2) there (3) they're (4) theyr'e
31. (1) No Change (2) . His (3) ,his (4) his
32. (1) No Change (2) do never (3) doesn't never (4) doesn't ever
33. (1) No Change (2) have only eaten (3)

CORRECTNESS AND EFFECTIVENESS OF EXPRESSION

these kind of cooky all eve-
(34)
ning.

Walking into the room,
(35)
our footsteps echoed
through the corridors.
Everyone in the class
which was dismissed left
(36)
for home except Morris
and he.
(37)
Due to the present con-
(38)
fusion in the office, we
(39)
were unable to find his
records.
Leave it lay where it has
(40)
fallen so that the police
may be better able to identify it.
Lets not lose any more
(41)
time in trying to solve this
difficulty.
I prefer ham and eggs than
(42)
any other breakfast dish.
Neither Albert or I are
(43) (44)
able to decide just where
your going.
(45)

I lived in this house until
(46)
my only surviving uncle,
who I admire very much,
(47) (48)
moved away.

There laid the pen and
(49)
book just where he
dropped them.
(50)
Whiskey and soda are a
(51)
dangerous stimulant for a
driver.
He owns less heads of
(52)
cattle then any man in his
(53)(54)

have eaten only (4)
only ate
34. (1) No Change (2)
this kind of a (3)
these kind of a (4)
this kind of
35. (1) No Change (2)
When walking (3) As
we walked (4) After
we walked
36. (1) No Change (2)
were
37. (1) No Change (2)
he and Morris (3)
Morris and him
38. (1) No Change (2)
Owing to (3) Since
(4) Because of
39. (1) No Change (2) .
We (3) we (4) ; we
40. (1) No Change (2)
Let it lay (3) Leave
it lie (4) Let it lie
41. (1) No Change (2)
Let's not lose (3)
Let's not loose (4)
Lets not loose
42. (1) No Change (2)
then (3) to (4) too
43. (1) No Change (2)
or me (3) nor I (4)
nor me
44. (1) No Change (2)
am (3) is (4) were
45. (1) No Change (2)
your'e (3) you're
46. (1) No Change (2)
have lived (3) had
lived (4) have been
living
47. (1) No Change (2)
whom (3) which
48. (1) No Change (2)
have been admiring
(3) had been admir-
ing (4) admired
49. (1) No Change (2)
lay (3) lays
50. (1) No Change (2)
had dropped (3)
drops (4) has dropped
51. (1) No Change (2) is
52. (1) No Change (2)
fewer
53. (1) No Change (2)
than

district.
I cannot forget that scene;
(55)
however much I try.
(56)
"It just cannot succeed",
(57)
exclaimed Phyllis. "It is
(58) (59)

too complicated!"
(60)

When preparing an aque-
(61)
ous solution, one must
check to see that you use
(62)
the right amounts.

Two-thirds of the prevail-
ing illnesses was caused by
(63)
this microbe!
He arrived late to work
(64)
that day, therefore, he
(65)
could not have been pres-
ent during the time of the
accident.
The books of Heming-
way are more simply writ-
ten than Dickens.
(66)
Knowing that we had
(67)
failed, there was nothing
to do but to depart.
Now that I know the
cause, I feel badly.
(68)
She said that she truly
objects to me telling others
(69)
what to do.
The play ended too
abruptly, which annoyed
(70)
me very much.
The reason one of the
balloons is falling is be-
(71)
cause the rope tore.
(72)

54. (1) No Change (2)
any other
55. (1) No Change (2)
seen
56. (1) No Change (2) ;
however, (3) , how-
ever (4) . However
57. (1) No Change (2)
," exclaimed (3) !",
exclaimed (4) !," ex-
claimed
58. (1) No Change (2)
Phyllis, (3) Phyllis!
59. (1) No Change (2)
"it (3) "It's (4) "it's
60. (1) No Change (2)
to (3) two
61. (1) No Change (2)
Being that you have
prepared (3) Being
that one has prepared
(4) When you pre-
pare
62. (1) No Change (2) it
is used in (3) one
uses (4) the mixture
uses
63. (1) No Change (2)
were
64. (1) No Change (2)
has arrived (3) was
arriving (4) had ar-
rived
65. (1) No Change (2) :
therefore (3) . There-
fore (4) ; Therefore
66. (1) No Change (2)
Dicken's (3) those of
Dickens' (4) those of
Dickens
67. (1) No Change (2)
Upon knowing (3)
When realizing (4)
When we knew
68. (1) No Change (2)
bad
69. (1) No Change (2)
my
70. (1) No Change (2) ;
which (3) which (4)
This ending
71. (1) No Change (2)
are
72. (1) No Change (2)
since (3) that (4)
why

TEST 3

DIRECTIONS: Each of the following paragraphs consists of three or four sentences with a dotted line to indicate that a sentence has been omitted. Below you will find four sentences, one of which is the original, but omitted, sentence. By circling the appropriate letter in the answer column, mark:

(a) if the sentence is the suitable one
(b) if the sentence is unsuitable because of meaning
(c) if the sentence is inappropriate in tone or diction
(d) if the sentence contains an error in grammatical usage

NOTE: In some of the exercises there may be more than two sentences belonging to one of the above categories, and therefore no sentence for another category.

The emancipation of Western woman from her bondage of centuries led many to believe that equal rights meant equal privileges. To them, women had won the right to carry their own heavy packages and to stand in a crowded bus while some men sat. To others it meant that man now would accept woman as an equal partner, both striving to accomplish a single goal that could be reached more easily if both had an equal voice in choosing the path. . . . .

1. Women could soon prove there true worth, with neither one of them claiming superiority.
    1. a b c d
2. The struggle which had seemed foreordained to subsist forever had now come to a peaceful solution.
    2. a b c d
3. Neither one would claim superiority; each would be the complement of the other.
    3. a b c d
4. They would soon learn to accept the inevitable, the innate superiority of the male.
    4. a b c d
5. They would soon learn to respect the ability of one another.
    5. a b c d

Before this he had thought that he could be right. Now, he knew that he was right. Being right did not come from physical superiority or well-phrased words. The march of events and the opinions of those whom he had learned to respect had given him the the necessary proof. . . . .

6. He walked away, smirking gleefully, exuberant in the strength that his new found paradox gave to him.
    6. a b c d
7. Walking into the room filled with the waiting delegates, a look of inner calm spread over his face.
    7. a b c d
8. He now had the key to success and he was going to push it for all that it was worth.
    8. a b c d
9. Walking into the room filled with the waiting delegates, he was unable to avoid communicating to them the sense of defeat that filled him.
    9. a b c d
10. With firm step and steady gait, he walked calmly into the room filled with the waiting delegates.
    10. a b c d

One man's word is no man's word; we should quietly hear both sides. Justice, however, is more than a willingness to be disinterested. Justice is the constant desire and effort to render to every man his due. . . . .

11. Justice is truth in action. 11. a b c d
12. Justice is mans only defense against intolerance and ignorance. 12. a b c d
13. That which cannot be cured must be endured.
    13. a b c d
14. The full flowering of man's intellect, the apex of man's earthly achievements, and the fulcrum of man's achievements are in justice.
    14. a b c d
15. We must do our duty and let the devil take the hindmost to achieve the basis for true justice.
    15. a b c d

At last I had found my haven. Here was a true company of the wisest and wittiest men. Here, ready at all times, were the thinkers and sages, waiting to impart their wisdom to me. . . . .

16. Here in the hallowed halls of tomes, the lofty library stacks were all the companionship I had sought.
    16. a b c d
17. Here in the library were the companions I needed they could give me all the knowledge I so desperately wanted. 17. a b c d
18. Here on the shelves of the library was the philosophers who held the key to the understanding that I had searched for so long. 18. a b c d
19. I was filled with a vague dread that here too I would find only disappointment and uncertainty.
    19. a b c d
20. Here was where I belonged. 20. a b c d
21. Here I could rest my wings and plow through to the core of the meaning of existence.
    21. a b c d

Poetry is music in words. Music is poetry in sound. Both make excellent sauces, but they lived and died poor who made the mistake of making them their meat. . . . .

22. Poetry and music may be our vocations but not our avocations. 22. a b c d e
23. Without music and poetry, man leds a partial life.
    23. a b c d e
24. Yet how intense must have been their few days!
    24. a b c d e
25. Poetry and music can give us insight into the very meaning of life. 25. a b c d e
26. Only through work, hard work, can we achieve greatness. 26. a b c d e

Youth is in danger until it learns to look upon debts as traps. Think of what you do when you run into debt! You give another power over your liberty. If you cannot pay at the time, you will be ashamed when you see your creditor and you will be in fear when you speak with him. . . . .

27. No man had ought to be put into a position in which he is ashamed to meet another or afraid to speak with another. 27. a b c d
28. The essential nature of debts is such that the debtor can exact an undue toll of the creditor.
    28. a b c d
29. The moral to draw is very simple don't allow your affairs to so deteriorate that you must be in debt to another. 29. a b c d

CORRECTNESS AND EFFECTIVENESS OF EXPRESSION

30. A freeborn man ought not to be ashamed or afraid to see or speak with any man living.
    30. a b c d
31. If you owe another fellow money, you can't look him in the eye or look at yourself in the mirror!
    31. a b c d

Today we all realize that democracy is not a self-perpetuating virus adapted to any body politic—that was the assumption of a previous generation. Democracy we now know to be a special type of organism ....

32. who can survive only when its environment is favorable to its growth.
    32. a b c d
33. which will last forever, despite the efforts of the totalitarian forces that now threaten its existence.
    33. a b c d
34. which can with a mailed fist defy the dictatorships of the world and gain sustenance from this defiance.
    34. a b c d
35. requiring specific nutriment materials—some economic, some social and cultural.
    35. a b c d
36. weak and unstable as it regenerates from generation to generation.
    36. a b c d

If you would relish food, labor for it before you take it. Things don't turn up in this world until somebody turns them up. The fact is, nothing comes: at least, nothing good. ....

37. If one really wants something, you have to fetch it yourself.
    37. a b c d
38. You must conclude then with that most elementary of realizations that if there is some worldly object that you truly want, it must be encumbent upon you to obtain it for yourself.
    38. a b c d
39. Only the lazy gain from doing nothing.
    39. a b c d
40. Everyone who wants something worthwhile must toil with their own hands to get it.
    40. a b c d
41. All has to be fetched.
    41. a b c d

To comprehend a man's life, it is necessary to know not merely what he does, but also what he purposely leaves undone. .... He is a wise man who wastes no energy on pursuits for which he is not fitted. He is still wiser who, from among the things that he can do well, chooses and resolutely follows the best.

42. Knowing when and where the limits of his endurance is can empower a man to do more than he would otherwise be able to.
    42. a b c d
43. There is a limit to the work that can be got out of a human body or a human brain.
    43. a b c d
44. There is little to be gained by trying to exceed beyond the limits of one's own physical and mental powers.
    44. a b c d
45. The purpose behind the activities of the doer determines its worth.
    45. a b c d
46. To know just how much his mind and body can accomplish are as important to man as to understand the worth of his accomplishments.
    46. a b c d

.... You gain not at all whether it be good, bad, or indifferent: nothing good, of what is vanity; nothing bad, for that is affectation; nothing indifferent for that is silly.

47. There is a joy in being able to tell others of your progress.
    47. a b c d
48. The mistake is when you make yourself a topic of conversation.
    48. a b c d
49. Due to the demands of society, it is best that you do not become the principal speaker when you are the topic of conversation.
    49. a b c d
50. One of the most important rules of manners is that you should be for the most part silent about yourself.
    50. a b c d

How easy to be amiable in the midst of happiness and success! .... He who seeks to do the amiable always can at times be successful only by the sacrifice of his individuality.

51. However I cannot become enthused about amiability at all times.
    51. a b c d
52. The real test comes when adversity follows on the heels of amiability.
    52. a b c d
53. However you can go too far amiability is not essential on all ocassions.
    53. a b c d
54. Yet amiability is not to be exercised at the expense of essential values.
    54. a b c d

A good talker or writer is only part of the team. Without the rest, little of effectiveness is ever accomplished. A good talker or writer is only a pitcher. ....

55. A man's character is revealed by his speech.
    55. a b c d
56. Unless his audience catches him with heart and mind, he is defeated.
    56. a b c d
57. Without an attentive audience, his words are like the cypress, tall and large, but they bear no fruit.
    57. a b c d
58. Everyone in the audience must do their part and be good receivers.
    58. a b c d
59. The lines of communication between the originator of the verbal impulses and the receiving audience must be direct and clear.
    59. a b c d

Now that the moment had come, he was pleased. .... Reality, once again, was less filled with terror. His imaginings had paralyzed him into inaction. The truth of the impending disaster freed him for action and the release that only action could give.

60. No more would fearful imaginings aggravate him into impotency.
    60. a b c d
61. He laughed with joy in anticipation of the pleasures to come.
    61. a b c d
62. The pangs of regret freed him from reality.
    62. a b c d
63. He had allowed dread for too long to fill his every waking hour.
    63. a b c d
64. If only it would have come sooner!
    64. a b c d

It is not what a man does that gives his actions dignity. .... Yet, without such dignity, I do not think that man could achieve any degree of happiness. Happiness is a reflection within us of group standards rather than self-centered ones of our own.

65. Dignity and personal liberty are interdependent.
    65. a b c d
66. It is rather societys evaluation of what he does that makes his actions significant and worthwhile.
    66. a b c d
67. Anyone can shoot off his mouth and claim that what he is doing is socially acceptable.
    67. a b c d
68. Rather it is what others judge as the worth of his actions that places such values.
    68. a b c d

69. It is no as much what a man does as what his neighbors think of what he does.   69. a b c d

    So many writers inveigh against man's inhumanity to man; and I agree so wholeheartedly with them. That we could allow a Hitler to fester even for a short while is more than I can bear to think about. Yet with the dawn of civilization only just past, we must realize how far we have actually gone in so short a time. . . . .

70. There has not been hardly enough time for man to advance to higher levels of conduct.
    70. a b c d
71. The boys who can only see what there is in it for them will soon give way to those who are willing to share and share alike with others.
    71. a b c d
72. The star of mercy will soon outshine all others.
    72. a b c d
73. I can confidently assert that we can prevent the rise of another Hitler if we band together and outlaw genocide.   73. a b c d
74. We should be more willing to praise man for his acts of humanity than to condemn him totally for his reversion to animalism.   74. a b c d

    . . . . However, you must not confuse an attempt to reach as far as you can with demanding that you reach that point. Low aim, half-hearted preparation, and early discouragement are the crimes that those who attempt to inspire us speak about. I would add to this the crime of perfectionism in which nothing but unachievably high goals are the only ones that are acceptable stopping points.

75. There is nothing wrong in seeking perfection.
    75. a b c d
76. Man must ever seek the ideal's set by his capabilities.   76. a b c d
77. To get ahead you must be ready to get your licks in before the other fellow, and on your own terms.
    77. a b c d

78. We must ever be aware of man's imperfections.
    78. a b c d
79. Knowing the furthest limits of your abilities, your work should be planned for that point and no further.   79. a b c d
80. Realizing the brief duration of man's stay on earth, you must be reasonable in your selection of goals.
    80. a b c d

    With the growth of modern science, the ancient problem of the extent of an individual's responsibility for his actions has once again become a topic of debate and discussion. If we believe that man has a degree of control over his actions and decisions, then he deserves punishment to the extent that he willfully decides to go counter to moral codes and laws. . . . . Then the responsibility for his conduct rests in the institutions, and these institutions must be changed to prevent further infringements by the individual. The individual cannot then be held responsible or be punished for his misconduct.

81. He must be compelled to obey the laws that are for the good of all.   81. a b c d
82. An eye for an eye and a tooth for a tooth must ever be the basis of laws.   82. a b c d
83. If one believes that social institutions control man, you must believe that man does not have freedom of the will.   83. a b c d
84. We could believe, however, that human nature results from the interplay of environment and biological mechanisms.   84. a b c d
85. At the extreme other end of the pole of man's metaphysical cogitations is the thesis or premise that behavior patterns result from the forces exerted by external factors upon the inherited physiological organism.   85. a b c d
86. If we believe, on the other hand, that man's spirit is as free as that of the birds, we must believe that freedom of the will is a reality.
    86. a b c d

TEST 4

DIRECTIONS: Beneath each of the following selections there are several sentences that might be used in place of the dotted lines. Classify each of the choices as

(a) if it is appropriate in tone, diction, style and ideas
(b) if it is inappropriate in meaning
(c) if it is inappropriate in tone, diction or style
(d) if it is defective in grammar or sentence structure
(e) if it is wordy

    We are confronted primarily with a moral issue. . . . The heart of the question is whether all Americans are to be afforded equal rights and equal opportunities; whether we are going to treat our fellow Americans as we want to be treated.

1. It is as old as the Scriptures and is as clear as the American Constitution.   1. a b c d e
2. We cannot continue to hesitate; we must get a move on.   2. a b c d e
3. Everyone must raise their hand to be counted on this issue.   3. a b c d e
4. This moral issue rises from the ashes of man's failures.   4. a b c d e
5. May I repeat again for emphasis that this in the first place must be considered primarily as a moral issue.   5. a b c d e
6. Not forgetting the basic issues involved, equality must be seen as the fundamental consideration.
    6. a b c d e
7. The forces of evil are rampant in the world around us, and we must swim against the tide.
    7. a b c d e
8. Our principle consideration must be based in equality.   8. a b c d e
9. We can't scarcely consider the problem from any other point.   9. a b c d e
10. It is not an issue of money or prestige, of wealth or power.   10. a b c d e

    But however close we sometimes seem to that dark and final abyss, let no man of peace and freedom despair. . . . If we all can persevere, if we can in every land and office look beyond our own shores and ambitions, then surely the age will dawn in which the strong are just and the weak secure, and the peace preserved.

11. A man of good will with all the forces of good at

his side have the power to triumph.
11. a b c d e
12. We must not disremember the power of good will. 12. a b c d e
13. Sing out sweet land, and watch the blues fade! 13. a b c d e
14. For he does not stand alone. 14. a b c d e
15. For no human can fear that he stands alone. 15. a b c d e
16. The clenched fist is merely a cloud of doubt. 16. a b c d e
17. Each one of us among the millions involved must keep their faith. 17. a b c d e
18. We must ascend up out of the depths of despair. 18. a b c d e
19. Throughout the ages, man has sidestepped and avoided facing the dangers in this issue. 19. a b c d e
20. It was nice of you to bring it to our attention. 20. a b c d e

The world is very different now. . . . And yet the same revolutionary beliefs for which our forebears fought are still at issue around the globe—the belief that the rights of man come not from the generosity of the state but from the hand of God.

21. The forces of poverty and misery have so much of man in their grasp. 21. a b c d e
22. The clutching hand of poverty and misery have farmers and workers, but not for long, in a deathlike vise. 22. a b c d e
23. For man holds in his mortal hands the power to abolish all forms of poverty and all forms of human life. 23. a b c d e
24. Man for the first time has the power to abolish poverty and of ending all forms of human life. 24. a b c d e
25. The coarse of history has taken a dramatic turn. 25. a b c d e
26. At the present time man can both end poverty and all forms of human life now. 26. a b c d e
27. O nations of the world! Now is the time to end the reign of dire poverty! 27. a b c d e
28. We have long waited for this moment of limitless power in controlling our destiny. 28. a b c d e
29. We dare not forget today that we are the heirs of that first revolution. 29. a b c d e
30. When considering the dynamics of change, now is the time to abolish poverty forever. 30. a b c d e
31. Are there any other group that is responsible for the production of wealth? 31. a b c d e
32. All other forces merely compliment the efforts of labor. 32. a b c d e
33. There just is no going anywhere without labor. 33. a b c d e
34. All the other forces in our economy must cooperate together with labor. 34. a b c d e
35. Under the leadership of the management class labor forges ahead. 35. a b c d e
36. Our meaning as a country rests on the shoulders of labor. 36. a b c d e
37. The seas of struggle throughout the world are manned by the sweating masses of laborers. 37. a b c d e
38. Our glory and power is created by our laboring class. 38. a b c d e
39. Our focus must be ever clear. 39. a b c d e
40. The consuls of state must reckon on the basis of labor's contribution. 40. a b c d e

There are two kinds of moral law, two kinds of consciences, in men and women, and they are altogether different. The two sexes do not understand each other. . . . But in practical life, the woman is judged by man's law, as if she were a man, not a woman.

41. Our concept of morality is based on double standards, one for the rich, another for the poor. 41. a b c d e
42. The rules of the man's world is superimposed on the lives of women. 42. a b c d e
43. In my opinion, I think that we believe that we are just when the same sets of law are applied to both. 43. a b c d e
44. We tend to believe that our standards are equally as just to both men and women. 44. a b c d e
45. Summarizing the total effect of these standards, a superficial fairness seems to exist. 45. a b c d e
46. Women are forced to distort themselves into the patterns set for men, if they want to compete with men in the business world. 46. a b c d e
47. Women soon get wise and recognize the double standards. 47. a b c d e
48. The tenor of laws passed by legislators point this out. 48. a b c d e
49. The laws on the statute books seem to be based on equality. 49. a b c d e
50. On the surface the moral law that governs our society seems to reflect the convictions of both man and woman. 50. a b c d e
51. You may or not concur with this interpretation. 51. a b c d e

There are revolutions that are sweeping the world and we in America have been in the position of trying to stop them. . . . Those revolutions are revolutions against a form of political and economic organization in the countries of Asia and the Middle East that are oppressive. They are revolutions against feudalism.

52. There is nothing that the in-group, the power-crowd in Washington can do to stop them. 52. a b c d e
53. If simple pressure from without would have been able to stop them, we could have succeeded. 53. a b c d e
54. The forces are led by fanatics who will stop at nothing less than total victory. 54. a b c d e
55. With all the wealth of America, with all the military strength of America, these revolutions cannot be stopped. 55. a b c d e
56. Our general staff with all the weapons and men at present in our arsenals and training camps are in no position to stop them. 56. a b c d e

57. The marching feet of freedom cannot be choked from the path of the inevitable.
57. a b c d e
58. The thunders of protest rising from the throats of men throughout the world must be audible to the ears of even the mightiest in the Pentagon.
58. a b c d e
59. Listening to the voices of protest, our efforts are doomed to failure.
59. a b c d e
60. It's time that we got off the backs of the progressive elements in the countries throughout the world.
60. a b c d e
61. When are we going to learn the lessons taught by history to former nations which show that people must determine their own destinies.
61. a b c d e

TEST 5

DIRECTIONS: Beneath each of the following selections there are several sentences that might be used in place of the dotted lines. Classify each of the choices as

(a) if it is appropriate in tone, diction, style and ideas
(b) if it is inappropriate in meaning
(c) if it is inappropriate in tone, diction or style
(d) if it is defective in grammar or sentence structure
(e) if it is wordy

Our institutions were not devised to bring about uniformity of opinion. . . . It is important to remember, as has well been said, "The essential characteristic of true liberty is that under its shelter many different types of life and character and opinion and belief can develop unmolested and unobstructed."

1. As they say in the books, its variety that makes the world interesting.
1. a b c d e
2. If they had been, we might well abandon hope.
2. a b c d e
3. The basic element of mutual living together lies in the variety rather than in the same conformity.
3. a b c d e
4. You can't hardly look anywhere without seeing diversity rather than variety as the rule.
4. a b c d e
5. Diversity rather than uniformity is the basis of rules that govern democratic societies.
5. a b c d e
6. They have expected stability and have found none within themselves or in their universe.
6. a b c d e
7. Each one among the living must bravely accept the changes time brings into their lives.
7. a b c d e
8. How can puny man reconcile the seeming stability of the heavenly spheres with the diversity which is time.
8. a b c d e
9. Get into the groove and spin around on the tides of time, not the desires for stability that delude man.
9. a b c d e
10. Serious good will come from the realization that there is permanence in change itself.
10. a b c d e
11. Man must not think that diversity is the rule for every particle in the universe but he.
11. a b c d e
12. Our beliefs must lay in acceptance of change rather than desire for stability.
12. a b c d e

We will make converts day by day. We will grow strong by the violence and injustice of our adversaries. And, unless truth be a mockery and justice a hollow lie, we will be in the majority after a while. . . . The battle of freedom is to be fought on principle.

13. The revolution which we will accomplish will be none the less radical from being the result of pacific measures.
13. a b c d e
14. Our strength lies in right rather then might.
14. a b c d e
15. Whose to say that we have chosen the wrong path toward success!
15. a b c d e
16. The affect of our program will be felt the more because of our reliance on peaceful measures.
16. a b c d e
17. In the cool of the night as our forces gather strength for the struggles of the next day, a fervent prayer will be answered as the forces of ignorance ebb into nothingness.
17. a b c d e
18. We are the radicals of our day, we are uprooting the evil practices of the past.
18. a b c d e
19. We do not seek strength from the multitudes; we are strong within ourselves.
19. a b c d e
20. When one is in the right, you do not need force to gain leadership.
20. a b c d e
21. If we would have used force, we never could achieve the moral strength that is ours.
21. a b c d e
22. We must never forget that the peoples' strength lies in numbers not arms.
22. a b c d e

According to the ancient Chinese proverb, a journey of 1,000 miles must begin with a single step. My fellow Americans, let us take that first step. . . . And if that journey is 1,000 miles or even more, let history record that we, in this land at this time, took the first step.

23. The reason is simply because the threats of war are all around us while we stand where we are.
23. a b c d e
24. We must take the bit between our own teeth and forge the chains of peace.
24. a b c d e
25. Let us, if we can, step back from the shadows of war and seek out the way of peace.
25. a b c d e
26. The time has come for us to move now away from the real threats of man's destruction of man in a final though brief war.
26. a b c d e
27. The merciless lords of war must be ignored if we are to proceed.
27. a b c d e
28. Walking toward peace together, the rough path ahead will not be impassable in our united effort.
28. a b c d e
29. We should take a lesson from the Chinese and not let fear of what happened to them make us timid.
29. a b c d e

CORRECTNESS AND EFFECTIVENESS OF EXPRESSION

30. Let's get our backs together and plan the combination that leads to lasting peace.
    30. a b c d e
31. In regards to peace, there can be no peace unless we take this decisive step. 31. a b c d e
32. If we walk forward and seek the way of peace, our positive act must be for the good of mankind.
    32. a b c d e

America was chosen to be, in many respects, and to many purposes, a nation; and for all these purposes, her government is complete; to all these objects, it is competent.... It can, then, in effecting these objects legitimately control all individuals or governments within the American territory.

33. The people has declared that the government represents them. 33. a b c d e
34. The people, the inhabitants to the country, have stated and declared that they are supreme and in full command at all times. 34. a b c d e
35. The people have declared that there shall be an end to poverty and want within the limits of their territory. 35. a b c d e
36. The people have declared that in the exercise of all powers given for these objects it is supreme.
    36. a b c d e
37. Is there any of these objects that the people cannot declare to the government?
    37. a b c d e
38. The people are more powerful than any group that constitutes the totality. 38. a b c d e
39. The people hold the reins of government and let their power flow into the agencies of government.
    39. a b c d e
40. Every individual together with all related to them make up the total called the people.
    40. a b c d e

41. It cannot be counted as a force that weakens the reputation of the country and its people.
    41. a b c d e
42. It can hardly never be denied that the nation exists for the benefit of the people.
    42. a b c d e

A man's own good-breeding is the best security against other people's ill-manners.... Ill-breeding invites and authorizes the familiarity of the most timid.

43. It carries along with it a dignity that is respected by the most petulant. 43. a b c d e
44. Do not do what I do; do what I say.
    44. a b c d e
45. Setting an example of good manners yourself, the first step toward politeness has been taken.
    45. a b c d e
46. You must blame it on yourself to a great extent if you are treated rudely. 46. a b c d e
47. The secret of polite responses lays in the example set by the questioner. 47. a b c d e
48. Even though youth of today ridicules the niceties of good breeding, we need not descend to the level of the uncouth. 48. a b c d e
49. To turn the other cheek is more preferable to descending to the level of the ill-breed.
    49. a b c d e
50. Good-breeding invites a response in kind. A pattern which then invites continuance.
    50. a b c d e
51. Good-breeding leads us safely past the crudities which ever threatens to wreck the vehicles of communication. 51. a b c d e
52. Men who are polite and well-mannered can expect others, the people they come in contact with, to be polite and well-mannered in return.
    52. a b c d e

TEST 6

DIRECTIONS: Each of the following paragraphs consists of three or four sentences with a dotted line to indicate that a sentence has been omitted. Below you will find four sentences, one of which is the original, but omitted, sentence. By circling the appropriate letter in the answer column, mark
  (a) if the sentence is the suitable one
  (b) if the sentence is unsuitable because of meaning
  (c) if the sentence is inappropriate in tone or diction
  (d) if the sentence is grammatically defective

NOTE: In some of the exercises there may be more than two sentences belonging to one of the above categories, and therefore no sentence for another category.

Success is a dangerous goal for all of one's endeavors. .... The joyous time comes when the plans are being made and the dreams beckon toward reality. The promise is always so much more alluring than the fulfillment.

1. We must ever strive to reach success, for it can be the pinnacle of our ambitions. 1. a b c d
2. It not only can mislead us into a false security but also into false values. 2. a b c d
3. It is a false snare that can lead us only to insecurity.
    3. a b c d
4. It lacks permanence, and the rewards too often come at the wrong time. 4. a b c d
5. We cannot make it last. However much we try.
    5. a b c d

.... Parents have given them their life and nurture. The true teacher has given the children even more. He has taught them the art of living well.

6. The teacher who educates children well is to be more honored even than parents.
    6. a b c d
7. The teacher of children who concentrate on teaching them well is most important in their lives.
    7. a b c d
8. You must learn to give credit where credit is due to the faithful pedagogue who sees what has to be done and does it. 8. a b c d
9. We must not belittle the importance of parents in shaping the lives of children. 9. a b c d
10. The wise parent has added responsibilities, irregardless of how fine the child's teacher may be.
    10. a b c d

Help from without in most instances can merely serve to give us direction. Often all that it does is merely to weaken whatever effort is made. The best type of help comes from within. ....

11. Do the best that you can and your conscience will never bother you.   11. a b c d
12. The spirit of self-help is the root of all genuine growth in the individual.   12. a b c d
13. The affect of self-help is much more lasting than guidance from others could ever be.   13. a b c d
14. If one wants to accomplish much, you must learn to depend upon yourself.   14. a b c d
15. Those who ascend up the ladder of improvement are usually motivated by their own actions.   15. a b c d

The purpose of true criticism is not to praise or blame. Too much emotionalism and subjectivity result when the supposed critic decides that an object of art is either good or bad. The primary function of criticism is to interpret for the layman the artist's purpose and the extent to which the artist achieves that purpose............

16. The sooner modern critics learn what we expect of them, the sooner they will be earning the money that they now charge us for their services.   16. a b c d
17. There is hardly no critic that I have read recently who I can truly say has assumed his rightful position in society.   17. a b c d
18. The critic proves his competency by proving that good art is good and bad art is truly bad.   18. a b c d
19. The critic, who decides on the true worth of a writer, is misusing his position.   19. a b c d
20. The critic must so prepare the public that it can appreciate and evaluate the work of the artist.   20. a b c d

.... Ours is a proud heritage that we shall pass on to future generations. We developed England's industrialization to greater heights. We carried Sweden's concern for public health to newer levels; but we did so much more than this. For the first time in the long history of man, Joe Average was important; Joe Average had comforts and a standard of living surpassing that of the kings of old.

21. When the chips are down and the boys in the backroom rate the governments of today, where will they find us?   21. a b c d
22. When present times become ancient history, what will ages to come say about the American way of life?   22. a b c d
23. With the passage of time, man always tends to evaluate what has gone before, what will then be the reaction to our American way of life?   23. a b c d
24. When time lends its perspective to the affairs of man, what then will be the consensus of opinion on the American way of life?   24. a b c d
25. When present day governmental structures have become outmoded. How will the historians rate the American way of life?   25. a b c d

.... It consists in an indifference about little things and in a well-proportioned concern about things of importance. Its pursuit is characterized by calmness and tranquility. Its pleasures last longest.

26. Moderation can do nothing but outrage humanity.   26. a b c d
27. Moderation the inseparable companion of wisdom is not achieved without effort.   27. a b c d
28. Mans search for happiness must begin and end in moderation.   28. a b c d
29. Moderation is the keystone to our pursuit of happiness.   29. a b c d
30. I am firmly convinced that it is an act of superfluousness on my part to remind a person of your ability and brilliance of the value of moderation.   30. a b c d

Yet, there are so many misguided people who have twisted their lives because they have had a false idea of what is meant by freedom............ True freedom consists with the observance of the law. It allows us to pursue our own good in our own way so long as we do not attempt to deprive others of their, or impede their efforts to obtain it.

31. None are more hopelessly enslaved than those who falsely believe that they are free.   31. a b c d
32. Freedom cannot desist where the rights of the individual are disregarded.   32. a b c d
33. Anyone who wants to be free must know their limitations.   33. a b c d
34. Freedom releases us from the bondage of obligations to others.   34. a b c d
35. Your flights towards freedom must not be at the expense of others.   35. a b c d

In times past inquisitiveness was a trait to be avoided. The inquisitive man was considered a creature empty of thought itself and therefore forced to apply for foreign assistance. Yet, when this willingness to pry into secrets of others is applied by a scientist in his attack on the unknown areas of the universe, inquisitiveness becomes an admired characteristic................

36. A man who is inquisitive should be an object of your caution.   36. a b c d
37. Your point of view depends upon which foot fits the shoe of ignorance.   37. a b c d
38. Purpose and intent can even make inquisitiveness healthy.   38. a b c d
39. Even this normally bad trait can be commendable when used to benefit all.   39. a b c d
40. Don't underestimate this trait, it can be put to a worthwhile social usefulness.   40. a b c d

Generalizations have their place as guides, but we must ever beware of using them as rules of conduct. All too often they are just not applicable to the present problem; almost as frequently, we may feel compelled to choose between one axiom or its opposite. Franklin said, "Never put off till tomorrow that which you can do today," ....

41. Hesiod replies, "The man who procastinates struggles with ruin."   41. a b c d
42. Aaron Burr replies, "Never do today what you can put off till tomorrow. Delay may give clearer light as to what is best to be done."   42. a b c d
43. Between late and too late are an immeasurable distance.   43. a b c d
44. Waste not thy precious hours today on that which thou canst best do in the day to come.   44. a b c d
45. The skater must wait until the water has froze before trying out his new iceskates.   45. a b c d

CORRECTNESS AND EFFECTIVENESS OF EXPRESSION

You must learn quickly that your focus must be on truth and not on pride of opinion. .... A wise man is ever willing to alter his opinions as the march of events causes values to change. The unwise fear to change their opinions lest they endanger their status in society.

46. It is common for men to make errors; only the unwise persevere in their errors.   46. a b c d
47. Private opinion is weak, but public opinion is all-powerful.   47. a b c d
48. He, who never changes his opinions, never corrects his mistakes.   48. a b c d
49. When you have pulled a boner, be the first to admit it.   49. a b c d
50. Pride always goeth before the fall.   50. a b c d

I lose patience with those who condemn the cities because they are filled with people and the creations of people .... The painter translates emotions and projects thoughts in lines and color. So—the metropolis shouts defiantly to the rest of insensate nature that man is willing to compete with universal forces in the creation of order and beauty.

51. Anyone who has spent time in our big cities know that they have their ugly seams.   51. a b c d
52. You got to realize that the man in the street can think too.   52. a b c d
53. A painter does not use words to express himself; man does not create trees and plants to reveal his identity.   53. a b c d
54. The poets pen forms meaningful wholes in word-pictures.   54. a b c d
55. The true beauty in this world is to be found outside the horrors and dirt of the cities.   55. a b c d

I go as a salesman with nothing to sell but myself. I knock on many doors, hoping to find friendliness and concern in the hearts of those I approach so shyly. Discouragement dogs my footsteps, and I falter often. However, I cannot give up, and on I go. ....

56. The human heart can absorb lots of punishment.   56. a b c d
57. Unconsciously I know that life without friends is no life at all.   57. a b c d
58. Will you offer me understanding when I knock, will you offer to share some moments with me as your equal?   58. a b c d
59. The search is painful, but without companionship life is bear of meaning.   59. a b c d
60. Only when I find companionship will I find the solace that I need.   60. a b c d

ANSWER KEY / REVIEW TESTS OF MASTERY

TEST 1 / Page 69

1. (1)	7. (1)	13. (1)	19. (3)	25. (3)	31. (2)	37. (2)	43. (1)
2. (2)	8. (2)	14. (2)	20. (2)	26. (2)	32. (2)	38. (2)	44. (4)
3. (2)	9. (4)	15. (2)	21. (1)	27. (2)	33. (3)	39. (2)	45. (1)
4. (2)	10. (3)	16. (3)	22. (1)	28. (1)	34. (2)	40. (1)	46. (2)
5. (2)	11. (2)	17. (2)	23. (2)	29. (1)	35. (2)	41. (4)	47. (4)
6. (2)	12. (2)	18. (4)	24. (1)	30. (1)	36. (1)	42. (2)	48. (3)

TEST 2 / Page 70

1. (4)	10. (2)	19. (3)	28. (3)	37. (3)	46. (3)	55. (1)	64. (4)
2. (1)	11. (4)	20. (3)	29. (3)	38. (4)	47. (2)	56. (3)	65. (3)
3. (4)	12. (4)	21. (2)	30. (1)	39. (1)	48. (1)	57. (2)	66. (4)
4. (1)	13. (3)	22. (1)	31. (3)	40. (4)	49. (2)	58. (1)	67. (4)
5. (1)	14. (2)	23. (3)	32. (4)	41. (2)	50. (2)	59. (1)	68. (2)
6. (3)	15. (2)	24. (4)	33. (3)	42. (3)	51. (2)	60. (1)	69. (2)
7. (1)	16. (2)	25. (3)	34. (4)	43. (2)	52. (2)	61. (3)	70. (4)
8. (3)	17. (3)	26. (3)	35. (3)	44. (2)	53. (2)	62. (3)	71. (1)
9. (2)	18. (3)	27. (2)	36. (1)	45. (3)	54. (2)	63. (2)	72. (3)

ANSWERS TO REVIEW TESTS OF MASTERY

TEST 3 / Page 72

1. (d)	12. (d)	23. (c)	34. (c)	45. (b)	56. (a)	67. (c)	78. (b)
2. (c)	13. (b)	24. (a)	35. (a)	46. (d)	57. (c)	68. (a)	79. (d)
3. (a)	14. (c)	25. (b)	36. (b)	47. (b)	58. (d)	69. (d)	80. (b)
4. (b)	15. (b)	26. (b)	37. (d)	48. (d)	59. (c)	70. (d)	81. (b)
5. (d)	16. (c)	27. (d)	38. (c)	49. (d)	60. (c)	71. (c)	82. (b)
6. (b)	17. (d)	28. (b)	39. (b)	50. (c)	61. (b)	72. (c)	83. (d)
7. (d)	18. (d)	29. (d)	40. (d)	51. (c)	62. (b)	73. (c)	84. (a)
8. (c)	19. (b)	30. (a)	41. (a)	52. (b)	63. (a)	74. (a)	85. (c)
9. (b)	20. (a)	31. (c)	42. (d)	53. (d)	64. (d)	75. (a)	86. (b)
10. (a)	21. (c)	32. (d)	43. (a)	54. (a)	65. (b)	76. (d)	
11. (a)	22. (b)	33. (b)	44. (c)	55. (b)	66. (d)	77. (c)	

TEST 4 / Page 74

1. (a)	9. (d)	17. (d)	25. (c)	33. (c)	41. (b)	49. (b)	57. (c)
2. (c)	10. (a)	18. (e)	26. (e)	34. (e)	42. (d)	50. (a)	58. (e)
3. (d)	11. (d)	19. (b)	27. (c)	35. (b)	43. (e)	51. (c)	59. (d)
4. (b)	12. (c)	20. (c)	28. (b)	36. (b)	44. (e)	52. (c)	60. (c)
5. (e)	13. (c)	21. (b)	29. (a)	37. (c)	45. (d)	53. (d)	61. (d)
6. (d)	14. (a)	22. (d)	30. (d)	38. (d)	46. (b)	54. (b)	
7. (c)	15. (c)	23. (a)	31. (d)	39. (a)	47. (c)	55. (a)	
8. (c)	16. (c)	24. (d)	32. (c)	40. (c)	48. (d)	56. (d)	

TEST 5 / Page 76

1. (d)	8. (c)	15. (c)	22. (d)	29. (b)	36. (a)	43. (a)	50. (d)
2. (a)	9. (c)	16. (c)	23. (d)	30. (c)	37. (d)	44. (b)	51. (d)
3. (e)	10. (b)	17. (c)	24. (c)	31. (c)	38. (b)	45. (c)	52. (e)
4. (c)	11. (d)	18. (d)	25. (a)	32. (a)	39. (c)	46. (d)	
5. (a)	12. (c)	19. (b)	26. (e)	33. (d)	40. (d)	47. (b)	
6. (b)	13. (a)	20. (c)	27. (b)	34. (e)	41. (b)	48. (b)	
7. (d)	14. (c)	21. (d)	28. (d)	35. (b)	42. (d)	49. (c)	

TEST 6 / Page 77

1. (b)	9. (b)	17. (d)	25. (d)	33. (d)	41. (b)	49. (c)	57. (c)
2. (d)	10. (d)	18. (b)	26. (b)	34. (b)	42. (a)	50. (b)	58. (b)
3. (c)	11. (b)	19. (d)	27. (d)	35. (c)	43. (d)	51. (d)	59. (d)
4. (a)	12. (a)	20. (a)	28. (d)	36. (b)	44. (c)	52. (c)	60. (a)
5. (d)	13. (c)	21. (c)	29. (a)	37. (b)	45. (d)	53. (a)	
6. (a)	14. (d)	22. (a)	30. (c)	38. (c)	46. (a)	54. (d)	
7. (d)	15. (c)	23. (d)	31. (a)	39. (a)	47. (b)	55. (b)	
8. (c)	16. (c)	24. (c)	32. (c)	40. (d)	48. (d)	56. (c)	

The English Composition Test

Section **TWO** : Practice Examinations for the English Composition Test

1. *Typical Questions*

2. *Ten Practice Examinations*

3. *Answers to Practice Examinations with Analyses of Answers*

There is ample drill in the following examinations for you to be able to evaluate your control of the skills required for communicating in Standard Written English on the college level. Before you begin to take any of them, you should familiarize yourself with the material in the preceding section.

After you have taken one of the examinations and have evaluated your results, turn to the preceding reviews for the knowledge your score revealed you lacked. By so doing, you will be making maximum use of these practice sessions. Use them to time yourself. Use them to familiarize yourself with the type of questions you will meet on the Achievement Test in English Composition. Use them to help yourself achieve your maximum.

To Do Your Best

1. The body of material being covered in the test remains the same, but the question items change. Therefore make certain that you read the directions before you begin to answer. Know what each of the letters in the Answer Key stands for before you block any one of them out.

2. The test must cover a wide range so that there can be a spread in student scores. Therefore, do not look for subtle variations first. Rather look for the obvious ones first! Unacceptable forms of agreement, tense, use of the apostrophe, confusion of common words will be much more frequent than stylistic changes. Only when you do not find the common blunder, then go toward the more sophisticated type of change.

3. Once you have found the "error" do not stop! Examine the other choices before you write your answer.

4. Do not mull over any one item. Remember the subtle is mixed with the obvious; you receive as much credit for one as the other. If you find one item difficult, skip it and then come back later if you have time.

5. Follow the suggested time schedule. It is better to go on to the next section when time is up. If you are permitted, you may be able to go back later.

6. There is a penalty for guessing. If you can narrow your choices down to two, then chance is on your side. If you cannot narrow your choices, do not fill in with a random answer. When you have guessed one of two, then do not go back and change the answer. Chance favors your first choice!

7. Rely upon your past training. Do not assume because it is a form that you normally use it must be unacceptable.

8. When in doubt, select the more formal item, the less colloquial choice. Remember that what is being tested is your control of Standard Written English.

NOTE: In College Board publications, the terms *correct* and *incorrect* are used interchangeably with *acceptable* and *not acceptable*, respectively, when referring to specific forms in usage, diction, and spelling. Thus, items labeled in this book as *acceptable* in current Standard Written English may be labeled as either *acceptable* or *correct* in directions and in test items of the English Composition Test; items labeled in this book as *not acceptable* may be identified as either *not acceptable* or *incorrect* in the explanatory material and directions of the English Composition Test.

TYPICAL QUESTIONS

The multiple-choice questions that follow are the type found on recent examinations. Study the directions and then the analysis so that you will have full comprehension of the tasks ahead.

Type One: Underlined Choices

The sentences in this kind of question may contain problems in grammatical relationships, usage, diction (choice of words) or idiom.

> DIRECTIONS: Each of the following sentences has four parts underlined and lettered. Each sentence may contain one or no underlined section containing parts that may be unacceptable. If there is no underlined part requiring change, then circle (E) showing no error. Otherwise circle the number of the underlined portion that is not correct or is poorly expressed.

SAMPLE ITEM:
It's certain that we're the group that are to represent our school in the contest. No error
(a,   b,   c,   d,   e)

ANALYSIS:
- (a) is correct since *it is* is appropriate.
- (b) is correct since *we are* is appropriate.
- (c) is correct since *group* is a word that fits in with the sense and style of the rest of the sentence
- (d) is incorrect since *group* is singular and should be followed by *is*.

SUMMARY: With this type of question, look for the obvious first!

Type Two: Variations

This question tests ability not only to identify standard usage but also to choose the best way of phrasing a sentence. The sentence presented may contain problems in grammatical relationships, usage, diction (choice of words), sentence construction, or punctuation.

> DIRECTIONS: Beneath each of the following sentences you will find five ways of rewriting the underlined part. Do not choose any change that alters the meaning of the original sentence.
>
> Select a — If you think that the original sentence is better than any of the changes.
>
> Otherwise select the letter of the choice that is most appropriate and effective.

SAMPLE ITEM:
Seeing how angry he had become, my fingers became more clumsy than ever, and I made a mess of the elements of the puzzle.
- (a) Seeing how angry he had become,
- (b) Seeing how angry he became,
- (c) Having seen how angry he had become
- (d) Seeing as how he was becoming angry,
- (e) When I saw how angry he had become,

ANALYSIS:
- (a) is incorrect since it contains a dangling participle *seeing* which seems to modify *fingers*.
- (b) is incorrect because *seeing* is a continuation of the dangling participle element.
- (c) is incorrect because *having seen* is another dangling participle.
- (d) is incorrect because not only is *seeing* dangling but *seeing as how* is unidiomatic.
- (e) is correct because of the elimination of the dangling participle.

SUMMARY: With this type of question, once you have identified the error, selection of the correct item is simple! The error can often be detected if you compare the various choices within the same range.

If the problem is not easily identified, then look for the sentence construction errors that cause awkwardness or ambiguity. Sometimes a choice can be eliminated because it changes the meaning of the original sentence.

Type Three: Labeling

This kind of question is based on a sentence that may contain any one of four kinds of unacceptable uses or no such usages. You are expected to identify and label, but not to correct the sentence. The unacceptable forms may be in

FAULTY DICTION:
Use of wrong synonym (*bring* for *take*)
Confusion of homonyms (*heard* for *herd*)
Use of nonstandard expressions (slang—*cop out*; clipped words—*phone*; nonstandard idioms—*different than*)

WORDINESS (unnecessary repetitions):
Word and definition (*fatigued* and *very tired*)

Word that repeats affix (descend *down*)
Lengthy definition instead of word itself (*discontinuance of his employment* for *dismissal*)

CLICHÉS:
Overused phrases (*trials and tribulations*)
Tired idioms (*talk a blue streak*)
Trite proverbs (*Clothes do not make the man*)

MIXED METAPHORS:
Absurd literal meaning of figurative comparison (*A twilight silence filled the room*)

FAULTY GRAMMATICAL RELATIONSHIPS OR SENTENCE STRUCTURE:
Wrong tense, case, or number
Lack of parallel structure
Misplaced or squinting modifiers

DIRECTIONS: Read each of the following sentences carefully. Then circle the appropriate letter in the answer column.
(a) if the sentence contains faulty diction
(b) if the sentence is wordy
(c) if the sentence contains clichés or inappropriate metaphors
(d) if the sentence contains faulty grammar or sentence structure
(e) if the sentence contains none of these errors

SAMPLE ITEM:
The man whom we had seen lying in the field had been placed in the ambulance and rushed to the hospital base.

(a) whom—correct—object of had seen
lying—correct—means resting
in—incorrect—into is the correct form
(b) is incorrect since each of the words carries a unique function.
(c) is incorrect since no comparisons are included or implied.
(d) is an incorrect choice since the words are all colloquial in tone.

Therefore, since this is an error in choice of word, the error is one of diction.

SUMMARY: Here more than in any other type of question, the best technique requires looking for an obvious error first!

You must be certain that you have a clear idea of each category involved. Before making your final selection, check to see that you plan to block out the appropriate letter.

Type Four: Editing

The fourth kind of question calls for editing or revising a correct and acceptable sentence. The revision should stay as close as possible to the meaning and language of the original. The traps planted in the unacceptable choices cover the errors found in each of the other types of questions, but the stress here is on the writing itself and not on the labels.

DIRECTIONS: Read each of the following sentences carefully. Then rephrase it according to the directions which follow it. Select from the choices A through E the word or entire phrase that is included in your revised sentence. The choice should be part of a sentence that is accurate and complete. Make only those changes that the directions require.

SAMPLE ITEM ONE:
When we approached the city, the stench of decaying flesh told us just where the ambush had occurred.

DIRECTIONS: Substitute <u>Approaching</u> for <u>When we approached</u>.
(a) city, the stench
(b) city the stench
(c) could have told
(d) ambush told
(e) we were told

ANALYSIS:
<u>Approaching</u> is a participle and must have a noun or pronoun to modify.
(a) and (b) would give us a dangling participle in Approaching the city(,) the stench . . .
(c) and (d) make unnecessary changes
(e) supplies the pronoun for approaching to modify <u>Approaching</u> the city, <u>we</u> were told by the stench . . .

SAMPLE ITEM TWO:
It seems to be inherent in human nature to want deity to worship and a devil to abhor. Machinery has become the devil of a widespread cult.

DIRECTIONS: Begin with <u>Since machinery had become</u>.
(a) cult. It seems
(b) worship, and a devil
(c) cult, it seemed
(d) worship. A devil
(e) cult; it had seemed

ANALYSIS:
<u>Since</u> introduces a subordinate clause that cannot be separated from the rest of the sentence.
(a) and (d) create sentence fragments
(b) introduces an irrelevant error, a comma separating compound items joined by <u>and</u>
(e) uses a semicolon to separate subordinate and main clause
(c) has the necessary past tense for <u>seemed</u> and

the comma to separate introductory adverb clause from main clause

SAMPLE ITEM THREE:

A hero is no braver than an ordinary man, but he is brave five minutes longer.

DIRECTIONS: Omit *but* and add *only*.
(a) braver. Than an ordinary man, only
(b) man; he is brave only
(c) braver, than an ordinary man, only
(d) man. He is only brave
(e) man, only he is brave

ANALYSIS:

The adverb *only* must be placed as close as possible to the phrase *five minutes longer*. Without the conjunction *but*, the two clauses become independent and have to be so punctuated: either as two separate sentences or as one sentence containing a semicolon.

(a) introduces irrelevant error with meaningless period after *brave* and capitalized *than*
(b) uses acceptable semicolon to separate the two independent clauses; *only* is placed close to *five minutes longer*
(c) introduces irrelevant error in use of commas
(d) *only* is misplaced changing meaning of sentence
(e) *only* is misplaced; comma is misused to separate the two independent clauses

SUMMARY:

If you can, follow the directions and evolve the sentence suggested. Then look through the choices for the one that fits. However, do not make your final selection before considering the other choices as well.

Not all possibilities of revision are included in the five choices. If you find that none of the choices fit your sentence, then rephrase it; begin your revision thinking with each of the choices offered.

PRACTICE EXAMINATION ONE

Total Time: One Hour
PART 1 *Suggested Time: 20 Minutes*
Time begun ..... Time ended ..... Time used .....
Did you complete the section within the time limit? ..

DIRECTIONS: Each of the sentences in this part is either correct or contains an unacceptable form of grammar, usage, diction (choice of words), or idiomatic usage. If there is an error, it will be found in one of the underlined sections, labeled (1), (2), (3), or (4); circle the number of the error. If there is no underlined section containing an error, then circle (5), showing no error.

1. Everyone in the class <u>looks</u> <u>well</u> in the graduation
(1) (2)
picture except Margie and <u>me</u>. <u>No error</u>
(3)   (4)   (5)

2. There <u>are</u> <u>fewer</u> items in this test <u>than</u> in the ones
(1) (2)   (3)
he had given <u>previously</u>. <u>No error</u>
(4)   (5)

3. Her cough so <u>aggravated</u> her condition that the doc-
(1)
tor had to <u>bring</u> her to the hospital where she <u>lay</u> in
(2)   (3)
the ward awaiting <u>further</u> treatment. <u>No error</u>
(4)   (5)

4. There is <u>really</u> no reason for <u>you</u> becoming so
(1)   (2)
<u>annoyed</u> with Bea and <u>me</u> that you can scarcely talk
(3)   (4)
with us. <u>No error</u>
(5)

5. We <u>lived</u> in this house for three years <u>before</u> my
(1)   (2)
father <u>decided</u> to have us move to a <u>newer</u> neigh-
(3)   (4)
borhood. <u>No error</u>
(5)

6. Sift two <u>cupsful</u> of flour, break the eggs very care-
(1)   (2)
<u>fully</u>, and then fill the <u>emptied</u> shells with the flour.
(3)   (4)
<u>No error</u>
(5)

7. Although Milton and I <u>are</u> deeply involved in this
(1)
matter, the <u>amount</u> of hours we have devoted to it
(2)   (3)
<u>is</u> negligible. <u>No error</u>
(4)   (5)

8. Hardly <u>no one</u> that I <u>have</u> seen in the <u>past</u> two hours
(1)   (2)   (3)
<u>had</u> witnessed the performance. <u>No error</u>
(4)   (5)

9. Some of the famous opera stars of the past <u>were</u>
(1)
<u>present</u>, they all approved <u>of</u> our proposal, a plan <u>to</u>
(2)   (3)   (4)
popularize good music. <u>No error</u>
(5)

10. The main difficulty <u>was</u> the barriers <u>which</u> <u>were</u>
(1)   (2) (3)
standing in the <u>center</u> of the crosswalk. <u>No error</u>
(4)   (5)

PRACTICE EXAMINATIONS FOR THE ENGLISH COMPOSITION TEST

11. The most exciting scene occurred <u>when</u> everyone in
    (1)
    the <u>cast</u> <u>was</u> told to disguise <u>themselves</u> as gypsies.
    (2) (3)   (4)
    <u>No error</u>
    (5)

12. In the newspaper <u>they</u> say that much more money
    (1)
    must be <u>spent</u> on research<u>;</u> hence<u>,</u> we may confi-
    (2)   (3)   (4)
    dently expect an increase in our present grant. <u>No
    error</u>
    (5)

13. <u>They're</u> the ones who <u>assert</u> that a better bridge
    (1)   (2)
    <u>could</u> have been built <u>had</u> we had their assistance.
    (3)   (4)
    <u>No error</u>
    (5)

14. She said, moreover, that I had not <u>even</u> tried, <u>which</u>
    (1)   (2)   (3)   (4)
    annoyed me very much. <u>No error</u>
                         (5)

15. Frances has <u>long</u> had the desire to become a famous
                (1)
    writer<u>_</u>even though the study of <u>it</u> would require
         (2)   (3)
    years of sacrifice on <u>her</u> part. <u>No error</u>
                         (4)   (5)

16. Realizing how little I <u>had been</u> able to accomplish<u>,</u>
                           (1)   (2)
    my <u>fears</u> of failure grew rapidly, <u>robbing</u> me of what
       (3)   (4)
    little confidence I had had. <u>No error</u>
                                 (5)

17. Even though it <u>may</u> be the <u>most</u> harmless of snakes<u>,</u>
                   (1)   (3)   (3)
    I am not <u>enthused</u> about having it in a cage in my
             (4)
    room. <u>No error</u>
          (5)

18. <u>Every one</u> who is anyone <u>was</u> invited to attend the
    (1)   (2)   (3)
    party for you and <u>me</u>. <u>No error</u>
                      (4)   (5)

19. The old tape recorder <u>seems</u> to be much better <u>then</u>
                          (1)   (2)
    any of the <u>newer</u> ones that <u>are</u> on display now.
               (3)   (4)
    <u>No error</u>
    (5)

20. He treats his pets <u>as though</u> they <u>were</u> <u>humans</u>,
                       (1)   (2)   (3)
    <u>showing</u> them every possible consideration. <u>No error</u>
    (4)   (5)

21. <u>In regards to</u> your recent request for assistance<u>,</u> I
    (1)   (2)
    have to report that Allan has stated <u>emphatically</u>
                                         (3)
    that he has no more money to give you or <u>me</u>. <u>No
                                             (4)
    error</u>
    (5)

22. <u>It</u> was <u>kind of a</u> shock to look <u>into</u> these matters and
    (1)   (2)   (3)
    <u>discover</u> that the fault was solely mine. <u>No error</u>
    (4)   (5)

23. "I cannot leave <u>now!</u>" she exclaimed<u>.</u> "Why must
                   (1)   (2)
    you insist that I do <u>so</u><u>?</u>" <u>No error</u>
                         (3) (4)   (5)

24. She will <u>definitely</u> <u>lose out</u> if she studies <u>less</u> than
             (1)   (2)   (3)
    any <u>other</u> girl in her class. <u>No error</u>
        (4)   (5)

25. Let it <u>lay</u> where it <u>has</u> <u>fallen</u> until the demolition
    (1)   (2)   (3) (4)
    squad arrives. <u>No error</u>
                   (5)

26. You <u>will</u> have to make the curves <u>rounder;</u> other-
        (1)   (2)   (3)
    wise, everyone will be copying your mistakes. <u>No
    (4)
    error</u>
    (5)

27. Grandmother and <u>I</u> enjoyed your letter <u>muchly</u><u>;</u> we
                    (1)   (2)   (3)
    are <u>eagerly</u> looking forward to your next communi-
        (4)
    cation. <u>No error</u>
            (5)

28. As he <u>neared</u> the end of the evening, his <u>voice</u>
          (1)   (2)
    echoed the hopes that filled <u>everyones'</u> heart <u>;</u> he
                                 (3)   (4)
    became the symbol of our hopes. <u>No error</u>
                                    (5)

29. Let's play <u>a</u> old record on the machine<u>_</u>so that we
               (1) (2)   (3)
    <u>can</u> discover the true worth of this latest gadget.
    (4)
    <u>No error</u>
    (5)

30. <u>Due to</u> carelessness, the couple will <u>lose</u> <u>their</u> <u>live's</u>
    (1)   (2)   (3)   (4)
    savings in this uncalled-for mess. <u>No error</u>
                                       (5)

31. Give it to <u>whoever</u> it really belongs to<u>;</u> it <u>little</u> mat-
               (1)   (2)   (3)

ters to me now <u>whose</u> it is. <u>No error</u>
      (4)   (5)

32. I <u>may</u> not <u>except</u> you from these regulations, <u>re-</u>
       (1)   (2)   (3)
<u>gardless</u> of how much pressure you put on me to do
 (4)
so. <u>No error</u>
     (5)

33. When you are <u>among</u> friends and the problem is
                   (1)
<u>all ready</u> to be solved, it is better that you do <u>as</u> you
  (2)   (3)
are told and not <u>aggravate</u> others. <u>No error</u>
                   (4)   (5)

PART 2   *Suggested Time: 20 Minutes*
Time begun ..... Time ended ..... Time used .....
Did you complete the section within the time limit? ..

DIRECTIONS: In each of the following sentences, there is an underlined section that presents a problem in acceptable usage in grammar, diction (choice of words), sentence construction, or punctuation. Beneath each sentence are five ways of writing the underlined part.
   Select   a   if you think the original is better than any of the changes.
   Otherwise   select the letter of the choice that is most effective and appropriate.
Do not select any change that alters the meaning of the original sentence.

34. Mrs. Fitzpatrick is one of those people <u>who is always willing</u> to help others.
  (a) who is always willing
  (b) which are always willing
  (c) whom are always willing
  (d) who are always willing
  (e) which is always willing

35. Having spoken to the <u>principle, our anger subsided</u>.
  (a) principle, our anger subsided
  (b) principal, we felt our anger subside
  (c) principal, our anger had subsided
  (d) principle, the discussion caused our anger to subside
  (e) principal, our anger could have subsided

36. A package finally arrived <u>however it is not the one I expected</u>.
  (a) however it is not the one I expected
  (b) which was not the one I had expected
  (c) , however it is not the one I expect
  (d) ; however it was not the one I expect
  (e) . However it was not the one I had expected

37. It was <u>a awesome sight, much too much</u> for my weakened condition.
  (a) a awesome sight, much too much
  (b) an awesome sight. Much too much
  (c) a awesome sight, much to much
  (d) an awesome sight, much too much
  (e) an awesome sight; much to much

38. If I <u>would have gone</u> there, we could have prevented all of this!
  (a) would have gone
  (b) would of gone
  (c) had gone
  (d) could have gone
  (e) could've gone

39. I can see hardly <u>any reason for their</u> listening to us.
  (a) any reason for their
  (b) no reason for them
  (c) no reason for their
  (d) any reason for them
  (e) any of the reasons for them

40. I hate to <u>loose the ring it really was quit valuable</u>.
  (a) loose the ring it really was quit valuable
  (b) loose the ring: it really was quit valuable
  (c) lose the ring. It really was quit valuable
  (d) lose the ring; it really was quite valuable
  (e) loose the ring. It really had been quit valuable

41. <u>Leave it lay there</u> until we are ready.
  (a) Leave it lay there
  (b) Let it lay their
  (c) Leave it lie their
  (d) Leave it lay there
  (e) Let it lie there

42. Alberta is <u>more sensitive than any girl</u> in her class.
  (a) more sensitive than any girl
  (b) most sensitive
  (c) more sensitive than any other
  (d) most sensitive than any girl
  (e) more sensitive than any girls

43. <u>Being Harold had invited me,</u> I had not anticipated such a curt reception.
  (a) Being Harold had invited me,
  (b) Being that Harold had invited me,
  (c) Being that Harold invited me,
  (d) Since Harold had invited me,
  (e) Since Harold invited me,

44. Everyone <u>except he and I</u> had the necessary visas.
  (a) except he and I
  (b) except him and I
  (c) except I and he
  (d) except me and him
  (e) except him and me

45. The results were better <u>then I should of expected</u>.
  (a) then I should of expected
  (b) than I should of expected
  (c) . Then I should have expected
  (d) Than I should of expected
  (e) than I should have expected

46. Is it <u>him who</u> I have to see this morning?
  (a) Is it him who
  (b) Was it he whom
  (c) Is it he whom
  (d) Is it he who
  (e) Was it him who

47. All I can say is that it is a womans' world after all.
    (a) that it is a womans' world after all.
    (b) "That it is a woman's world after all."
    (c) "That it is a woman's world after all".
    (d) that it is a women's world after all.
    (e) that it is a woman's world after all.

48. When the damage is assessed you pay the costs.
    (a) When the damage is assessed,
    (b) After the damage has been assessed,
    (c) After the damage is assessed,
    (d) When the damage had been assessed,
    (e) By the time the damage is assessed,

49. Is he one of those doctors who have been experimenting on humans?
    (a) who have been experimenting on humans?
    (b) who has been experimenting on humans?
    (c) who have been experimenting on human beings?
    (d) who has been experimenting on human beings?
    (e) which has been experimenting on humans?

50. He told us that its a kind of a fools' paradise.
    (a) its a kind of a fools' paradise
    (b) it's a kind of fools' paradise
    (c) its a kind of a fool's paradise
    (d) it's kind of a fool's paradise
    (e) its a kind of fools' paradise

51. Being as everyone of my friends were there, I felt confident.
    (a) Being as everyone of my friends were there,
    (b) Being that everyone of my friends was there,
    (c) Being that everyone of my friends were there,
    (d) Since every one of my friends was there,
    (e) Since everyone of my friends were there,

52. The case has been decided in our favor; however, it can still be appealed.
    (a) ; however, it can still be appealed.
    (b) however it can still be appealed.
    (c) ; However, it can still be appealed.
    (d) , and however, it can still be appealed.
    (e) , however, it could have been still appealed.

53. We must make our peace with Mr. Shaw the leader of the opposition.
    (a) with Mr. Shaw the leader of the opposition
    (b) with Mr. Shaw who had been leader of the opposition
    (c) with Mr. Shaw. The leader of the opposition
    (d) with Mr. Shaw. Who has been leader of the opposition
    (e) with Mr. Shaw, the leader of the opposition

54. His favorite complimentary close is that old favorite, sincerely yours'.
    (a) that old favorite, sincerely yours'
    (b) that old favorite sincerely yours
    (c) that old favorite sincerely your's
    (d) that old favorite Sincerely yours'
    (e) that old favorite, Sincerely yours

55. If I was he, I would drop the discussion at this point.
    (a) If I was he,
    (b) If I were he,
    (c) If I was him,
    (d) If I had been him,
    (e) If I were him,

56. You will find these here somewhere near the new school.
    (a) these here somewhere near the new school
    (b) these somewhere near the new school
    (c) these here somewheres near the new school
    (d) these here someplace near the new school
    (e) these someplace near the new school

57. He always finds the negative values in whatever I suggest, which annoys me no end.
    (a) which annoys me no end
    (b) . Which annoys me no end
    (c) , an action which annoys me no end
    (d) ; which annoys me no end
    (e) ; an action which annoys me no end

58. The most exciting scene is when the hero's horse stumbles.
    (a) is when the hero's horse stumbles
    (b) occurs when the heroes' horse stumbles
    (c) is when the heroes' horse stumbles
    (d) occurs when the hero's horse stumbles
    (e) was when the hero's horse stumbles

PART 3 *Suggested Time: 20 Minutes*
Time begun ..... Time ended ..... Time used .....
Did you complete the section within the time limit? ..

DIRECTIONS: Read each of the following sentences carefully. Then circle the appropriate letter in the answer column.

Select a if the sentence contains an unacceptable form of diction (use of a word or phrase that does not make sense, is not idiomatic, or is not acceptable in Standard Written English).
        b if the sentence is verbose (wordy) or contains a redundant phrase (unjustifiable repetition).
        c if the sentence contains clichés (trite, overused words or phrases) or mixed metaphors (misused figurative language).
        d if the sentence contains an unacceptable form of grammar or sentence structure: lack of parallel structure; wrong tense, case or number; misplaced modifiers or similar errors.
        e if the sentence contains none of these unacceptable forms.

59. What gives him the right to think that he alone among men can use his corrosive wit on others while sitting in a self-made judgment seat!
    59. a b c d e

60. It was just that sort of an argument that leaves me drained of all energy.   60. a b c d e
61. How quickly do my spirits descend down the steps of despair, leaving me without hope or fear.   61. a b c d e
62. I shall fight tooth and nail to defend your right to express your opinions in an atmosphere of calm reason.   62. a b c d e
63. How can you claim that all is lost when every one of your companions still have their weapons and will to fight!   63. a b c d e
64. Why must this be another of those marriages that terminate in divorce!   64. a b c d e
65. Despite all of the optimistic evaluations that have bombarded me, I cannot become enthused over these results.   65. a b c d e
66. Being as the answer was obvious to all but me, I could not claim full understanding at that moment.   66. a b c d e
67. Caught in the turmoil of the battle, he soon discovered that his mind and body had the suppleness of the superman he had dreamed of.   67. a b c d e
68. Coming to the end of the examination, my fatigue was more than I could bear.   68. a b c d e
69. I have known for quit some time of his decision to resign at the end of the semester.   69. a b c d e
70. When caught on the anvil of misfortune, you must learn to swim with the current.   70. a b c d e
71. Only when you brought both samples into close scrutiny did I realize how much mine differs to his!   71. a b c d e
72. How quickly can we settle up the estate so that the company can once again be adequately financed?   72. a b c d e
73. I had hoped that this would be the occasion on which I would be formerly presented to the king.   73. a b c d e
74. I still affirm that we hold no brief for modern writings.   74. a b c d e
75. Grasp time firmly in your fingers lest evening arrive before you have felt the warmth of the daily sun.   75. a b c d e
76. He inferred in his comments that I could win the nomination if I so desired at this moment.   76. a b c d e
77. Like a dog in the manger he refused to give to us what was so necessary to our plans and so unessential to his.   77. a b c d e
78. When I hear of such happenings, I cannot help but think of what the final compromise must be.   78. a b c d e
79. I was unavailable at that moment, moreover even if I had been there, I could not have been of much assistance.   79. a b c d e
80. Do I have to remind you that you must endorse every check on the back?   80. a b c d e
81. How could I not tell him that he would come to grief if he continued along this collision path!   81. a b c d e
82. He has always been the kind of person whom I could trust with all of my confidences.   82. a b c d e
83. Is this an artificial man-made fabric that can be used throughout the year?   83. a b c d e
84. Did Margie tell Edna that she was expected to be at the exhibition hall all morning?   84. a b c d e
85. We expect to reach the actual beginning initial stage of the construction by noon tomorrow.   85. a b c d e
86. Swimming against the current of popular opinion, you must expect to be a target for all types of criticism.   86. a b c d e
87. He had told us that there was scarcely no food left by the time they had arrived in port.   87. a b c d e
88. With that kind of a temperament, he can hardly be considered a reasonable man.   88. a b c d e
89. Who can claim that he has the answers to the burning issues of our day?   89. a b c d e
90. This basic principle must not be violated if we are ever to move in the direction of total employment.   90. a b c d e

ANSWER KEY AND ANALYSIS OF ANSWERS / *Page 127*

PRACTICE EXAMINATION TWO

Total Time: One Hour
PART 1   *Suggested Time: 25 Minutes*
Time begun ..... Time ended ..... Time used .....
Did you complete the section within the time limit? ..

DIRECTIONS: Read each of the following sentences carefully. Then circle the appropriate number in the answer column.

Select 1 if the sentence contains an unacceptable form of diction (use of a word or phrase that does not make sense, is not idiomatic, or is unacceptable in Standard Written English).

2 if the sentence contains an unacceptable form of grammar or sentence structure; wrong tense, case or number; misplaced modifiers or similar errors.

3 if the sentence contains clichés (trite, overused phrases) or mixed metaphors (misused figurative language).

4 if the sentence is verbose (wordy) or contains a redundant phrase (unjustifiable repetition).

5 if the sentence contains none of these forms.

1. Now that time is running out and the minutes have ticked their way into the inevitable hours, we should be taking stock of what we have done and begin to reach some definitive conclusions.
   1. 1 2 3 4 5
2. Sailing into the fight with youthful confidence, he quickly ran the gauntlet of anticipated difficulties and rose to the top as victor.
   2. 1 2 3 4 5
3. The best that we could promise under these circumstances was to terminate all activities around ten in the evening. 3. 1 2 3 4 5
4. I shall try to prevent a recurrence of this unfortunate mix-up. 4. 1 2 3 4 5
5. I am convinced that we can bank on your full cooperation when you are called upon to assist us.
   5. 1 2 3 4 5
6. We had tried to please him in every possible way, which gave us a distinct advantage over our nearest competitors. 6. 1 2 3 4 5
7. Regardless of how often I called to him, he refused to let us know where he was.
   7. 1 2 3 4 5
8. He was most impressive when he handled with lightning speed all the complaints of the tenants whom he was responsible for.
   8. 1 2 3 4 5
9. Adding meat to the very foundations of our complaints, Helen accused all of us of having slighted her at every opportunity. 9. 1 2 3 4 5
10. When the reporters arrive, will you please give them copies of the mimeographed report so that when they write up their articles there can be no doubt in their minds of the facts in this case.
    10. 1 2 3 4 5
11. He is looking for a companion to type his letters, to read his mail to him, and who can do simple bookkeeping at the same time. 11. 1 2 3 4 5
12. When the sands of time run out, you will then realize what you had lost when you forsook your loyal friends. 12. 1 2 3 4 5
13. By the time I had taken my pen in hand and had prepared myself mentally for the task of putting into words the basic objections that I have to you taking my place, the storm broke and I had to run for shelter. 13. 1 2 3 4 5
14. Since the aged conductor had been unprepared for the speed with which we dispatched the first number, he asked us to repeat it again at a much slower tempo. 14. 1 2 3 4 5
15. His swan song may have heralded his ultimate failure, but it shall merely serve as a spring board for our successes to come. 15. 1 2 3 4 5
16. With most unwilling steps and a heaviness of heart that I am unaccustomed to, I plan to bring to a termination this journey with you through the thoroughfares of our beloved city.
    16. 1 2 3 4 5
17. The tree that we planted in the fall was sturdy, fully formed, and it should have survived the wintry blasts with ease. 17. 1 2 3 4 5
18. The actual performance of this group will never compare favorably with the inspired work of those who preceded. 18. 1 2 3 4 5
19. Like a battering ram of old, he groped his way unmercifully and tore open the weakest chinks in their armor. 19. 1 2 3 4 5
20. Sheldon angrily told the group leader, Mr. Allerton, that he was being blamed for the entire difficulty.
    20. 1 2 3 4 5
21. What angered me was not his refusal but the speed with which he was willing to cop out.
    21. 1 2 3 4 5
22. I am certain that you will like the new plans and will be very much pleased with them.
    22. 1 2 3 4 5
23. Without appearing impatient, the counselor asked his client how long he would have to be waiting on her answer. 23. 1 2 3 4 5
24. When the jury filed into the room, the judge asked whether it was prepared to present its verdict.
    24. 1 2 3 4 5
25. The student insisted that Lake Erie was larger than the Mediterranean. 25. 1 2 3 4 5
26. Although the expedition was doomed to failure from its very inception, the untiring efforts of the leader almost carried it off.
    26. 1 2 3 4 5
27. Her anxieties had taken such control that she was incapable of viewing my efforts as being in her behalf. 27. 1 2 3 4 5
28. Finding the happy medium is easier said than done.
    28. 1 2 3 4 5
29. A large plaque has been placed on the building where the first county school had been originally located. 29. 1 2 3 4 5
30. So long as I continue to have my self-respect, I can never lose out completely.
    30. 1 2 3 4 5
31. From all sections of the country came the letters of protest that overflowed the mail bins in the alumni office. 31. 1 2 3 4 5
32. Paul told his brother that he was the one who would pay the bill. 32. 1 2 3 4 5
33. When waiting for the results of a medical examination, even a favorite television program seems dull and trivial. 33. 1 2 3 4 5
34. The instructor was near the end of his patience and did not know how much longer he could put up with Harold's inane comments.
    34. 1 2 3 4 5
35. Lake Placid is one of the most beautiful, if not the most beautiful town in the Adirondacks.
    35. 1 2 3 4 5
36. The wheels of misfortune swept over him and ground his hopes into the mire.
    36. 1 2 3 4 5
37. The truth shall be shouted from the roof tops and freedom's ring will be heard throughout the length and breadth of the land. 37. 1 2 3 4 5
38. The doctor called the family together to let them know that the end was eminent.
    38. 1 2 3 4 5

39. How different our outlook would be had ours not been the house destroyed by the fire caused by his carelessness! 39. 1 2 3 4 5
40. By the time he was twenty, Van Cinter's style was ranked with the greatest painters.
   40. 1 2 3 4 5
41. The chief of police suspicioned that the witness had been evading his questions.
   41. 1 2 3 4 5
42. Who has the ability to comfort the hypochondriac who constantly worries about his health?
   42. 1 2 3 4 5
43. Considering all of the dangers that the explorers had faced, it is a miracle that so many of them survived. 43. 1 2 3 4 5
44. Would that I could outrun the difficulties that bog me down! 44. 1 2 3 4 5

PART 2 *Suggested Time: 20 Minutes*
Time begun ..... Time ended ..... Time used .....
Did you complete the section within the time limit? ...

DIRECTIONS: In each of the following sentences there is an underlined section that presents a problem in acceptable usage or grammar, diction (choice of words), sentence construction, or punctuation. Beneath each sentence are five ways of writing the underlined part.

Select **A** if you think that the original is better than any of the changes.
Otherwise select the letter of the choice that is most effective and appropriate.

Do not select any change that alters the meaning of the original sentence.

45. The young reporter went out on many routine assignments until his ability to grasp essentials was proved.
   (A) until his ability to grasp essentials was proved.
   (B) . Until his ability to grasp essentials was proved.
   (C) until his ability to grasp essentials was proven.
   (D) until he proved his ability to grasp essentials.
   (E) ; until his ability to grasp essentials was proven.

46. If the car would have been moved on time, we would not have received the ticket.
   (A) If the car would have been moved on time,
   (B) If the car could have been moved on time,
   (C) If the car had been moved on time,
   (D) If the car were moved on time,
   (E) If the car was moved on time,

47. Neither Janet nor Merwin have been in this office all day.
   (A) have been in this office
   (B) could have been in this office
   (C) has been in this office
   (D) have been in this here office
   (E) has been in this here office

48. The condenser was just installed, therefore it is the part to be checked first.
   (A) installed, therefore
   (B) installed therefore,
   (C) installed, therefore,
   (D) installed and therefore
   (E) installed; therefore,

49. He answered me before I had completed my question, which annoyed me very much.
   (A) question, which annoyed me very much.
   (B) question, which annoyed me muchly.
   (C) question which annoyed me muchly.
   (D) question. His impatience annoyed me very much.
   (E) question, this annoyed me very much.

50. The reason the machine failed is because the motor had overheated.
   (A) the machine failed is because
   (B) why the machine failed is because
   (C) the machine failed is that
   (D) that the machine failed is because
   (E) for the machine's failure is because

51. No sooner had the door opened than the nurse ordered us to close it.
   (A) than the nurse ordered us to close it.
   (B) when the nurse ordered us to close it.
   (C) when the nurse orders us to close it.
   (D) then the nurse ordered us to close it.
   (E) than the nurse orders us to close it.

52. To drive a tractor, your patience must match your skill.
   (A) To drive a tractor, your patience must match your skill.
   (B) When you drive a tractor, your patience must match your skill.
   (C) When driving a tractor, your patience must match your skill.
   (D) To drive a tractor; your patience must match your skill.
   (E) Driving a tractor, your patience must match your skill.

53. No one, including Harriet and I, have the right to make this decision for him.
   (A) one, including Harriet and I, have
   (B) one, including Harriet and me, have
   (C) one including Harriet and I have
   (D) one, including Harriet and me have
   (E) one, including Harriet and me, has

54. Your results must be as good or even better than those of your predecessor.
   (A) must be as good or even better than
   (B) must be as good as or even better then
   (C) has to be as good or even better then
   (D) must be as good as or even better than
   (E) must be as good or better then

55. Not one of the woman in the room smiled when the speaker used the phrase, "the man's world of sports."
   (A) woman in the room smiled when the speaker used the phrase, "the man's world
   (B) women in the room smiles when the speaker used the phrase, "the man's world
   (C) women in the room smiled when the speaker used the phrase, "the man's world
   (D) woman in the room smiles when the speaker mentions, "the man's world
   (E) woman in the room smiled when the speaker made mention of "the man's world

56. You must admit that he is by far a better passer than any of the other players on his squad.
   (A) than any of the other players
   (B) then any of the players

(C) then any of the other players
(D) than any of the players
(E) than any of the players'

57. However difficult the task may be perseverance is its own reward.
(A) However difficult the task may be perseverance
(B) However, difficult the task may be perseverance
(C) However, difficult the task may be, perseverance
(D) However difficult the task may be. Perseverance
(E) However difficult the task may be, perseverance

58. She is one of the delegates who was chosen to attend the convention.
(A) who was chosen to attend
(B) who were chosen to attend
(C) that was chosen to attend
(D) whom was chosen to attend
(E) which were chosen to attend

59. Because we saw the accident, the judge ordered us to testify at the hearing.
(A) Because we saw the accident, the
(B) Because we saw the accident. The
(C) Because we saw the accident the
(D) Because we had seen the accident; the
(E) Because we had seen the accident, the

60. When I take into consideration all of the factors involved, I neither have the inclination nor the insensitivity to interfere.
(A) neither have the inclination nor the insensitivity to interfere.
(B) neither have the inclination or the insensitivity to interfere.
(C) have neither the inclination or the insensitivity to interfere.
(D) have neither the inclination nor the insensitivity to interfere.
(E) have neither inclination or the insensitivity to interfere.

61. The state of the economy being what it is, I feel that further commitment of fiduciary sums would be unwise at this time.
(A) The state of the economy being what it is, I
(B) The economy being what it is, I
(C) The state of the economy being what it is; I
(D) The economy being what it is I
(E) Thing being what they are. I

62. Ever since the reorganization was planned, there has been too many promises made and too few problems solved.
(A) there has been too many promises made
(B) there was to many promises made
(C) there had been too many promises
(D) there was too many promises made
(E) there have been too many promises made

63. After considering most carefully the arguments on both sides there is only one decision that could be reached.
(A) sides there
(B) sides, there
(C) sides. There
(D) sides, we realized that there
(E) sides. We concluded that there

64. Not only Lucy but her friends and relatives as well was aware of your need for assistance.
(A) was aware of your need for
(B) were aware of your need for
(C) have been aware of your need of
(D) is aware of your need of
(E) are aware of your need for

65. The intended victims of this crude practical joke seem to be Paul and I.
(A) Paul and I.
(B) I and Paul.
(C) Paul and me.
(D) me and Paul.
(E) Paul or I.

66. Milton told me when I arrived I was to go directly to the office.
(A) Milton told me when I arrived I was to go directly to the office.
(B) Milton told me when I arrived, I was to go directly to the office.
(C) Milton told me, when I arrived I was to go directly to the office.
(D) Milton told me, "When I arrive I was to go directly to your office."
(E) Milton told me I was to go directly to your office when I arrived.

67. Has any of our friends expressed his views in this matter?
(A) Has any of our friends expressed his views in this matter?
(B) Have any of our friends expressed his views, in this matter?
(C) Have any of our friends expressed their views in this matter?
(D) Has any of our friends expressed his views, in this matter?
(E) Has any of our friends expressed views in this matter?

68. Upon receiving the letter of acceptance from the college of my choice my cup of happiness was filled to overflowing.
(A) choice my cup of happiness was filled to overflowing.
(B) choice. My cup of happiness was filled to overflowing.
(C) choice, my cup of happiness was filled to overflowing.
(D) choice I was overjoyed.
(E) choice, I was overjoyed.

69. Marvin Aarons is the member of the group whom I think can best advise you.
(A) whom I think can best advise you.
(B) who I think can best advise you.
(C) whom I think can best advice you.
(D) whom, I think, can best advice you.
(E) which, I think, can best advise you.

70. To be able to live with myself comfortably is more important than earning additional income.
(A) than earning additional income.
(B) then earning additional income.
(C) then to earn additional income.
(D) than earning some extra money.
(E) than to earn additional income.

PART 3 Suggested Time: 15 Minutes

Time begun .... Time ended .... Time used ....
Did you complete the section within the time limt? ..

DIRECTIONS: Read each of the following sentences carefully. Then rephrase it according to the directions which follow it. Select from the choices (a) through (e) the word or entire phrase that is included in your revised sentence. The choice should be part of a sentence that is accurate and complete. Make only those changes that the directions require.

71. Everyone of the soldiers was given his full set of equipment. Begin with All of the soldiers
    (a) were given his
    (b) will be given their
    (c) was given their
    (d) were given their
    (e) will have been given their

72. Ben is the most egotistical man I know.
    Substitute more egotistical for the most egotistical
    (a) than any man I know
    (b) than any man I have ever known
    (c) than any other man I have known
    (d) than any other man I know
    (e) than any man I had ever known

73. Running up the steps, he soon found himself out of breath.
    Begin with He ran
    (a) and then he was found
    (b) and soon found
    (c) and could have found
    (d) which found him
    (e) and then had found

74. Miss Muller, our college adviser and guidance counselor, addressed the assembly.
    Begin with Because
    (a) counselor addressed
    (b) counselor, she could have
    (c) counselor she
    (d) counselor was addressed
    (e) counselor, she

75. Dave along with several other members of the class was seen loitering in the vicinity of the lockers.
    Begin with Dave and
    (a) has been
    (b) are
    (c) is
    (d) were
    (e) was often

76. To be used effectively, the solution must be kept at full strength.
    Substitute you must for the solution must
    (a) When used effectively
    (b) the solution effectively
    (c) strength of full solution
    (d) To have been used
    (e) When used as a solution,

77. I saw the accident, and therefore I expected to be called as a witness.
    Begin the sentence with Because
    (a) ; and therefore
    (b) . Therefore
    (c) accident, I
    (d) and expected
    (e) I saw

78. The body which had been found lying face down in the stagnant pool at the edge of town was finally identified as that of an itinerant day laborer.
    Begin the sentence with Found
    (a) town, the body
    (b) which had been identified
    (c) town, itinerant day laborer
    (d) An itinerant day laborer
    (e) town. Body

79. Was there anyone in the group ready to describe the project at that time?
    Substitute any for anyone
    (a) Had there been
    (b) Were there
    (c) of the group
    (d) Have there been
    (e) . Ready to describe

80. I was unprepared for the report, and this soon became very obvious to the members of the committee.
    Begin with That I was unprepared
    (a) report, and this
    (b) report; and this
    (c) report soon
    (d) report and soon
    (e) report, soon

81. I agreed to purchase the new equipment from them, but I really thought that the price was too high.
    Substitute however for but
    (a) , however, I
    (b) ; however, the price
    (c) . However, the new equipment
    (d) . However I
    (e) ; however I

82. Frances felt that she was ready, and she asked her instructor to give her the makeup test.
    Omit the second she
    (a) , and asked
    (b) and had asked
    (c) but asked
    (d) and asked
    (e) ; and asked

83. Being my best friend, Marvin helped me plan my strategy.
    Substitute who is for Being
    (a) Marvin who is
    (b) friend, helped
    (c) . Helped
    (d) strategy, who
    (e) strategy who

PRACTICE EXAMINATIONS FOR THE ENGLISH COMPOSITION TEST

84. I was so angry that I wrote a letter to the company and mailed it immediately.
Substitute which I for and
(a) company which
(b) company, which
(c) which I had
(d) immediately to
(e) . Which I

85. How can we measure the worth of the hours which have been frittered away in useless worry!
Substitute time for hours
(a) time. Which
(b) time, which
(c) which has
(d) which would have been
(e) frittering away

ANSWER KEY AND ANALYSIS OF ANSWERS / *Page* 129

PRACTICE EXAMINATION THREE

Total Time: One Hour
PART 1 *Suggested Time: 25 Minutes*
Time begun .... Time ended .... Time used ....
Did you complete the section within the time limit? ..

DIRECTIONS: Read each of the following sentences carefully. Then circle the appropriate number in the answer column

1. if the sentence contains an error in agreement.
2. if the sentence contains an error in comparison.
3. if the sentence contains a faulty parallelism.
4. if the sentence contains an error in punctuation.
5. if the sentence contains none of these errors.

1. Among the thousands of unemployed was the group of men whose hands were trained to tasks that are no longer being performed. 1. 1 2 3 4 5
2. Helen is more capable than any member of her family, bar none. 2. 1 2 3 4 5
3. We were fully prepared for the storm, because the weather reports had reached us a full twenty-four hours before the first drops of rain fell.
3. 1 2 3 4 5
4. You must remember that he has always been a man of integrity, honor, and courage. 4. 1 2 3 4 5
5. I hope that I have convinced you that Ellen is better or at least as good as any of the successful candidates of the past. 5. 1 2 3 4 5
6. There must be another way out; and I shall find it! 6. 1 2 3 4 5
7. Anybody who is ready at this moment to hand in their projects may do so if they have completed the heading. 7. 1 2 3 4 5
8. Relaxing in the sun, sleeping late, and to be able to read some of the books around me constitute the basis of my idea of a real vacation.
8. 1 2 3 4 5
9. He assured me that my sisters' chances are as good as anyones. 9. 1 2 3 4 5
10. Phyllis could see only one way out of all of her difficulties; resigning from her position on the Membership Committee. 10. 1 2 3 4 5
11. In a summer camp the head counselor is as important, if not more important than the owner himself. 11. 1 2 3 4 5
12. I was so surprised, I did not expect so curt an answer. 12. 1 2 3 4 5
13. Irene and Danny who live around the corner have been my friends for many years.
13. 1 2 3 4 5
14. Ben, as well as his brother Henry, know the route; and I have the utmost confidence in him, regardless of when he gives the signal to begin.
14. 1 2 3 4 5
15. The development of the new suburbs along with the industrial centers on the outskirt of town and our new school system are the result of Ida's untiring efforts. 15. 1 2 3 4 5
16. When do you plan to read "Of Human Bondage?" 16. 1 2 3 4 5
17. The music that he had planned for the program was intensely beautiful and of great variety. 17. 1 2 3 4 5
18. The true end of his career, came when he allowed his followers to dip into the county treasury in order to fill their own pockets. 18. 1 2 3 4 5
19. "When you reach the turn in the road", she warned me, "don't follow the signs up on the embankment." 19. 1 2 3 4 5
20. Yesterday in algebra we learned the method of adding like terms, the dangers involved in subtracting like terms, and how to multiply unlike terms.
20. 1 2 3 4 5
21. When in New York do as the New Yorkers do. 21. 1 2 3 4 5
22. At what age do a boys' thoughts turn toward occupational choices? 22. 1 2 3 4 5
23. When one is in a difficult situation, you must learn to avoid making hasty decisions. 23. 1 2 3 4 5
24. This story is as interesting if not more interesting than any of the ones Duane Decker ever wrote. 24. 1 2 3 4 5
25. You will have to work most carefully and with the greatest speed. 25. 1 2 3 4 5
26. Every student in the school must do their own studying for the tests to come. 26. 1 2 3 4 5
27. To be able to visit Wales in the spring is one of my lifelong ambitions. 27. 1 2 3 4 5
28. Did you see the look on that womans' face! 28. 1 2 3 4 5
29. Anyone seen without their protective gloves will be fired. 29. 1 2 3 4 5
30. This is one of the tapedecks that has been repaired. 30. 1 2 3 4 5
31. It was all over our scheme had backfired and destroyed everything that we had been working for. 31. 1 2 3 4 5

32. If you strike lighted matches, you must expect to be burned.   32. 1 2 3 4 5
33. William, the Conqueror, helped to perpetuate the caste system in England.   33. 1 2 3 4 5
34. He could have made a more final judgment at that time.   34. 1 2 3 4 5
35. Which department store specializes in ladies ski jackets?   35. 1 2 3 4 5
36. Do not do it again; the risks are not worth it.   36. 1 2 3 4 5
37. It is up to we seniors to stop all of this nonsense!   37. 1 2 3 4 5
38. It is no worse or better than any of the others.   38. 1 2 3 4 5
39. Phil is capable, sensitive, and does not let his emotions control his professional decisions.   39. 1 2 3 4 5
40. Coming to the end of the road, gives the traveller a chance to pause.   40. 1 2 3 4 5
41. You will have to act quickly, decisively, but with the greatest caution.   41. 1 2 3 4 5
42. The house is built high on a hill; the only hill for miles around.   42. 1 2 3 4 5
43. The man, who owns this gun, will be accused of murder.   43. 1 2 3 4 5
44. Will the someone who borrowed these pamphlets please be courteous enough to raise their hands.   44. 1 2 3 4 5

PART 2   *Suggested Time: 20 Minutes*

Time begun .... Time ended .... Time used ....
Did you complete the section within the time limit? ..

DIRECTIONS: Each of the sentences in this part is either correct or contains one error in grammar, usage, diction (choice of words), or idiomatic usage. If there is an error, it will be found in one of the underlined sections, labeled (A), (B), (C), or (D). If there is an error, circle the letter of the underlined section that is not correct. If there is no underlined section containing an error, then circle (E), showing no error.

45. I <u>cannot</u> argue <u>with</u> what he <u>said,</u> but I object to
    (A)   (B)   (C)
how he said <u>it.</u> <u>No error</u>
    (D)   (E)

46. Neither he <u>nor</u> I <u>am</u> unwilling to <u>accept</u> <u>these</u> reasonable suggestions. <u>No error</u>
    (A)   (B)   (C)   (D)
    (E)

47. When the pipes <u>burst</u>, the sound was so <u>loud</u> that
    (A)   (B)
I <u>could not</u> hardly <u>bear</u> the pain in my ears. <u>No</u>
  (C)   (D)   (E)
error

48. My grandparents <u>had lived</u> in Brooklyn <u>long before</u>
    (A)   (B)
any bridge <u>connected up</u> Manhattan <u>with</u> Long
    (C)   (D)
Island. <u>No error</u>
    (E)

49. <u>May</u> we say that we do not want to <u>hear</u> <u>any more</u>
  (A)   (B)   (C)
about how she blames everything that goes wrong on him. <u>No error</u>
  (D)   (E)

50. Alice, accompanied by her classmates, <u>are</u> here concerning <u>your</u> objections to the <u>guests</u> they <u>chose</u> to
  (A)
  (B)   (C)   (D)
invite to the school dance. <u>No error</u>
  (E)

51. Without telling Rose or <u>us,</u> Frances <u>had sent</u> a
  (A)   (B)
note to everyone except <u>me</u>, demanding immediate
  (C)
payment of <u>their</u> pledge. <u>No error</u>
  (D)   (E)

52. In this <u>modern world of today</u>, there <u>is</u> so many
  (A)   (B)
more gadgets <u>than</u> our grandparents <u>had ever</u>
  (C)   (D)
<u>dreamed</u> possible. <u>No error</u>
    (E)

53. <u>Being a sensible person</u> does not mean <u>that you</u>
    (A)   (B)
<u>intend to</u> allow others to <u>push you</u> around. <u>No error</u>
  (C)   (D)   (E)

54. He <u>could have</u> <u>chosen</u> another <u>equally as good</u> without having to take <u>ours.</u> <u>No error</u>
    (A)   (B)   (C)
  (D)   (E)

55. It would be wise to decide that everyone <u>except</u> <u>her</u>
    (A)   (B)
<u>is</u> to be permitted to have <u>access</u> to the records.
  (C)   (D)
<u>No error</u>
  (E)

56. There <u>are</u> <u>nowheres</u> <u>nearly</u> enough food supplies
    (A)   (B)   (C)
for the long, cold months <u>ahead.</u> <u>No error</u>
    (D)   (E)

57. Who other than Jack and <u>I</u> <u>can</u> enjoy being isolated <u>by themselves</u> for hours <u>on end.</u> <u>No error</u>
    (A)(B)
  (C)   (D)   (E)

58. The problem <u>was when</u> a series of films <u>was</u> transferred <u>into</u> the permanent <u>files.</u> <u>No error</u>
    (A)   (B)
  (C)   (D)   (E)

59. The song he <u>wrote</u> was <u>sung</u> <u>continually</u> <u>over</u> this
    (A)   (B)   (C)   (D)
station until it caught the public's favor. <u>No error</u>
    (E)

60. When I <u>was graduated</u> <u>from</u> high school, there
    (A)   (B)
were scarcely <u>no</u> jobs <u>that</u> I could qualify for. <u>No</u>
(C)   (D)
error
(E)

61. Bring this recording to the dean so that he can
    (A)
    hear for himself what had really been said. No
    (B)   (C)   (D)
    error
    (E)

62. If anyone is interested, it has been quite some time
                   (A)   (B)   (C)
    since Henry and I had visited the farm. No error
                    (D)   (E)

63. Our old apartment is so large in size that we may
                                 (A)
    have to give away much of our furniture when we
    (B)   (C)
    move. No error
    (D)   (E)

64. His conception of the work to be done differs so
        (A)   (B)
    greatly with mine that I am completely perplexed.
           (C)   (D)
    No error
    (E)

65. This incredible record had been compiled at a
         (A)
    time when the company had many less employees.
        (B)   (C)   (D)
    No error
    (E)

66. You may have a loan of these data since they have
            (A)   (B)   (C)
    been adjusted for the latest changes. No error
                         (D)   (E)

67. The old car is lying somewheres on the desert
                   (A)   (B)   (C)
    floor, turning slowly into red dust. No error
                   (D)   (E)

68. Since I do not feel well, you had ought not to
                        (A)   (B)
    expect me to do so much of the organizing. No error
    (C)   (D)   (E)

69. A set of the company's books is in the safe so that
                                 (A)
    everyone of the officials is able to use it at all times.
    (B)   (C)   (D)
    No error
    (E)

70. Since there are only three to choose from, may I
                    (A)   (B)   (C)
    claim the latter. No error
              (D)   (E)

71. It does not make sense to me that up until yester-
                 (A)   (B)
    day he could have been jailed for life for this act!
           (C)   (D)
    No error
    (E)

72. To invest in a mutual fund as a kind of a forced
                   (A)   (B)
    savings, you must make arrangements with your
             (C)
    bank for an automatic withdrawal of funds. No
         (D)
    error
    (E)

73. The selfish acts perpetrated by Pauline and him
                     (A)   (B)
    should have resulted in the sort of behavior that
                                (C)
    mirrors what they have done. No error
                    (D)   (E)

74. If they had stayed at home more often, the situa-
           (A) (B)   (C)
    tion would be far different than it is. No error
                   (D)   (E)

PART 3 Suggested Time: 15 Minutes
Time begun .... Time ended .... Time used .....
Did you complete the section within the time limit? ..

DIRECTIONS: In each of the following sentences there is an underlined section that presents a problem in acceptable usage, diction (choice of words), sentence construction, or punctuation. Beneath each sentence are five ways of writing the underlined part.

Select A   if you think that the original is better
           than any of the changes.
Otherwise select the letter of the choice that is
           more effective and appropriate.

Do not choose any change that alters the meaning of the original sentence.

75. I had been reading widely for years which stood
    me in good stead when I went for the college
    interview.
    (a) which stood me in good stead when I went
    (b) , which stood me in good stead when I went
    (c) , which stood me in good stead when I had gone
    (d) which stayed me in good stead when I went
    (e) , a fact which stood me in good stead when I
        went

76. Henry's car is as good as if not better than that
    of his neighbor
    (a) Henry's car is as good as if not better than
    (b) Henry's car is as good if not better then
    (c) Henry's car is as good as if not better then
    (d) Henrys' car is as good as if not better then
    (e) Henrys' car is as good if not better than

77. Eating starchy foods, working long hours and
    without recreation makes any teenager much less
    efficient than he could be.
    (a) and without recreation makes any teenager
    (b) and without recreation make any teenager
    (c) without recreation makes any teenager
    (d) and avoiding recreation make
    (e) and avoiding recreation makes

78. This fact shall remain a barrier in the way of a peaceful setting, irregardless of where the blame lays.
    (a) , irregardless of where the blame lays
    (b) regardless of where the blame lays
    (c) regardless of where the blame has been laid
    (d) , regardless of where the blame lies
    (e) irregardless of where the blame lies

79. It is the kind of a argument that I find to painful to attempt to analyze or refute.
    (a) kind of a argument that I find to painful
    (b) kind of a argument that I find too painful
    (c) kind of argument that I find too painful
    (d) kind of an argument that I find to painful
    (e) kind of an argument that I find too painful

80. "You cannot do that!" he exclaimed. "You are destroying public property!"
    (a) that!" he exclaimed. "You
    (b) that!" he exclaimed, "you
    (c) that," he exclaimed! "you
    (d) that," he exclaimed" "You
    (e) that"! he exclaimed. "You

81. Everybody except Alan and she knew the effect of the drug.
    (a) except Alan and she knew the effect
    (b) except Alan and her knew the affect
    (c) except Alan and she knew the affect
    (d) except Alan and her knew the effect
    (e) except Alan and her new the affect

82. You cannot claim that you knew nothing about this, moreover you will have to share the responsibility for affecting a cure.
    (a) , moreover
    (b) moreover
    (c) ; moreover
    (d) . However
    (e) ; moreover,

83. The set of documents that you must not loose is on the desk.
    (a) that you must not loose is on
    (b) which you must not loose is on
    (c) that you must not lose is on
    (d) that you must not lose are on
    (e) which you must not lose are on

84. I plan to bring these here notes with me to the counsel.
    (a) bring these here notes with me to the counsel
    (b) take these notes with me to the council
    (c) take these here notes with me to the council
    (d) bring these notes with me to the consul
    (e) transport these here notes with me to the council

85. Dora is the sort of a secretary which I can trust.
    (a) sort of a secretary which I can trust.
    (b) sort of secretary who I can trust
    (c) sort of a secretary whom I can trust
    (d) sort of a secretary I can trust
    (e) sort of secretary I can trust

86. Knowing the cost of Tom's college education, his failure notice caused his parents untold anguish
    (a) Knowing the cost of Tom's college education,
    (b) Knowing the cost of Tom's college education
    (c) Since we knew the cost of Tom's college education,
    (d) Knowing the cost of Tom's college education, we realized that
    (e) Knowing the cost of Toms' college education,

ANSWER KEY AND ANALYSIS OF ANSWERS / *Page 131*

PRACTICE EXAMINATION FOUR

Total Time: One Hour
PART 1 *Suggested Time: 20 Minutes*
Time begun .... Time ended .... Time used ....
Did you complete the section within the time limit? ..

DIRECTIONS: Each of the following sentences has four parts underlined and numbered. Each sentence may contain *one* or *no* underlined section containing parts that may be unacceptable. If there is no underlined part requiring change, then circle (5) showing no error. Otherwise circle the number of the underlined portion that is not correct or is poorly expressed.

1. Everyone of us who were(1) present assumes(2) that the winner will be she,(3) barring(4) any unexpected turn of events. No error(5)

2. Alfred is one who(1) seems to like Helen better than(2) us, irregardless(3) of how much we try to please(4) him. No error(5)

3. The decision must be their's(1) ;(2) however much we try(3) , our next step can only be made with their full(4) consent. No error(5)

4. "May I have the next dance?(1) " he asked?(2) "It(3) is the last one of the evening.(4) " No error(5)

5. If the loser in the contest turns out to be him(1) ;(2) I shall(3) have had hardly any(4) opportunity to speak with

him. No error
      (5)

6. I just cannot leave the book lay on the floor without
                 (1)   (2)
   telling you and her that you had better pick it up
                    (3)   (4)
   immediately. No error
                (5)

7. That there is a army of ants sharing our lunch with
   (1)   (2)
   us would have come to my attention sooner or later.
      (3)   (4)
   No error
   (5)

8. Flying high above the weather, clouds obscured our
                         (1)   (2)
   view of the earth below ; consequently , we had to
                          (3)   (4)
   rely solely upon the instruments. No error
                                     (5)

9. Providing you listen carefully, you will be able to do
   (1)   (2)
   the work as well as I without any assistance from
                       (3)
   them. No error
   (4)   (5)

10. Dickens's books are among my brother's most pre-
    (1)   (2)
    cious possessions. Each being more cherished than
                       (3)   (4)
    the next. No error
              (5)

11. Worrying , fretting , and unable to stop talking,
    (1)   (2)   (3)
    Harry paced up and down the corridor. No error
    (4)   (5)

12. Because I had hardly no time to lose . Paula, along
                         (1)   (2) (3)
    with the fourteen other members of the committee,
    was notified of our decision. No error
    (4)   (5)

13. Who shall I blame when it's time for the group and
    (1)   (2)
    us to make our report , and we shall have to report
    (3)   (4)
    that we are unprepared? No error
                            (5)

14. My brothers-in-law's storage facilities far exceeds
       (1)   (2)   (3)
    ours. No error
    (4)   (5)

15. There are three errors in the manuscript : there
                                              (1) (2)
    are four misspelled do's ; two words omitted, and a
                         (3) (4)

period used instead of a question mark. No error
                                        (5)

16. You will be graduated from high school in a few
                (1)
    days; you should make an appointment to see the
        (2)   (3)
    officer , who is in charge of the trainee program.
            (4)
    No error
    (5)

17. Let's come to one basic conclusion : if we're to
    (1)   (2)   (3)
    put our savings in stocks and bonds, we must first
                    (4)
    hire a qualified consultant. No error
                                 (5)

18. One of the workers has accidently overturned the
                       (1) (2)
    pail which was laying on the kitchen floor. No error
    (3)   (4)   (5)

19. He spoke out of turn when he allowed that except
              (1)   (2)
    for you and me none of the members was interested
              (3)   (4)
    in the matter. No error
                   (5)

20. Anyone who asserts that he may become mad every-
                (1)   (2)   (3)
    time a friend disagrees with him will soon be with-
                                  (4)
    out friends. No error
                 (5)

21. My old , brown hat and several of my sisters' skirts
        (1)   (2)
    were badly soiled when the package fell from the
    (3) (4)
    back of the truck. No error
                       (5)

22. His father , whose a well-known philanthropist, do-
              (1) (2) (3)   (4)
    nated the initial sum to our building fund. No error
                                                (5)

23. My marks in English and Mathematics were higher
                            (1)
    than or equal to theirs. No error
    (2)   (3) (4)   (5)

24. Anywheres you travel in this area you will lose much
    (1)   (2)   (3)
    time if you fail to read the road signs carefully. No
                                            (4)
    error
    (5)

25. Since they had arrived at around seven in the eve-
                 (1)   (2)
    ning, everybody but you and us was at the station
                                (3) (4)
    to greet them. No error
                   (5)

26. I may not be so capable as you, but when I want to
    (1)   (2)
    do something badly enough, my work is superior to
                  (3)
    yours. No error
    (4)   (5)

27. Being that neither Herbert nor I am scheduled to
    (1)   (2) (3)
    play in that game, the coach told Herbert and me
                                                  (4)
    that we were excused from the practice sessions.
    No error
    (5)

28. I do not question but what he has made a serious
                      (1)
    error in assuming that the man whom we had seen
              (2)   (3)
    could be responsible for this confusion. No error
             (4)   (5)

29. Is it I who am to ever stand between you and him?
         (1) (2) (3)   (4)
    No error
    (5)

30. Am I to assume, therefore, that it is the consensus
            (1)   (2)
    of opinion in this group that they are more accurate
    (3)
    than we? No error
         (4) (5)

31. Thomas' method differs with yours in one very im-
    (1)   (2)
    portant aspect—his greater emphases in the fields of
                  (3)   (4)
    safety. No error
            (5)

32. Here come the group of astronauts who are to lead
         (1)   (2)
    in man's exploration of outer space. No error
    (3) (4)   (5)

33. The committee are unable to agree on whom they
                   (1)   (2) (3)
    should elect to replace Jensen and her. No error
                                       (4) (5)

PART 2 *Suggested Time: 20 Minutes*
Time begun .... Time ended .... Time used .....
Did you complete the section within the time limit? ..

DIRECTIONS: Read each of the following sentences carefully. Then circle the appropriate letter in the answer column

(a) if the sentence contains faulty diction
(b) if the sentence is wordy
(c) if the sentence contains cliches or inappropriate metaphors
(d) if the sentence contains faulty grammar or sentence structure
(e) if the sentence contains none of these errors

34. Ever since that incident she is seldom ever at home alone.   34. a b c d e
35. Paul along with his three brothers was summoned to appear in court to testify in this case.   35. a b c d e
36. He tried to swim in the treacherous channels of international intrigue before his wings had mature strength.   36. a b c d e
37. I know that somewheres in this vast city there must be someone who will believe my side of the story.   37. a b c d e
38. We put all of our hopes in this one basket and waited for either success or abject failure.   38. a b c d e
39. Of all the possible avenues of escape, you chose the one with the least chance of success.   39. a b c d e
40. If he would have listened to the instructions, this model would be on display by now.   40. a b c d e
41. This is another one of those cases that are beyond my belief.   41. a b c d e
42. The final conclusion was reached when we realized that there was nothing to be gained by continuing our efforts.   42. a b c d e
43. His answer was basically the same as mine; however, his delivery was much smoother.   43. a b c d e
44. Too long have I looked at the seamy side of life, and I yearn to see signs that could point toward the existence of simple joys.   44. a b c d e
45. These kinds of explanations always make me suspect the motives of the speakers.   45. a b c d e
46. His approach is different in various ways from the one that we advocate at the present.   46. a b c d e
47. The seas of uncertitude engulf me and fill my being with the black thoughts of despair.   47. a b c d e
48. She is another one of those people which I have learned to admire for their depth of understanding and tact.   48. a b c d e
49. Following the last curtain call of the star of the show, what additional attraction could be appropriate and timely!   49. a b c d e
50. The dean told him that he would be the one who would be responsible for any damage that resulted from the effort.   50. a b c d e
51. He chose a model that was an appropriate gray in color.   51. a b c d e
52. The meeting will commence after we have combined together the three proposals into one.   52. a b c d e
53. All that I can say is that these here are the very ones I would have chosen.   53. a b c d e
54. He hopes to follow in the footsteps of his father who had been an instructor in the local high school for many years.   54. a b c d e
55. Irregardless of what you say, I intend to see that these instructions are carried out.   55. a b c d e
56. This is another problem that can be settled only if there is understanding between you and I.   56. a b c d e

57. Optimism is that cheerful frame of mind that enables a tea kettle to sing though in hot water up to its nose. 57. a b c d e
58. The opportunity for doing mischief is found a hundred times a day, and to do good only once in a year. 58. a b c d e
59. It did my heart good to hear the children tell of the advantages found in living in our country. 59. a b c d e
60. When in doubt, three spoons of the medicine is the maximum that can be given to adults. 60. a b c d e
61. How long do you intend to continue blaming your own weaknesses on others! 61. a b c d e
62. Morality is the best of all devices for leading mankind by the nose. 62. a b c d e
63. She acts toward me as though I was a complete stranger. 63. a b c d e
64. Either treat them both alike or you will have serious misunderstandings with them. 64. a c b d e
65. He plans to arrive in town at about three in the afternoon. 65. a b c d e
66. The thoughts flowed through his mind with such intensity that they pushed all else out of his consciousness. 66. a b c d e
67. Shouting from the bottom of the stairwell, his voice could be heard on the top floor. 67. a b c d e
68. Nowheres in the entire world is there another like him! 68. a b c d e
69. The greater the philosopher, the harder it is for him to answer the questions of the average man. 69. a b c d e

PART 3 Suggested Time: 20 Minutes
Time begun .... Time ended .... Time used ....
Did you complete the section within the time limit? ..

DIRECTIONS: Read each of the following sentences carefully. Then rephrase it according to the directives which follow it. Select from the choices (A) through (E) the word or entire phrase that is included in your revised sentence. The choice should be part of a sentence that is accurate and complete. Make only those changes that the directions require.

70. To do good is merely to feed one's ego.
    Begin with *He insists that doing*.
    (A) to feed merely
    (B) merely to have fed
    (C) merely to have been feeding
    (D) feeding my ego merely
    (E) merely feeding

71. Giant turtles move so slowly on land that we often come to the conclusion that they are ill-adapted to their environment.
    Begin with *That they move so slowly*.
    (A) is the reason why
    (B) reason for our coming
    (C) conclusion; giant turtles
    (D) conclusion giant
    (E) environment, is

72. The performance scheduled for tonight may have to be postponed; the star performer was taken ill suddenly.
    Begin with *Because*.
    (A) had to be
    (B) postponing the performance
    (C) suddenly, the
    (D) would have been
    (E) ill, and the

73. If I am called in as a witness, I shall testify that no one of my friends has even seen a copy of the letter.
    Substitute *some* for *no one*.
    (A) friends, has even
    (B) friends have even
    (C) friends had even
    (D) friends even has
    (E) friends has even

74. With the approach of autumn, the nights have become cold and crisp, and the leaves of the surrounding forest are beginning to turn.
    Begin with *When the nights became*.
    (A) autumn, and the
    (B) turn with the approach
    (C) leaves began
    (D) crisp; with
    (E) autumn, the

75. We did not need an expensive survey team to tell us that Mr. Pollett is the most efficient diagnostician in our division.
    Substitute *more efficient* for *the most efficient*.
    (A) than any one
    (B) than some of
    (C) any diagnostician
    (D) any other diagnostician
    (E) diagnostician

76. I just do not know what he was referring to when he asked who can measure the worth of the dollars that are squandered in the name of vanity.
    Change *dollars* to *money*.
    (A) that have been squandered
    (B) squandering
    (C) which has been squandered
    (D) that is squandered
    (E) money, which

77. It was evidenced in his disregard of our comfort that he was willing to be impatient with us.
    Begin with *when*.
    (A) us. It was
    (B) us, and this was
    (C) us and it was
    (D) us; and it was
    (E) us, it

78. These songs are the ones that we remember longest since they are the ones which were taught us in our childhood.
    Begin with *These songs taught*.
    (A) childhood are
    (B) childhood; are
    (C) ones. We
    (D) ones, we
    (E) longest are

79. Known for the excellence of its products, this fine small company employs only people living in the surrounding community.
    Substitute *which is known* for *known*.
    (A) company is
    (B) company, which
    (C) products. Employs
    (D) has been employing
    (E) company. Which
80. Harold insisted on continuing the journey even though he knew what my reaction would be.
    Omit *even though*, and use *nevertheless*.
    (A) journey, nevertheless,
    (B) be; nevertheless,
    (C) journey; nevertheless
    (D) continuing, nevertheless,
    (E) Nevertheless Harold
81. The Pulvers are the ones who will have to determine the lowest selling price since they are the owners of the property.
    Omit *since they are*.
    (A) price. The
    (B) price, the
    (C) property. The
    (D) Pulvers, the
    (E) ones, owners
82. Speaking before huge audiences of students, the Rhodes scholar tried to communicate to them his intense insights into world problems.
    Substitute *The Rhodes scholar spoke* for *Speaking*.
    (A) after he tried
    (B) having tried
    (C) and tried
    (D) while he was trying
    (E) since he tried
83. Mr Arnold is my former college counselor, and I often turn to him for advice.
    Begin with *Because*.
    (A) advice, Mr. Arnold
    (B) counselor, I
    (C) Mr. Arnold, counselor
    (D) Mr. Arnold, I
    (E) advice. I
84. Fashions are not brought about by changes in man's needs, but they come about as the result of whim and chance.
    Omit *they*.
    (A) needs. But
    (B) but coming
    (C) needs; but
    (D) needs, but
    (E) but come
85. The task became an endless series of trials and errors when we tried to assemble the mechanism without resorting to the set of instructions.
    Begin with *Without resorting*.
    (A) instructions. We
    (B) instructions. The
    (C) errors, when
    (D) mechanism when
    (E) mechanism, the

ANSWER KEY AND ANALYSIS OF ANSWERS / Page 133

PRACTICE EXAMINATION FIVE

Total time: One Hour
PART 1 *Suggested Time: 20 Minutes*
Time begun .... Time ended .... Time used ....
Did you complete the section within the time limit? ..

DIRECTIONS: Each of the following sentences has four parts underlined and numbered. Each sentence may contain one or no underlined section containing parts that may be unacceptable. If there is no underlined part requiring change, then circle (5) showing no error. Otherwise circle the number of the underlined portion that is not correct or is poorly expressed.

1. We felt <u>like</u> we <u>had</u> lost a friend when the foreman
         (1)   (2)
    along with his four assistants <u>was</u> <u>summarily</u> discharged. <u>No error</u>
         (3)   (4)
         (5)

2. <u>Except</u> you follow directions, the set of books <u>which</u>
     (1)   (2)
    <u>are</u> now on the shelves <u>is</u> going to be assigned to another class. <u>No error</u>
     (3)   (4)
         (5)

3. I insist that there <u>are</u> <u>less</u> errors <u>being</u> made in our division than in <u>yours</u>. <u>No error</u>
                   (1) (2)   (3)
                (4)   (5)

4. Three men entered the room — his commanding
                          (1)
    officer, his <u>buddy</u>, and his <u>fellow</u> prisoner. <u>No error</u>
          (2)   (3)   (4)   (5)

5. Anyone who <u>thinks</u> that I am <u>in back of</u> all of this
            (1)   (2)
    planning is <u>reckoning</u> in the wrong <u>set</u> of books.
          (3)   (4)
    <u>No error</u>
    (5)

6. His contention <u>is</u> that clothes <u>does</u> not make the
         (1)   (2)
    man<u>;</u> consequently<u>,</u> I do not see how you can convince him to buy that new suit. <u>No error</u>
     (3)   (4)
         (5)

7. The moment at which Albert and <u>she</u> could <u>have</u>
                            (1)   (2)
    interfered <u>was</u> when the car left without <u>us</u>. <u>No error</u>
         (3)   (4)
    (5)

8. "Nelson," she shouted, "<u>how</u> can you <u>let</u> this op-
     (1)   (2) (3)   (4)

portunity slip out of your grasp!" No error
                                      (5)

9. Either Jane or her brother is to be here inside of ten
                               (1)   (2)
   minutes to speak to you in regard to the kind of re-
                            (3)   (4)
   ception we should be planning. No error
                                  (5)

10. The summer residents of Luzerne, they told the
                                      (1)
    supervisor to let matters lie just as they are for the
                   (2)   (3)   (4)
    time being. No error
                (5)

11. All that they could see were their chances of losing
                              (1) (2)   (3)
    out without support from you and us. No error
    (4)   (5)

12. If they had only listened to me, we would have seen
            (1) (2)   (3)
    a most interesting film, because he was prepared
                           (4)
    to show it to us at that time. No error
                                   (5)

13. Helen, one of the girls in the office, told Mrs.
         (1)   (2)
    Mackey that she had mistakenly identified the
                  (3)   (4)
    wrong person. No error
                  (5)

14. The advise that he gave us to accept your apologies
        (1)   (2)
    was altogether unfortunate and should have in no
        (3)   (4)
    way affected our decision. No error
                               (5)

15. Neither of the boys who have been helping us knows
                              (1)   (2)
    when this game will be over with. No error
                              (3) (4) (5)

16. Standing beside the machine, we could not identify
             (1)   (2)(3)
    any of the occupants except Lucy and her. No error
                                           (4) (5)

17. Whenever we watch an exciting television pro-
    gram, the main concern of my cousin is whether the
         (1)   (2)   (3)   (4)
    advertisement will break in before or after the big
    rescue scene. No error
                  (5)

18. "I should never have listened to you, George," Mr.
                                       (1)   (2)
    Worthington exclaimed. "You misled me com-
                          (3) (4)
    pletely!" No error
              (5)

19. The counsel for the defense complemented Joyce's
        (1)   (2)   (3)
    father for his disinterested presentation when he
                   (4)
    was a witness giving testimony. No error
                                    (5)

20. The porter told us that he had not felt good when
                                (1)   (2)(3)
    the effect of the injection finally wore off. No error
        (4)   (5)

21. Repeating again the main point of my argument,
              (1)
    the danger that faces us can hardly be overcome by
        (2)   (3)   (4)
    men of good will without training in the tactics of
    modern warfare. No error
                    (5)

22. This sort of nonsense usually appeals to those stu-
         (1)
    dents who I referred to earlier in this article. No
         (2)   (3) (4)
    error
    (5)

23. Please try and understand; there was so little that
               (1)   (2)(3)
    we guards were able to do to prevent such an out-
    (4)
    break. No error
           (5)

24. One of the workers has hung the curtains that had
                       (1) (2)   (3)
    been laying on the floor. No error
         (4)   (5)

25. The well-trained nurse quickly noticed the change
         (1)   (2)
    in the babies' behavior; and called for the doctor
           (3)   (4)
    immediately. No error
                 (5)

26. Victor commented: "Let's end this petty quarrel-
                   (1) (2)
    ing; there's so many things that we really have do
    (3) (4)
    be doing!" No error
               (5)

27. Neither Edna nor her sisters knows to whom this
                 (1)   (2)   (3)
    kind of note must be sent. No error
    (4)   (5)

28. The ending is so different from the one that you and
                                (1)
    I am willing to accept, even in a third-rate story. No
      (2)   (3)   (4)
    error
    (5)

29. Take this book to the principal who was so aggra-
    (1)   (2)   (3)   (4)
    vated when he discovered that it had been borrowed

without his permission. No error
                   (5)

30. Since one of the teachers has objected to him having
    (1)   (2)
    the main role in the varsity play, we have had to
        (3) (4)
    make a last-minute substitution. No error
                                     (5)

31. If you would have listened, you too would have con-
           (1)   (2)
    cluded that Peter is more capable than any other
                      (3)   (4)
    boy in his class. No error
                      (5)

32. I had not drank more than half the coffee in the
                 (1)   (2)
    container when the alarm sounded , sending me
              (3)   (4)
    hurtling through space! No error
                            (5)

33. The e's in this manuscript look too much like i's ,
        (1)   (2)(3)
    moreover , the spacing between the words is much
            (4)
    too cramped. No error
                 (5)

PART 2 Suggested Time: 20 Minutes
Time begun .... Time ended .... Time used .....
Did you complete the section within the time limit? ..

DIRECTIONS: In each of the following sentences there is an underlined section that presents a problem in acceptable usage in grammar, diction (choice of words), sentence construction, or punctuation. Beneath each sentence are five ways of writing the underlined part.
  Select A   if you think the original is better than any of the changes.
  Otherwise   select the letter of the choice that is more effective and appropriate.
Do not choose any change that alters the meaning of the original sentence.

34. They must either choose the plans we proposed or the ones approved by the preceding administration.
 (A) must either choose the plans we proposed
 (B) either must choose the plans we proposed
 (C) must choose either the plans we proposed
 (D) either have to chose the plans we proposed
 (E) have either to choose the plans we proposed

35. If the official would have consulted his staff, this embarrassing situation would never have arisen.
 (A) If the official would have consulted his staff, this
 (B) If the official would have consulted his staff this
 (C) If the official would have consulted his staff. This
 (D) If the official were to consult his staff, this
 (E) If the official had consulted his staff, this

36. The contractor hoped to have completed the building on schedule, but the floods were disrupting deliveries of supplies.
 (A) hoped to have completed
 (B) had hoped to complete
 (C) had hoped to have completed
 (D) would have completed
 (E) could have completed

37. Due to his carelessness, the form of the data is different from what the computer can assimilate.
 (A) Due to his carelessness, the form of the data is different from what
 (B) Because of his carelessness, the form of the data is different from what
 (C) Due to his carelessness. The form of the data is different from what
 (D) Due to his carelessness, the form of the data are different from that which
 (E) Because of his carelessness, the form of the data is different than that which

38. They claimed that it was the responsibility of us students to see that no one of the intruders were admitted.
 (A) us students to see that no one of the intruders were
 (B) us students, to see that not one of the intruders were
 (C) we students, to see that no one of the intruders were
 (D) us students to see that no one of the intruders was
 (E) we students to see that no one of the intruders was

39. My family lived in this town for three generations.
 (A) lived in this town
 (B) is living in this town
 (C) is living in this here town
 (D) has been living in this here town
 (E) has lived in this town

40. The salesman assured us that if we placed the order by nine we could have the car fully equipped.
 (A) that if we placed the order by nine
 (B) that, if we placed the order by nine;
 (C) that if we had placed the order by nine
 (D) that if we were to place the order by nine
 (E) that if by nine we had placed the order

41. The director stated that he had never been consulted on the changes before they were made.
 (A) he had never been consulted on the changes before they were made.
 (B) he was never consulted on the changes before they had been made.
 (C) he had never been consulted on the changes before they had been made.
 (D) he was never consulted on the changes before they were made.
 (E) he was never consulted on the changes, before they were being made.

42. When in doubt, the best approach is to consult an expert.
 (A) when in doubt, the
 (B) When in doubt the
 (C) When you are in doubt, the

(D) When you are in doubt the
(E) When one is in doubt; the

43. There must be a moral to this story, but somehow it eludes me.
(A) moral to this story, but somehow it
(B) moral to this story but somehow it
(C) moral to this story, however, it somehow
(D) moral to this story because it
(E) moral to this story. Since it somehow

44. Everyone of her classmates except Edna and me were invited to the gathering.
(A) except Edna and me were invited
(B) except Edna and I was invited
(C) except Edna and me was
(D) accept Edna and me were
(E) except Edna and I, were

45. Statistics the invention of devils and saints can easily confuse us into inactivity.
(A) Statistics the invention of devils and saints can
(B) Statistics, the invention of devils and saints, can
(C) Statistics are the invention of devils and saints, and can
(D) Statistics, the invention of devils and saints can
(E) Statistics—the invention of devils and saints, can

46. You hadn't ought to have said that the candidate must be him.
(A) You hadn't ought to have said that the candidate must be him.
(B) You hadn't ought to say that he must be the candidate.
(C) You shouldn't have said that the candidate must be him.
(D) You hadn't ought to have said that the candidate must be he.
(E) You should not have said that the candidate must be he.

47. At thirty, his reputation for honesty and forthrightness was one of his most valuable business assets.
(A) At thirty, his reputation for honesty and forthrightness was
(B) On reaching thirty, his reputation for honesty and forthrightness was
(C) When he was thirty, his reputation for honesty and forthrightness was
(D) When he reached his thirtieth birthday, he was known for the honesty and forthrightness which were
(E) By the time he was thirty, his reputation for honesty and forthrightness were

48. If I was the chairperson, I would never have tolerated such rowdyism and flagrant disregard of decorum.
(A) If I was the chairperson, I
(B) If I were the chairperson, I
(C) If I had been the chairperson, I
(D) If I am chosen as chairperson, I
(E) If I was the chairperson; I

49. This pottery is better or at least equal to the very best that was produced in the last generation.
(A) better or at least equal to
(B) better than or at least equal to
(C) at least better than or equal to
(D) at least better or equal to
(E) better or at least the equal to

50. Having worked beside him for years, his decision to leave the firm does not surprise me.
(A) Having worked beside him for years, his
(B) Having worked beside him for years. His
(C) Having worked beside him for years his
(D) Since I had worked beside him for years, his
(E) Because of my having worked besides him for years, his

51. His reasoning during the discussion was logical, clear, and with much persuasive power.
(A) was logical, clear, and with much persuasive power.
(B) logical and clear and with much persuasive power.
(C) logical, clear, and highly persuasive.
(D) logical, clear; and highly persuasive power.
(E) logical, clear, and with much persuasion.

52. The slow solemn strains of the organ music flooded the room; it was a time for quiet meditation.
(A) room; it was
(B) room, and it was
(C) room, when it was
(D) room since it became
(E) room while it was

53. There never has been as far as I know any other short story collections to match these.
(A) There never has been as far as I know any
(B) Never has there been, as far as I know, any
(C) There never have been as far as I know
(D) Never has there been as far as I know any
(E) There never could have been—as far as I know—any

54. Without him helping us, everyone in our squad know that we could never have succeeded.
(A) Without him helping us, everyone in our squad know that
(B) Without him helping us everyone in our squad knows that
(C) Unless he helped, everyone in our squad know that
(D) Without help from him everyone in the squad knows that
(E) Without his help, everyone in our squad knows that

55. We not only enjoyed seeing our relatives but also visiting their homes.
(A) We not only enjoyed seeing our relatives but also visiting their homes.
(B) We not only enjoyed seeing our relatives but also to visit their homes.
(C) We not only enjoyed to see our relatives, but also to visit their homes.
(D) We enjoyed seeing our relatives and to visit their homes.
(E) We enjoyed not only seeing our relatives but also visiting their homes.

56. Because of the weakness of the UN, man's inhumanity to man reigns unabated.
(A) Because of the weakness of the UN, man's
(B) Because of the weakness of the UN. Man's
(C) Because of the weakness of the UN mans'
(D) Due to the weakness of the UN man's
(E) The weakness of the UN causes mans'

57. <u>Neither Sheldon nor I is ready to decide who is to be the winner.</u>
 (A) Neither Sheldon nor I is ready to decide who is
 (B) Neither Sheldon nor I is ready to decide whom is
 (C) Neither Sheldon or I is ready to decide who is
 (D) Neither Sheldon nor I am ready to decide who is
 (E) Neither Sheldon or me is ready to decide who is

58. <u>He accepted full responsibility for something he had not done, which</u> surprised me very much.
 (A) He accepted full responsibility for something he had not done, which
 (B) His accepting full responsibility for something he had not done
 (C) He excepted responsibility for something he had not done, which
 (D) He accepted responsibility for something he had not done, this
 (E) He accepted responsibility for something he had not done; which

59. <u>Had he spoken up, there</u> would have been no confusion.
 (A) Had he spoken up, there
 (B) He could have spoken up, so that there
 (C) If he would have spoken up, there
 (D) Had he spoken up; there
 (E) If he were to speak up, there

60. The most exciting scene <u>is when the countdown begins.</u>
 (A) is when the countdown begins.
 (B) was when the countdown begins.
 (C) occurs when the countdown begins.
 (D) is where the countdown began.
 (E) is where the countdown begins.

61. <u>My parents lived in that house before I was born!</u>
 (A) My parents lived in that house before I was born!
 (B) My parents had lived in that house before I was born!
 (C) Before I was born my parents lived in that house!
 (D) My parents lived in that house, before I was born!
 (E) Before I was born, my parents lived in that house!

62. <u>Being Harriet had warned me, I was not</u> surprised by what I saw.
 (A) Being Harriet had warned me, I was
 (B) Being Harriet warned me, I am
 (C) Since Harriet warned me, I am
 (D) Since Harriet had warned me, I was
 (E) Being Harriet warned me, I was

63. Feigning illness, procrastinating at every opportunity, and <u>without any of the controls that truth sets, he</u> amazed us by retaining the job for three whole days!
 (A) without any of the controls that truth sets, he
 (B) without the controls that truth sets. He
 (C) prevaricating constantly, he
 (D) without the controls that truth sets; he
 (E) lying, he

PART 3 *Suggested Time: 20 Minutes*
Time begun ..... Time ended ..... Time used .....
Did you complete the section within the time limit?...

DIRECTIONS: Read each of the following sentences carefully. Then rephrase it according to the directions which follow it. Select from the choices (A) through (E) the word or entire phrase that is included in your revised sentence. The choice should be part of a sentence that is accurate and complete. Make only those changes that the directions require.

64. Everyone of the men caught in the deadly trap will be remembered as heroes who died for their countrymen.
 Begin with <u>We will remember</u>.
 (A) were caught
 (B) men, who
 (C) had been caught
 (D) remember, everyone
 (E) trap, as

65. Calling him a falsifier did not help to make our relationships any the more cordial.
 Begin with <u>I had not helped</u>.
 (A) by having called him
 (B) by calling him
 (C) falsifier I had
 (D) because I could have called
 (E) although I called

66. The new evidence along with the facts that had been gathered for the earlier trial is sufficient to free him.
 Change <u>along with</u> to <u>and</u>.
 (A) facts, that
 (B) facts, which
 (C) evidence, and
 (D) trial, is
 (E) trial are

67. Hoping to end the tournament quickly, the champion defeated his first opponent in straight sets.
 Begin with <u>His first opponent was defeated</u>.
 (A) champion, who
 (B) who had hoped
 (C) quickly in straight sets
 (D) sets, by
 (E) champion who

68. Konner is one of those men who have devoted a lifetime to the study of past cultures.
 Substitute <u>a man</u> for <u>one of those men</u>.
 (A) to have devoted
 (B) who has
 (C) that have
 (D) devoting
 (E) , devoting

69. Paul and Dave have been selected to represent us at the conference.
 Substitute <u>Either Paul or Dave</u> for <u>Paul and Dave</u>.
 (A) have been selected
 (B) had been selected
 (C) were selected
 (D) has been selected
 (E) is selected

PRACTICE EXAMINATIONS FOR THE ENGLISH COMPOSITION TEST

70. Mel told Margie, "You are to leave at ten tonight."
    Substitute <u>Margie that she</u> for <u>Margie, "You.</u>
    (A) is to leave
    (B) could leave
    (C) had to leave
    (D) was leaving
    (E) should have left
71. This model, like all the others that preceded it, is too bulky and fragile.
    Substitute <u>and its predecessors</u> for <u>like all the others that preceded it</u>.
    (A) model, and
    (B) which are
    (C) predecessors, is
    (D) are too
    (E) had been too
72. Mahogany is the best wood for making this type of castenet.
    Substitute <u>better than</u> for <u>the best</u>.
    (A) any other
    (B) any wood
    (C) could be
    (D) type of a
    (E) wood, for
73. I read all the directions, and I could find no mention of a set of gears.
    Use the present thought sequence, and begin with <u>Although</u>.
    (A) I read
    (B) I would read
    (C) I was reading
    (D) I had read
    (E) directions I
74. To be able to sing like Joan Sutherland is beyond my wildest dream.
    Begin with <u>I cannot imagine</u>.
    (A) as Joan Sutherland
    (B) ever being able
    (C) never being able
    (D) Sutherland's singing
    (E) my having been able
75. He answered me in anger, a fact that irritated me very much.
    Begin with <u>His answering</u>.
    (A) which
    (B) I was very much irritated
    (C) anger he
    (D) the fact
    (E) anger irritated
76. They came into the house and were greeted by the visitor from their hometown.
    Begin with <u>The visitor who had just arrived</u>.
    (A) greeted from their hometown
    (B) when they had come
    (C) from his hometown
    (D) when they did come
    (E) greeted them
77. If you had listened to me, we could have completed the project in record time.
    Change <u>If</u> to <u>Because</u>.
    (A) completed
    (B) should have completed
    (C) had been completing
    (D) would have been able to complete
    (E) you would have listened
78. Both Edna and her sisters are insisting that we join them in the hike.
    Change <u>Both Edna and</u> to <u>Edna along with</u>.
    (A) had been insisting
    (B) sisters,
    (C) is insisting
    (D) insisting. We
    (E) insisting, we

ANSWER KEY AND ANALYSIS / *Page 135*

PRACTICE EXAMINATION SIX

Total Time: One Hour
PART 1 *Suggested Time: 25 Minutes*
Time begun ..... Time ended ..... Time used .....
Did you complete the section within the time limit? ...

DIRECTIONS: Read each of the following sentences carefully. Then circle the appropriate number in the answer column
1. if the sentence contains an error in diction
2. if the sentence contains an error in grammatical usage
3. if the sentence contains a cliche or a mixed metaphor
4. if the sentence is verbose or contains a redundant phrase
5. if the sentence contains none of these errors

1. Gentlemen, let us concentrate on these data that we have before us and use them as the sole bases for our conclusions.   1. 1 2 3 4 5
2. From all indications it would seem like they will win unless they become impatient and rush into battle before they are fully prepared.
    2. 1 2 3 4 5
3. Magellan may very well have circumnavigated around the globe with greater safety than I negotiated the distance from town to our house over that icy road.   3. 1 2 3 4 5
4. In our final report we plan to state that we have found that your workmanship is equally as good as it was last year.   4. 1 2 3 4 5
5. Only after long hours of tedious research was the historian able to ascertain that at the age of ten, Clark's father had died.   5. 1 2 3 4 5
6. Cancer, the scourge of modern man, has swept too many of our leaders to untimely deaths.
    6. 1 2 3 4 5
7. The dean told the gathering of student leaders that this was the kind of a meeting that would lead to an improvement in student government.
    7. 1 2 3 4 5
8. I hope that once you have come to a full realization of the fix that I am in you will understand why I have become so short-tempered.
    8. 1 2 3 4 5
9. I can never have enough activity crammed into my waking hours when I realize the brevity of life, the

unexpected quirks of fate, and friends who soon turn faithless. 9. 1 2 3 4 5

10. Using the atom bomb as his key to world conquest, the dictator attempted to stamp out the democratic elements of the world. 10. 1 2 3 4 5

11. I still insist that his workmanship is better or a least equal to the very best that they are capable of producing. 11. 1 2 3 4 5

12. When you leave this room, you will definitely discover inside of a very brief time how little you contributed to the discussion. 12. 1 2 3 4 5

13. Now that we have reached the moment when frankness is essential, I can tell you that the reason you were not elected president is simply because we had felt that you were much too self-centered. 13. 1 2 3 4 5

14. So long as there is an ounce of strength left in my body, I shall do all that I can to thwart your vicious schemes! 14. 1 2 3 4 5

15. Sylvia Warner finally admitted that she is not so agile as she had once been. 15. 1 2 3 4 5

16. When the committee had launched its inquiry into malpractices among local physicians, the welfare department proved a mine of information for the investigators. 16. 1 2 3 4 5

17. I shall be forced to answer in the negative if I am one of those requested to express a willingness to participate in the approaching festivities. 17. 1 2 3 4 5

18. Sleep is truly the balm of hurt minds, soothing with drops of forgetfulness where no man-made remedy may be effective. 18. 1 2 3 4 5

19. It was an sordid story of ever-mounting troubles and incredulous courage in the face of inevitable defeat. 19. 1 2 3 4 5

20. If I was the writer of that story, I am certain that I could have evolved a more logical conclusion. 20. 1 2 3 4 5

21. Tired as we were, we could not refuse their gracious offer and joined them at the festive table as they partook of the abundant supply of refreshments. 21. 1 2 3 4 5

22. If you are willing to conform and think exactly what the other members do and think, you will never be singled out for censure. 22. 1 2 3 4 5

23. The tickets will be sent to whomever the treasurer declares eligible. 23. 1 2 3 4 5

24. Only one who had experienced the horrors of withdrawal would have recoiled so forcefully at the sight of the pep pills. 24. 1 2 3 4 5

25. When our ship comes in, I expect to be firmly established in the driver's seat. 25. 1 2 3 4 5

26. Our mayor has always had a deep interest for youth's struggle for identity. 26. 1 2 3 4 5

27. By the time he was twenty, Van Cinter's style was ranked with the greatest painters. 27. 1 2 3 4 5

28. The orchestra will be led by a local conductor whom in my opinion is as good as or even better than those with international reputations. 28. 1 2 3 4 5

29. Asiatic influenza is a dreaded communicable disease that is transferred from one person to another. 29. 1 2 3 4 5

30. For over a year now, ham and eggs have been in short supply throughout our urban areas. 30. 1 2 3 4 5

31. The outcome is so different than what I had hoped it would be! 31. 1 2 3 4 5

32. Fanned by the heat of ambition, he spent endless hours in a vain attempt to achieve perfection. 32. 1 2 3 4 5

33. We may have lost in this last election; nevertheless, we are now planning our campaign for the next one. 33. 1 2 3 4 5

34. The mechanic proved easily that the old engine could be made to run as smooth as ever. 34. 1 2 3 4 5

35. What could be more preferable to a life of self-fulfillment through helping others. 35. 1 2 3 4 5

36. The least we can promise youth is economic security from the cradle to the grave. 36. 1 2 3 4 5

37. It is up to we students to see that our school does not become a symbol of bigotry and prejudice. 37. 1 2 3 4 5

38. My grandfather is one of the men who was fortunate enough to have worked with John Kennedy. 38. 1 2 3 4 5

39. When I consider how fortunate we are in our choice of city officials, I shudder to think of what the consequences would have been had the tides of fortune brought less capable men into the arena. 39. 1 2 3 4 5

40. A disaster was narrowly averted only through the efforts of the gangleader who ordered his followers to cool it. 40. 1 2 3 4 5

41. Had the jet plane landed on the runway a moment later, it would have collided with the careening escape car. 41. 1 2 3 4 5

42. When the storekeeper saw ruin staring him in the face, he turned to his suppliers for financial assistance. 42. 1 2 3 4 5

43. The walls of the canyon echoed back the shrieks of horror of the trapped miners. 43. 1 2 3 4 5

44. Is any of the doctors available to handle an emergency case? 44. 1 2 3 4 5

PART 2 *Suggested Time: 15 Minutes*
Time begun ..... Time ended ..... Time used .....
Did you complete the section within the time limit? ...

DIRECTIONS: Each of the following sentences has four parts underlined and lettered. Each sentence may contain one or no underlined section containing parts that may be unacceptable. If there is no underlined part requiring change, then choose (E) showing no error. Otherwise select the letter of the underlined portion that is not correct or is poorly expressed.

45. Coming to my final reason, the solution to the
    (A)   (B)   (C)
    puzzle lies right before our eyes! No error
    (D)   (E)

46. There is hardly no reason that I can think of for
          (A)   (B)
    his refusing Dave's offer. No error
    (C)   (D)   (E)

47. I lived in this neighborhood for more than 27
      (A)   (B) (C)
    years, and I will not move now! No error
    (D)   (E)

48. Go slow, don't be hasty; and you won't have re-
       (A)   (B)   (C) (D)
    grets. No error
           (E)

49. If you would have listened to me then, we would
            (A)   (B)(C) (D)
    not be in danger now. No error
                          (E)

50. Before they had began, she was ready to complain
                    (A) (B)   (C)   (D)
    to the authorities. No error
                        (E)

51. Here is another one of those items which have
         (A)   (B)   (C)
    been the basis of our weakness. No error
             (D)   (E)

52. I was very much annoyed; moreover, it wasn't my
                  (A)   (B)   (C) (D)
    turn! No error
          (E)

53. This healthy climate will restore not only his health
             (A)   (B)   (C)
    but his good nature as well. No error
    (D)   (E)

54. He pored over the law books, studying each statue
        (A)   (B)   (C)   (D)
    and hoping to find the loophole that could save
    his client. No error
                (E)

55. His three assets are: his ability to read quickly, his
                         (A)
    never-failing good humor, and his endless energy.
          (B)   (C)(D)
    No error
    (E)

56. He was formerly introduced to the president of the
               (A)
    college which he had applied to only a few days
            (B)   (C) (D)
    before. No error
            (E)

57. In times passed, I would have refused to raise a
             (A)(B)   (C)   (D)
    finger to help them. No error
                         (E)

58. The bell had rung, and the classes had begun by
                 (A)(B)   (C) (D)
    the time I had reached the corner. No error
                                       (E)

59. Somebody has gone and left his hat on the rack
             (A) (B)   (C)
    without asking permission. No error
    (D)   (E)

60. In our city, they treat strangers very politely. No
           (A)(B)(C)   (D)
    error
    (E)

61. They said that I had sung a song in the wrong key,
                         (A)   (B)   (C)
    which annoyed me very much. No error
    (D)   (E)

62. I was not so willing as he to place blame in this
               (A)   (B)(C)
    case. No error
    (D)   (E)

63. They had seen all of their friends except Lucy and
                (A)   (B)
    I at the festival. No error
    (C)(D)   (E)

64. It's one of them things that I always find so fright-
    (A)   (B)   (C)   (D)
    ening. No error
           (E)

65. These flowers do not smell so sweetly as did those
                         (A)   (B) (C)   (D)
    we bought last night. No error
                          (E)

66. You will have to settle this issue between Henry
        (A)   (B)   (C)
    and me. No error
        (D)   (E)

67. They had brought the picture of a airplane into
                (A)   (B) (C)   (D)
    the classroom. No error
                   (E)

68. There wasn't anything I could do to help, we were
              (A)   (B)   (C)
    all caught up in that maze from which there seemed
    to be no escape. No error
          (D)   (E)

69. There was scarcely no time left for them to leave
              (A)   (B)   (C)
    before the fighting would begin. No error
                               (D)   (E)

70. Have there ever been any others just like you and
              (A)   (B)   (C)
    me? No error
    (D) (E)

71. I had to lay down on the couch for ten minutes
    (A)   (B)
    before going into the room in which the meeting
          (C)   (D)
    was being held. No error
                    (E)

72. I disapprove of your claiming that the set of papers
                      (A)   (B)
    were corrected with supervision. No error
    (C)   (D)   (E)

PART 3 Suggested Time: 15 Minutes
Time begun ..... Time ended ..... Time used .....
Did you complete the section within the time limit? ...

DIRECTIONS: Read each of the following sentences carefully. Then rephrase each according to the directions which follow it. Select from the choices (A) through (E) the word or entire phrase that is included in your revised sentence. The choice should be part of a sentence that is accurate and complete. Make only those changes that the directions require.

73. The American Secretary of State and the world's leading revolutionary hero could meet in a friendly atmosphere which was made possible by the pace of changing times.
    Begin with Such was.
    (A) that it was possible
    (B) could have met
    (C) atmosphere made possible
    (D) times, the
    (E) meeting in

74. The American people and their institutions have as their most urgent business a resolution of the crisis in the Presidency.
    Begin with A resolution.
    (A) Presidency, the
    (B) is the
    (C) people, and
    (D) Presidency would be
    (E) business. The

75. Any human product worth the price of the degree will soon cease to be supplied to the nation by a campus that barters away its autonomy.
    Begin with A campus.
    (A) campus, bartering
    (B) product, worthy of
    (C) cease to supply
    (D) to have supplied to
    (E) autonomy. Any

76. Over the years the Air Force has built ever more complex machines which were planned to gain relatively minor tactical advantages against an enemy.
    Begin with To gain.
    (A) advantages. The
    (B) Force—over
    (C) advantages. Over
    (D) enemy, over
    (E) gain, over

77. On the contrary, the present crisis is merely making us face a little sooner a long-term problem with the most profound implications for human society.
    Begin with We are.
    (A) sooner. A
    (B) made on the
    (C) . With the most
    (D) society on the
    (E) contrary, merely being

78. These difficult questions are a reason, rather, to stop pretending that all will soon be for the best in the best of all possible worlds, and to start telling ourselves the truth.
    Begin with We should.
    (A) truth even though
    (B) truth, difficult
    (C) all would be
    (D) since these
    (E) rather than stopping

79. Our conventional military forces were an expensive, empty shell of a shield providing little protection at all from the threat of another superpower.
    Begin with Little protection.
    (A) superpower,
    (B) provided in
    (C) was providing
    (D) providing, by
    (E) forces, an

80. Campaigns are the public's business and are one of the few examples of public business not financed by public funds.
    Begin with One of.
    (A) campaigns;
    (B) funds is
    (C) and campaigns
    (D) which have been
    (C) business, not

81. The handclasp at Kilometer 10 symbolizes a spirit that could substantially enhance the prospects for the eventual outlawing of war as means of negotiation among nations.
    Substitute was symbolized for symbolizes.
    (A) nations; the
    (B) symbolized for the
    (C) could have enhanced
    (D) spirit; which
    (E) had enhanced

82. The revised rules were open to valid complaint on the grounds that too little of the extra income that accrued to owners was applied to the correction of violations and improvements of buildings.
    Begin with Because.
    (A) income, accrued to owners,
    (B) were applied
    (C) buildings. The
    (D) will be open
    (E) buildings, the

83. The power plant reversed the flow of the Forked River, and it drew into the river channel salt water from the nearby sea.
    Substitute drawing for drew.

(A) sea, the
(B) would have
(C) having reversed
(D) sea, and
(E) sea; the

84. A byproduct of economic growth is the pollution of the oceans, like other forms of pollution which are thus to an extent inevitable.
Begin with *Like other forms of pollution*.
(A) pollution. Which
(B) growth. The
(C) could have been
(D) inevitable, a
(E) pollution; which

85. The very essence of this series of events is that the people involved keep meeting each other in encounters over which they have little conscious control.
Substitute *had been* for *is*.
(A) people who were
(B) could keep
(C) had had
(D) events,
(E) have kept

86. In 1941 Prokofiev undertook the huge task of converting *War and Peace* into an opera, out of the conviction that the vastness of Russia would frustrate Hitler as it had Napoleon.
Begin with *Convinced that*.
(A) task, in 1941
(B) Napoleon, in 1941
(C) opera in 1941
(D) Russia, in 1941
(E) Prokofiev, in 1941,

87. Most astronomers these days accept the probability that life exists elsewhere in the universe and the corollary probability that some of these presumed beings have reached a higher state of intelligence than ours.
Begin with *That life exists*.
(A) ours. Probability
(B) and its corollary,
(C) is a probability
(D) are, probabilities
(E) , and

ANSWER KEY AND ANALYSIS OF ANSWERS / *Page 137*

PRACTICE EXAMINATION SEVEN

Total Time: One Hour
PART 1 *Suggested Time: 25 Minutes*
Time begun ..... Time ended ..... Time used .....
Did you complete the section within the time limit? ..

DIRECTIONS: Read each of the following sentences carefully. Then circle the appropriate number in the answer column

1. if the sentence contains an error in diction.
2. if the sentence contains an error in grammatical usage.
3. if the sentence contains a cliché or a mixed metaphor.
4. if the sentence is verbose or contains a redundant phrase.
5. if the sentence contains none of these errors.

1. We were all as close to the point of exhaustion as we could possibly be when the news of our success reached our ears, reviving both our spirit and our energies.   1. 1 2 3 4 5
2. The audio tube he has patented is so small that it is almost invisible to the eye.   2. 1 2 3 4 5
3. I bridled at having him tug at our heartstrings with his pained expressions and tales of deprivation.
   3. 1 2 3 4 5
4. The data that we have collected so far all points to a rapid resolution of our present problem.
   4. 1 2 3 4 5
5. As soon as you are already, we shall apply for permission to use the rehearsal hall.
   5. 1 2 3 4 5
6. Although we have not cleared all of the hurdles that face us, with a firm hand on the helm, we shall soon be out of danger.   6. 1 2 3 4 5
7. Once we have learned how to face our problems squarely, we shall be able to combine many small items together and ease our present administrative burdens.   7. 1 2 3 4 5
8. Since he had formally been the mainstay of the attorney general's office, we can turn to him for sound legal advice.   8. 1 2 3 4 5
9. Juvenile delinquency is the cancer in society's vitals and it must be surmounted if ever we are to avoid the danger of totalitarianism.   9. 1 2 3 4 5
10. Are you certain that he inferred in his speech that we are incapable of managing the student publications if ever we are elected to office?
    10. 1 2 3 4 5
11. Patience is required more of the teacher than of any other profession.   11. 1 2 3 4 5
12. Unless you know the full set of exercises to be executed during the ceremony, you are liable to misjudge the dexterity of the participants.
    12. 1 2 3 4 5
13. Once again I take my pen in hand to give you an opportunity to keep abreast of the flow of events that have made my present existence so filled with exhilarating joy.   13. 1 2 3 4 5
14. My head may be bloody but it is unbowed as I face, with the confidence of youth, the trials ahead.
    14. 1 2 3 4 5
15. They should not change their horses in midstream when their ideas float through the sieve of uncertainty.   15. 1 2 3 4 5
16. We most respectively submit this request for an interview at your earliest convenience so that we may acquaint you more fully with the details so that your ultimate decision may be a truly just one.
    16. 1 2 3 4 5

17. To our utter amazement, we were told of how he met his death this morning by telephone.
    17. 1 2 3 4 5
18. Now that we have reached the climax in our struggles, I am certain that he will either declare us the winner or co-winner.
    18. 1 2 3 4 5
19. As they walk through the corridor, Jane will precede ahead of her squad to the appointed station and wait there for them to reach her.
    19. 1 2 3 4 5
20. The council adopted the tenets and principles that had gone into effect at our last convocation.
    20. 1 2 3 4 5
21. As luck would have it, Mother Nature clothed all outdoors in a white mantle that evening and caused us to postpone our trip.
    21. 1 2 3 4 5
22. Since Paul really did not want to antagonize the faculty, at the very moment that we were requesting their cooperation, he carefully avoided the labels of *square* and *egghead*.
    22. 1 2 3 4 5
23. Most of the preliminary planning had been accomplished by only two members of the committee, Helen and I.
    23. 1 2 3 4 5
24. The new houses are so attractive in appearance that many of the neighbors offered to act as selling agents for the development company.
    24. 1 2 3 4 5
25. The young lawyer climbed to the top of his profession in such short time that none of his colleagues had the opportunity to be envious.
    25. 1 2 3 4 5
26. After swimming in deep water for so long, I was pleased to be able to turn over a new leaf and begin afresh.
    26. 1 2 3 4 5
27. The candidate for political office gained in statue as a result of his courageous stand on the equal rights issue.
    27. 1 2 3 4 5
28. Just when the alumnus and his son walked up to the coach, he fell to the ground in a dead faint.
    28. 1 2 3 4 5
29. In discussing outcomes, we must not overlook the fact that we were given television time equal to that given to our more powerful opponents.
    29. 1 2 3 4 5
30. Those who are prejudiced are impaled in the quicksands of ignorance.
    30. 1 2 3 4 5
31. At the present time neither Henry nor I am ready to accede to these unreasonable demands.
    31. 1 2 3 4 5
32. His anger was so conspicuously obvious that we could not ignore it.
    32. 1 2 3 4 5
33. Having read *Manchild in the Promised Land*, my attitude toward life in Harlem changed completely.
    33. 1 2 3 4 5
34. May his prophesies of doom never come to pass!
    34. 1 2 3 4 5
35. Those who know a foreign language are often tempted to garnish plain English with an exotic word or two.
    35. 1 2 3 4 5
36. The giant redwoods grown on our West Coast can be matched by no other area in the world.
    36. 1 2 3 4 5
37. Rather than bang my head against a stone wall, I was willing to accept a compromise just to save face.
    37. 1 2 3 4 5
38. The carburetor has been cleaned and the tires rotated.
    38. 1 2 3 4 5
39. In that the seams had split in various places, the operator was told to redo the stitching again with stronger thread.
    39. 1 2 3 4 5
40. Our cautious friend always carries a spare pair since he is as blind as a bat without his eyeglasses.
    40. 1 2 3 4 5
41. Having had a frank talk with his employee, the apprentice saw clearly just what his chances of advancement were.
    41. 1 2 3 4 5
42. I placed the key in the desk drawer which would open the closet.
    42. 1 2 3 4 5
43. Purists in the language of cookery insist that eggs should be labeled hard-cooked rather than hard-boiled since at no time in the cooking process does the liquid part of the egg boil.
    43. 1 2 3 4 5
44. On these momentous occasions that are so significant in our lives, we must not forget or lose sight of those who had contributed so much to our success.
    44. 1 2 3 4 5

PART 2 *Suggested Time: 15 Minutes*
Time begun ..... Time ended ..... Time used .....
Did you complete the section within the time limit? ..

DIRECTIONS: Read each of the following sentences carefully. Then rephrase it according to the directions which follow it. Select from the choices (A) through (E) the word or entire phrase that is included in your revised sentence. The choice should be part of a sentence that is accurate and complete. Make only those changes that the directions require.

45. They carried out 45 painstaking experiments, and then they finally succeeded in synthesizing the enzyme.
    Begin with Only after.
    (A) ; and then
    (B) they carried
    (C) , did they
    (D) they had finally
    (E) they synthesized

46. When we viewed the substance without the aid of the microscope, it seemed no different from any other colorless liquid.
    Substitute Viewing for When we viewed.
    (A) microscope, it
    (B) microscope it
    (C) different than
    (D) it had seemed
    (E) we found it

47. It turned out to be one of those toys that glut the market for a short while and then disappear.
    Substitute a toy for one of those toys.
    (A) disappears
    (B) and then would disappear
    (C) , and then they disappear
    (D) glut the market
    (E) could glut

48. It was a secret that was well kept, known to everyone except Edna and me.
    Substitute but for except.
    (A) well-kept
    (B) everyone,
    (C) and I
    (D) me
    (E) secret, that

49. The child whose personality traits do not match the values of his society is not likely to be well adjusted.
    Substitute who has for whose.
    (A) child, whose
    (B) society, is
    (C) who do not
    (D) that have not
    (E) which do not

50. Coming at the end of a long string of disappointments, this failure was more than I could bear.
    Begin with I could not bear.
    (A) bear which
    (B) failure, coming
    (C) failure coming
    (D) which could come
    (E) more failure

51. A minority culture striving to maintain a viable and creative presence in the midst of a rich majority culture will inevitably find itself in a constant state of war.
    Begin with A minority culture inevitably finds itself.
    (A) majority culture striving
    (B) when it strives
    (C) if it would strive
    (D) war striving
    (E) war when striving

52. Except for the faded green of its foliage, the scenery is all in black and white in order to challenge the story's main characters with the cruelty of nature and the bleakness of death.
    Begin with In order to challenge.
    (A) challenge, except
    (B) foliage the
    (C) death, except
    (D) which is all
    (E) because it is all

53. Man with all the resources at his command is unable to prevent war from making a mockery of all of his pious utterings.
    Begin with War still makes.
    (A) despite
    (B) man and all his resources
    (C) man who has
    (D) utterings;
    (E) , considering

54. Many critics argue that the only sound criterion for banning strikes should be the essentiality of the service at stake, whether in the public or private sector.
    Begin with The essentiality of the service.
    (A) argue many critics
    (B) sector is
    (C) according to
    (D) which is argued by
    (E) could be considered

55. Interpolated in the main story is a set of lurid tales told by each of the major characters.
    Begin with Each of the main characters.
    (A) have told
    (B) are interpolated
    (C) that is
    (D) which could have been
    (E) are a

56. The two themes in this brief essay stress the dramatic psychological growth that occurs in the opening years and the importance of the parent-child relationship for that growth.
    Substitute One of the two themes for The two themes.
    (A) themes,
    (B) that had occurred
    (C) but the other
    (D) years while
    (E) years because

PART 3 *Suggested Time: 20 Minutes*
Time begun ..... Time ended ..... Time used .....
Did you complete the section within the time limit? ..

DIRECTIONS: In each of the following sentences there is an underlined section that presents a problem in acceptable usage in grammar, diction (choice of words), sentence construction, or punctuation. Beneath each sentence are five ways of writing the underlined part.

Select A if you think that the original is better than any of the other changes.
Otherwise select the letter of the choice that is most effective and appropriate.

Do not choose any change that alters the meaning of the original sentence.

57. We concluded that the amount of mistakes he made was almost equal to the maximum allowed by probability.
    (A) the amount of mistakes he made was almost equal
    (B) the amount of mistakes which he had made were almost equal
    (C) the amount of mistakes made were almost equal
    (D) the number of mistakes made were almost equal
    (E) the number of mistakes he made was almost equal

58. Frances told her sister that she was scheduled to leave on the afternoon plane.
    (A) sister that she was scheduled to leave on the afternoon plane.
    (B) her sister, "You are scheduled to leave on the afternoon plane."
    (C) her sister. That she was scheduled to leave on the afternoon plane.
    (D) her sister she had been scheduled to leave on the afternoon plane.
    (E) her sister, that she was scheduled to leave on the afternoon plane.

59. You can readily recognize the package since it is red in color and with exceptional bulk.
    (A) package since it is red in color and with exceptional bulk.

(B) package. Since it is red in color and with exceptional bulk.
(C) package since it is red and exceptionally bulky.
(D) package since it is red and with exceptional bulk.
(E) package since it is red in color, and exceptionally bulky.

60. He has proven that the accused was seen placing the money in his pocket.
(A) proven that the accused was seen placing the money in his pocket.
(B) proved that the accused was seen placing the money in his pocket.
(C) proved that the accused was seen placing the money into his pocket.
(D) proven, that the accused was placing the money in his pocket when he was seen.
(E) proven that the accused was seen placing the money into his pocket.

61. He must either find a more economical way to produce his wares or a financial backer to pay for his subsequent losses.
(A) either find a more economical way to produce his wares
(B) either find a more economical way to produce his wares;
(C) be finding either a more economical way to produce his wares
(D) find either a more economical way to produce his wares
(E) have found either a more economical way to produce his wares,

62. We are compelled to conclude that he must respect them much more than me.
(A) that he must respect them much more than me.
(B) that he respects them much more than I.
(C) that he has respected them more than I.
(D) that he respects them much more then me.
(E) that he has been respecting them much more than I.

63. My father worked in that factory until the year in which I was born.
(A) worked in that factory until
(B) worked in that factory; until
(C) has been working in that factory, until
(D) had been working in that factory; until
(E) had worked in that factory until

64. The salesman spoke softly and with politeness to the group of potential customers.
(A) spoke softly and with politeness to
(B) spoke softly and politely to
(C) had spoken softly and with politeness with
(D) speaking softly and politely with
(E) was speaking softly and with politeness with

65. Of the three men who had been working as coaches at that time—Grant, Smieds, and Lurie—only the latter is still working in this area.
(A) time—Grant, Smieds, and Lurie—only the latter is
(B) time, Grant, Smieds, and Lurie only the latter is
(C) time. Grant, Smieds, and Lurie, only the latter is
(D) time—Grant, Smieds, and Lurie—only the last is
(E) time—Grant, Smieds, and Lurie—only the last had been

66. His sense of humor, together with his tact and ready wit, make him a deservedly popular leader.
(A) humor, together with his tact and ready wit, make him
(B) humor together with his tact and ready wit make him
(C) humor, tact, and ready wit makes him
(D) humor, together with his tact and ready wit, makes him
(E) humor together with his tact and ready wit making him

67. The only logical solution to this dilemma is to declare the winner to be her.
(A) is to declare the winner to be her.
(B) would be to declare the winner to be she.
(C) is to declare she to be the winner.
(D) would be to declare that the winner will be she.
(E) should be to declare her to be the winner.

68. To be effective as a speaker, your message must have prime significance for your audience.
(A) speaker, your message must have
(B) speaker, you must deliver a message that has
(C) speaker. You must deliver a message that has
(D) speaker your message must have
(E) speaker, what is said must have

69. I knew that I made a mistake when that peculiar smile spread across his face.
(A) that I made a mistake when
(B) that I made a mistake. When
(C) that I made a mistake; when,
(D) that I had made a mistake as
(E) that I had made a mistake when

70. In this article it states that a strong UN is our only hope for peace in our time.
(A) In this article it states
(B) In this article, it states
(C) In this article, the author states
(D) In this article it is stated
(E) In this article, they quote that

71. Between you and me, there is definitely fewer chances for survival than at any time since the end of World War II.
(A) me, there is definitely fewer chances
(B) me, there are fewer chances
(C) I, there is less chances
(D) me, there are less chances
(E) I, there are less chances

72. The counselor characterized Mr. Gardiner as being friendly, easy-going, and likely to be cooperative.
(A) as being friendly, easy-going, and likely to be cooperative.
(B) as being friendly, easy-going and likely to be cooperative.
(C) for being friendly, easy-going and likely to be cooperative.
(D) by being friendly, easy-going, and likely to be cooperative.
(E) as being friendly, easy-going and potentially cooperative.

73. No sooner had the truck arrived than the children clamored for a ride.
(A) No sooner had the truck arrived than the children
(B) No sooner had the truck arrived when the children
(C) Just as the truck was arriving, the children
(D) No sooner had the truck arrived. When the

children
(E) Just as the truck arrived; the children

74. For many years now, the chances of a <u>war of annihilation erupting in the Middle East has filled</u> my dreams with nightmares.
(A) war of annihilation erupting in the Middle East has filled
(B) war of annihilation to erupt in the Middle East has filled
(C) annihilating war erupting in the Middle East has filled
(D) war of annihilation erupting in the Middle East have filled
(E) war of annihilation that may erupt has filled

75. There is one cardinal rule of safety <u>involved here you must not allow</u> fear to be the decision-maker.
(A) involved here you must not allow
(B) involved, here you must not allow
(C) involved, here, you must not let
(D) involved here, you must not let
(E) involved here: you must not allow

76. In the 1920s, there were very few business <u>machines; they did not have any casette recorders.</u>
(A) machines; they did not have any casette recorders.
(B) machines and no casette recorders.
(C) machines. They did not have any casette recorders.
(D) machines since they did not have any casette recorders.
(E) machines, and they did not have any casette recorders.

77. We have the responsibility of choosing a representative <u>who will see that our needs are recognized and our point of view respected.</u>
(A) who will see that our needs are recognized and our point of view respected.
(B) to see that our needs are recognized and our point of view respected.
(C) whom will see our needs recognized and point of view respected.
(D) who will see that our needs are recognized and that our point of view is respected.
(E) to see, our needs recognized, and our point of view respected.

ANSWER KEY AND ANALYSIS OF ANSWERS / *Page* 139

PRACTICE EXAMINATION EIGHT

Total Time: One Hour
PART 1   *Suggested Time: 20 Minutes*
Time begun .... Time ended .... Time used .....
Did you complete the section within the time limit?

DIRECTIONS: Each of the following sentences has four parts underlined and numbered. Each sentence may contain *one* or *no* underlined section containing parts that may be unacceptable. If there is no underlined part requiring change, then circle (5) showing no error. Otherwise circle the number of the underlined portion that is not correct or is poorly expressed.

1. Because we had left early, there <u>were</u> three items
   (1)   (2)
   included in the agenda <u>without</u> <u>us</u> having a chance
                          (3)   (4)
   to vote for or against them. <u>No error</u>
                                 (5)

2. They are not <u>so</u> willing <u>as</u> <u>us</u> to have this picture
   (1)   (2)(3)
   <u>hung</u> in the corridor. <u>No error</u>
   (4)   (5)

3. Everyone <u>except</u> <u>her</u> realized that the data <u>were</u>
             (1)   (2)   (3)
   different <u>than</u> the professor had anticipated. <u>No error</u>
             (4)   (5)

4. Between you and <u>me</u>, neither Paul nor Frances
                    (1)
   <u>knows</u> to <u>whom</u> this letter should be addressed <u>to</u>.
   (2)   (3)   (4)
   <u>No error</u>
   (5)

5. I am <u>positive</u> that the cat had not <u>drank</u> all of <u>its</u>
         (1)   (2)   (3)
   milk before the alarm <u>was</u> sounded. <u>No error</u>
                          (4)   (5)

6. <u>All together</u> there <u>have</u> been three <u>cases</u> of typhus
   (1)   (2)   (3)
   reported during the <u>past</u> two weeks. <u>No error</u>
                        (4)   (5)

7. They <u>reassured</u> us that it is <u>I</u> who <u>am</u> to be <u>their</u>
         (1)   (2)   (3)   (4)
   choice for candidate. <u>No error</u>
                          (5)

8. The coach <u>emphasized</u> that all <u>we</u> varsity players
              (1)   (2)
   must <u>cooperate</u> with <u>each other</u>. <u>No error</u>
         (3)   (4)   (5)

9. <u>Regardless</u> of <u>whom</u> he thinks is guilty, I <u>shall</u> never
   (1)   (2)   (3)
   for a moment consider that it could be <u>she</u>. <u>No error</u>
                                           (4)   (5)

10. To read a poem well, <u>your</u> <u>attention</u> must <u>center</u>
                          (1)   (2)   (3)
    <u>upon</u> the mood created by the thought patterns de-
    (4)
    veloped by the poet. <u>No error</u>
                          (5)

11. <u>There</u> is no doubt <u>but</u> that ham and eggs <u>is</u> the
    (1)   (2)   (3)
    favorite <u>morning</u> food of many Americans. <u>No error</u>
             (4)   (5)

12. Did Lucy <u>say,</u> "<u>I'm</u> going to travel <u>almost</u> the entire
             (1)   (2)   (3)

distance"? No error
           (4)   (5)

13. The set of twelve books which were written in the
                                  (1)
    Erse almost was lost during the moving. No error
    (2)   (3) (4)   (5)

14. The male willingness to avoid foods with high-fat
        (1)   (2)
    content is a healthful sign in the national welfare
                 (3)   (4)
    picture. No error
             (5)

15. Suzie, the tallest of the three speakers, was the one
        (1)   (2)   (3)
    who hadn't ought to be the first one called upon to
         (4)
    address the group. No error
                       (5)

16. Whenever he comes into the room; his older sister
                (1)   (2) (3)
    finds any excuse to leave immediately. No error
                             (4)   (5)

17. This group, among whom are Jean and Eadie, cer-
        (1)   (2) (3)
    tainly were the life of the party. No error
           (4)   (5)

18. It's an occurrence most unique in the annals of our
    (1) (2)   (3)
    club's long existence. No error
    (4)   (5)

19. One must be very careful to do his work step by step
                     (1)   (2)
    lest you attempt more than can be done within the
    (3) (4)
    given time limits. No error
                       (5)

20. "I have never before in my life," she shouted, "Seen
                 (1)   (2)(3)   (4)
    such a disregard of the rights of others!" No error
                                               (5)

21. Neither Alan nor his classmates enjoy the kind of a
                 (1)   (2)   (3)
    display that you have been planning. No error
                      (4)   (5)

22. The officer told the private that he would have to
                                      (1)
    lie where he had fallen until the arrival of an am-
    (2)   (3)   (4)
    bulance. No error
             (5)

23. There is hardly any reason for you to feel badly and
                     (1)   (2)
    blame yourself for this mishap. No error
    (3)   (4)   (5)

24. Being that he is sensible, you're going to find that it
    (1)   (2)

is he who will assume most of the responsibility.
   (3)   (4)
No error
(5)

25. Put the book that is now lying on the shelf in the
                        (1) (2)   (3)
    closet before Edna returns. No error
                       (4)   (5)

26. Of course, we shall have to agree with you when
                  (1)   (2)   (3)
    you say that he is taller than any boy in his class.
                                  (4)
    No error
    (5)

27. Coming to the affects of the Civil War upon in-
                  (1)
    dustry, I shall merely say in passing that much more
                    (2)   (3)   (4)
    research is needed in this area. No error
                                     (5)

28. Being tired, Herb listened heedlessly to the words
    (1)   (2)
    that had sounded so meaningfully to him only a
                        (3)   (4)
    brief two hours before. No error
                            (5)

29. "Two-thirds of our money have been stolen!"
                             (1)   (2)
    shouted the leader. "We must recover it at once."
                (3)   (4)
    No error
    (5)

30. In the meantime, my brother and I , we had at-
        (1)   (2) (3) (4)
    tended to the most pressing of the matters on hand.
    No error
    (5)

31. Whoever has been responsible for this mistake, re-
    (1)   (2)
    gardless of who he is, shall be punished most severely
                 (3)
    by the provost and I. No error
                       (4)   (5)

32. Before baking a cake, the ingredients must be
                    (1)   (2)
    listed, gathered, and measured. No error
    (3)   (4)   (5)

33. If you would have listened to me, no one but me
           (1)   (2)
    would have been involved in this experience which
    (3)   (4)
    has taken such a toll of our energy. No error
                                         (5)

34. They had not come but once before; yet they were
         (1)   (2) (3)
    able to negotiate the difficult trail without diffi-
                                    (4)
    culty. No error
           (5)

35. When the three brothers spoke to each other,
    ___(1)___   ___(2)___
    there was only the highest respect in their words.
    ___(3)___   ___(4)___
    No error
    ___(5)___

36. He never refused to help us when every so often
    ___(1)___   ___(2)___ ___(3)___
    we had to turn to him for advice. No error
    ___(4)___   ___(5)___

37. Not daring to challenge his statements, we were
    ___(1)___   ___(2)___
    completely overawed by the presence of this emi-
    ___(2)___ ___(3)___   ___(4)___
    nent authority. No error
    ___(5)___

38. Not one of the counselors who was there has ever
    ___(1)___   ___(2)___   ___(3)___
    deduced fully the implications in that simple ges-
    ___(4)___
    ture. No error
    ___(5)___

39. Without consulting the doctor or us, one of the
    ___(1)___
    nurses who has been on the case revealed the gov-
    ___(2)___ ___(3)___   ___(4)___
    ernor's true condition to the press. No error
    ___(5)___

40. In this televised series, they follow the age-old for-
    ___(1)___   ___(2)___
    mula of romantic love, a formula that rarely ever
    ___(3)___   ___(4)___
    fails. No error
    ___(5)___

41. His principal concern were the rumors of impend-
    ___(1)___ ___(2)___ ___(3)___
    ing jurisdictional disputes between the unions in-
    ___(4)___
    volved. No error
    ___(5)___

42. Here lie the ruins of hope destroyed by our naive
    ___(1)___   ___(2)___   ___(3)___
    confidence in the integrity of our fellow humans.
    ___(4)___
    No error
    ___(5)___

43. Would that the judge had not raised these ques-
    ___(1)___   ___(2)___
    tions that have so upset all of our neighbors and
    ___(3)___
    us. No error
    ___(4)___ ___(5)___

44. Even if the infantry were deployed properly the
    ___(1)___   ___(2)___
    concentrated mass of tanks would have broken
    ___(3)___   ___(4)___
    through the thin defenses. No error
    ___(5)___

PART 2 *Suggested Time: 20 Minutes*
Time begun .... Time ended .... Time used .....
Did you complete the section within the time limit?

DIRECTIONS: Read each of the following sentences carefully. Then rephrase it according to the directions which follow it. Select from the choices (A) through (E) the word or entire phrase that is included in your revised sentence. The choice should be part of a sentence that is accurate and complete. Make only those changes that the directions require.

45. The depression seriously cut funds for medical research; nevertheless, the thirties were another decade of advance.
    Omit *nevertheless* and use *even though* instead.
    (A) advance; the
    (B) research, the
    (C) cutting funds
    (D) had been
    (E) advance, the

46. A peace which is merely founded on superpower military and economic equilibrium is necessarily put into question if the bases of that equilibrium undergo a change.
    Begin with *When a peace* and omit *necessarily*.
    (A) equilibrium, it
    (B) because the bases
    (C) which is necessarily
    (D) peace, which
    (E) will have undergone

47. The only people who buy and read first-aid manuals are the ones who already know what to do in an emergency and just want to reinforce their knowledge.
    Begin with *First-aid manuals*.
    (A) only
    (B) who have known
    (C) emergency, and just wanted
    (D) only by the people
    (E) which are the ones

48. The World Trade Center when it is completely lighted up night after night probably consumes more of our energy resources than all the homes in a large-sized suburbia.
    Begin with *More of our energy resources*.
    (A) Center, when
    (B) night, than
    (C) than by all
    (D) had been consumed
    (E) were probably consumed

49. The political leaders face serious dilemmas when they attempt to control limited supplies of essential commodities in a vast continental country like the United States with its diverse climates and attitudes.
    Begin with *Had they attempted*.
    (A) would have faced
    (B) attitudes; the
    (C) attitudes. The
    (D) leaders faced
    (E) country. Like the

50. Lawyers in general do not look at their work as moral or immoral. That often allows them to act in a way that the rest of us would consider immoral.
Begin with *The fact that*.
(A) allowing them
(B) immoral often
(C) way, that
(D) allow them
(E) immoral; that

51. Preliterate hunting and gathering tribes offer the best speculation on how our prehistoric forebears may have lived. They are highly pacific people by our "civilized standards."
Change *offer* to *that offer*.
(A) lived are
(B) tribes; who
(C) lived, they
(D) tribes. Who
(E) who are highly

52. No government office and especially not the highest in the land carries with it the right to ignore the law's command.
Change *and especially* to *not even*.
(A) command, not even
(B) right not even
(C) office, not
(D) command; not even
(E) office carries

53. National security has become a kind of talisman invoked by officials at widely disparate levels of government service to justify a wide range of apparently illegal activities.
Begin with *Invoked by*.
(A) service; national
(B) service, which can justify
(C) security would become
(D) talisman to justify
(E) service; to justify

54. The enormous scientific value of the achievements in space of the crews of Skylab was made abundantly evident years ago.
Begin with *That the achievements*.
(A) achievements were made
(B) have been made
(C) ago has
(D) value, was
(E) Skylab have

55. For nearly four decades, other American workers have had machinery for free elections and enforcement of fair labor practices. The basic need remained for passage by Congress of a law extending to farm workers the same machinery.
Omit the period after *the same machinery* and begin with *The basic need*.
(A) law; extending
(B) practices that other
(C) elections, enforcement
(D) machinery for nearly
(E) having had

56. All you hear are crisp leaves skittering or a few flakes nudging each other as they fall when winter comes over the hill and down the valley so quietly.
Begin with *So quietly does*.
(A) because all you
(B) valley that
(C) skittering, or a
(D) hills, and
(E) coming over

57. In asking us to consume less fuel in order to avert a real fuel crisis, the President has made a logical and reasonable request.
Begin with *In order to*.
(A) had made
(B) to make a logical
(C) request in asking
(D) who has made
(E) shortage. The

58. The United States is about to embark on a momentous program to render itself independent of foreign energy supplies, by the end of a decade if possible.
Begin with *To render the United States*.
(A) possible, a
(B) supplies is about to be
(C) about to have been
(D) by the end is about
(E) embarked upon a momentous program

59. The two-party system has become a major stabilizing influence in the nation's conduct of Constitutional government; however, political parties are not mentioned in the written Constitution.
Change *however* to *although*.
(A) Constitution, the
(B) government; although
(C) not being mentioned
(D) parties, the
(E) government. Although

60. The first impression that one gets of a ruler and of his brains is from seeing the men he has about him.
Begin with *When we*.
(A) from getting
(B) him, we
(C) we seeing
(D) ruler, and
(E) men he had

61. Mao Tse-tung has set the stamp of his personality on modern China just as Lenin had set the stamp of his intellect on modern Russia.
Omit *just as*.
(A) Lenin setting
(B) Mao Tse-tung had set
(C) China; Lenin
(D) Lenin set
(E) China, Lenin

62. Yet we all should be reminded that the shock waves of change are not a sudden occurrence and not limited to the United States. Their origin was in World War II.
Change *Their origin* to *had their origin* and combine the sentences.
(A) States; had
(B) yet had
(C) change which is
(D) not being
(E) who are

PRACTICE EXAMINATIONS FOR THE ENGLISH COMPOSITION TEST

63. Hoping that it will be stronger for the ordeal it has suffered, we Americans seem to like to put our political system to the test now and then.
Change *Hoping* to *hope*.
 (A) suffered we
 (B) seeming to like
 (C) hope now and then
 (D) putting our
 (E) then and

PART 3 Suggested Time: 20 Minutes
Time begun .... Time ended .... Time used .....
Did you complete the section within the time limit? ..

DIRECTIONS: Read each of the following sentences carefully. Then circle the appropriate letter in the answer column
 (a) if the sentence contains cliches or inappropriate metaphors.
 (b) if the sentence contains faulty grammar or sentence structure.
 (c) if the sentence contains faulty diction.
 (d) if the sentence is wordy.
 (e) if the sentence contains none of these errors.

64. If I would have listened to him, this never could have happened.   64. a b c d e
65. Leave us do it now, and you will never be sorry.   65. a b c d e
66. Neither Henry nor I am ready to leave at this time.   66. a b c d e
67. We all agreed that the recipient of the medal had to be she.   67. a b c d e
68. Commence at the beginning and tell me how it all started.   68. a b c d e
69. Henry is much more in favor of Helen than me.   69. a b c d e
70. Each of the customers waiting in the anteroom has paid completely.   70. a b c d e
71. There was never any doubts in my mind once I had heard all the evidence.   71. a b c d e
72. Once they threw caution to the wind, I knew that we were in a different ball game.   72. a b c d e
73. Far out to sea was the earthly remains of their victim.   73. a b c d e
74. The price they asked is far less then what I had been prepared to pay.   74. a b c d e
75. I hope to be able to give the book to whomever you designate.   75. a b c d e
76. Either Tom or his brothers have been told all the facts in this case.   76. a b c d e
77. You too will have a turn, however I am still convinced that you do not deserve such consideration.   77. a b c d e
78. You haven't scarcely any time to lose at this moment.   78. a b c d e

79. The capital at the top of the marble column was destroyed by the exploding missile.   79. a b c d e
80. He is in eminent danger of being arrested as a spy.   80. a b c d e
81. He does not know the simplest words that are basic to the beginning vocabulary.   81. a b c d e
82. When in a hurry, the scenery seems to rush by at an incredible rate.   82. a b c d e
83. Helen is definitely not so active as Bernie.   83. a b c d e
84. Paul asked where I put the copy of the letter.   84. a b c d e
85. The additional squad brought the ship's complement up to it's full quota.   85. a b c d e
86. It is she who must apologize this time.   86. a b c d e
87. I cannot except your apology when it is offered so cynically.   87. a b c d e
88. Correct punctuation results from nothing more or less then careful practice.   88. a b c d e
89. It is amazing how soon my hands felt as cold as ice.   89. a b c d e
90. Leave it lie just where it has fallen unless you want to be accused of having tampered with the evidence.   90. a b c d e
91. May I thank you for a most perfect evening.   91. a b c d e
92. Talking as rapidly as I could, the emergency message was broadcast over the facilities of the improvised radio station.   92. a b c d e
93. Her principal reason for wanting to join us was never made clear to me.   93. a b c d e
94. He chose the most melodious of the two selections for presentation during the school assembly period.   94. a b c d e
95. This interpretation is as good if not better than the one that had won the prize.   95. a b c d e
96. It could so easily have been I who was left in a lurch as a result of his carelessness.   96. a b c d e
97. If he was as capable as you, he never would have been found wanting at so embarrassing a moment.   97. a b c d e
98. There was a sudden sound behind me, I tried to turn quickly to discover where it had come from.   98. a b c d e
99. Who would have thought that everyone except me could go to the affair!   99. a b c d e
100. How conspicuously obvious do you have to be when you want to let others know how you feel about me!   100. a b c d e

ANSWER KEY AND ANALYSIS OF ANSWERS / *Page 141*

PRACTICE EXAMINATION NINE

Total Time: One Hour
PART 1 *Suggested Time: 25 Minutes*
Time begun .... Time ended .... Time used .....
Did you complete the section with the time limit? ..

DIRECTIONS: Read each of the following sentences carefully. Then circle the appropriate number in the answer column

1. if the sentence contains an error in tense or mood.
2. if the sentence contains a dangling element.
3. if the sentence contains a double negative.
4. if the sentence contains an error in case.
5. if the sentence contains none of the above errors.

1. He hadn't ought to listen to those who are so envious of him. 1. 1 2 3 4 5
2. I so want the winner to be he that I can scarcely count the ballots. 2. 1 2 3 4 5
3. There is hardly no one left in our neighborhood once the hot weather comes in. 3. 1 2 3 4 5
4. I truly wish I was in his place; I could then show you who is really the more capable! 4. 1 2 3 4 5
5. To enjoy modern music, it is necessary to know the purpose of the composer. 5. 1 2 3 4 5
6. I thought it was inconsiderate of her to complain about me leaving when I did. 6. 1 2 3 4 5
7. After waiting for three hours, the train finally arrived on Track 4. 7. 1 2 3 4 5
8. I don't doubt that nothing good will come of all of his efforts. 8. 1 2 3 4 5
9. I am convinced that he hurt his hand after I came into the house. 9. 1 2 3 4 5
10. This never would have happened if you would have given me the moment of advice that I had asked for. 10. 1 2 3 4 5
11. Of course, I knew all the time that the next contestant had to be me. 11. 1 2 3 4 5
12. Driving along the icy mountain road, the car almost skidded over the edge of the cliff. 12. 1 2 3 4 5
13. One of the announcers who work in the local studio is going to address our Speakers' Bureau. 13. 1 2 3 4 5
14. At forty, his career as an artist came to an abrupt end when he was seriously injured in a freak fall. 14. 1 2 3 4 5
15. Between you and I, the solution that he suggested is so fantastic that I believe we now have a decided advantage over him. 15. 1 2 3 4 5
16. Could you tell me the name of the man who they selected to run for office? 16. 1 2 3 4 5
17. Six of us boys were among those who had been chosen as finalists. 17. 1 2 3 4 5
18. His parents spoke to him before he had left, but, being unable to prove their contentions, they could only reveal their innermost fears. 18. 1 2 3 4 5
19. Had it only been they, there could scarcely be any other solution, for they are the ones who's fortune is now at stake. 19. 1 2 3 4 5
20. While reading the report of his experiment, our tentative conclusion was that he could very well be on the verge of a break-through in man's fight against cancer. 20. 1 2 3 4 5
21. My parents moved to New York City the year before my sister was born. 21. 1 2 3 4 5
22. By doubling the recipe, the quantity and not the quality is increased. 22. 1 2 3 4 5
23. They had declared that their next victims would be we. 23. 1 2 3 4 5
24. He knows as much as me about this incident. 24. 1 2 3 4 5
25. This summary of the minutes is for whomsoever desires it. 25. 1 2 3 4 5
26. My fervent wish is that she was here to lend me support. 26. 1 2 3 4 5
27. After verifying my answer, the problem no longer seemed difficult. 27. 1 2 3 4 5
28. I am certain that I will have scarcely ten minutes to prepare for the conference. 28. 1 2 3 4 5
29. When undecided as to where to eat, the taxi driver can always make knowledgeable suggestions. 29. 1 2 3 4 5
30. The visitor spoke as though he had never been here before. 30. 1 2 3 4 5
31. It was only years later that I learned what he said. 31. 1 2 3 4 5
32. In order to sell competitively, production costs must be kept to their minimums. 32. 1 2 3 4 5
33. After the session with the chiropractor, I could not scarcely walk the short distance to my home. 33. 1 2 3 4 5
34. Having read every book Robert Nathan had had published, my reaction to the negative evaluation by the critic was immediate and defensive. 34. 1 2 3 4 5
35. He was willing to bet that Lake George was closer to Warrensburg than to Hadley. 35. 1 2 3 4 5
36. To have lasting friendships, you must be more willing to give than to receive. 36. 1 2 3 4 5
37. I had often wished that I was three inches taller. 37. 1 2 3 4 5
38. As the sun sinks below the horizon, the cowhands chose the camping ground for the night. 38. 1 2 3 4 5
39. Not counting the water boys, there are 34 men on the squad. 39. 1 2 3 4 5
40. He acts as though he really is the owner of my car. 40. 1 2 3 4 5
41. Upon arriving in the Adirondacks, for the first time in years, tears of nostalgia filled my eyes. 41. 1 2 3 4 5
42. It must have been wonderful to have been alive during those days of decision! 42. 1 2 3 4 5
43. When all is said and done, we must conclude that there is not but one way out of these complications. 43. 1 2 3 4 5
44. If he really wanted to go, he would have spoken up sooner. 44. 1 2 3 4 5

PART 2 *Suggested Time*: 15 Minutes
Time begun .... Time ended .... Time used .....
Did you complete the section within the time limit? ..

DIRECTIONS: Read each of the following sentences carefully. Then circle the appropriate letter in the answer column

(a) if the sentence contains faulty diction
(b) if the sentence is wordy
(c) if the sentence contains cliches or inappropriate metaphors
(d) if the sentence contains faulty grammar or sentence structure
(e) if the sentence contains none of these errors.

45. Is there any object to him joining us at this time?   45. a b c d e
46. I enjoy watching baseball games and to go to dances.   46. a b c d e
47. How long can he continue to drown his sorrows in drink!   47. a b c d e
48. He is a man completely without principals.   48. a b c d e
49. They walked slowly with measured paces up the path to the house on top of the hill.   49. a b c d e
50. At this time we are now ready to act in his favor.   50. a b c d e
51. I was strongly effected by his stirring speech.   51. a b c d e
52. Alex, bring this note home to your parents.   52. a b c d e
53. The teacher asked both of us, Tom and I, to carry the packages to the office.   53. a b c d e
54. It came as sort of a surprise to all of us.   54. a b c d e
55. The weight of his opinions carried him along on the tide of popularity.   55. a b c d e
56. For a moment he thought that Tom was me.   56. a b c d e
57. I could not help but agree with him when he said that we had based our conclusions on unproved opinions.   57. a b c d e
58. This package has been lying on the shelf for weeks.   58. a b c d e
59. He really felt badly when he realized the damage his remarks had caused.   59. a b c d e
60. She is more studious than any girl in her class.   60. a b c d e
61. Alex together with the other members of the team plans to arrive here at ten.   61. a b c d e
62. Neither John nor I am willing to listen to such gossip.   62. a b c d e
63. Here are the set of papers that you asked me to mark.   63. a b c d e
64. In a flash I instantly saw what they were planning to do.   64. a b c d e
65. My decision is final and unalterable.   65. a b c d e
66. On this festive occasion I am delighted to be able to tell you the story of how this castle changed hands.   66. a b c d e
67. Each of us who are here is obligated to silence until the news is published in the newspapers.   67. a b c d e
68. Who but he could have dared to speak so bluntly to the king!   68. a b c d e

PART 3   *Suggested Time: 20 Minutes*
Time begun .... Time ended .... Time used .....
Did you complete the section within the time limit? ..

DIRECTIONS: In each of the following sentences there is an underlined section that presents a problem in acceptable usage in grammar, diction (choice of words), sentence construction, or punctuation. Beneath each sentence are five ways of writing the underlined part.

Select A   if you think the original is better than any of the changes.
Otherwise   select the letter of the choice that is most effective and appropriate.

Do not choose any change that alters the meaning of the original sentence.

69. The politician assured his constituents that their letters <u>may and had influenced his voting record.</u>
(A) may and had influenced his voting record.
(B) may, and had, influenced his voting record.
(C) may, and had influenced his voting record.
(D) may have and had, influenced his voting record.
(E) may have and had influenced his voting record.

70. To prove the effectiveness of the current <u>research, the death rate has been</u> lowered among those in the project.
(A) research, the death rate has been
(B) research, we can show that the death rate has been
(C) research. The death rate has been
(D) research, the death rate have been
(E) research we can show that the death rate have been

71. <u>The inspector announced after a thorough investigation he</u> would submit his report to his superiors.
(A) The inspector announced after a thorough investigation he
(B) The inspector announced, after a thorough investigation. He
(C) Investigating thoroughly, the inspector announced he
(D) After a thorough investigation, the inspector announced that he
(E) The announcement by the inspector stated after a thorough investigation he

72. From all the major <u>highways of the state come the multitude who overflow</u> our metropolitan area
(A) highways of the state come the multitude who overflow
(B) highways of the state comes the multitude that overflows
(C) highways of the state comes the multitude which overflow
(D) highways of the state come the multitude which overflows
(E) highways of the state come the multitude overflowing

73. The recipient of the award <u>could so easily have been I—or you!</u>
(A) could so easily have been I—or you!
(B) could so easily have been any one of us!
(C) could have so easily been I—or you!
(D) could have been so easily me—or you!
(E) so easily could have been me—or you!

74. <u>No one, but him and me knew, the</u> combination to the strong box.
(A) No one, but him and me knew, the
(B) No one but he and me knew the

(C) No one but him and me knew the
(D) No one but he and I knew the
(E) No one, but he and I, knew the

75. It was one of those ideas that is ignored because it was proposed before its time.
(A) that is ignored because it was proposed
(B) which is ignored because it was proposed
(C) that are ignored, because it was proposed
(D) that was ignored because it was proposed
(E) that are ignored because it had been proposed

76. Being it was Saturday night, the shopping center did not close until midnight.
(A) Being it was Saturday night, the
(B) Being Saturday night, the
(C) Since it was Saturday night, the
(D) Being that it was Saturday night, the
(E) Being it was Saturday night. The

77. Not one of the soldiers that were called up was aware of the gravity of the situation.
(A) soldiers that were called up was
(B) soldiers which were called up was
(C) soldiers that was called up were
(D) soldiers that were called up were
(E) soldiers being called up were

78. Things being the way they are, we shall have to be satisfied with crumbs and not feasts from now on.
(A) they are, we shall have to be
(B) they are. We shall have to be
(C) they are; we shall have to be
(D) they are we shall have to be
(E) that they are we shall have to be

79. He readily accepted my offer to help him, which pleased me greatly.
(A) He readily accepted my offer to help him, which
(B) That he readily accepted my offer to help him which
(C) He readily accepted my offer to help him. Which
(D) He readily accepted my offer to help him, this
(E) He excepted readily my offer to help him; which

80. It is the sort of a bargain that no one except him could resist.
(A) the sort of a bargain that no one except him
(B) It is a bargain that no one
(C) the sort of bargain that no one except him
(D) the sort of a bargain that no one except he
(E) sort of bargain that no one except he

81. I had to drive to town immediately, otherwise I would never meet him.
(A) immediately, otherwise
(B) immediately: otherwise
(C) immediately. Otherwise
(D) immediately otherwise
(E) immediately. Otherwise,

82. I knew I made my offer out of turn when the chairman ignored my remarks.
(A) I made my offer out of turn when
(B) I made my offer out of turn. When
(C) I had made my offer out of turn when
(D) I made my offer out of turn since
(E) I made my offer out of turn; however,

83. Will you please send me a list of the pamphlets which deals with this topic.
(A) pamphlets which deals with this topic.
(B) pamphlets which deal with this topic.
(C) pamphlets which deal on this topic.
(D) pamphlets which is relevant.
(E) pamphlets which deals with this here topic.

84. I still do not see the reason for him being released on parole.
(A) reason for him being released on parole.
(B) why he is being released on parole.
(C) for his having been released on parole.
(D) for him having been released on parole.
(E) for his being released on parole.

85. I found the cruel narrative excruciating; it was more than I could endure.
(A) excruciating; it was
(B) tortuous. It was
(C) excruciating, it was
(D) excruciating it was
(E) tortuous; it was

86. Paula is more sensitive by far than any girl in her sorority.
(A) more sensitive by far than any girl
(B) by far more sensitive then any other girl
(C) more sensitive, by far, then any girl
(D) more sensitive by far than any other girl
(E) more sensitive by far than any of the girls

87. When you have raised the necessary capitol, the offer will be renewed.
(A) have raised the necessary capital, the offer
(B) have raised the necessary capitol the offer
(C) have raised the necessary capital, the offer
(D) raised the necessary capital the offer
(E) raised the necessary capitol; the offer

88. Having taken a firm stand, we were reluctant to re-open the issue.
(A) Having taken a firm stand, we
(B) Because we were taking a firm stand we
(C) Having taken a firm stand. We
(D) Because we had taken a firm stand. We
(E) Because our stand was firm; we

89. The seer prophesied dire events to follow if his warnings were ignored.
(A) prophesied dire events to follow if
(B) prophesied dire events to follow, if
(C) prophesied dire events to follow. If
(D) prophecied dire events to follow when
(E) prophecied dire events to follow if

PRACTICE EXAMINATION TEN

Total Time: One Hour
PART 1 *Suggested Time: 20 Minutes*
Time begun .... Time ended .... Time used .....
Did you complete the section within the time limit? ..

DIRECTIONS: Each of the following sentences has four parts underlined and numbered. Each sentence may contain *one* or *no* underlined section containing parts that may be unacceptable. If there is no underlined part requiring change, then circle (5) showing no error. Otherwise circle the number of the underlined portion that is not correct or is poorly expressed.

1. The percentage(1) of saving is too(2) slight in this process,(3) moreover,(4) the bookkeeping involved becomes much more difficult for us to perform accurately. No error(5)

2. May I have a loan(1) of your(2) book so that I can study for the test on(3) capitals(4) of the world. No error(5)

3. Bring(1) the results to his office so that the council(2) can(3) examine the details for themselves.(4) No error(5)

4. Arlene accompanied(1) by her brother and sister are(2) in the foyer,(3) waiting to discuss with you the plans for the costume(4) ball. No error(5)

5. Not caring(1) what happened to them,(2) I(3) was completely disinterested(4) in their tale of woe. No error(5)

6. The would-be(1) rescuers formed a continuous(2) chain by holding hands; Henry,(3) acting as lead man,(4) reached cautiously over the edge of the cliff. No error(5)

7. "Take me to your leader,(1)" she commanded quietly,(2) "I have an important message for him and him alone!"(3) No error(4) (5)

8. Is(1) there no one among you to whom(2) I can turn to(3) for advice(4) and comfort? No error(5)

9. You're(1) in eminent(2) danger of being accused of a crime you did not commit;(3) therefore,(4) you must find out who is behind this foul plotting. No error(5)

10. The less(1) mistakes one makes, the greater(2) is his(3) chance of unraveling this incredible(4) mix-up. No error(5)

11. Neither you nor(1) I are(2) capable of ridding(3) the city of this unhealthful(4) situation. No error(5)

12. A set of his fingerprints are(1) on file in the office,(2) and everyone of the officers of the law is(3) able to examine it at any time. No error(4) (5)

13. Between you and me,(1) he is seldom ever(2) wrong when he decides on(3) whom(4) to reject. No error(5)

14. I still think it would be all right(1) if no one but him(2) was(3) permitted to eat their(4) lunch in the office. No error(5)

15. Bagels and lox is(1) my favorite midnight snack due to(2) my having been(3) brought up(4) in Brooklyn, the home of wholesome foods. No error(5)

16. I read in the paper that(1) the killer and his accomplices are(2) to be hung(3) at noon by order of(4) the governor. No error(5)

17. Do just like(1) I(2), and you will(3) have little if any(4) difficulty. No error(5)

18. Is(1) there any other set of tests that I could have(2) used to see the affect(3) of tension on those who(4) are involved in this project? No error(5)

19. Is it she(1) who spoke so indistinct(2) that we did not know whether(3) we were to precede(4) or follow the procession. No error(5)

20. Each of them has(1) ever(2) resented you(3) daring to tell them what had(4) to be done. No error(5)

21. Among the three of them I would judge him to be
    (1)   (2)
    the more intelligent, especially where abstract con-
        (3)
    cepts are concerned. No error
          (4)   (5)

22. Everyone of the boys in the class who have passed
                                     (1) (2)   (3)
    the test are to receive certificates. No error
             (4)   (5)

23. Larry can drive the car as well as you or I ; when-
                                (1)   (2)(3)
    ever he is permitted to borrow it. No error
                             (4)   (5)

24. To pass such a test, it is necessary that each candi-
                         (1)
    date be prepared to do his utmost. No error
         (2)   (3) (4)   (5)

25. He felt so badly that Ethel and I had to ask whom-
                (1)   (2)
    ever we met to do the work for him. No error
    (3)   (4)   (5)

26. Whether you agree or not , this was a most perfect
    (1)   (2)   (3)
    arrangement for him and Paul under the circum-
                    (4)
    stances. No error
              (5)

27. If you would have told me just what I was to do,
            (1)   (2)
    they would never have found fault with my handling
         (3)   (4)
    of the case. No error
                  (5)

28. Somewheres in my notes there is a statement that
    (1)   (2)
    we seniors may use any of the lockers that are left
    (3)   (4)
    open. No error
           (5)

29. Every candidate who has swam the length of the
                         (1) (2)
    pool will be given a certificate stating that he has
                                                 (3)
    proved his competence. No error
    (4)   (5)

PART 2   Suggested Time: 20 Minutes
Time begun .... Time ended .... Time used .....
Did you complete the section within the time limit? ..

DIRECTIONS: Read each of the following sentences carefully. Then rephrase it according to the directions which follow it. Select from the choices (A) through (E) the word or entire phrase that is included in your revised sentence. The choice should be part of a sentence that is accurate and complete. Make only those changes that the directions require.

30. Neither of the drivers who are being held by the
                                (1)
    police knows whom to blame for his plight. No error
           (2)   (3)   (4)   (5)

31. He is the sort of a person who I suspect would be
              (1) (2)   (3)   (4)
    capable of making such a remark. No error
                                      (5)

32. The danger is when there is a series of cars that are
                   (1)   (2)   (3)
    ready to cross an obstructed area. No error
                      (4)   (5)

33. Without consulting Margie or us, Phyllis asserted
                                 (1)
    that everyone except her had to contribute one-
                         (2)
    tenth of his earnings to the fund. No error
    (3)   (4)   (5)

34. The Navy had intercepted Japanese messages after the Battle of the Coral Sea, and it knew the next move and rushed every available plane and vessel into the Central Pacific.
    Begin with *The Navy, having intercepted.*
    (A) moved, and
    (B) knowing the next
    (C) vessel; into the
    (D) messages. After the
    (E) Sea, knew

35. The Germans created a critical oil shortage by mid-January because they had moved so many submarines to the Atlantic Coast, where at night they torpedoed tankers silhouetted against the light of cities.
    Begin with *By mid-January, the Germans had moved.*
    (A) cities, that they created
    (B) coast. Where
    (C) tankers; silhouetted
    (D) cities, that
    (E) coast; where

36. Prophets have cried out in the wilderness, and they despaired of TV's lost opportunities during its first twenty-five years.
    Omit *they*, and begin with *During.*
    (A) wilderness; and
    (B) opportunities prophets
    (C) wilderness. Despairing
    (D) wilderness and despaired
    (E) years. Prophets

37. All too often those who want to suppress a repugnant doctrine only succeed in giving it more notoriety.
    Begin with *Those who would want.*
    (A) succeed all too often
    (B) doctrine all too often
    (C) had only succeeded
    (D) to suppress all too often
    (E) only have succeeded

38. Moral issues can be debated endlessly with no resolution, but there is also a material side to this problem.

Substitute *even though* for *but*.
(A) resolution; even though
(B) there had been
(C) With no resolution
(D) resolution even
(E) would have been debated

39. Winter does not wait on the calendar. You need no almanac to recognize its coming.
Change *Winter does not* to *since it does not*.
(A) needing no almanac
(B) Winter since
(C) waiting on the calendar
(D) recognize. The coming
(E) calendar. You

40. John F. Kennedy considered the Test Ban Treaty not the most historic act since Creation but a single step on a journey of a thousand miles.
Begin with *The Test Ban Treaty*.
(A) act, since Creation
(B) step. On a journey
(C) Kennedy as not the most
(D) Kennedy. Not the most
(E) Creation, but a single

41. We hesitate like Hamlet whipsawed by conflicting emotions of desire to avenge his father's death and guilt at having desired that very death.
Begin with *Like Hamlet*.
(A) father's death; and guilt
(B) guilt at desiring
(C) death, we
(D) father's death, and guilt
(E) death; we

42. His skepticism, his sense of the absurd in life, his recognition of failure were all directed at himself as much as anyone.
Begin with *He directed*.
(A) recognition of failure.
(B) anyone: his
(C) life; and his
(D) skepticism; his
(E) anyone; his

43. A quiet revolution in American life, the four-day week, could come to pass a decade before its time, hurried along by a sustained fuel shortage.
Begin with *Had a sustained fuel shortage resulted*.
(A) life. The four-day week
(B) could be coming to pass
(C) life; the four-day week
(D) resulted. A
(E) week, could have come

44. There is no need for Americans to fear economic disaster when there is effective national leadership and a sustained and cooperative response from business and the public.
Change *when there is a sustained leadership* to *Given effective national leadership*.
(A) leadership, and a
(B) public, there is
(C) Americans. To fear
(D) a sustaining and cooperative
(E) there had been no need

45. The shot that claimed the life of John F. Kennedy will be remembered for more than the murder of a charismatic and promising young President; it marked the beginning of the end of an era filled with ebullient optimism and confidence.
Begin with *Having marked the beginning*.
(A) confidence. The shot
(B) shot that claims
(C) remembered, for more
(D) confidence, the shot
(E) era, filled with

46. The old police headquarters on Centre Street is an architectural gem in an otherwise drab area. It should be preserved as an important New York City landmark.
Combine both sentences by eliminating *is* and *It*.
(A) area, should be
(B) Street an architectural gem
(C) gem; in
(D) area;
(E) landmark should be

47. We must give up the demand for right answers and instead encourage students to explore many ways of viewing an issue or problem.
Eliminate *and instead* and begin with *Our obligation is to encourage*.
(A) explore. Many ways
(B) students exploring
(C) problem; we
(D) problem, nor must we
(E) giving up the demand

48. That today's young people communicate more sensitively and more comfortably through visual media than through the printed page is one of the obvious results of the massive, pervasive influence of television.
Begin with *Is it true that one of the obvious*.
(A) page, is
(B) television?
(C) television, is that
(D) media; rather than
(E) printed page?

49. The true genius of America lies in its ability to organize free and strong-minded men to solve great problems. It also lies in its ability to meet and overcome challenges.
Begin with *In its ability to meet* and combine the two sentences.
(A) problems; are where
(B) America lie
(C) challenges, and
(D) problems is where
(E) problems, are where

50. In America our race relations are not perfect, but constructive processes are at work, and we are narrowing the gap in opportunity and in education, and in income, and in the day-to-day relations.
Omit *but* and all *and's*.
(A) gap, in
(B) perfect constructive
(C) work: we
(D) we will have narrowed
(E) education, in

51. When a train approaches a Paris subway station, gates at the ticket window automatically swing shut. Only those already on the platform may board the train.
Combine both sentences, and begin with *Because the gates*.
(A) approaches; only
(B) shut. When
(C) approaches, only
(D) the gates, at the
(E) shut, when

52. It is an accepted fact that the rate of gasoline consumption increases with an increase in speed; and, therefore, over any given distance the higher the speed, the more gasoline will be used.
Change *It is an accepted fact that* to *Because*.
(A) gasoline could have been used
(B) given distance, the more
(C) speed; and therefore over any
(D) gasoline would have been used
(E) speed. Therefore, over any

53. The opportunity for a significant international effort at cooperation exists because of mutual need and shared emergency.
Change *because of* to *Since this is a time of*.
(A) need, and
(B) emergency the
(C) was this
(D) exists. Since this
(E) emergency, the

54. The chickadees and the juncos have come down from the woodlands and the hills, back to the dooryard feeders where they were welcomed last year.
Change *have come* to *came*.
(A) year, the
(B) Welcomed last year,
(C) feeders; where
(D) had been welcomed
(E) feeders. Where

55. Political appeals to ignorance and selfishness needlessly divided the nation and thereby substituted neglect for compassion.
Change *thereby substituted* to *By substituting*.
(A) dividing needlessly
(B) compassion, political
(C) ignorance; and selfishness
(D) ignorance, and selfishness
(E) needlessly dividing

56. More of our people have lost their lives in automobile accidents than in all the wars in United States history.
Begin with *Automobile accidents have claimed*.
(A) claimed more of our people losing
(B) than have all the wars
(C) claimed. The lives of more
(D) people. Than
(E) lives than all

57. Consequently we cannot come to grips with the real issues until we first face the urgent need to make drastic changes in our energy economy.
Begin with *First we had to face*.
(A) Economy, coming to grips
(B) economy; therefore, we cannot
(C) economy before we could come to grips
(D) economy, as we came
(E) economy, as we come

58. Reports from transplant surgeons that immunosuppressive drugs given to patients to suppress organ rejection foster the rise of cancer are additional evidence of the relationship between cancer and immunity and the need for moderation in drug therapy.
Begin with *Additional evidence*.
(A) therapy, came from
(B) drugs, given to patients
(C) therapy comes from
(D) cancer, and immunity, and the
(E) surgeons. That

PART 3   *Suggested Time: 20 Minutes*
Time begun ..... Time ended ..... Time used .....
Did you complete the section within the time limit? ...

DIRECTIONS: Beneath each of the following sentences you will find five ways of rewriting the underlined part. Do not choose any change that alters the meaning of the original sentence.

Select **a**   if you think the original sentence is better than any of the changes.
Otherwise   select the letter of the choice that is most correct and effective.

59. <u>Seeing as how he disliked the camp site, I</u> suggested that we repack and move.
(a) Seeing as how he disliked the camp site, I
(b) Seeing as how he had disliked the camp site, I
(c) Since he had disliked the campsite, I
(d) Seeing as how he disliked the camp site. I
(e) Since he disliked the camp site, I

50. The book was written <u>by an obscure scholar Lillian Reinisch</u>.
(a) by an obscure scholar Lillian Reinisch.
(b) by an obscure scholar, Lillian Reinisch.
(c) by the obscure scholar Lillian Reinisch.
(d) by a obscure scholar, Lillian Reinisch.
(e) by a obscure scholar—Lillian Reinisch.

61. <u>Between you and I, there was</u> no other books on the shelf.
(a) Between you and I, there was
(b) Between you and me, there was
(c) Between us, there could not have been
(d) Between you and me, there were
(e) Between you and I there was

62. We should like to know <u>whether he is one of the men, who are</u> responsible for this confusion!
(a) whether he is one of the men, who are
(b) whether he is one of the men that has been
(c) if he is one of the men which are
(d) whether he is one of the men who are
(e) if he is one of the men whose

63. <u>In our city they are very much concerned</u> over the increase in the number of street crimes.
(a) In our city they are very much concerned
(b) In our city the people are very much concerned
(c) In our city people are very concerned
(d) In our city they are much concerned
(e) In our city, they are very concerned

64. If you would have listened to me, we could have prevented this mishap.
    (a) If you would have listened to me,
    (b) If you'd listened to me,
    (c) If you would've listened to me,
    (d) If you would of listened to me,
    (e) If you had listened to me,

65. When Tom, Helen's brother came into the room, I left.
    (a) When Tom, Helen's brother came into the room,
    (b) When Tom, Helens' brother, came into the room,
    (c) When Tom, Helen's brother, came into the room,
    (d) When Tom Helen's brother came into the room,
    (e) When Tom, Helen's brother, came into the room

66. Being a sensible person, I did not argue with them at the time.
    (a) Being a sensible person,
    (b) Being that I am a sensible person,
    (c) Being as I am a sensible person
    (d) Because I am a sensible person
    (e) Since I am a sensible person

67. They told me the entire story at that time, which surprised me very much.
    (a) , which surprised me very much
    (b) which surprised me very much
    (c) ; a revelation which surprised me very much
    (d) . This revelation surprised me very much
    (e) . Which surprised me very much

68. In our town they are very much interested in the current college crises.
    (a) In our town they are very much interested in
    (b) In our town they are very interested in
    (c) The people who live in our town are very much interested in
    (d) Our town is very interested in
    (e) They are very much interested in our town in

69. He told Alex that he was foolish to become so angry.
    (a) that he was foolish to become so angry
    (b) he was foolish to become so angry
    (c) "That he was foolish to become so angry."
    (d) "That he was foolish to become so angry."
    (e) "I was foolish to become so angry."

70. I bought a copy of the book of poems he had printed.
    (a) book of poems he had printed
    (b) book of poems that he had printed
    (c) book of Poems that he had printed
    (d) book of poems. He had printed
    (e) poetry book he had printed

71. All of the possible angles having been explored, we sat by and waited for results.
    (a) All of the possible angles having been explored, we
    (b) When all of the possible angles would have been explored, we
    (c) All of the possible angles having been explored. We
    (d) All of the possible angles having been explored; we
    (e) Since we were exploring all of the possible angles,

72. We plan to visit the house on the hill that she just bought.
    (a) house on the hill that she just bought.
    (b) house on the hill she just bought.
    (c) house on he hill which she just bought.
    (d) house she just bought on the hill.
    (e) house on the hill. That she just bought.

73. This one is rounder than the others.
    (a) rounder than the others
    (b) more round than the others
    (c) round
    (d) the roundest of them all
    (e) the most round

74. He is as eligible or even more eligible than the other candidates.
    (a) as eligible or even more eligible than
    (b) as eligible or even more eligible as
    (c) more eligible than
    (d) as eligible or even more eligible then
    (e) as eligible as or even more eligible than

75. He spoke ever so clearly and with emphasis.
    (a) ever so clearly and with emphasis
    (b) ever so clearly and emphatically
    (c) never so clearly and with emphasis
    (d) never so clearly and emphatically
    (e) He spoke ever so clear and with emphasis

76. We lived on Martense Street for seven years before we moved here.
    (a) We lived on .... before we moved
    (b) We would have lived on .... we had moved
    (c) We lived on .... before we had moved
    (d) We had lived on .... before moving
    (e) We lived on .... before we would have moved

77. Everyone except you and me has been told the formula.
    (a) Everyone except you and me has been told
    (b) Everyone except you and I has been told
    (c) Everyone except you and me have been told
    (d) Everyone except you and I have been told
    (e) Everyone except I and you have been told

78. There isn't scarcely a penny left in the larder.
    (a) isn't scarcely a penny left
    (b) is scarcely a penny left
    (c) is scarcely no pennies left
    (d) isn't scarcely no penny left
    (e) isn't a penny left

79. <u>Between you and I, nobody in this class knows</u> the right procedure.
    (a) Between you and I, nobody in this class knows
    (b) Between you and me, nobody in this class know
    (c) Between you and I, nobody in this class know
    (d) Between I and you, nobody in this class knows
    (e) Between you and me, nobody in this class knows

80. <u>Seeing as how they did not enjoy our company,</u> I soon excused myself and retired early.
    (a) Seeing as how they did not enjoy our company,
    (b) Seeing as how they did not enjoy our company.
    (c) Seeing as they did not enjoy our company,
    (d) Seeing as they did not enjoy our company.
    (e) Seeing that they did not enjoy our company,

81. We will have <u>to let it lie</u> just where it has fallen until we notify the police.
    (a) to let it lie
    (b) to leave it lay
    (c) to leave it lie
    (d) to let it lay
    (e) to have let it lay

82. <u>They stood on that farm for three weeks a year ago.</u>
    (a) They stood on that farm for three weeks a year ago.
    (b) A year ago they stood on that farm for three weeks.
    (c) For three weeks they had stood on that farm a year ago.
    (d) A year ago, they had stayed on that farm for three weeks
    (e) A year ago, they stayed on that farm for three weeks.

83. <u>Take the package off of the shelf and put it in</u> the desk drawer.
    (a) Take the package off of the shelf and put it in
    (b) Take the package off the shelf and put it into
    (c) Take the package off the shelf, and put it in
    (d) Take the package off from the shelf and put it in
    (e) Take the package off of the shelf and put it in

84. <u>That there article is the type of a satire that</u> I enjoy least
    (a) That there article is the type of a satire that
    (b) That there article is the type of a satire which
    (c) That article is the type of a satire that
    (d) That article is the type of a satire which
    (e) That article is the type of satire that

85. <u>They put on quite a act during their half hour on the stage.</u>
    (a) They put on quite a act during their half hour on the stage.
    (b) They put on quiet an act during there half-hour on the stage.
    (c) They put on quite a act during their half-hour on the stage.
    (d) They put on quite an act during there half an hour on the stage.
    (e) They put on quite an act during their half hour on the stage.

86. There should be <u>no mans' or womans' privileges but privileges for all humans.</u>
    (a) no mans' or womans' privileges but privileges for all humans
    (b) no mans' or womans' privileges but privileges for all human beings
    (c) no man's or woman's privileges but privileges for all humans
    (d) no men's or women's privileges but privileges for all human beings
    (e) no mens or womens privileges but privileges for all human beings

87. They say <u>were all together wrong in the advise</u> we plan to give the others.
    (a) were all together wrong in the advise
    (b) we're all together wrong in the advise
    (c) we're altogether wrong in the advice
    (d) we're all together wrong in the advise
    (e) were altogether wrong in the advice

88. <u>Is anyone of the members of the committee able to loan us</u> a copy of the report?
    (a) Is anyone of the members of the committee able to loan us
    (b) Are anyone of the members of the committee able to loan us
    (c) Is anyone of the members of the committee capable of loaning us
    (d) Are anyone of the members of the committee able to lend us
    (e) Is any one of the members of the committee able to lend us

89. Can you <u>learn me how to spill this liquid into the dish</u> without losing any of it?
    (a) learn me how to spill this liquid into the dish
    (b) teach me how to spill this liquid in the dish
    (d) learn me how to pour this liquid into the dish
    (c) teach me how to pour this liquid into the dish
    (e) teach me to pour this liquid in the dish

90. He <u>read all of Dicken's works before writing</u> the report.
    (a) read all of Dicken's works before writing
    (b) had read all of Dicken's works before writing
    (c) had read all of Dickens' works before he had written
    (d) had read all of Dickens's works before writing
    (e) read all of Dickens' works before he had written

ANSWER KEY AND ANALYSIS OF ANSWERS / *Page 146*

PRACTICE EXAMINATIONS FOR THE ENGLISH COMPOSITION TEST

ANSWERS TO PRACTICE EXAMINATIONS WITH ANALYSES OF ANSWERS

ANSWER KEY: PRACTICE EXAMINATION ONE / Page 84

Part 1
1. (2)
2. (5)
3. (2)
4. (2)
5. (1)
6. (1)
7. (3)
8. (1)
9. (2)
10. (5)
11. (4)
12. (1)
13. (5)
14. (4)
15. (3)
16. (3)
17. (4)
18. (1)
19. (2)
20. (3)
21. (1)
22. (2)
23. (5)
24. (2)
25. (2)
26. (2)
27. (2)
28. (3)
29. (2)
30. (1)
31. (1)
32. (5)
33. (4)

Part 2
34. (d)
35. (b)
36. (e)
37. (d)
38. (c)
39. (a)
40. (d)
41. (e)
42. (c)
43. (d)
44. (e)
45. (e)
46. (c)
47. (e)
48. (b)
49. (c)
50. (b)
51. (d)
52. (a)
53. (e)
54. (e)
55. (b)
56. (b)
57. (c)
58. (d)

Part 3
59. (e)
60. (a)
61. (b)
62. (c)
63. (d)
64. (c)
65. (a)
66. (a)
67. (e)
68. (d)
69. (a)
70. (c)
71. (a)
72. (b)
73. (a)
74. (c)
75. (c)
76. (a)
77. (c)
78. (a)
79. (d)
80. (b)
81. (c)
82. (e)
83. (b)
84. (d)
85. (b)
86. (c)
87. (d)
88. (a)
89. (c)
90. (d)

Summary of Results

Section	Number Correct	Number Wrong	Number Omitted
1			
2			
3			

Total correct: _____

Conversion Chart

The total number correct on the exam is converted to a scaled score ranging from 20 to 80. This conversion enables you to compare your results with those of other candidates who have taken the test. Half the scores fall above 50, half fall below; two-thirds of the candidates score between 40 and 69. The more competitive colleges usually prefer candidates who achieve 65 or above.

The following conversion chart can give you a rough approximation of what your English Composition score should be for this practice exam.

Number Correct	Test Score	Number Correct	Test Score
89	80	77	64
88	79	76	63
87	78	75	60
86	77	74	59
85	76	73	58
84	75	72	54
83	74	71	54
82	73	70	52
81	72	69	52
80	70	68	51
79	69	67	51
78	67	66	50

Self-appraisal Chart

Total Correct	Percentile
86–89	99
81	90
66	50
53	25
41	10

ANALYSIS OF ANSWERS: PRACTICE EXAMINATION ONE

Part 1
1. (2) The adjective *good* describes *everyone*.
2. (5) No error
3. (2) The verb *take* rather than *bring* is correct since the action is not toward the speaker.
4. (2) Possessive *your* is required as subject of gerund *becoming*.

5. (1) The past perfect *had lived* is required since the action preceded past action.
6. (1) Since cupful is a unit word, the sign of the plural is added at the end—*cupfuls*.
7. (3) The noun *number* rather than *amount* is used since units (*hours*) are involved.
8. (1) *Hardly* is followed by the positive *anyone*, not the negative *no one*.
9. (2) The run-on sentence must be corrected (present. They).
10. (5) No error
11. (4) The pronoun *everyone* requires singular *himself*, not the plural *themselves*.
12. (1) The pronoun *they* lacks an antecedent.
13. (5) No error
14. (4) The pronoun *which* must relate back to a specific word and not to the general idea of the sentence.
15. (3) The pronoun *it* lacks an antecedent.
16. (4) The participle *Realizing* dangles since *fears* can do no realizing.
17. (4) The term *enthused* is nonstandard.
18. (1) The pronoun *everyone* should be spelled as one word.
19. (2) In comparisons *than* rather than *then* is used.
20. (3) The standard term is *human beings*, not *humans*.
21. (1) The standard phrase is *in regard to*.
22. (2) The idiom *kind of a* is nonstandard.
23. (5) No error
24. (2) The word *out* is unnecessary.
25. (2) The verb *lie* (rest) and not *lay* (put) is required.
26. (2) Something is either round or not round; it cannot be rounder in Standard Written English.
27. (2) The term *muchly* is nonstandard.
28. (3) The pronoun *everyone* ends in *e*; therefore, the possessive form is *everyone's*.
29. (2) The article *an* and not *a* is needed because the first letter in *old* is a vowel.
30. (1) The phrase *due to* is nonstandard as a synonym for *since* or *because*.
31. (1) The pronoun *whomever* is required since it belongs to him (whomever).
32. (5) No error
33. (4) Nonstandard as a synonym for *irritate* is *aggravate*.

Part 2
34. (d) The pronoun *who* refers to the plural *people*, and therefore it should be followed by a plural verb form.
35. (b) A noun is needed for the participle to modify.
36. (b) The conjunctive adverb *however* can separate, not unite completely; therefore it cannot be used as a coordinating conjunction.
37. (d) The article *an* is needed because of the initial vowel in *awesome*.
38. (c) The past subjunctive *had* is required since the sentence describes action contrary to what had really happened.
39. (a) No error
40. (d) The word *loose* (lax) is used incorrectly; the two ideas must be punctuated as semi-dependent.
41. (e) The verb let (allow), not leave (depart), and lie (rest)—not lay (put)—are required.
42. (c) She could not be brighter than herself.
43. (d) The word *being* cannot be used as a substitute for *since* or *because* in standard usage.
44. (e) The preposition *except* should be followed by the objective form.
45. (e) Required are *than* (comparison) and *have*.
46. (c) The subject form is needed for the verb *is*.
47. (e) The noun *woman* ends in a consonant; the possessive form, therefore, is *woman's*.
48. (b) The present perfect tense is required to describe action that preceded the present action in the main verb.
49. (c) The plural verb form (have) is required; *humans* is not an acceptable standard synonym for *human beings*.
50. (b) The standard term is *kind of*.
51. (d) The term *being as* is a nonstandard synonym for *since*.
52. (a) No error
53. (e) Appositives are set off by commas.
54. (e) The possessive pronoun *yours* does not require an apostrophe; the complimentary close has an introductory capital letter.
55. (b) The present subjunctive form is required in untrue conditional clauses in the present tense.
56. (b) The word *these* means *the ones here*; therefore, *here* is unnecessary.
57. (c) The pronoun *which* must refer back to a specific word.
58. (d) The idiom *is when* is a nonstandard synonym for *occurs when*.

Part 3
59. (b) The phrase *alone among men* is wordy.
60. (a) The phrase *sort of* is not followed by *a* or *an* in standard use.
61. (b) The verb *descend* means *go down* and should not be followed by *down*.
62. (c) The term *tooth and nail* is a cliché.
63. (d) The pronoun *everyone* should be followed by the singular *has*.
64. (c) The phrase *terminate in a divorce* is a cliché.
65. (a) The verb *enthused* is nonstandard.
66. (a) The term *being as* is not a standard synonym for *since* or *because*.
67. (e) No error
68. (d) The participle *coming* has no word to modify logically.
69. (a) Required is *quite* (almost) and not *quit* (stop, leave).
70. (c) When caught on an anvil, one is in no position to swim.
71. (a) The standard idiom is *differ from*.
72. (b) The word *up* is unnecessary.
73. (a) The term *formally* (in a formal manner), not *formerly* (at one time) is required.
74. (c) The idiom *hold no brief* is overused.
75. (c) *Grasp time firmly in your fingers* and *felt the warmth of the sun* are clichés.
76. (a) The verb *infer* is not synonymous with *hint* or *insinuate*.

PRACTICE EXAMINATIONS FOR THE ENGLISH COMPOSITION TEST

77. (c) The dog in the manger has barked too often.
78. (a) The idiom *cannot help but* is nonstandard.
79. (d) The conjunctive adverb *moreover* cannot be used to join two independent ideas when it is preceded by a comma.
80. (b) The phrase *on the back of* repeats part of the meaning of *endorse*.
81. (c) The idiom *come to grief* is a cliché.
82. (e) No error
83. (b) The term *man-made* means artificial.
84. (d) As the sentence stands, *she* can refer to either Edna or Margie.
85. (b) The terms *beginning* and *initial* repeat each other.
86. (c) *Swimming against the current of public opinion* is a cliché.
87. (d) The term *scarcely* should be followed by *any*, not by another negative (*no*).
88. (a) The standard phrase is *kind of*.
89. (c) The expression *burning issues of the day* is a cliché.
90. (d) The adverb *ever* was misplaced.

ANSWER KEY: PRACTICE EXAMINATION TWO / *Page* 88

Part 1

1. (3)	12. (3)	23. (1)	34. (1)
2. (3)	13. (2)	24. (5)	35. (2)
3. (1)	14. (4)	25. (2)	36. (3)
4. (5)	15. (3)	26. (3)	37. (3)
5. (1)	16. (4)	27. (5)	38. (1)
6. (2)	17. (2)	28. (3)	39. (5)
7. (5)	18. (5)	29. (4)	40. (2)
8. (5)	19. (3)	30. (1)	41. (1)
9. (3)	20. (2)	31. (5)	42. (4)
10. (1)	21. (1)	32. (2)	43. (2)
11. (2)	22. (4)	33. (2)	44. (3)

Part 2

45. (E)	52. (B)	59. (E)	66. (E)
46. (C)	53. (E)	60. (D)	67. (C)
47. (C)	54. (D)	61. (A)	68. (E)
48. (E)	55. (C)	62. (E)	69. (B)
49. (D)	56. (A)	63. (D)	70. (E)
50. (C)	57. (E)	64. (A)	
51. (A)	58. (B)	65. (C)	

Part 3

71. (d)	74. (e)	77. (c)	80. (c)	83. (b)
72. (d)	75. (d)	78. (a)	81. (d)	84. (d)
73. (b)	76. (b)	79. (b)	82. (d)	85. (c)

Summary of Results

Section	Number Correct	Number Wrong	Number Omitted
1			
2			
3			

Total correct: _____

Self-appraisal Chart

Total Correct	Percentile
81–85	99
76–80	90
60–63	50
49–52	25
40	10

Conversion Chart

The total number correct on the exam is converted to a scaled score ranging from 20 to 80. This conversion enables you to compare your results with those of other candidates who have taken the test. Half the scores fall above 50, half fall below; two-thirds of the candidates score between 40 and 69. The more competitive colleges usually prefer candidates who achieve 65 or above.

The following conversion chart can give you a rough approximation of what your English Composition score should be for this practice exam.

Number Correct	Test Score	Number Correct	Test Score
85	80	72	64
84	80	71	64
83	79	70	62
82	79	69	61
81	79	68	60
80	78	67	59
79	77	66	57
78	75	65	55
77	74	64	53
76	73	63	51
75	71	62	51
74	69	61	50
73	67	60	50

ANALYSIS OF ANSWERS: PRACTICE EXAMINATION TWO

Part 1

1. (3) Among the clichés are *time is running out* and *inevitable hours.*
2. (3) Among the clichés are *sailing into the fight* and *rose to the top.*
3. (1) The term *around* is colloquial when used as a synonym of *about.*
4. (5) No error
5. (1) The idiom *bank on* is nonstandard.
6. (2) The pronoun *which* does not have a definite antecedent.
7. (5) No error
8. (5) No error
9. (3) When *meat* is added to a *foundation* a mixed metaphor results.
10. (1) The preposition *up* is superfluous after *write.*
11. (2) Parallel construction requires *to type* and *to read* after *to do.*
12. (3) The phrases *sands of time running out* and *forsaking loyal friends* are clichés.
13. (2) The gerund *taking* requires the possessive *your* as subject.
14. (4) The adverb *again* repeats the idea of *repeat.*
15. (3) Only in a mixed metaphor can a *swan song* be a *spring board.*
16. (4) The idiom *bring to a termination* is wordy for *end.*
17. (2) Parallel construction is violated by *it should have survived.*
18. (5) No error
19. (3) The phrases *like a battering ram* and *weakest chinks* are among the clichés in this sentence.
20. (2) The pronoun *he* can refer to either Sheldon or Mr. Allerton.
21. (1) The idiom *cop out* is nonstandard.
22. (4) The terms *like* and *very much pleased* are repetitious.
23. (1) The standard idiom is *to wait for* not *to wait on.*
24. (5) No error
25. (2) The verb should be *is*, present tense, since the statement deals with something that is always true.
26. (3) The phrases *doomed to failure* and *untiring efforts* are clichés.
27. (5) No error
28. (3) The phrases *happy medium* and *easier said than done* are clichés.
29. (4) The terms *first* and *originally* are repetitious.
30. (1) The standard term is *lose*, not *lose out.*
31. (5) No error
32. (2) The pronoun *he* can refer to either Paul or his brother.
33. (2) The term *when waiting* has no noun to show who was waiting.
34. (1) The idiom *put up with* is nonstandard.
35. (2) The noun *towns* must follow *one of the most beautiful.*
36. (3) Wheels do not sweep over other than in mixed metaphors.
37. (3) The idiom *shout from the roof tops* is among the clichés in this sentence.
38. (1) The term *imminent* (about to happen) and not *eminent* (famous) is required.
39. (5) No error
40. (2) The man and not the style was ranked high.
41. (1) The term *suspicioned* is nonstandard.
42. (4) The clause *who constantly worries about his health* repeats the idea in *hypochondriac.*
43. (2) The participle *considering* has no noun or pronoun to modify.
44. (3) The words *run* and *bog* result in a mixed metaphor.

Part 2

45. (D) Both verbs should be active.
46. (C) The subjunctive past is *had* in a conditional clause.
47. (C) The verb is controlled by the singular noun Merwin.
48. (E) The conjunctive adverb *therefore* cannot be used as a coordinating conjunction.
49. (D) The pronoun *which* cannot be used to refer to the idea of the rest of the sentence.
50. (C) In standard usage *is because* cannot be used as an equivalent for *is that.*
51. (A) No error
52. (B) Patience cannot drive a tractor. Mixed metaphor.
53. (E) The preposition *including* is followed by the object *me*; *one* is the singular subject.
54. (D) The phrase *as good as* must be completed.
55. (C) The plural form is *women.*
56. (A) No error
57. (E) An introductory adverb clause is set off by a comma.
58. (B) The plural *delegates* requires the plural *were*; *who* refers to people and is subject of *were chosen.*
59. (E) The introductory clause contains precedent action and therefore the past perfect *had seen* is required.
60. (D) The correlatives *neither . . . nor* must be placed before the words they balance.
61. (A) No error
62. (E) The plural *promises* requires the plural *have.*
63. (D) The introductory gerund phrase must have a noun or pronoun to modify.
64. (A) No error
65. (C) The subject of the infinitive *to be* is in the object form (*me*).
66. (E) In its given position, *when I arrived* could modify either clause.
67. (C) The pronoun *any* is plural and requires *have* and *their.*
68. (E) The gerund phrase *upon receiving* requires a noun or pronoun to modify.
69. (B) Omission of parenthetical *I think* uncovers *who* as subject of *can advise.*
70. (E) Parallel construction requires *to be able* and *to earn.*

Part 3
71. (d) The pronoun *all* is plural and requires *were* and *their*.
72. (d) The term *more* requires the addition of *other*.
73. (b) The compound verb *ran and found* is the result.
74. (e) Because Miss Muller is our college adviser and guidance counselor, she addressed the assembly.
75. (d) The sentence contains a plural subject *Dave and several other members*.
76. (b) The infinitive phrase *to be used effectively* must not be converted into a dangling infinitive phrase.
77. (c) Because I saw the accident, I . . . .
78. (a) Found lying face down in the stagnant pool at the edge of town, the body was finally identified . . . .
79. (b) The plural *any* requires the plural verb *were*.
80. (c) That I was unprepared for the report soon became very obvious . . . .
81. (d) The conjunctive adverb cannot be punctuated as a coordinating conjunction.
82. (d) The compound verb *felt and asked* requires no comma before *and*.
83. (b) Marvin, who is my best friend, helped me plan our strategy.
84. (d) I was so angry that I wrote a letter which I mailed immediately to the company.
85. (c) The singular *time* requires the singular *has*.

ANSWER KEY: PRACTICE TEST THREE / Page 93

Part 1

1. (5)	12. (4)	23. (1)	34. (2)
2. (2)	13. (4)	24. (2)	35. (4)
3. (4)	14. (1)	25. (3)	36. (5)
4. (5)	15. (1)	26. (1)	37. (1)
5. (2)	16. (4)	27. (5)	38. (5)
6. (4)	17. (3)	28. (4)	39. (3)
7. (1)	18. (4)	29. (1)	40. (4)
8. (3)	19. (4)	30. (1)	41. (3)
9. (4)	20. (3)	31. (4)	42. (4)
10. (4)	21. (4)	32. (5)	43. (4)
11. (2)	22. (4)	33. (4)	44. (1)

Part 2

45. (B)	53. (D)	61. (A)	69. (E)
46. (E)	54. (C)	62. (C)	70. (D)
47. (C)	55. (E)	63. (A)	71. (B)
48. (C)	56. (B)	64. (C)	72. (B)
49. (D)	57. (C)	65. (D)	73. (D)
50. (A)	58. (A)	66. (A)	74. (C)
51. (D)	59. (A)	67. (B)	
52. (B)	60. (D)	68. (B)	

Part 3

75. (e)	78. (d)	81. (d)	84. (b)
76. (a)	79. (c)	82. (e)	85. (e)
77. (d)	80. (a)	83. (c)	86. (d)

Summary of Results

Section	Number Correct	Number Wrong	Number Omitted
1			
2			
3			

Total correct: _____

Self-appraisal Chart

Total Correct	Percentile
83–86	99
80	90
65	50
54	25
45	10

Conversion Chart

The total number correct on the exam is converted to a scaled score ranging from 20 to 80. This conversion enables you to compare your results with those of other candidates who have taken the test. Half the scores fall above 50, half fall below; two-thirds of the candidates score between 40 and 69. The more competitive colleges usually prefer candidates who achieve 65 or above.

The following conversion chart can give you a rough approximation of what your English Composition score should be for this practice exam.

Number Correct	Test Score	Number Correct	Test Score	Number Correct	Test Score
86	80	79	70	72	59
85	79	78	67	71	56
84	79	77	65	70	55
83	78	76	63	69	54
82	76	75	60	68	53
81	74	74	59	67	52
80	72	73	58	66	51
				65	50

ANALYSIS OF ANSWERS: PRACTICE EXAMINATION THREE

Part 1

1. (5) No error
2. (2) Helen is more capable than any *other* member.
3. (4) No comma is needed after *storm* since the *because* clause is in its natural position at the end of the sentence.
4. (5) No error
5. (2) Ellen is better *than* or at least as good as . . . .
6. (4) Without internal punctuation in the independent clauses, the conjunction (*and*) joining them should be preceded by a comma.
7. (1) The singular *anybody* should be followed by singular *his, he, has*.
8. (3) *To be able* must be changed to the participial *being able* to be parallel with *Relaxing* and *sleeping*.
9. (4) The possessive form is *anyone's*.
10. (4) A comma should separate *difficulties* and *resigning* since *resigning* is in apposition with *one way*.
11. (2) The phrase *as important* must be completed by *as*.
12. (4) A period, not a comma, should separate two independent clauses.
13. (4) The clause *who live around the corner* is a nonrestrictive clause and should be set off by commas.
14. (1) *Ben* is subject and should be followed by *knows*.
15. (1) *The development* is the subject and should be followed by *is*.
16. (4) *Of Human Bondage* is the title of a novel and should be underlined or italicized.
17. (3) The phrase *beautiful and varied* would be in parallel construction.
18. (4) There is no need of a comma to separate the subject from the verb.
19. (4) The comma after *road* should be inside the quotation marks.
20. (3) The phrase *and the multiplication of unlike terms* would continue the parallel construction.
21. (4) Introductory elliptical clause should be set off by a comma.
22. (4) The singular possessive form is *boy's*.
23. (1) *One* and *you* do not mix.
24. (2) The term *as interesting* must be followed by *as*.
25. (1) The adverb *carefully* requires *speedily* in parallel construction.
26. (1) The singular *student* requires *his*.
27. (5) No error
28. (4) The possessive of both *woman* and *women* ends in *'s*.
29. (1) The singular *anyone* requires *his*, not *their*.
30. (1) The plural *tapedecks* requires the plural *have*.
31. (4) The two independent ideas must be separated: *over. Our*.
32. (5) No error
33. (4) Since *William the Conqueror* is a composite name, no commas of separation are needed.
34. (2) The adjective *final* is one of the words that cannot logically be preceded by *more* or *most*.
35. (4) The possessive form is *ladies'*.
36. (5) No error
37. (4) The phrase *us seniors* is required as object of preposition.
38. (5) No error
39. (3) In parallel structure, *capable, sensitive* must be followed by another adjective, such as *controlled*.
40. (4) No comma is needed to separate subject from verb.
41. (3) The adverbs *quickly* and *decisively* require *cautiously* to continue the parallel construction.
42. (4) A comma, not a semicolon, is required to separate a noun from its appositive.
43. (4) A restrictive clause is not set off by commas.
44. (1) The pronoun *someone* requires singular *his*, not plural *their*.

Part 2

45. (B) We argue *with* a person and *against* an idea.
46. (E) No error
47. (C) The adverb *hardly* does not need *not* to carry negative values.
48. (C) The idiom *connect up* is nonstandard.
49. (D) The idiom *blame on* is nonstandard.
50. (A) The singular *Alice* requires the singular *is*.
51. (D) The pronoun *everyone* as subject requires *his*.
52. (B) The plural *gadgets* as subject requires the plural *are*.
53. (D) The idiom *push around* is nonstandard.
54. (C) The phrase *equally as* is not standard as a synonym for *equally*.
55. (E) No error
56. (B) The term *nowheres* is a nonstandard equivalent for *nowhere*.
57. (C) The phrase *by themselves* should be omitted since it repeats the idea in *isolated*.
58. (A) The idiom *was when* is a nonstandard equivalent for *occurred when*.
59. (A) The past perfect *had written* is required since it involves action precedent to past action.
60. (D) The adverb *scarcely* is followed by *any*, not *no* or *not*.
61. (A) The verb *take*, not *bring*, is required since the action is not toward the speaker.
62. (C) The expression *quite some time* is nonstandard.
63. (A) The terms *large* and *in size* repeat each other: omit *in size*.
64. (C) The standard idiom is *differs from*.
65. (D) The term *fewer* is required, not *less*, since units (*employees*) are involved.
66. (A) The idiom *have a loan of* is nonstandard as an equivalent for *borrow*.
67. (B) The term *somewheres* is nonstandard for *somewhere*.

68. (B) The defective verb *ought* cannot be preceded by *had*.
69. (E) No error
70. (D) The word *last* is required since *latter* can refer to two only.
71. (B) The term *up until* is not a standard equivalent for *until*.
72. (B) The idiom *kind of a* is nonstandard as an equivalent for *kind of*.
73. (D) Since action precedent to past action is described the past perfect tense is required.
74. (C) The standard idiom is *far different from*.

Part 3
75. (e) The pronoun *which* must refer to a specific word.
76. (a) The expression *as good* requires *as*: *than*, not *then*, is used in comparisons.
77. (d) Parallel structure and compound subject require this answer.
78. (d) The term *irregardless* is nonstandard.
79. (c) The idiom *kind of a* is nonstandard.
80. (a) No error
81. (d) The pronoun *her* is object of preposition *except*; the noun *effect* is required in the phrase *the effect of*.
82. (e) The conjunctive adverb *moreover* cannot function as a coordinating conjunction.
83. (c) The singular *set* requires the singular *is*; *lose* (*misplace*) and not *loose* (*lax, free*) is required.
84. (b) The verb *take* is required since the action is not toward the speaker; *these here* is nonstandard.
85. (e) The idiom *sort of a* is nonstandard; as a pronoun *which* refers to things or ideas while *who* refers to people.
86. (d) The participle *knowing* requires a logical word for it to modify.

ANSWER KEY: PRACTICE EXAMINATION FOUR / *Page* 96

Part 1
1. (5)	10. (3)	19. (2)	28. (1)	
2. (4)	11. (3)	20. (3)	29. (3)	
3. (1)	12. (1)	21. (1)	30. (3)	
4. (2)	13. (1)	22. (2)	31. (2)	
5. (2)	14. (3)	23. (1)	32. (1)	
6. (1)	15. (4)	24. (1)	33. (5)	
7. (2)	16. (4)	25. (2)		
8. (2)	17. (4)	26. (5)		
9. (1)	18. (2)	27. (1)		

Part 2
34. (a)	43. (b)	52. (b)	61. (a)	
35. (e)	44. (c)	53. (a)	62. (e)	
36. (c)	45. (e)	54. (c)	63. (d)	
37. (a)	46. (b)	55. (a)	64. (b)	
38. (a)	47. (c)	56. (d)	65. (b)	
39. (e)	48. (a)	57. (e)	66. (e)	
40. (d)	49. (e)	58. (d)	67. (d)	
41. (e)	50. (d)	59. (c)	68. (a)	
42. (b)	51. (b)	60. (d)	69. (e)	

Part 3
70. (E)	74. (E)	78. (A)	82. (C)
71. (B)	75. (D)	79. (B)	83. (B)
72. (C)	76. (D)	80. (B)	84. (E)
73. (B)	77. (E)	81. (D)	85. (E)

Summary of Results

Section	Number Correct	Number Wrong	Number Omitted
1			
2			
3			

Total correct: _____

Self-appraisal Chart

Total Correct	Percentile
83–85	99
81	90
68	50
55	25
42	10

Conversion Chart

The total number correct on the exam is converted to a scaled score ranging from 20 to 80. This conversion enables you to compare your results with those of other candidates who have taken the test. Half the scores fall above 50, half fall below; two-thirds of the candidates score between 40 and 69. The more competitive colleges usually prefer candidates who achieve 65 or above.

The following conversion chart can give you a rough approximation of what your English Composition score should be for this practice exam.

Number Correct	Test Score	Number Correct	Test Score
85	80	76	69
84	79	75	68
83	79	74	65
82	78	73	63
81	77	72	60
80	75	71	57
79	75	70	54
78	73	69	53
77	72	68	50

ANALYSIS OF ANSWERS: PRACTICE EXAMINATION FOUR

Part 1

1. (5) No error
2. (4) The word *irregardless* is nonstandard for *regardless*.
3. (1) The possessive *theirs* does not require an apostrophe.
4. (2) The question mark after *he asked* is in error.
5. (2) A comma, not a semicolon, sets off an introductory clause.
6. (1) The verb *let* (*allow*), not *leave* (*go*), is needed.
7. (2) The noun *army* must be preceded by *an* since *army* has an initial vowel.
8. (2) The participle *flying* has no word that it can modify logically.
9. (1) The standard term is *provided*, not *providing*.
10. (3) The pronoun *each* introduces a sentence fragment.
11. (3) Parallel construction requires *being able*.
14. (3) The plural *facilities* requires the plural *exceed*.
15. (4) Since *omitted* is followed by a comma, *do's* should also be so followed.
16. (4) A restrictive clause should not be set off by a comma.
17. (4) The preposition *into*, not *in*, is required in standard use.
18. (2) The standard term is *accidentally*.
19. (2) The verb *allowed* means *permitted* in standard usage.
20. (3) The adjective *mad* is a nonstandard synonym for *angry*.
21. (1) The adjectives *old* and *brown* should not be separated by a comma.
22. (2) The pronoun *who's* (*who is*) and not the possessive *whose* is required.
23. (1) The noun *mathematics* as a school subject is not capitalized.
24. (1) The adverb *anywheres* is nonstandard.
25. (2) The word *around* is not a standard equivalent for *about*.
26. (5) No error
27. (1) The idiom *being that* is a nonstandard equivalent for *since* or *because*.
28. (1) The term *but that* is not a standard equivalent for *that*.
29. (3) There is no apparent reason for splitting the infinitive *to stand*.
30. (3) The nonstandard *consensus of opinion* should be replaced by *opinion*.
31. (2) The standard idiom is *differs from*.
32. (1) The singular *group* requires the singular *comes*.
33. (5) No error

Part 2

34. (a) The term *seldom ever* is not a standard equivalent for *rarely*.
35. (e) No error
36. (c) *Swimming* and *flying* are confused into a mixed metaphor.
37. (a) The word *somewheres* is nonstandard.
38. (a) The preposition *into*, not *in*, is intended.
39. (e) No error
40. (d) The past subjunctive form is *had*, not *would have*.
41. (e) No error
42. (b) The additional *final* is superfluous.
43. (b) The adverb *basically* is unnecessary.
44. (c) The phrases *seamy side of life* and *simple joys* are clichés.
45. (e) No error
46. (b) The phrase *in various ways* is superfluous.
47. (c) The expressions *seas of uncertainty* and *black thoughts of despair* are prime clichés.
48. (a) The pronouns *that* or *whom* (*people*) are required in place of *which* (*things*).
49. (e) No error
50. (d) The pronoun *he* lacks a definite antecedent.
51. (b) The phrase *in color* is unnecessary.
52. (b) The word *together* is superfluous.
53. (a) The term *these here* is nonstandard for *these*.
54. (c) The idiom *follow in the footsteps* is a cliché.
55. (a) The term *irregardless* is nonstandard.
56. (d) The preposition *between* should be followed by *me*.
57. (e) No error

PRACTICE EXAMINATIONS FOR THE ENGLISH COMPOSITION TEST

58. (d) Parallel construction requires *and for doing good*.
59. (c) The idiom *does my heart good* is a cliché.
60. (d) Spoons cannot be in doubt.
61. (a) The idiom *blame on* is nonstandard.
62. (e) No error
63. (d) The present subjunctive form is *were*.
64. (b) The word *both* is superfluous.
65. (b) The preposition *at* is unnecessary.
66. (e) No error
67. (d) The participle *shouting* is a dangling modifier.
68. (a) The term *nowheres* is a nonstandard equivalent for *nowhere*.
69. (e) No error

Part 3
70. (E) He insists that doing good is merely feeding one's ego.
71. (B) That they move so slowly is often the reason for our coming to the conclusion that giant turtles . . . .
72. (C) Because the star performer has been taken ill suddenly, the performance . . . .
73. (B) . . . some of my friends have . . . .
74. (E) When the nights became cold and crisp with the approach of autumn, the leaves of the surrounding forest began to turn.
75. (D) . . . Mr. Pollett is more efficient than any other diagnostician in our division.
76. (D) . . . money that is squandered . . . .
77. (E) When he was willing to be impatient with us, it . . . .
78. (A) These songs taught us in our childhood are the ones we remember longest.
79. (B) This fine small company, which is known for the excellence of its products, employs . . . .
80. (B) Harold knew what my reaction would be; nevertheless, he insisted . . . .
81. (D) The Pulvers, the owners of the property, are the ones . . . .
82. (C) The Rhodes scholar spoke before huge audiences of students and tried . . . .
83. (B) Because Mr. Arnold is my former college counselor, I often . . . .
84. (E) Fashions are not brought about by changes in man's needs but come about . . . .
85. (E) Without resorting to the set of instructions when we tried to assemble the mechanism, the task became . . . .

ANSWER KEY: PRACTICE EXAMINATION FIVE / Page 100

Part 1
1. (1)
2. (1)
3. (2)
4. (5)
5. (2)
6. (2)
7. (3)
8. (5)
9. (2)
10. (1)
11. (3)
12. (4)
13. (3)
14. (1)
15. (4)
16. (5)
17. (3)
18. (5)
19. (2)
20. (2)
21. (1)
22. (2)
23. (1)
24. (4)
25. (4)
26. (4)
27. (2)
28. (2)
29. (4)
30. (2)
31. (1)
32. (1)
33. (3)

Part 2
34. (C)
35. (E)
36. (B)
37. (B)
38. (D)
39. (E)
40. (E)
41. (A)
42. (C)
43. (A)
44. (C)
45. (B)
46. (E)
47. (C)
48. (C)
49. (B)
50. (D)
51. (C)
52. (A)
53. (C)
54. (E)
55. (E)
56. (A)
57. (D)
58. (B)
59. (A)
60. (C)
61. (B)
62. (D)
63. (C)

Part 3
64. (c)
65. (b)
66. (e)
67. (e)
68. (b)
69. (d)
70. (d)
71. (d)
72. (a)
73. (d)
74. (b)
75. (e)
76. (e)
77. (a)
78. (c)

Summary of Results

Section	Number Correct	Number Wrong	Number Omitted
1			
2			
3			

Total correct: _____

Self-appraisal Chart

Total Correct	Percentile
76–78	99
74	90
65	50
48	25
39	10

Conversion Chart

The total number correct on the exam is converted to a scaled score ranging from 20 to 80. This conversion enables you to compare your results with those of other candidates who have taken the test. Half the scores fall above 50, half fall below; two-thirds of the candidates score between 40 and 69. The more competitive colleges usually prefer candidates who achieve 65 or above.

The following conversion chart can give you a rough approximation of what your English Composition score should be for this practice exam.

ANSWERS TO PRACTICE EXAMINATION FIVE

Number Correct	Test Score	Number Correct	Test Score
78	80	71	66
77	79	70	65
76	78	69	62
75	75	68	59
74	73	67	56
73	72	66	52
72	69	65	50

ANALYSIS OF ANSWERS: PRACTICE EXAMINATION FIVE

Part 1

1. (1) The term *like* is not a standard equivalent for *as if*.
2. (1) The term *except* is not a standard equivalent for *unless*.
3. (2) The term *fewer*, not *less*, is required with units (errors).
4. (5) No error
5. (2) The idiom *in back of* is a nonstandard equivalent for *behind*.
6. (2) The plural *clothes* requires the plural *do*.
7. (3) The standard form is *occurred when*, not *was when*.
8. (5) No error
9. (2) The phrase *inside of* is not a standard synonym for *within*.
10. (1) The pronoun *they* is an unnecessary appositive.
11. (3) The standard form is *losing*, not *losing out*.
12. (4) The subordinating conjunction *because* should not be preceded by a comma when the clause it introduces is in its natural order.
13. (3) The pronoun *she* has no antecedent.
14. (1) The noun *advice*, not the verb *advise*, is needed.
15. (4) The term *over with* is nonstandard for *over*.
16. (5) No error
17. (3) The word *concern* is not in standard usage in this sentence.
18. (5) No error
19. (2) The term required is *complimented (praised)* and not *complemented (completed)*.
20. (2) When referring to health, *well*, not *good*, is used.
21. (1) The word *again* is superfluous.
22. (2) I referred to him (*whom*).
23. (1) The standard idiom is *try to*.
24. (4) The participle *lying (resting)*, not *laying (putting)*, is required.
25. (4) A compound verb (*noticed and called*) is not separated by a semicolon (or a comma).
26. (4) The plural *there are*, not the singular *there's (there is)*, is required.
27. (2) The plural *sisters* requires *know*.
28. (2) Required is *you and I are*.
29. (4) The word *aggravated* is nonstandard as an equivalent for *annoyed*, *irritated*, or *exacerbated*.
30. (2) The pronoun *his*, not *him*, is the subject of the gerund *having*.
31. (1) The past subjunctive form is *had*, not *would have*.
32. (1) The standard past perfect is *had drunk*.
33. (3) The punctuation should be ; *moreover*, in this instance.

Part 2

34. (C) Parallel construction requires *either the plans or the ones*.
35. (E) The standard form for the past subjunctive is *had consulted*.
36. (B) The past perfect *had hoped* is required for action precedent to past action (*were disrupting*).
37. (B) The standard idiom is *because of*, not *due to*; required is the standard *different from*, not *different than*.
38. (D) The pronoun *us* is required as object of *of*; *was* is required to follow the singular *no one*.
39. (E) The present perfect *has lived* is required for action begun in the past and carried into the present.
40. (E) The phrase *by nine* must be so placed that it can refer to only one of the three verbs in the sentence.
41. (A) No error
42. (C) The elliptical clause *When in doubt* must refer to a specific noun or pronoun.
43. (A) No error
44. (C) The pronoun *everyone* requires *was*; the preposition *except* should be followed by the object form (*me*).
45. (B) The nonrestrictive appositive phrase, *the invention of devils and saints*, should be set off by commas.
46. (E) The verb form *hadn't ought* is nonstandard for *ought not*; *he* is predicate nominative after *must be*.

47. (C) Because *At thirty* dangles, *When he was thirty* is required; the singular *reputation* requires singular *was*.
48. (C) The past subjunctive is required.
49. (B) The standard idiom is *better than: at least* should be close to the word modified (*equal*).
50. (D) The participle phrase *Having worked* dangles.
51. (C) Construction requires *persuasive* (adjective) to parallel *logical* (adjective) and *clear* (adjective).
52. (A) Two closely related independent clauses may be separated by a semicolon.
53. (C) The plural *collections* requires the plural *have*.
54. (E) The object form *him* cannot be the subject of gerund *helping*; the singular *everyone* requires the singular *knows*.
55. (E) Parallel construction requires *not only seeing but also visiting*.
56. (A) An introductory clause is set off by a comma.
57. (D) With the correlatives *neither . . . nor*, the verb agrees with the noun or pronoun (*I*) following *nor*.
58. (B) The pronoun *which* cannot refer to the main idea in the rest of the sentence.
59. (A) An introductory clause is set off by a comma.
60. (C) The standard idiom is *occurs when*, not *is when*.
61. (B) The past perfect *had lived* is required for past action preceding past action (*was*).
62. (D) The expression *being that* is not a standard equivalent for *since* or *because*.
63. (C) Parallel construction requires the participle *prevaricating*.

Part 3
64. (c) We will remember as heroes who died for their countrymen everyone of the men who had been caught in the deadly trap.
65. (b) I had not helped to make our relationships any the more cordial by calling him a falsifier.
66. (e) The new evidence and the facts . . . are sufficient . . . .
67. (e) His first opponent was defeated by the champion who hoped . . . .
68. (b) Konner is a man who has devoted . . . .
69. (d) Either Paul or Dave has been selected . . . .
70. (d) Mel told Margie that she was leaving . . . .
71. (d) This model and its predecessors are too . . . .
72. (a) Mahogany is better than any other wood for making . . . .
73. (d) Although I am reading all the directions, I can . . . .
74. (b) I cannot imagine my ever being able to sing like Joan . . . .
75. (e) His answering me in anger irritated me very much.
76. (e) The visitor who had just arrived from their hometown greeted them as they came into the house.
77. (a) Because you had listened to me, we completed . . . .
78. (c) Edna along with her sister is insisting that we . . . .

ANSWER KEY: PRACTICE EXAMINATION SIX / Page 105

Part 1

1. (5)
2. (1)
3. (4)
4. (4)
5. (2)
6. (3)
7. (1)
8. (1)
9. (2)
10. (3)
11. (1)
12. (1)
13. (1)
14. (3)
15. (5)
16. (3)
17. (3)
18. (5)
19. (1)
20. (2)
21. (3)
22. (4)
23. (5)
24. (1)
25. (3)
26. (1)
27. (2)
28. (2)
29. (4)
30. (5)
31. (1)
32. (3)
33. (4)
34. (2)
35. (1)
36. (3)
37. (2)
38. (2)
39. (3)
40. (1)
41. (5)
42. (3)
43. (4)
44. (2)

Part 2

45. (C)
46. (B)
47. (A)
48. (C)
49. (A)
50. (A)
51. (E)
52. (E)
53. (A)
54. (D)
55. (A)
56. (A)
57. (A)
58. (B)
59. (B)
60. (C)
61. (D)
62. (E)
63. (C)
64. (B)
65. (C)
66. (E)
67. (B)
68. (E)
69. (B)
70. (E)
71. (A)
72. (C)

Part 3

73. (A)
74. (B)
75. (C)
76. (B)
77. (E)
78. (D)
79. (E)
80. (B)
81. (D)
82. (E)
83. (A)
84. (D)
85. (C)
86. (E)
87. (B)

Summary of Results

Section	Number Correct	Number Wrong	Number Omitted
1			
2			
3			

Total correct: _____

Self-appraisal Chart

Total Correct	Percentile
84–87	99
80	90
70	50
52	25
40	10

ANSWERS TO PRACTICE EXAMINATION SIX

Conversion Chart

The total number correct on the exam is converted to a scaled score ranging from 20 to 80. This conversion enables you to compare your results with those of other candidates who have taken the test. Half the scores fall above 50, half fall below; two-thirds of the candidates score between 40 and 69. The more competitive colleges usually prefer candidates who achieve 65 or above.

The following conversion chart can give you a rough approximation of what your English Composition score should be for this practice exam.

Number Correct	Test Score	Number Correct	Test Score
87	80	78	67
86	80	77	66
85	79	76	63
84	77	75	60
83	75	74	58
82	74	73	55
81	73	72	53
80	71	71	50
79	69		

ANALYSIS OF ANSWERS: PRACTICE EXAMINATION SIX

Part 1

1. (5) No error
2. (1) The term *like* is not a standard equivalent for *as if*.
3. (4) The word *around* is unnecessary.
4. (4) The term *equally* is unnecessary.
5. (2) Clark's father had not died at the age of ten.
6. (3) The expression *untimely deaths* is a cliché.
7. (1) The idiom *kind of a* is nonstandard.
8. (1) The word *fix* is in nonstandard use in this sentence.
9. (2) To continue the parallel construction, and the *faithfulness of friends* is required.
10. (3) A key can be used to stamp out only in a mixed metaphor.
11. (1) The standard idiom is *better than*.
12. (1) The phrase *inside of* is in nonstandard use.
13. (1) The standard form is *reason is that*, not *reason is because*.
14. (3) The expression *an ounce of strength* is a cliché.
15. (5) No error
16. (3) The expression *a mine of information* is a cliché.
17. (3) The expressions *answer in the negative* and *approaching festivities* are clichés.
18. (5) No error
19. (1) The article *a*, and not *an*, precedes a word beginning with a consonant.
20. (2) The present subjunctive form is *If I were*.
21. (3) The expressions *gracious offer* and *festive table* are clichés.
22. (4) The idea of *conform* is repeated in *think exactly what other members do and think*.
23. (5) No error
24. (1) The phrase *pep pills* is nonstandard.
25. (3) Ship and driver's seat result in a mixed metaphor.
26. (1) The standard idiom is *deep interest in*.
27. (2) A style cannot rank with painters, only with *that of other painters*.
28. (2) He (*who*) is as good as . . . .
29. (4) The word *communicable* means the same as transferred from one person to another.
30. (5) No error
31. (1) The idiom is *different from*.
32. (3) The expressions *endless hours* and *vain attempt* are clichés.
33. (4) The word *last* is unnecessary.
34. (2) The adverb *smoothly* is required to modify *to run*.
35. (1) In standard usage *preferable* is not preceded by *more*.
36. (3) The idiom *from the cradle to the grave* is a cliché.
37. (2) *It is up to us . . . to see . . . .*
38. (2) *. . . men who are . . . .*
39. (3) The idiom *tides of fortune* is a cliché.
40. (1) The word *cool* is in nonstandard use.
41. (5) No error
42. (3) The expression *ruin staring him in the face* is a cliché.

43. (4) The word *back* is unnecessary.
44. (2) The plural *any* requires the plural *are*.

Part 2
45. (C) The solution did not come to a reason.
46. (B) The term *hardly* is followed by *any*, not *no*.
47. (A) The present perfect *have lived* is required to describe action begun in the past and continued onto the present.
48. (C) A comma, not a semicolon, is required to continue the parallel construction.
49. (A) The form for the past subjunctive is *had*, not *would have*.
50. (A) The past perfect is *had begun*.
51. (E) No error
52. (E) No error
53. (A) A person is *healthy*; climate is *healthful*.
54. (D) The term *statute* (*law*), not *statue* (*monument*) is required.
55. (A) In a listing *are* is not followed by a colon.
56. (A) The word *formally* (*in a formal manner*), and not *formerly* (*at one time*), is required.
57. (A) The form *past*, not *passed*, is required.
58. (B) The compound verbs *had rung* and *had begun* should not be separated by a comma.
59. (B) The expression *had gone and* is nonstandard.
60. (C) The pronoun *they* lacks an antecedent.
61. (D) The pronoun *which* lacks an antecedent.
62. (E) No error
63. (C) The preposition *except* should be followed by *me* as an object.
64. (B) The adjective *those*, and not the pronoun *them*, is required to modify the noun *things*.
65. (C) The predicate adjective form is *sweet*, not *sweetly*.
66. (E) No error
67. (B) . . . *an airplane* . . . .
68. (E) no error
69. (B) The term *scarcely* is followed by *any*, not *no*.
70. (E) No error
71. (A) The verb *lie* (*rest*), not *lay* (*put*), is required.
72. (C) The singular *set* requires the singular *was*.

Part 3
73. (A) Such was the pace of changing times that it was possible for that . . . .
74. (B) A resolution of the crisis in the Presidency is the most urgent business . . . .
75. (C) A campus that barters away its autonomy will soon cease to supply any . . . .
76. (B) To gain relatively minor tactical advantages against an enemy, the Air Force, over the years, has built . . . .
77. (E) We are, on the contrary, merely being made by the present crisis to face a little sooner . . . .
78. (D) We should start telling ourselves the truth since these difficult questions . . . .
79. (E) Little protection at all from the threat of another superpower was proved by our conventional military forces, an expensive, empty shell of a shield.
80. (B) One of the few examples of public business not financed by public funds is the campaigns which are public business.
81. (D) A spirit which was symbolized by the handclasp at Kilometer 10 could substantially enhance . . . .
82. (E) Because too little of the extra income that accrued to owners was applied to the correction of violations and improvement of buildings, the revised rules . . . .
83. (A) Drawing into the river channel salt water from the nearby sea, the power plant . . . .
84. (D) Like other forms of pollution, which are thus to an extent inevitable, a byproduct of economic growth . . . .
85. (C) . . . over which they had had . . . .
86. (E) Convinced that the vastness of Russia would frustrate Hitler as it had Napoleon, Prokofiev, in 1947, undertook . . . .
87. (B) That life exists elsewhere in the universe and corollary, that some of the presumed beings have reached a higher state of intelligence than ours, are probabilities accepted these days by astronomers.

ANSWER KEY: PRACTICE EXAMINATION SEVEN / Page 109

Part 1
1. (3)
2. (4)
3. (3)
4. (2)
5. (1)
6. (3)
7. (4)
8. (1)
9. (3)
10. (1)
11. (2)
12. (1)
13. (3)
14. (3)
15. (3)
16. (1)
17. (2)
18. (2)
19. (1)
20. (5)
21. (3)
22. (5)
23. (4)
24. (4)
25. (5)
26. (3)
27. (1)
28. (2)
29. (4)
30. (3)
31. (5)
32. (4)
33. (2)
34. (1)
35. (5)
36. (2)
37. (3)
38. (2)
39. (4)
40. (3)
41. (1)
42. (2)
43. (5)
44. (4)

Part 2
45. (c)
46. (e)
47. (a)
48. (d)
49. (e)
50. (c)
51. (b)
52. (c)
53. (a)
54. (c)
55. (b)
56. (d)

Part 3
57. (E)
58. (B)
59. (C)
60. (C)
61. (D)
62. (A)
63. (E)
64. (B)
65. (D)
66. (D)
67. (A)
68. (B)
69. (E)
70. (C)
71. (B)
72. (E)
73. (A)
74. (D)
75. (E)
76. (B)
77. (D)

Summary of Results

Section	Number Correct	Number Wrong	Number Omitted
1			
2			
3			

Total correct: _____

ANSWERS TO PRACTICE EXAMINATION SEVEN

Conversion Chart

The total number correct on the exam is converted to a scaled score ranging from 20 to 80. This conversion enables you to compare your results with those of other candidates who have taken the test. Half the scores fall above 50, half fall below; two-thirds of the candidates score between 40 and 69. The more competitive colleges usually prefer candidates who achieve 65 or above.

The following conversion chart can give you a rough approximation of what your English Composition score should be for this practice exam.

Number Correct	Test Score	Number Correct	Test Score
77	80	64	64
76	79	63	62
75	77	62	60
74	76	61	59
73	75	60	57
72	74	59	56
71	73	58	54
70	72	57	54
69	72	56	53
68	70	55	52
67	69	54	51
66	67	53	50
65	65		

Self-appraisal Chart

Total Correct	Percentile
75–77	99
70	90
48	50
40	25
32	10

ANALYSIS OF ANSWERS: PRACTICE EXAMINATION SEVEN

Part 1

1. (3) Among others, *to the point of exhaustion* is a cliché.
2. (4) The phrase *to the eye* is unnecessary.
3. (3) Among others, *tug at our heartstrings* is a cliché.
4. (2) The plural *data* requires the plural *point*.
5. (1) The required term is *all ready*.
6. (3) Among others, *firm hand on the helm* is a cliché.
7. (4) An unnecessary addition to *combine* is *together*.
8. (1) The required term is *formerly* (at one time), not *formally* (in a formal manner).
9. (3) Surmounting (climbing above) a cancer results in a mixed metaphor.
10. (1) Required is *insinuated* (hinted), not *inferred* (deduced).
11. (2) . . . *than any other professional.* . . .
12. (1) A standard synonym for *likely* is not *liable*.
13. (3) Among others, *take my pen in hand* is a cliché.
14. (3) Among others, *face the trials ahead* is a cliché.
15. (3) *Changing horses in midstream* and *floating through a sieve* result in a mixed metaphor.
16. (1) Required is *respectfully* (with respect) and not *respectively* (severally).
17. (2) The phrase *by telephone* must be placed closer to the word it modifies, *told*.
18. (2) The required correlation is *either the winner or co-winner*.
19. (1) The required term is *proceed* (walk), not *precede* (go ahead of).
20. (5) No error
21. (3) The phrases *clothed all outdoors* and *in a white mantle* are clichés.
22. (5) No error
23. (4) The word *preliminary* is unnecessary.
24. (4) The phrase *in appearance* is unnecessary.
25. (5) No error
26. (3) Swimming in deep water and turning over a new leaf result in a mixed metaphor.
27. (1) Required is *stature* (height) and not *statue* (monument).
28. (2) The pronoun *he* may refer to *alumnus, son,* or *coach*.
29. (4) The phrase *the fact* is unnecessary.
30. (3) One can be impaled (stuck on a pole) in quicksand only in a mixed metaphor.

31. (5) No error
32. (4) The word *conspicuously* is unnecessary.
33. (2) There is no noun for *Having read* to modify.
34. (1) The word required is *prophecies*.
35. (5) No error
36. (2) ... *by trees in no other area in the world.*
37. (3) The idiom *bang my head against a stone wall* is a cliché.
38. (2) ... *and the tires have been rotated.*
39. (4) The word *again* is unnecessary.
40. (3) The phrase *blind as a bat* is a cliché.
41. (1) Required is *employer* (one who hires others) and not *employee* (one who is hired).
42. (2) The clause *which would open the closet* should follow *key*, not *desk drawer: I placed in the desk drawer the key which....*
43. (5) No error
44. (4) The idea of *momentous* is repeated in the clause *that are so significant in our lives.*

Part 2

45. (c) Only after they had carried out 45 painstaking experiments, did they....
46. (e) Viewing the substance without the aid of a microscope, we found it no different from....
47. (a) It turned out to be a toy that gluts the market for a short while and then disappears.
48. (d) ... everyone but Edna and me.
49. (e) The child who has personality traits which do not match....
50. (c) I could not bear this failure coming at the end....
51. (b) A minority culture inevitably finds itself in a constant state of war when it strives to maintain....
52. (c) In order to challenge the story's main characters with the cruelty of nature and the bleakness of death, except for the faded green of its foliage, the scenery is all in black and white.
53. (a) War still makes a mockery of all of man's pious utterings because, despite all his resources, he is unable to prevent it.
54. (c) The essentiality of the service at stake, whether in the public or private sector, should be the only sound criterion for banning strikes according to the critics.
55. (b) Each of the main characters which are interpolated into the main story tells a set of lurid tales.
56. (d) One of the two themes in this brief essay stresses the dramatic psychological growth that occurs in the opening years while the other theme emphasizes the importance....

Part 3

57. (E) Required is *number* (units), not *amount* (quantity).
58. (B) The pronoun *she* could refer either to *Frances* or her *sister*.
59. (C) The phrase *in color* is unnecessary; the adjective *red* requires the adjective *bulky* for parallel construction.
60. (C) The standard term is *proved*; required is *place into* not *place in.*
61. (D) The parallel construction is *either a more economical way or a financial backer.*
62. (A) No error
63. (E) The past perfect *had worked* is required for past action preceding past action.
64. (B) The adverb *softly* requires adverb *politely* for parallel construction.
65. (D) The noun *latter* refers to two only.
66. (D) The singular *sense of humor* requires the singular verb *makes.*
67. (A) No error
68. (B) The phrase *To be effective* must have a noun or pronoun that it can modify logically.
69. (E) The past perfect *had made* is required for action that preceded past action.
70. (C) The pronoun *it* lacks a definite antecedent.
71. (B) Required as plural verb is *are* for plural *fewer chances.*
72. (E) The adjective *friendly* and the adjective *easygoing* require adjective *cooperative* in parallel construction.
73. (A) No error
74. (D) The word *chances* (plural) requires *have* (plural).
75. (E) Two closely related independent clauses can be separated by a semicolon.
76. (B) In the 1920s there were very few business machines and no casette recorders.
77. (D) The word *needs* should be followed by *are*; singular *point of view* requires singular *is.*

ANSWER KEY: PRACTICE EXAMINATION EIGHT / Page 112

Part 1

1. (4)	12. (5)	23. (2)	34. (2)	
2. (3)	13. (3)	24. (1)	35. (2)	
3. (4)	14. (2)	25. (3)	36. (3)	
4. (4)	15. (4)	26. (4)	37. (5)	
5. (2)	16. (2)	27. (1)	38. (2)	
6. (1)	17. (4)	28. (3)	39. (3)	
7. (5)	18. (3)	29. (1)	40. (2)	
8. (4)	19. (4)	30. (3)	41. (3)	
9. (2)	20. (4)	31. (4)	42. (4)	
10. (1)	21. (3)	32. (2)	43. (5)	
11. (2)	22. (1)	33. (1)	44. (1)	

Part 2

45. (B)	50. (B)	55. (B)	60. (B)
46. (E)	51. (A)	56. (B)	61. (C)
47. (D)	52. (C)	57. (C)	62. (C)
48. (C)	53. (D)	58. (A)	63. (E)
49. (A)	54. (E)	59. (A)	

Part 3

64. (b)	68. (d)	72. (a)	76. (e)
65. (c)	69. (e)	73. (b)	77. (b)
66. (e)	70. (e)	74. (c)	78. (b)
67. (b)	71. (b)	75. (e)	79. (c)

ANSWERS TO PRACTICE EXAMINATION EIGHT

80. (c) 83. (e) 86. (e) 89. (a) 92. (b) 95. (c) 98. (b)
81. (d) 84. (b) 87. (c) 90. (c) 93. (e) 96. (a) 99. (e)
82. (b) 85. (b) 88. (c) 91. (c) 94. (c) 97. (b) 100. (d)

Summary of Results

Section	Number Correct	Number Wrong	Number Omitted
1			
2			
3			

Total correct: _____

Self-appraisal Chart

Total Correct	Percentile
96–100	99
88–92	90
70–72	50
42	25
35	10

Conversion Chart

The total number correct on the exam is converted to a scaled score ranging from 20 to 80. This conversion enables you to compare your results with those of other candidates who have taken the test. Half the scores fall above 50, half fall below; two-thirds of the candidates score between 40 and 69. The more competitive colleges usually prefer candidates who achieve 65 or above.

The following conversion chart can give you a rough approximation of what your English Composition score should be for this practice exam.

Number Correct	Test Score	Number Correct	Test Score
100	80	86	73
99	79	85	71
98	79	84	70
97	79	83	69
96	78	82	69
95	78	81	67
94	78	80	65
93	77	79	63
92	77	78	60
91	76	77	59
90	76	76	57
89	75	75	54
88	75	74	53
87	74	73	50

ANALYSIS OF ANSWERS: PRACTICE EXAMINATION EIGHT

Part 1

1. (4) The subject of the gerund *having* should be in the possessive case (*our*).
2. (3) . . . as we are. . . .
3. (4) The idiom is *different from*.
4. (4) The last *to* is repetitious.
5. (2) After the helping verb *had*, *drunk* is the required form.
6. (1) The adverb *altogether* is required.
7. (5) No error
8. (4) The phrase *each other* can refer to two only.
9. (2) . . . he thinks he (who) is guilty. . . .
10. (1) Subject *you* must agree with participle. Should be rephrased so that sentence reads *to read a poem well, you* . . .
11. (2) The term *but that* is in nonstandard use.
12. (5) No error
13. (3) The subject *set* (singular) requires the singular *was*.
14. (2) No hyphen is needed.
15. (4) The verb form *hadn't ought* is nonstandard.
16. (2) An introductory adverb clause is followed by a comma.
17. (4) The singular subject (*group*) is followed by a singular verb (*was*).
18. (3) In standard use *unique* cannot be compared and cannot thus be used with *more* or *most*.
19. (4) The pronoun *one*, not *you*, is required for consistency.
20. (4) The word *seen* should not be capitalized.
21. (3) The standard idiom is *kind of*.
22. (1) The pronoun *he* could refer to either the officer or the private.
23. (2) The standard idiom is *to feel bad*.
24. (1) The term *being that* is nonstandard when used as an equivalent of *since* or *because*.
25. (3) The standard phrase is *put into*.

26. (4) Logic requires *than any other*.
27. (1) The phrase to remember is *the effects of*.
28. (3) The adjective *meaningful* is required since the words did not make the sounds.
29. (1) The singular unit *two-thirds* should be followed by the singular verb *has*.
30. (3) The pronoun *we* is unnecessary.
31. (4) The objective *me* should follow the preposition *by*.
32. (2) Ingredients cannot bake the cake.
33. (1) The standard form for a condition contrary to fact is *If I had*.
34. (2) The negative *but* cannot follow the negative *not*.
35. (2) The phrase *each other* can refer to only two.
36. (3) The idiom *every so often* is nonstandard.
37. (5) No error
38. (2) The plural *counselors* is followed by *who were*.
39. (3) The plural *nurses* is followed by *who have been*.
40. (2) The pronoun *they* lacks an antecedent.
41. (3) The singular *concern* requires the singular verb *was*.
42. (4) The standard term is *human beings*, not *humans*.
43. (5) No error
44. (1) The past tense *had been deployed* is required.

Part 2
45. (B) Even though the depression seriously cut funds for medical research, the thirties. . . .
46. (E) When a peace . . . is put into question, the bases will have undergone a change.
47. (D) First-aid manuals are bought and read only by people who already know what to do in an emergency and just want. . . .
48. (C) More of our energy resources are consumed by the World Trade Center when it is completely lighted up night after night than by all the homes in a large-sized suburbia.
49. (A) Had they attempted to control . . . attitudes, the political leaders would have faced serious dilemmas.
50. (B) The fact that lawyers in general . . . immoral often allows them to act. . . .
51. (A) Preliterate hunting and gathering tribes that offer the best speculation . . . have lived are the highly pacific people. . . .
52. (C) No government office, not even the highest in the land, carries with it the right . . .
53. (D) Invoked by officials at widely disparate levels of government service, national security has become a kind of talisman to justify a wide range of apparently illegal activities.
54. (E) That the achievements in space of the crews of Skylab have enormous scientific value was made abundantly clear years ago.
55. (B) The basic need remained for passage by Congress of a law extending to farm workers the same machinery that other American workers have had for nearly four decades for. . . .

56. (B) So quietly does winter come over the hill and down the valley that all you hear are crisp leaves skittering or. . . .
57. (C) In order to avert a real fuel crisis, the President has made a logical and reasonable request in asking us. . . .
58. (A) To render the United States independent of foreign energy supplies, by the end of this decade if possible, a momentous program is about to be embarked upon.
59. (A) Although political parties are not mentioned in the written Constitution, the two-party system has become. . . .
60. (B) When we see the men about a ruler, we get our first impression of him and his brains.
61. (C) Mao Tse-tung . . . China; Lenin had set. . . .
62. (C) Yet we all should be reminded that the shock waves of change that had their origin in World War II are not. . . .
63. (E) We Americans seem to like to put our political system to the test now and then and hope that. . . .

Part 3
64. (b) The past subjunctive form is *If I had listened*.
65. (c) The word required is *let* (*allow*), not *leave* (*go*).
66. (e) No error
67. (b) After the infinitive *to be* the object *her* is required.
68. (d) The word *beginning* repeats the idea of *how it all started*.
69. (e) . . . *much more in favor of Helen than of me*.
70. (e) The singular *each* requires the singular *has*.
71. (b) The plural *doubts* requires plural *were*.
72. (a) The idioms *throwing caution to the wind* and *a different ball game* are clichés.
73. (b) The plural *remains* requires plural *were*.
74. (c) . . . *far less than*. . . .
75. (e) No error
76. (e) The plural *brothers* determines the plural verb form (*have*).
77. (b) The conjunctive adverb cannot be used along with a comma to join two complete ideas.
78. (b) The phrase *scarcely any* cannot be preceded by *not*.
79. (c) A *capital* is always *on top of* a column.
80. (c) The word required is *imminent* (*about to happen*).
81. (d) The words *simplest, basic, beginning* are repetitious.
82. (b) Scenery cannot be in a hurry.
83. (e) No error
84. (b) Action preceding past action must be in the past perfect tense (*had put*).
85. (b) The pronoun required is *its* (possessive), not *it's* (*it is*).
86. (e) No error
87. (c) The word *accept* (*receive*), and not the ex-

cept meaning *exclude*, is required.
88. (c) . . . more or less than. . . .
89. (a) The idiom *as cold as ice* is a cliché.
90. (c) The standard expression is *Let it lie*.
91. (c) In standard use *perfect* cannot be preceded by *more* or *most*.
92. (b) The participle *talking* requires a word that it can logically modify.
93. (e) No error

94. (c) When two are being compared *more*, not *most*, is required.
95. (c) . . . *is as good as* . . .
96. (a) The idiom *left in a lurch* is a cliché.
97. (b) The present subjunctive is *If he were*. . . .
98. (b) A comma cannot join two complete ideas.
99. (e) No error
100. (d) The word *conspicuously* is unnecessary.

ANSWER KEY: PRACTICE EXAMINATION NINE / Page 117

Part 1
1. (1)   12. (2)   23. (5)   34. (2)
2. (4)   13. (5)   24. (4)   35. (1)
3. (3)   14. (2)   25. (4)   36. (5)
4. (1)   15. (4)   26. (1)   37. (1)
5. (2)   16. (4)   27. (2)   38. (1)
6. (4)   17. (5)   28. (5)   39. (2)
7. (2)   18. (1)   29. (2)   40. (1)
8. (5)   19. (4)   30. (5)   41. (2)
9. (1)   20. (2)   31. (1)   42. (1)
10. (1) 21. (1)   32. (2)   43. (3)
11. (5) 22. (2)   33. (3)   44. (1)

Part 2
45. (d)   51. (a)   57. (a)   63. (d)
46. (d)   52. (a)   58. (e)   64. (b)
47. (c)   53. (d)   59. (a)   65. (b)
48. (a)   54. (a)   60. (d)   66. (c)
49. (b)   55. (c)   61. (e)   67. (e)
50. (b)   56. (d)   62. (e)   68. (d)

Part 3
69. (E)   75. (E)   80. (C)   85. (A)
70. (B)   76. (C)   81. (E)   86. (D)
71. (D)   77. (A)   82. (C)   87. (C)
72. (B)   78. (A)   83. (B)   88. (A)
73. (A)   79. (B)   84. (E)   89. (E)
74. (C)

Summary of Results

Section	Number Correct	Number Wrong	Number Omitted
1			
2			
3			

Total correct: _____

Self-appraisal Chart

Total Correct	Percentile
87–89	99
83–85	90
55	50
38	25
29	10

Conversion Chart

The total number correct on the exam is converted to a scaled score ranging from 20 to 80. This conversion enables you to compare your results with those of other candidates who have taken the test. Half the scores fall above 50, half fall below; two-thirds of the candidates score between 40 and 69. The more competitive colleges usually prefer candidates who achieve 65 or above.

The following conversion chart can give you a rough approximation of what your English Composition score should be for this practice exam.

Number Correct	Test Score	Number Correct	Test Score	Number Correct	Test Score
89	80	79	73	70	64
88	80	78	72	69	63
87	79	77	72	68	62
86	78	76	70	67	60
85	77	75	69	66	58
84	77	74	69	65	56
83	76	73	68	64	54
82	76	72	67	63	53
81	75	71	66	62	51
80	74				

PRACTICE EXAMINATIONS FOR THE ENGLISH COMPOSITION TEST

ANALYSIS OF ANSWERS: PRACTICE EXAMINATION NINE

Part 1
1. (1) In standard use the defective verb *ought* is not preceded by *had* or *had not*.
2. (4) The objective *him*, not the subjective *he*, follows the infinitive *to be*.
3. (3) The term *hardly* is negative in itself.
4. (1) The present subjunctive form is *I were*.
5. (2) The infinitive *to enjoy* lacks a word to modify.
6. (4) She complained about the *leaving*, not about *me*.
7. (2) The train did not wait.
8. (5) The negative *don't* should not be followed by the negative *nothing*.
9. (1) Past action preceding past action requires the past perfect *I had come*.
10. (1) The past subjunctive form is *if you had given*.
11. (5) No error
12. (2) The car did not do the driving.
13. (5) No error
14. (2) His career was not intended as forty.
15. (4) The preposition *between* requires *me* as object.
16. (4) They selected him (*whom*).
17. (5) No error
18. (1) Action precedent to past action requires *had spoken*.
19. (4) The possessive *whose*, not *who is* (*who's*), is required.
20. (2) The conclusion did not read the report.
21. (1) Action preceding past action requires *had moved*.
22. (2) The quantity did not double the recipe.
23. (5) No error
24. (4) . . . *as much as I do*. . . .
25. (4) He (*whosoever*) desires it.
26. (1) The subjunctive present form required is *that she were here*.
27. (2) The problem did not verify the answer.
28. (5) No error
29. (2) The driver was not undecided.
30. (5) No error
31. (1) The past perfect *had said* is required.
32. (2) Costs do not sell.
33. (3) Only one of the adverbs *not* or *scarcely* is needed.
34. (2) Reaction had not done the reading.
35. (1) Since geographical distance is always true, *is closer* is required.
36. (5) No error
37. (1) The subjunctive present *that I were* is required.
38. (1) The present tense *sinks* requires the present *choose*.
39. (2) The participle *counting* lacks word to modify.
40. (1) The present subjunctive *he were* is required.
41. (2) Tears did not arrive.
42. (1) The standard sequence of tenses requires *must have been wonderful to be alive*.
43. (3) The adverb *but* in standard use is not preceded by *not*.
44. (1) The past subjunctive *If I had wanted* is required.

Part 2
45. (d) The subject of the gerund (*joining*) is in the possessive case (*his*).
46. (d) Parallel construction requires *watching* and *going*.
47. (c) The idiom *drown his sorrows in drink* is a cliché.
48. (a) The noun principle (*standards*) is required.
49. (b) The adverb *slowly* is unnecessary.
50. (b) The adverb *now* is unnecessary.
51. (a) The past participle *affected* (*moved*) is required.
52. (a) The verb *take* is required since the carrying is not toward the speaker.
53. (d) The objective form *me* is required to be in the same case as *us*.
54. (a) The standard idiom is *sort of*, not *sort of a*.
55. (c) The expressions *weight of his opinions* and *tide of popularity* are clichés.
56. (d) The subject form *I*, not *me*, follows *was*.
57. (a) The idiom *could not help but* is nonstandard.
58. (e) No error
59. (a) The standard idiom is *to feel bad*.
60. (d) . . . *than any other girl*. . . .
61. (e) The singular *Alex* requires the singular *plans*.
62. (e) No error
63. (d) The singular *set* requires the singular *is*, not the plural *are*.
64. (b) The adverb *instantly* is repetitious of *in a flash*.
65. (b) The adjective *unalterable* is repetitious of *final*.
66. (c) The phrase *on this festive occasion* is a cliché.
67. (e) No error
68. (d) The preposition *but* is followed by an object (*him*).

Part 3
69. (E) The completion of the helping verb is *may have*, not *may had*.
70. (B) The death rate is not being proved effective.
71. (D) The phrase *after a thorough investigation* must be so placed that it modifies only one part of the sentence.
72. (B) The singular *multitude* requires the singular *comes* and *overflows*.
73. (A) No error
74. (C) The preposition *but* requires the objective *me*.
75. (E) Action precedent to past action requires the past perfect *had been proposed*.
76. (C) *Being* is a nonstandard equivalent for *since* or *because*.
77. (A) No error
78. (A) The nominative absolute *things being the way they are* is an independent construction.
79. (B) the pronoun *which* lacks a definite antecedent.
80. (C) the standard idiom is *sort of*.
81. (E) Example (E) is standard when *otherwise* connects two independent ideas.
82. (C) The past perfect *had made* is required for action preceding past action (ignored).

83. (B) The plural *pamphlets* requires the plural *deal*.
84. (E) The subject of a gerund (*being released*) is in the possessive case (*his*).
85. (A) No error
86. (D) . . . *than any other girl*. . . .
87. (C) The term *capital* (money) is required.
88. (A) No error
89. (E) The verb *prophesy* is required.

ANSWER KEY: PRACTICE EXAMINATION TEN / Page 120

Part 1

1. (3)	10. (1)	19. (2)	28. (1)
2. (1)	11. (2)	20. (3)	29. (2)
3. (1)	12. (1)	21. (3)	30. (5)
4. (2)	13. (2)	22. (4)	31. (2)
5. (4)	14. (4)	23. (3)	32. (1)
6. (5)	15. (2)	24. (1)	33. (5)
7. (2)	16. (3)	25. (1)	
8. (3)	17. (1)	26. (3)	
9. (2)	18. (3)	27. (1)	

Part 2

34. (E)	41. (C)	48. (E)	55. (B)
35. (D)	42. (A)	49. (D)	56. (B)
36. (D)	43. (E)	50. (E)	57. (C)
37. (A)	44. (B)	51. (C)	58. (C)
38. (D)	45. (D)	52. (B)	
39. (B)	46. (A)	53. (E)	
40. (C)	47. (C)	54. (D)	

Part 3

59. (e)	67. (d)	75. (b)	83. (b)
60. (b)	68. (c)	76. (d)	84. (e)
61. (d)	69. (e)	77. (a)	85. (e)
62. (d)	70. (e)	78. (b)	86. (d)
63. (e)	71. (a)	79. (e)	87. (c)
64. (e)	72. (d)	80. (e)	88. (e)
65. (c)	73. (c)	81. (a)	89. (c)
66. (a)	74. (e)	82. (d)	90. (d)

Summary of Results

Section	Number Correct	Number Wrong	Number Omitted
1			
2			
3			

Total correct: _____

Self-appraisal Chart

Total Correct	Percentile
88–90	99
82–86	90
69	50
52	25
40	10

Conversion Chart

The total number correct on the exam is converted to a scaled score ranging from 20 to 80. This conversion enables you to compare your results with those of other candidates who have taken the test. Half the scores fall above 50, half fall below; two-thirds of the candidates score between 40 and 69. The more competitive colleges usually prefer candidates who achieve 65 or above.

The following conversion chart can give you a rough approximation of what your English Composition score should be for this practice exam.

Number Correct	Test Score	Number Correct	Test Score	Number Correct	Test Score
90	80	81	72	73	60
89	79	80	70	72	59
88	79	79	69	71	57
87	78	78	68	70	55
86	77	77	67	69	53
85	76	76	65	68	52
84	76	75	64	67	51
83	75	74	62	66	50
82	74				

PRACTICE EXAMINATIONS FOR THE ENGLISH COMPOSITION TEST

ANALYSIS OF ANSWERS: PRACTICE EXAMINATION TEN

Part 1
1. (3) The conjunctive adverb should be preceded by a semicolon.
2. (1) The idiom *have a loan of* is a nonstandard equivalent for *borrow*.
3. (1) The verb *bring* is used to convey action toward the speaker.
4. (2) The subject is the singular *Arlene*.
5. (4) The term required is *uninterested (apathetic)*, not *disinterested (impartial)*.
6. (5) No error
7. (2) A period must be placed at the end of the sentence.
8. (3) The first two *to*'s are repetitious.
9. (2) The adjective *imminent (about to happen)* is required.
10. (1) The term *less* refers to quantity; *fewer* refers to units.
11. (2) . . . I am . . . .
12. (1) The singular noun *set* requires the singular verb *is*.
13. (2) The term *ever* is superfluous.
14. (4) The singular pronoun *one* requires the singular *his*.
15. (2) The phrase *due to* is a nonstandard equivalent for *since* or *because*.
16. (3) People are *hanged*.
17. (1) . . . *just as I (do)*. . . .
18. (3) The phrase to remember is *the effect (result) of*.
19. (2) The adverb *indistinctly* is required to modify the verb *spoke*.
20. (3) The subject of the gerund *daring* is in the possessive case (*your*).
21. (3) The adverb *most* is required when reference is to three or more.
22. (4) The pronoun *everyone* requires the singular *is*.
23. (3) In this sentence the subordinating adverb *whenever* should not be preceded by a semicolon.
24. (1) The pronoun *it* cannot pass the test for dangling infinitive.
25. (1) The standard idiom is *to feel bad*.
26. (3) Something is *perfect* or *not perfect*; it cannot be *most perfect*.
27. (1) The form of the past subjunctive is *If you had*.
28. (1) The standard term is *somewhere*.
29. (2) The standard present perfect is *has swum*.
30. (5) No error
31. (2) The standard idiom is *sort of*, not *sort of a*.
32. (1) A clause beginning with *when* following *is* is a nonstandard synonym for *occurs when*.
33. (5) No error

Part 2
34. (E) The Navy, having intercepted Japanese messages after the Battle of the Coral Sea, knew the next move and rushed . . . .
35. (D) By mid-January the Germans had moved so many submarines to the Atlantic Coast, where at night they torpedoed tankers silhouetted against the light of the cities, that they created an oil shortage.
36. (D) During its first twenty-five years, prophets cried out in the wilderness and despaired of TV's lost opportunities.
37. (A) Those who would want to suppress a repugnant doctrine only succeed all too often in giving it more notoriety.
38. (D) Moral issues can be debated endlessly with no resolution even though there is . . . .
39. (B) You need no almanac to recognize the coming of winter since it does not wait on the calendar.
40. (C) The Test Ban Treaty was considered by John F. Kennedy as not the most historic since Creation but as a single . . . .
41. (C) Like Hamlet whipsawed by conflicting . . . death, we hesitate.
42. (A) He directed at himself as much as anyone his skepticism . . . recognition of failure.
43. (E) Had a sustained fuel shortage resulted, a quiet revolution in American life, the four-day week, could have come to pass . . . .
44. (B) Given effective national leadership and a sustained and cooperative response from business and the public, there is no need for Americans to fear economic disaster.
45. (D) Having marked the beginning of the end of an era filled with ebullient optimism and confidence, the shot that claimed the life of John F. Kennedy will be remembered for more . . . .
46. (A) The old police headquarters on Centre Street, an architectural gem in an otherwise drab area, should be . . . .
47. (C) Our obligation is to encourage students to explore many ways of viewing an issue or problem; we must give up . . . .
48. (E) Is it true that one of the obvious results of the massive, pervasive influence of television is that today's? . . .
49. (D) In its ability to meet and overcome challenge and in its ability to organize free and strong-minded men to solve great problems are where the true genius of America lies.
50. (E) In America our race relations are not perfect. Constructive processes are at work; we are narrowing the gap in opportunity, in education, in income, in the day-to-day relations.
51. (C) Because the gates at the ticket window automatically swing shut when a train approaches a Paris subway station, only those . . . .
52. (B) Because the rate of gasoline consumption . . . speed, the higher the speed over any given distance, the more . . . .
53. (E) Since this is a time of mutual need and shared emergency, the opportunity . . . .
54. (D) The chickadees . . . came . . . where they had been welcomed . . . .
55. (B) By substituting neglect for compassion, political appeals to ignorance and selfishness needlessly divided the nation.
56. (B) Automobile accidents have claimed more of the lives of our people than have all . . . .
57. (C) First we had to face the urgent needs to make drastic changes in our energy economy before we could come . . . .

58. (C) Additional evidence . . . in drug therapy comes from the reports from . . . .

Part 3

59. (e) The term *Seeing as* is considered nonstandard usage; use of the simpler past tense is preferred to the subjunctive as in choice (c).
60. (b) Comma is used to set off an appositive.
61. (d) Preposition *between* is followed by objective *me*; plural noun *books* requires plural *were*.
62. (d) The plural *men* requires *who are*.
63. (b) The pronoun *they* lacks an antecedent.
64. (e) The past subjunctive form required is *If you had*.
65. (c) Appositive should be set off by commas; the apostrophe is placed after a final consonant (Helen's).
66. (a) No error
67. (d) The relative pronoun *which* lacks a stated antecedent.
68. (c) The pronoun *they* lacks an antecedent.
69. (e) The second pronoun *he* could refer to either the speaker or Alex.
70. (e) The clause (*that*) *he had printed* should follow the word it modifies (*book*).
71. (a) A clause in absolute construction needs no word for it to modify.
72. (d) She had not just bought the hill.
73. (c) In standard usage *round* is an absolute term.
74. (e) . . . as eligible as . . . .
75. (b) The adverbs *clearly* and *emphatically* are required for parallel construction.
76. (d) Action preceding past action requires the past perfect tense.
77. (a) No error
78. (b) In standard usage the adverb *scarcely* is not preceded by *not*.
79. (e) The preposition *between* is followed by the object form *me*.
80. (e) The conjunctive *seeing as* is nonstandard.
81. (a) The standard phrase is *to let it lie*.
82. (d) The verb *stayed* (*remained*), not *stood* (*on one's feet*), is required.
83. (b) The preposition *off of* is nonstandard; the idiom is *put into*, not *put in*.
84. (e) The additional *there* is unnecessary; the standard idiom is *type of*, not *type of a*.
85. (e) The pronunciation should fit the spelling.
86. (d) The possessive forms of *man, men, woman, women* all end in *'s*.
87. (c) The adverb *altogether* and the noun *advice* are required; *we are* contracts into *we're*.
88. (e) The verb *to loan* is a nonstandard equivalent of *to lend*.
89. (c) The phrase to remember is we *learn from and teach to; spill* implies an accidental act.
90. (d) Since the name *Dickens* ends in *s*, the possessive is *Dickens'* or *Dickens's*.

The English Composition Test

Section THREE : Writing the Essay

1. A Closer Look

2. Improving Prose Style and Organization

3. Steps in Planning Your Essay

4. Practice Essay Assignments

1. A Closer Look

Although this section can be helpful to all test candidates since it reviews the organization of topics covered in college-level expository writing courses, it is planned primarily for those candidates who will be taking the form of the English Composition Achievement Test that includes the writing of an essay.

The previous sections of this book reviewed the aspects of writing tested on the multiple-choice questions. The essay question measures all of these aspects and, in addition, the ability to express ideas clearly and effectively, to organize ideas, and to marshall evidence and present proof to support ideas. This section of the book will give you a closer look at the methods of handling ideas and putting them into an essay.

THE ACHIEVEMENT TEST ESSAY AND COLLEGE THEMES

A college theme differs in several important aspects from this essay. The typical college theme results from a unit of work during which the student is given time to select a topic, to think about its various ramifications, to write a rough outline, to write a rough draft, and then to plan the revision. The final copy is then prepared. The college theme may result from research or it may be based upon any analysis of one of the four basic types of writing—narration, description, exposition, argumentation.

This essay is written during a limited period of time. You do not have time to read widely or to weigh and consider for a length of time. All you have is 20 minutes! It resembles an impromptu theme, one given to test your ability to write a good answer to an examination question demanding a fairly extensive statement. It resembles exposition more than any other form of writing; it requires an explanation of why you think the way you do about a definite ideal or question of morality.

THE ACHIEVEMENT TEST ESSAY AND HIGH SCHOOL COMPOSITIONS

Many high school themes are of the narrative variety. You are required to recall an incident or retell a highlight in your experiences. The high school theme, then, tends to deal with concrete incidents or facts. It can be organized around the original timetable of the events you describe.

This essay, on the other hand, requires an ability to discuss at length ideas, abstractions. This essay must be organized using the ideas discussed, and this process becomes a difficult one for those who have had little experience in organizing such a theme.

HOW THE ESSAY IS RATED

The essay will be read separately by several experienced high school and college instructors. Each will give it a numerical rating. These will be reconciled, and the grade will be part of your total English Composition Test score.

The graders will have a set of criteria for judging. They will rate several papers and then discuss their ratings to help them set their standards. The following is a sample of the type of standards set. This is a scale recently adopted by several colleges.

4. *Generally Excellent*: Writing containing originality of thought, correctness of expression, and freshness of expression

3. *Competent*: Correct expression with soundness of thought and clear organization

2. *Interesting but incorrect*: Imagination and ability to think clearly combined with a lack of the formal requirements of correctness

1. *Inadequate*: Borderline in thought, content and organization; thinness of thought coupled with a lack of organization and errors typical of illiteracy

ERRORS TO BE AVOIDED

Technical Errors—in Order of Seriousness

1. Sentence Errors—run-on, sentence fragments
2. Misuse of apostrophe
3. Word Confusion, errors in case and agreement
4. Dangling Elements
5. Vague Reference
6. Misspelling
7. Additional errors in punctuation
8. Incorrect paragraphing—over or under paragraphing
9. Incorrect capitalization
10. Trite expressions
11. Mixed metaphors

Errors in Content

1. Irrelevancies—additions to content that are not related to the ideas of the theme, lack of unity
2. Lack of coherence—lack of transitional words or phrases
3. Needless repetition of ideas
4. Superficiality—saying only the obvious
5. Incorrect statements of fact
6. Illogical deductions
7. Facile generalizations, overgeneralizing

2. Improving Prose Style and Organization

When writing the essay, the student will probably be most aware of avoiding errors in usage, diction, and sentence structure. However, the student should also attempt to display a sensitivity to the use of language and an effectiveness in organizing thoughts. Effective organization of thoughts comes through systematic consideration of the topic, compilation of evidence to support or attack the idea, and planned presentation of this evidence. Additional suggestions and practice material on planning your essay can be found in the following section. In this section, we consider the elements that go into producing varied, interesting prose style.

SENTENCE VARIETY

An experienced writer conveys a message most effectively by varying the types of sentences he or she uses. By varying your sentence types, you will achieve a certain rhythm and flow to your writing. There is some practice in varying sentence types given earlier in the book; we suggest that you review that section (Section One; Sentence Variety and Styling Problems), again considering the following sentence patterns:

Simple Sentence: Maria walked to the store.
Simple Sentence with Compound Subject: *Maria and Sylvia* walked to the store.
Simple Sentence with Compound Verb: Maria *walked* to the store and *bought* two onions.
Simple Sentence with Compound Object: Maria walked to the store and bought two *onions* and three *potatoes*.
Compound Sentence: Maria walked to the store, and Sylvia followed her.
Complex Sentence: As soon as Maria left for the store, Sylvia began to follow her.
Compound-Complex Sentence: If Maria walks to the store, Sylvia will follow her; but Maria wants to be alone.

Practice changing simple sentences to complex; change compound sentences to complex. Remember that an essay with only simple sentences will sound immature, so vary your sentences!

PARAGRAPHS FOR PRACTICE

Using the various methods suggested in this book, recast the following paragraphs to gain maximum emphasis and variety.

1. Jonas Salk is a true hero in my opinion. He worked unselfishly. He worked for mankind. He wanted to better the lot of his fellow men. The grate-

ful public showered honors on him. He avoided the limelight. He acknowledged the help he had received from others. He gave the money prizes to charity. His main request was a simple one. He wanted to continue to do his research in quiet and without interruptions. He set a good example. Many young people will follow in his footsteps. He is a hero in the best sense.

2. Cowardice is considered as having many facets today. It was easier to define years ago. It meant not being able to face a situation. The coward ran away. The brave man stayed to face the consequences. The test was clearcut, and it was easy to apply. The word *foolhardy* was not used, but *rash* was used in its place. *Rash* was not correlated with being brave, nor was it connected with being a coward. We now realize more subtle values, and the picture changes. One man may run and be brave and another may stay and be a coward. The man may run, and he can plan to face the foe at a more advantageous position. The man may stay, and he may cover his cowardice by blustering and shouting. He may stay, and he can sacrifice the lives of others. This sacrifice may be unnecessary, but it could make the situation safer for the coward. We know more today, and we know that rashness and foolhardiness are not bravery. It is the motive and it is not the deed that should determine what is to be labeled cowardice.

3. The Nineteenth Century had its physical frontiers, and we today have political, social, scientific frontiers. The pioneers settled our country, and they faced the dangers on the frontiers of our land. The pioneers of today face similar dangers and these dangers require a similar courage. Some people see social injustice around us, and they devote their lives to fighting for equality for others. Some people see political tyranny, and they see others deprived of their right to vote by tricks. They plan long campaigns, and they try to educate the public. Freedom cannot belong to a few. Freedom must belong to all. These political and social frontiers are being explored, and others explore the frontiers of space and others explore the frontiers found in the laboratory. There are many frontiers today, and no one can say that frontiers no longer exist.

4. You can lead a horse to the well. You cannot make the horse drink. This is a homely analogy. It fits the present situation. Some colleges allow students very little choice of subjects to be taken, and other colleges give the students wide latitude. Some students are more advanced in their studies, and some students have to begin at the beginning. All students must take the same subjects in the tightly structured school. The advanced students learn bad habits, and the other students gain no advantage from having the advanced ones in their classes. The picture is almost the same in the more lax colleges, and the advanced student can go ahead on his own, and the undeveloped student still has little to guide him. There is a better procedure, and this could be a compromise between the two. The advanced could take some discussion seminars, and the undeveloped student could be in the course. The advanced would take electives, and the beginner could take the required, and each would then be developing at a pace best for him.

5. War is a costly luxury, and man must realize this. The winner loses, and so does the loser lose. There is no victor in a war, and we should realize it. Inflation eats away the life savings in the land of the winner, and it does the same in the land of the conquered. The men had been in the army, and they feel that they have been deprived. They become civilians, and they look for the good times that they had missed. Morality reaches a low ebb, and the winners talk about a lost generation, and the losers complain about a generation that is without moral fibers. Fads sweep the country, and worthwhile social advances are neglected. Money is spent on more and more armaments, and needed civic improvements are neglected. War does not end with the firing of the last gun, but it continues to wreak havoc for years afterward. We should realize this, and we should be resolved to fight war at all costs, and we should fight war at all turns. We should fight poverty, hunger, and ignorance, and we should not fight other human beings. The fight against other human beings is wasteful, and all who are in it suffer.

NOTE: *Answers to this exercise will vary too greatly to allow for an Answer Key.*

PROPER PARAGRAPHING

In writing the essay, the student faces a practical test of the ability to arrange ideas within a sentence and within a paragraph with appropriate connectives. The material that follows will give you practice in developing the correct habits for mature thought sequences. It will familiarize you with the level of development expected of you in your paragraph work on the college level.

Scan the following data. Do not spend much time on items that you already know. Concentrate on what you have to learn. The *Mastery Tests* that follow will help you to discover how effective your study has been.

Elements of Correct Paragraphing

Unity A theme has unity when each sentence and each paragraph in it is related to the topic under discussion. Sentences or paragraphs that are not related to the topic are *irrelevant*. Unity is obtained in a paragraph by excluding extraneous material.

Coherence Each part of a theme should lead logically to the next. Each thought should lead to the one that follows. Each sentence in a paragraph should follow this logical type of pattern. Coherence is gained by the logical arrangement of material, by the judicious use of transitional words and phrases, linking words and expressions.

Coherence is gained through the use of linking expressions such as

therefore, moreover, consequently, in addition to, furthermore, for example, for instance, as a result, nevertheless, obviously, first, on the whole, at any rate, naturally, of course, however, yet, at length, in conclusion, finally, next, first.

Length There is no prescribed length for a paragraph. The average paragraph length, however, is about 100 words. A theme should normally consist of more than one paragraph. A paragraph should normally consist of more than one sentence.

The rule of thumb used by most students is that a paragraph of more than a page in long-hand is probably too long; a paragraph of two or three sentences is probably too brief.

Topic sentence The usual paragraph contains one sentence that summarizes the ideas of the paragraph. That sentence is called the topic sentence. If all of the ideas of the paragraph relate to that sentence, then the sentence contains unity. If the ideas of the paragraph lead to or from that sentence then the paragraph contains coherence. The topic sentence is usually found at the beginning of the paragraph. It may be placed at the end or at any other point in the paragraph.

Developing the paragraph Although each of the parts of a composition serves varied purposes, typical paragraphs usually contain only one of the ideas to be developed in the theme. Each of these paragraphs may explain, develop, defend, attack, or illustrate one idea. The paragraph may be developed

1. by giving examples of the idea stated in the topic sentence
2. by defining one or more of the terms in the topic sentence
3. by giving details to support the topic sentence
4. by giving examples
5. by giving cause and effect
6. by giving the steps in a process
7. by comparison and contrast
8. by presenting details or facts and also conclusions to be drawn from those details or facts

Introductory paragraph The introductory paragraph serves two main functions. The first is to delimit the topic, to explain just what the writer hopes to accomplish by writing the theme. The second is to interest the reader. Too often students are overconcerned with the need to interest the reader. If the introductory paragraph states the purpose of the theme succinctly, then that would be sufficient to create reader interest!

Concluding paragraph The final paragraph should *not* contain new ideas. It should serve to summarize the theme. It should also contain a concluding sentence that "clinches" the writer's main point.

WRITING THE ESSAY

Rhetorical question A rhetorical question is one that a writer uses in a theme for dramatic purposes but does not expect the reader to answer. A rhetorical question at the end of the introductory paragraph acts as an excellent connective. It joins the body of the composition to the introduction when the body of the composition actually is an answer to that question.

Transitions *Transitions* are words and expression that make the direction and organization of the theme absolutely clear to the reader. A good example of a transitional phrase is the use of *in conclusion* or *therefore* as part of the topic sentence in the conclusion.

Emphasis Emphasis can be gained within a paragraph by employing the unexpected. Emphasis can be gained through the use of

- Rhetorical Question: Who is responsible for the failure of the UN?
- Repetition: His coach refused him. His teachers refused him. His parents had refused him. Now his best friend had just refused him!
- Words Placed Out of Order: *Tired and frightened*, the prisoner was thrust into a cell.
  In September, I expect to leave for Europe.
  Whenever I come to that town, I visit my former colleague.
  Swiftly came the night.

TEST OF MASTERY

I. Underline the irrelevant sentences in each of the following paragraphs.

1. I look forward to the time that I can retire. I shall seek a cabin somewhere and let others worry about budgets. He who has been gifted with the love of retirement possesses as it were another sense. I then shall do all the reading that I have missed for the past three years.

2. The wise disregard nothing that concerns the welfare of mankind. Proverbs are but rules, and rules do not create character. They prescribe conduct, but do not furnish a full and proper motive. They are usually but half-truths and seldom contain the principle of the action they teach.

3. The morality of an action depends upon the motive from which we act. Let us with caution indulge the supposition that morality can be maintained without religion. Let us suppose that I fling a few dollars to a beggar with the intention of breaking his head. He escapes my intention and picks the money up. If he buys food with the money, the physical effect of my deed is good. However, with respect to me, the action was morally wrong.

4. Of course there is no one facet of a person's activities that can reveal him completely to others. However, what a person praises is perhaps a surer standard, even, than what he condemns. His praise can so often reveal his character, information, and abilities. No ashes are lighter than those of incense, and few burn out sooner. No wonder, then, that most people are so shy of praising anything.

5. Do not wait for a day of reckoning. Sum up at night what you have done by day. In the morning, plan reflectively what you are to do during that day. It is easier to enrich ourselves with a thousand virtues than to correct ourselves of a single fault. Dress and undress your inner being; mark well its decay and growth. You never know when your conscience will catch up with your deeds. Judged you will be, but by yourself, and on that day, beware of finding yourself wanting. There can be no sterner judge of your true accounts than you.

II. Underline the topic sentence in each of the following.

1. Hail can destroy one farmer's prospects of a harvest in a matter of seconds. It can leave his neighbor's unimpaired. It can slay a flock of sheep in one field, while the sun continues to shine in the next. To the harassed meteorologist its behavior is even more Machiavellian than that of the ice storm. He cannot predict the onset of a hailstorm, nor can he tell its course nor duration once it has started. He is not even too sure any more about the way in which hail forms. Hail is at once the cruelest weapon in Nature's armory, and the most incalculable.

2. The preservation of even small bits of marshlands or woods representing the last stands of irreplaceable biotic communities is interwoven with the red tape of law, conflicting local interests, the overlapping jurisdiction of governmental and private conservation bodies, and an intricate tangle of economic and social considerations. The problems we face in conserving natural resources are laborious and complex. During the time spent in desolving these factors, it often happens that the area to be preserved is swallowed up. Even more formidable is the broad-scale conservation problem raised by the spread of urban belts. The presures of human growth are so acute in such instances that they raise issues which would tax the wisdom of Solomon.

3. Farmers raising crops from the same type of seed will often band together into an association. The purpose of the association is to spread the cost of advertising their product. The growers of navel oranges in California have helped to make Sunkist known in every home in the land. The American growers of one of the pima cottons have banded to-

gether in the SuPima Association of America, and garments made of this superior cotton often carry the SuPima label.

4. I have a rich neighbor who is always so busy that he has no leisure to laugh. The entire business of his life is to get money. The more money he amasses, the more he seems to want. He fails to consider that it is not in the power of riches to make a man happy. How wise were they that said, "There are as many miseries beyond riches as on this side of them." The search for happiness or contentment must not center upon worldly wealth.

5. I am so tired of having to argue with others on unequal terms. The moment my adversary centers his thoughts upon self-interest, how can I continue to discuss with him! I am lost from the start. He will never accept my premises as I cannot accept his. My facts are not facts to him. My conclusions are just as absurd when he weighs them in terms of only himself. Yet, how can humanity strive to reach a goal in which all will have an equal chance to live fully unless we keep our thoughts centered upon all and not one. We can march forward together only when we think of *we* and not *me*.

III. Rearrange the following sentences into logical order. In the space to the left, write the number that would represent that sentence's place in the paragraph.

.... 1. (a) Great Britain declared war against the Netherlands a few months later.
.... (b) He was a former Vice President of South Carolina and President of the Continental Congress.
.... (c) Laurens was put into the Tower of London when the British discovered the projected treaty.
.... (d) In 1778 Henry Laurens was chosen to go to Holland to negotiate a $10,000,000 loan and a treaty of amity.
.... (e) He was captured off Newfoundland by the British frigate V*estal*.

.... 2. (a) For many years it was described as a hereditary disease, the result of some unknown defect in the germ plasm.
.... (b) Mongolism is a congenital malformation that blights approximately one in 650 births.
.... (c) Proof is now at hand to show that the disease is neither typically hereditary nor environmental.
.... (d) Other investigators have often argued an opposite explanation, that the disease was environmental, caused by accidents during gestation.
.... (e) It arises from a defect in the mechanism by which the hereditary material is passed on from parent to offspring.

.... 3. (a) One of the topics discussed was the development of methods that would elevate world fishing from a hunting industry to an agricultural technology.
.... (b) The group, known as the Conference of Science and World Affairs, convened for its seventh conference.
.... (c) Another topic discussed was the internationalization of the moon under the basic principles of the International Antarctic Treaty.
.... (d) The first conference had been held at Pugwash in Nova Scotia in 1957.
.... (e) In September 1961, 41 scientists from 12 countries met under skies darkened by distrust among nations.
.... (f) The purpose of these conferences is to foster the constructive use of science and help in preventing its destructive use.

.... 4. (a) Its width varies from 1,200 miles to 2,500 miles.
.... (b) The waters of the Pacific off North and South America conceal a low bulge in the crust of the earth.
.... (c) The Rise runs roughly north and south for 8,000 miles.
.... (d) But it is not its size that is at present considered so significant; its crest is a region of high earthquake activity.
.... (e) This bulge is as extensive as both of the continents.
.... (f) The East Pacific Rise is the name given to this vast feature.

.... 5. (a) They were supposed to live in the land of the Alps in houses built on stilts out over the water of the lakes.
.... (b) Recent findings tend to disprove Keller.
.... (c) These dwellings seemed to resemble those of South Sea Islanders.
.... (d) For over a century anthropologists have believed that there were prehistoric Swiss lake dwellers.
.... (e) This comparison resulted from the findings of Ferdinand Keller in 1854 along the shore of the Lake of Zurich.
.... (f) Research seems to point to these houses having been built on the shores of lakes that have since grown larger.

WRITING THE ESSAY   155

ANSWER KEY: TEST OF MASTERY / *Pages 153-154*

I.
1. He who has been gifted with the love of retirement possesses as it were another sense.
2. The wise disregard nothing that concerns the welfare of mankind.
3. Let us with caution indulge the supposition that morality can be maintained without religion.
4. No ashes are lighter than those of incense, and few burn out sooner.
5. It is easier to enrich ourselves with a thousand virtues, than to correct ourselves of a single fault.

II.
1. Hail is at once the cruelest weapon in Nature's armory, and the most incalculable.
2. The problems we face in conserving natural resources are laborious and complex.
3. Farmers raising crops from the same type of seed will often band together into an association.
4. The search for happiness or contentment must not center upon worldly wealth.
5. We can march forward together only when we think of *we* and not *me*.

III.
(1) 5, 2, 4, 1, 3   (3) 5, 2, 6, 3, 1, 4   (5) 2, 5, 3, 1, 4, 6
(2) 3, 1, 5, 4, 2   (4) 5, 1, 4, 6, 2, 3

PRACTICE IN ORGANIZATION

TEST 1 *Suggested Time: 20 Minutes*

The sentences in each unit below all belong to a well-organized paragraph. However, they are presented out of their correct order. You are to re-arrange them into the best possible order. As you do the exercises, before you begin to answer the questions that follow, you should write in the space below the correct order of the sentences. In answering the questions, circle *N* if nothing follows the given sentence.

A] The reaction of the American public to these disarmament proposals has ranged from great expectation to deep-seated lack of interest.
B] Yet we know that if the United States and Russia were to fire all their weapons at each other, there would be over 90% population destruction in both countries.
C] This is the grim fact that characterizes today's world.
D] Disarmament discussions have been in the headlines perhaps more than any other issue ever since the cold war began.
E] The failure of our leaders to inform and educate adequately on the complexities of this contemporary world problem has helped to cause the public mood.

1. Which sentence did you put first?   1. a b c d e N
2. Which sentence did you put after [A]?   2. a b c d e N
3. Which sentence did you put after [B]?   3. a b c d e N
4. Which sentence did you put after [C]?   4. a b c d e N
5. Which sentence did you put after [D]?   5. a b c d e N
6. Which sentence did you put after [E]?   6. a b c d e N

A] The average number of moves is usually somewhere around forty-five, although the shortest game can consist of only two moves.
B] A common saying among those who know the game best is that the winner of the game is the one who makes the next to the last blunder.
C] It is rare, therefore, that a game lasts for considerably more than 100 moves.
D] The end of the game is heralded by the opponent's skillful exploitation of a mistake made at any point in the game.
E] Even among grand masters the secret of success is not superior strategy but the persistent omission of tactical errors.

7. Which sentence did you put first?   7. a b c d e N
8. Which sentence did you put after [A]?   8. a b c d e N
9. Which sentence did you put after [B]?   9. a b c d e N
10. Which sentence did you put after [C]?   10. a b c d e N
11. Which sentence did you put after [D]?   11. a b c d e N
12. Which sentence did you put after [E]?   12. a b c d e N

A] The early hunter could do little more than forage for berries, fruits, and edible animals.
B] Later agriculture emerged as man's dominant activity, and he learned to control and direct living matter around him.
C] Primitive man lived in bondage to nature.
D] This complex and broad interaction between man and nature is still going on today.
E] He did nothing to interfere with the course of natural processes.

13. Which sentence did you put first?   13. a b c d e N
14. Which sentence did you put after [A]?   14. a b c d e N
15. Which sentence did you put atfer [B]?   15. a b c d e N
16. Which sentence did you put after [C]?   16. a b c d e N
17. Which sentence did you put after [D]?   17. a b c d e N
18. Which sentence did you put after [E]?   18. a b c d e N

A] This procedure may lessen the number of freshmen who will be asked to leave, but it throws into the discard many who could have made the grade.
B] The drop-out rate has long been a major concern of most of our colleges.
C] In addition to carrying only 12 instead of 16 credits, they are also enrolled in noncredit reading and study

skills programs to help them improve their general academic competence.

D] One way in which they have been facing the problem has been to restrict enrollments to those students whose previous academic record shows promise of success.

E] A growing number of colleges have begun, instead, to offer marginal students a chance to prove themselves through restricted programs.

19. Which sentence did you put first? 19. a b c d e N
20. Which sentence did you put after [A]? 20. a b c d e N
21. Which sentence did you put after [B]? 21. a b c d e N
22. Which sentence did you put after [C]? 22. a b c d e N
23. Which sentence did you put after [D]? 23. a b c d e N
24. Which sentence did you put after [E]? 24. a b c d e N

A] Our present research has enabled us to identify the Sun as a large body of gas with a surface temperature of about 11,000 degrees F.

B] Artificial satellites tell us that the corona envelops the Earth and extends far out into the solar system.

C] Above this visible Sun is a thinner layer called the chromosphere where our rocket-directed cameras reveal the temperature rises to about 30,000 degrees F.

D] Man's probing into space with rockets and satellites has helped to add much to his knowledge about the star nearest us, the Sun.

E] Beyond is the corona, an extremely hot region with a kinetic temperature measured in millions of degrees.

25. Which sentence did you put first? 25. a b c d e N
26. Which sentence did you put after [A]? 26. a b c d e N
27. Which sentence did you put after [B]? 27. a b c d e N
28. Which sentence did you put after [C]? 28. a b c d e N
29. Which sentence did you put after [D]? 29. a b c d e N
30. Which sentence did you put after [E]? 30. a b c d e N

A] The great majority of bills die in committee.

B] When a bill is introduced in either house, it is identified by a number and then referred to a committee.

C] It may on the other hand decide to ignore the measure altogether.

D] The committee may amend, or even rewrite a bill before reporting it for final debate and vote.

31. Which sentence did you put first? 31. a b c d N
32. Which sentence did you put after [A]? 32. a b c d N
33. Which sentence did you put after [B]? 33. a b c d N
34. Which sentence did you put after [C]? 34. a b c d N
35. Which sentence did you put after [D]? 35. a b c d N

TEST 2 *Suggested Time: 15 Minutes*

The sentences in each unit below all belong to a well-organized paragraph. However, they are presented out of their correct order. You are to re-arrange them into the best possible order. As you do the exercises, before you begin to answer the questions that follow, you should write in the space below the correct order of the sentences. In answering the questions, circle N if nothing follows the given sentence.

A] One of the main arguments in support of the new plan is that unicameral legislature would centralize legislative responsibility.

B] In 1934 Nebraska broke with a traditional feature of state as well as Federal government.

C] However, although many states have evinced an interest in Nebraska's system, no other state has followed her lead.

D] It replaced its bicameral legislature with an assembly of one house, with representatives chosen in a general election.

E] It would also make the legislature less dependent upon professional politicians.

1. Which sentence did you put first? 1. a b c d e N
2. Which sentence did you put after [A]? 2. a b c d e N
3. Which sentence did you put after [B]? 3. a b c d e N
4. Which sentence did you put after [C]? 4. a b c d e N
5. Which sentence did you put after [D]? 5. a b c d e N
6. Which sentence did you put after [E]? 6. a b c d e N

A] A shell of burning hydrogen encloses the helium core, allowing none of the energy released by the thermonuclear burning of the helium to escape from the star.

B] At such temperatures, the star begins to expand and the runaway climb in temperature stops and reverses itself.

C] The birth of a red giant star begins when the inner core of a star mass contains helium that has reached approximately 150 million degrees.

D] As the star cools down, it becomes a red giant in a process that lasts a mere 3,000 years.

E] The helium burning becomes more and more rapid with the temperature rising to about 630 million degrees.

7. Which sentence did you put first? 7. a b c d e N
8. Which sentence did you put after [A]? 8. a b c d e N
9. Which sentence did you put after [B]? 9. a b c d e N
10. Which sentence did you put after [C]? 10. a b c d e N
11. Which sentence did you put after [D]? 11. a b c d e N
12. Which sentence did you put after [E]? 12. a b c d e N

A] He thus had to find his way from theatricalism to a purer and more simplified film style.

B] He gives visible form to the inner conflicts of human beings in a genuine cinematic language.

C] He rejected the theatrical tradition which for too long had dominated film making with a consequent sterility in form.

D] At his peak, now, the result is a clarity of both substance and form unrealized by any other film director.

E] Films as an art form have achieved their highest peak to date under the direction of Sweden's Ingmar Bergman.

13. Which sentence did you put first?   13. a b c d e N
14. Which sentence did you put after [A]?   14. a b c d e N
15. Which sentence did you put after [B]?   15. a b c d e N
16. Which sentence did you put after [C]?   16. a b c d e N
17. Which sentence did you put after [D]?   17. a b c d e N
18. Which sentence did you put after [E]?   18. a b c d e N

A] Wow is a slow waver of the pitch; flutter is a fast, stuttery tremolo resulting from rapid speed variations.

B] At present there are varying and often opposing views of what constitutes the best in turntable design.

C] Flutter and wow are pitch variations caused by inconstant turntable speed.

D] Rumble which sounds like distant rolling of thunder is the result of vibration picked up by the phono cartridge.

E] The common purpose of these differing design approaches is to banish rumble, flutter and wow—the consequences of turntable malfunction.

19. Which sentence did you put first?   19. a b c d e N
20. Which sentence did you put after [A]?   20. a b c d e N
21. Which sentence did you put after [B]?   21. a b c d e N
22. Which sentence did you put after [C]?   22. a b c d e N
23. Which sentence did you put after [D]?   23. a b c d e N
24. Which sentence did you put after [E]?   24. a b c d e N

TEST 3 *Suggested Time: 20 Minutes*

The sentences in each unit below all belong to a well-organized paragraph. However, they are presented out of their correct order. You are to re-arrange them into the best possible order. As you do the exercises, before you begin to answer the questions that follow, you should write in the space below the correct order of the sentences. In answering the questions, circle N if nothing follows the given sentence.

A] This decline which began in 1914 is attributed by some scholars to the failure of the alliance system which the political leaders had toiled to create.

B] Gradually, before our very eyes Europe has disappeared as the over-lord of the world.

C] They claim that the nineteenth century was not a period of placidity and stability, as is commonly assumed, but one of deep and bitter discord.

D] Its cultural, political, and economic achievements had been accepted universally as the measure of human progress.

E] Others seem to feel that the basic cause lies in the undermining of traditional values by the intellectual giants of the preceding century—Darwin, Marx, Nietzsche.

1. Which sentence did you put first?   1. a b c d e N
2. Which sentence did you place after [A]?   2. a b c d e N
3. Which sentence did you place after [B]?   3. a b c d e N
4. Which sentence did you place after [C]?   4. a b c d e N
5. Which sentence did you place after [D]?   5. a b c d e N
6. Which sentence did you place after [E]?   6. a b c d e N

A] Even among these large groupings called varieties there are subgroups that differ from other subgroups in many fundamental respects.

B] Not only was this true, but when the experimenters tried to mate males of one kind with the females of another, they found sterility barriers in every case.

C] Even among the anopheles mosquitoes, for example, there are some populations that do not bite man under any circumstances, with several preferring to bite cattle, pigs, or goats instead.

D] Even though mosquitoes look the same everywhere, different varieties can be distinguished by microscopic examination of the patterns of spots on the eggs.

E] One of the most striking discoveries was that each kind had characteristic mating habits.

7. Which sentence did you put first?   7. a b c d e N
8. Which sentence did you place after [A]?   8. a b c d e N
9. Which sentence did you place after [B]?   9. a b c d e N
10. Which sentence did you place after [C]?   10. a b c d e N
11. Which sentence did you place after [D]?   11. a b c d e N
12. Which sentence did you place after [E]?   12. a b c d e N

A] When the rising cone of water and the cloud tip meet, a fountain of spray much wider than the spout itself is produced.

B] The water-spout is a marine relative of the tornado although it is not so fierce as its unholy relative.

C] As the lower tip of the cloud approaches the surface, the water churns and seems to boil upward.

D] Despite this heavy spray and the accompanying average winds of one hundred miles an hour, the waterspout is much less dangerous than tornadoes since their energy is usually lost on the waves in the water wastes of the empty oceans.

E] A snakelike cloud that writhes and dips toward the sea, it is in shape and appearance very much like a tornado.

13. Which sentence did you put first?   13. a b c d e N
14. Which sentence did you place after [A]?   14. a b c d e N
15. Which sentence did you place after [B]?   15. a b c d e N
16. Which sentence did you place after [C]?   16. a b c d e N

17. Which sentence did you place after [D]? 17. a b c d e N
18. Which sentence did you place after [E]? 18. a b c d e N

A] When a proposal is introduced in either the House of Representatives or the Senate, it is called a bill.
B] Once it has been passed by that House, it is reprinted as an act.
C] It becomes a law when it has finally passed both Houses and has satisfactorily passed the scrutiny of the President and he has signed it.
D] It remains a bill until it has been passed by that House.
E] An act, therefore, means that it is a measure that has been enacted by one branch of the Legislature.

19. Which sentence did you put first? 19. a b c d e N
20. Which sentence did you place after [A]? 20. a b c d e N
21. Which sentence did you place after [B]? 21. a b c d e N
22. Which sentence did you place after [C]? 22. a b c d e N
23. Which sentence did you place after [D]? 23. a b c d e N
24. Which sentence did you place after [E]? 24. a b c d e N

A] It furnished a faithful image of the deceased to aid his survival in the afterworld.
B] Etruscan sculptors preferred to work in clay or bronze rather than in stone.
C] The art of portraiture was deeply involved in their funeral rites.
D] They were particularly fond of the bas-relief, in which they filled the scene with delightfully animated figures.
E] They, however, did their best work in portraits.

25. Which sentence did you put first? 25. a b c d e N
26. Which sentence did you place after [A]? 26. a b c d e N
27. Which sentence did you place after [B]? 27. a b c d e N
28. Which sentence did you place after [C]? 28. a b c d e N
29. Which sentence did you place after [D]? 29. a b c d e N
30. Which sentence did you place after [E]? 30. a b c d e N

A] Frequently the supply is limited by natural or social circumstances beyond the control of its users.
B] Running the gamut of animal, vegetable, and mineral matter in the live, raw, and processed states, the forms of the currencies are as diverse as any of man's inventions.
C] Often, however, scarcity must be maintained by some convention that through consumption or destruction renders the currency valueless and withdraws it from circulation.
D] Many, but by no means all, primitive peoples have devised moneys of their own.
E] The maintenance of these primitive monetary systems requires the same balancing of supply and demand that confronts the United States Treasury.

31. Which sentence did you put first? 31. a b c d e N
32. Which sentence did you place after [A]? 32. a b c d e N
33. Which sentence did you place after [B]? 33. a b c d e N
34. Which sentence did you place after [C]? 34. a b c d e N
35. Which sentence did you place after [D]? 35. a b c d e N
36. Which sentence did you place after [E]? 36. a b c d e N

TEST 4 *Suggested Time: 15 Minutes*

The sentences in each unit below all belong to a well-organized paragraph. However, they are presented out of their correct order. You are to re-arrange them into the best possible order. As you do the exercises, before you begin to answer the questions that follow, you should write in the space below the correct order of the sentences. In answering the questions, circle N if nothing follows the given sentence.

A] Because the pleuropneumonia organism passes through filters, it resembles viruses.
B] It is, therefore, considered to be a bridge between these two large classes of organism.
C] A laboratory rat is a billion times heavier than a protozoan; the latter is a billion times heavier than a pleuropneumonia organism.
D] Since it can grow in non-living media, it is similar to bacteria.
E] But because it shows obvious differences from both bacteria and viruses, it has been accorded the status of a separate and distinct order: *mycroplasmatales*.

1. Which sentence did you put first? 1. a b c d e N
2. Which sentence did you place after [A]? 2. a b c d e N
3. Which sentence did you place after [B]? 3. a b c d e N
4. Which sentence did you place after [C]? 4. a b c d e N
5. Which sentence did you place after [D]? 5. a b c d e N
6. Which sentence did you place after [E]? 6. a b c d e N

A] This is the agent in the serum that brings about the transformation of fibrinogen to fibren.
B] Of the ten or more clotting factors present in the serum, the best known is the protein, prothrombin.
C] The latter is the material that forms one structure of the clot.
D] When the blood leaves the circulation and comes in contact with the surface of the wound, this substance is converted into thrombin.
E] It causes the independent molecules of fibrinogen to link up together in long fibers.

7. Which sentence did you place first? 7. a b c d e N
8. Which sentence did you place after [A]? 8. a b c d e N
9. Which sentence did you place after [B]? 9. a b c d e N
10. Which sentence did you place after [C]? 10. a b c d e N

11. Which sentence did you place after [D]? 11. a b c d e N
12. Which sentence did you place after [E]? 12. a b c d e N

A] In 1959 one investigator set up a computer so that it not only played a fair game of checkers but it was capable of looking over its past games and modifying its strategy in the light of this experience.
B] Has man boasted for too long of his thinking ability as his biggest advantage over machines?
C] Although at first the inventor was able to beat his machine with ease, it improved so rapidly that it soon reached the point at which it was beating him in every game.
D] Such machines not only do what they have been told to do, but also what they have learned to do.
E] The greatest threat to man comes from the learning machines, computers that improve with experience.

13. Which sentence did you place first? 13. a b c d e N
14. Which sentence did you place after [A]? 14. a b c d e N
15. Which sentence did you place after [B]? 15. a b c d e N
16. Which sentence did you place after [C]? 16. a b c d e N
17. Which sentence did you place after [D]? 17. a b c d e N
18. Which sentence did you place after [E]? 18. a b c d e N

A] It also includes a brief summary of the Congressional activities of the previous day as well as a list of scheduled committee hearings.
B] A bound edition is published for each session in volumes of convenient size for permanent preservation.
C] The Congressional Record contains, in addition to an official record of everything said on the floors of both houses, the roll call on all questions.
D] The appendix contains the extension of remarks, material not spoken on the floor but inserted by permission.
E] Bi-monthly, the daily records are bound in paper covers with an index covering the given period.

19. Which sentence did you place first? 19. a b c d e N
20. Which sentence did you place after [A]? 20. a b c d e N
21. Which sentence did you place after [B]? 21. a b c d e N
22. Which sentence did you place after [C]? 22. a b c d e N
23. Which sentence did you place after [D]? 23. a b c d e N
24. Which sentence did you place after [E]? 24. a b c d e N

TEST 5 *Suggested Time: 15 minutes*
The sentences in each unit below all belong to a well-organized paragraph. However, they are presented out of their correct order. You are to re-arrange them into the best possible order. As you do the exercises, before you begin to answer the questions that follow, you should write in the space below the correct order of the sentences. In answering the questions, circle N if nothing follows the given sentence.

A] The snake overcomes the difficulty by throwing forward lateral loops of its body.
B] However, it is the only way in which this snake can move satisfactorily over the yielding surfaces.
C] One of the members of the rattlesnake family is called the side-winder because of its method of traveling across the terrain in which it lives.
D] It is an inhabitant of the southwestern United States, and it is usually found on soft soil or sand, bad surfaces for a thick-bodied snake to travel across if it uses the usual snake methods of progression.
E] The effect of this "side-winding" makes it appear as if the snake were trying to walk.

1. Which sentence did you place first? 1. a b c d e N
2. Which sentence did you place after [A]? 2. a b c d e N
3. Which sentence did you place after [B]? 3. a b c d e N
4. Which sentence did you place after [C]? 4. a b c d e N
5. Which sentence did you place after [D]? 5. a b c d e N
6. Which sentence did you place after [E]? 6. a b c d e N

A] Spawned in the Sargasso Sea area, they soon become tiny, transparent eel larva, called *leptocephali,* and are part of the ocean plankton.
B] When they make their way up the rivers, they become darker and are called elvers.
C] Eels show a pattern that is the reverse of the one followed by salmon and shad.
D] As they grow in size, they collect around the estuaries of rivers in a form recognizable as that of an eel, the transparency still persisting in these *glass eels.*
E] The life cycle is completed when they come down the streams and rivers to the ocean in a one-way journey to reach their spawning grounds thousands of miles away.

7. Which sentence did you put first? 7. a b c d e N
8. Which sentence did you place after [A]? 8. a b c d e N
9. Which sentence did you place after [B]? 9. a b c d e N
10. Which sentence did you place after [C]? 10. a b c d e N
11. Which sentence did you place after [D]? 11. a b c d e N
12. Which sentence did you place after [E]? 12. a b c d e N

A] The Confederates almost succeeded in their plans, for on its first day as a destroyer of the old, the *Merrimac* quickly destroyed two wooden warships, and would have wiped out more of them if she had not met the *Monitor* the second day.
B] For four hours the ironclads pounded each other with shot and shell, with little apparent damage.
C] As an act of desperation in its attempt to end the Federal blockade that was strangling her commerce, the Confederacy placed all of its hopes in the *Merrimac.*

D] However, the *Merrimac* left leaking badly, unable to attack any more warships, thus failing to accomplish its primary mission.
E] It was a 3,500 ton steam-propelled vessel that had been abandoned and then sunk by the Federals before it was refitted by the Southerners with a coating of four inches of railroad iron.

13. Which sentence did you place first?   13. a b c d e N
14. Which sentence did you place after [A]?   14. a b c d e N
15. Which sentence did you place after [B]?   15. a b c d e N
16. Which sentence did you place after [C]?   16. a b c d e N
17. Which sentence did you place after [D]?   17. a b c d e N
18. Which sentence did you place after [E]?   18. a b c d e N

A] Many other post-war periods have been labeled "The Age of Anxiety," but the atom bomb, Communism, Asian and African self-assertion, and the downfall of Europe have given us an insecurity never felt before by man to the same depth as this.
B] None of our old formulas seem capable of holding the powers of destruction in check: alliances, United Nations, arsenals, armies, religious revivals—all have failed to lessen our fear of the imminent downfall of man.
C] Our basic premise has been that somehow each new invention and each new discovery was leading to progress, a desirable goal.
D] Suddenly we awoke to discover that progress has brought us to the brink of self-destruction both as a basic civilization pattern based on European culture and as a species of animal life inhabiting a planet in the Solar System.
E] Without any foreplanning or vision on our part, we could create a better world for our children if we adjusted quickly to the latest advances.

19. Which sentence did you put first?   19. a b c d e N
20. Which sentence did you place after [A]?   20. a b c d e N
21. Which sentence did you place after [B]?   21. a b c d e N
22. Which sentence did you place after [C]?   22. a b c d e N
23. Which sentence did you place after [D]?   23. a b c d e N
24. Which sentence did you place after [E]?   24. a b c d e N

TEST 6 *Suggested Time: 20 Minutes*

In each of the following exercises, the sentences form the sentence outline for a theme or composition. The sentences are out of their proper order. By circling the appropriate letter in the answer column, mark:
(*a*) if the sentence contains the central idea of the theme
(*b*) if the sentence contains a main supporting idea that points directly to the central idea
(*c*) if the sentence contains an example or illustrative fact that acts as proof
(*d*) if the sentence contains a statement that is unrelated to the central idea

EXERCISE 1
1. The peasantry were overburdened by taxes from many sources.   1. a b c d
2. Monarchs such as Peter the Great of Russia and Frederick II of Prussia supported the arts and sciences.   2. a b c d
3. All men were subject to military duty in the destructive wars carried on by these rulers.   3. a b c d
4. They spent millions of dollars in building magnificent palaces as monuments to remind people of their greatness.   4. a b c d
5. While the Eighteenth Century saw many advances in literature, science, and art, the common people were oppressed by continuing burdens.   5. a b c d
6. Voltaire was one of the intellectual leaders who revolted against the oppressive forces of the current rulers.   6. a b c d
7. These enlightened despots sponsored writers and artists who praised their reigns.   7. a b c d
8. They refused to change old, obsolete forms of government.   8. a b c d

EXERCISE 2
9. The earth could be blanketed in the space of an hour with a deadly cloud of radioactive fall-out poisons.   9. a b c d
10. Nearly half the population of America live or work in environments polluted to some degree by man-made fumes.   10. a b c d
11. Unfriendly nations have at their disposal even more dangerous pollutive forces.   11. a b c d
12. Bombs filled with bacterial agents can be exploded over vast areas, spreading disease and death for months and years.   12. a b c d
13. Modern industrialized society has forced equally large segments of peoples of other countries to breathe in chemical fumes, from factories, automobile exhausts and processing plants.   13. a b c d
14. Air pollution has become a social evil of widespread consequences.   14. a b c d
15. The average person daily breathes about twenty pounds of air.   15. a b c d
16. Airborne contaminants blanket large portions of the world.   16. a b c d

EXERCISE 3
17. The reasons for public indifference reach deep into the private lives of the citizens.   17. a b c d
18. In mid-term Congressional elections even fewer people take the trouble to cast their ballots.   18. a b c d
19. The average person is so deeply absorbed in his personal affairs that he sees little connection between what he is doing and governmental operations.   19. a b c d
20. Too often elections reveal an apathy on the part of the voters.   20. a b c d

WRITING THE ESSAY

21. The strength of a democracy lies in the intelligence of its citizens.   21. a b c d
22. America suffers from a widespread indifference to political affairs.   22. a b c d
23. Fewer than 65% of those eligible to vote take the trouble to do so in important presidential election years.   23. a b c d
24. Governmental agencies do not reach the people with the facts and figures needed to dispel ignorance of their principles and practices, so that the importance of their actions is unknown to the average voters.   24. a b c d

EXERCISE 4
25. Silver and gold coins are milled around the edges because they contain valuable metal.   25. a b c d
26. No one can pare a quarter or half-dollar without it being seen at once by anyone handling the coin.   26. a b c d
27. Unless they were so treated, people could pare the edges of these coins and sell the precious metal.   27. a b c d
28. Pennies and nickels have smooth edges, however.   28. a b c d
29. Have you ever wondered why some coins have grooved edges while others do not?   29. a b c d
30. Pennies and nickels are not milled because it would not be economically worthwhile to the thieves to pare the edges of these coins.   30. a b c d
31. The cost of coinage is kept to a minimum because it is done exclusively by the government with no middleman to make a profit.   31. a b c d

TEST 7   *Suggested Time: 20 Minutes*
In each of the following exercises, the sentences form the sentence outline for a theme or composition. The sentences are out of their proper order. By circling the appropriate letter in the answer column, mark:
(*a*) if the sentence contains the central idea of the theme
(*b*) if the sentence contains a main supporting idea that points directly to the central idea
(*c*) if the sentence contains an example or illustrative fact which acts as proof
(*d*) if the sentence contains a statement that is unrelated to the central idea

EXERCISE 1
1. The nuclear physicist holds a high priority in the group who center their interests in discovering more and more of the universe's until now unknown principles.   1. a b c d
2. The teacher of science and mathematics in the schools and colleges prepares the next generation for the tasks ahead of them.   2. a b c d
3. The man of science plays just as important a role in the practical world of everyday.   3. a b c d
4. The theoretical mathematician and the biochemist searching for the cure of man's physical ills meet here to exchange their ideas for the betterment of man.   4. a b c d
5. The student interested in science and mathematics has many areas open to him, depending upon his interests and aptitudes.   5. a b c d
6. The technician, the pharmacist, the laboratory assistant, and the nurse have their roles to play in safeguarding man from physical ills.   6. a b c d
7. Those who decide to go into research may work in private or public laboratories.   7. a b c d
8. The paths that lead to science and mathematics begin in the earliest school grades.   8. a b c d
9. The physician makes his daily rounds, applying his knowledge to the immediate health problems that cannot wait for a future solution.   9. a b c d

EXERCISE 2
10. The bells also signified the passing of every half hour during each watch.   10. a b c d
11. The time between four in the afternoon and eight in the early evening was often divided into two two-hour periods called dog watches.   11. a b c d
12. Each watch consisted of four hours, and there were six watches in each day.   12. a b c d
13. One bell meant the passing of the first half-hour in each watch.   13. a b c d
14. Time on board ship was once based solely on the bell system.   14. a b c d
15. Eight bells marked the end of each watch and the beginning of the next, when the man who was on duty departed and the next man came to relieve him.   15. a b c d
16. Three bells would mean, for example, that an hour and a half had passed during the watch.   16. a b c d
17. The bells were used to signal the end of the watches.   17. a b c d
18. Eight bells then meant that eight-half-hours had passed.   18. a b c d

EXERCISE 3
19. The impermanence of Federal employment discouraged the more qualified and pressured them to seek employment elsewhere, where their salaries and position would depend more upon their ability as workers.   19. a b c d
20. Before 1883 the spoils system prevailed, and nearly all positions in the Federal service were filled on the basis of political patronage.   20. a b c d
21. By 1933, nearly 80% of the positions in the executive branches of government were under the merit system.   21. a b c d
22. To maintain his job, the office holder had to contribute money and time to the political party in power.   22. a b c d
23. It has only been within recent years that government service has attracted career men and highly qualified personnel.   23. a b c d
24. With the passage of the Pendleton Act and the establishment of the Civil Service Commission, the end of the spoils system began.   24. a b c d
25. Even then, when the party that had given him his job was defeated at the polls, he would most likely

lose his job, regardless of how competent he might be.   **25.** a b c d
26. In recent years there has been considerable criticism directed against the administration of the Federal civil service system.   **26.** a b c d
27. However, there are still thousands of positions that are filled by the politicians who are interested in votes and not in ability to produce on the job.   **27.** a b c d

EXERCISE 4
28. Ability to receive sounds not only varies from person to person but from age group to age group.   **28.** a b c d
29. Sound is the result of air-molecule motion and cannot spread faster than the air's molecules move collectively.   **29.** a b c d
30. Sound waves are waves of energy that are received differently by different organisms.   **30.** a b c d
31. Sounds are audible to the average adult as continuous tones when they contain between twenty and thirty vibrations per second.   **31.** a b c d
32. Cats, small dogs, and guinea pigs detect better than thirty thousand vibrations per second.   **32.** a b c d
33. For ordinary sounds the energy involved is incredibly small.   **33.** a b c d
34. Brown bats have given evidence of hearing vibrations that are as high as a hundred thousand vibrations per second.   **34.** a b c d
35. Young children catch the more shrill sounds, sounds with the highest number of vibrations much better than adults do.   **35.** a b c d
36. Five thousand people speaking over the telephone for one year would develop only enough energy to bring a gallon of water to boil.   **36.** a b c d
37. Animals, particularly the small mammals, hear sounds even higher than those heard by children.   **37.** a b c d

TEST 8   *Suggested Time: 15 Minutes*
In each of the following exercises, the sentences form the sentence outline for a theme or composition. The sentences are out of their proper order. By circling the appropriate letter in the answer column, mark:
(*a*) If the sentence contains the central idea of the theme
(b) if the sentence contains a main supporting idea that points directly to the central idea
(c) if the sentence contains an example or illustration that acts as proof
(d) if the sentence contains a statement that is unrelated to the central idea

EXERCISE 1
1. The lawyers, dentists, and doctors continue to receive their initial college training in the liberal arts.   **1.** a b c d
2. Other four-year institutions have been springing up.   **2.** a b c d
3. Parents have led their children to realize that within a rather short period of time, the average white-collar worker will be college-trained.   **3.** a b c d
4. The liberal arts college is still a stepping stone to traditional professional training.   **4.** a b c d
5. The many fields of business education can now be pursued following training in a college of business.   **5.** a b c d
6. Not only are there colleges of engineering but some institutions now offer a four-year course in technology, the handmaiden to engineering   **6.** a b c d
7. Formal education beyond high school has been undergoing a rapid change within recent years.   **7.** a b c d

EXERCISE 2
8. History has demonstrated that peace cannot be maintained by a combination of victorious powers.   **8.** a b c d
9. The rift between the Western nations and the Soviet Union has been widening through the years.   **9.** a b c d
10. Military alliances have invariably fallen apart.   **10.** a b c d
11. Peace in our time must rest upon the success or failure of the UN.   **11.** a b c d
12. Our former policy of isolation is outworn.   **12.** a b c d
13. The balance of power arrangement has inevitably led to an arms race.   **13.** a b c d
14. Science and invention have overcome the barriers of geography.   **14.** a b c d

EXERCISE 3
15. A jet pilot trying to leave a disabled plane has little chance of climbing out against the pressure of the hurricane of air rushing by.   **15.** a b c d
16. Ejecting him with a charge of gunpowder only partially solves the difficulties.   **16.** a b c d
17. Survival of man after a supersonic bail-out has been a serious problem when a failure occurs in jet planes.   **17.** a b c d
18. An unprotected man cannot depend on surviving the effects of being hit by the wind of present plane speeds.   **18.** a b c d
19. The speed generated by the plane is a basic cause of the difficulty.   **19.** a b c d
20. In February 1955, a test pilot was the first man to survive a forced bail-out while his plane was traveling at supersonic speeds.   **20.** a b c d
21. Even if he did succeed in getting out of the cabin, the tail assembly would most probably cut him in two.   **21.** a b c d

EXERCISE 4
22. Hitler and his corps of followers destroyed the machinery that allowed nations to live at peace with each other.   **22.** a b c d
23. Six million Jews were not their only victims.   **23.** a b c d
24. Deceit and bullying, treachery and war replaced humanitarianism and Christian ethics as the principles the Nazis brought to the conference table when countries met to iron out their differences.   **24.** a b c d
25. Each succeeding generation must be taught to recoil at the horror that was unleashed on the world by the forces of Nazism.   **25.** a b c d
26. Many millions more from Russia, Poland, France and England were slaughtered like cattle and burned

WRITING THE ESSAY

in ovens built to convert their bodies into fertilizer.
26. a b c d
27. Innocent people throughout Europe were ground into slavery and dust because they stood in the path of these ruthless would-be conquerors of the world.
27. a b c d
28. By January 1933, the Nazis had formed the largest single political party in Germany.
28. a b c d

TEST 9 *Suggested Time: 20 Minutes*

In each of the following exercises, the sentences form the sentence outline for a theme or composition. The sentences are out of their proper order. By circling the appropriate letter in the answer column, mark:

(*a*) if the sentence contains the central idea of the theme
(*b*) if the sentence contains a main supporting idea that points directly to the central idea
(*c*) if the sentence contains an example or illustrative fact which acts as proof
(*d*) if the sentence contains a statement that is unrelated to the central idea.

EXERCISE 1

1. He hurried his family out of the house and into the cyclone cellar. 1. a b c d
2. Before he realized what had happened, the great funnel was hanging directly over him. 2. a b c d
3. Not many men have been as fortunate as the Kansas farmer, Will Keller, who escaped unharmed even though a tornado passed directly over him. 3. a b c d
4. All wind had ceased, and he caught a very distinctive pungent odor. 4. a b c d
5. He took one last look through the barn and hurried to the cellar himself. 5. a b c d
6. When he saw a greenish black cloud in the southwest, Keller suspected a tornado. 6. a b c d
7. A line of thunderheads, at first low on the horizon, soon appears in the west. 7. a b c d
8. He looked directly into the circular opening of the tornado, and saw small twisters form and writhe their way around inside the rim of the funnel. 8. a b c d
9. He stopped at the cellar door before going down to safety. 9. a b c d

EXERCISE 2

10. The late eighteenth and early nineteenth centuries were characterized by a relatively simple agricultural economy that did not require economic controls. 10. a b c d
11. To outlaw practices which endangered the public health, Congress enacted the Meat Inspection Act. 11. a b c d
12. The role of the government in assuring social justice for all has undergone marked changes during the last 75 years. 12. a b c d
13. The important issues of that day seemed to be mainly political rather than in the area of the national economy. 13. a b c d
14. The leaders felt that the government should try to encourage agriculture and commerce without restricting the individual farmer. 14. a b c d
15. The earlier approach was based on the Jeffersonian idea that the best form of government is the one which disturbs the individual the least. 15. a b c d
16. The government must exert controls in our social and economic organization to protect the individual. 16. a b c d
17. The governments must concern themselves with everyday factors of living and earning a living. 17. a b c d
18. The basic issues which confront the nation today are mainly economic, the outgrowth of a highly complex industrial civilization. 18. a b c d

EXERCISE 3

19. The freshwater angler who enjoys walking along rocks or streambeds wanders with a box of flies into isolated areas in search of trout. 19. a b c d
20. He casts his heavily weighted line out beyond the breakers and trolls it in, catching unwary fish that have come close to the beach in search of food. 20. a b c d
21. The fisherman of today has a variety of tackle and types of fishing activities to choose from. 21. a b c d
22. The surfcaster, equipped with heavy boots, and the longest rod of them all, stands in the white water on the beach's edge. 22. a b c d
23. The sportsman with the big-game hunter instinct is usually attracted to the swivel chair and the deep-sea launches. 23. a b c d
24. The flyfisherman can use either the traditional long bamboo pole or the modern spinning equipment with a spun-glass rod. 24. a b c d
25. The laker finds his fun and enjoyment by having a sport that has some of the characteristics usually found mainly among the other three types of fishing. 25. a b c d
26. The fishing widow is the wife who has resigned herself to being left stranded by her husband while he searches for the big one and for release of his tensions. 26. a b c d
27. The rod is secured to a harness that is part of the chair, and the line is usually of metal to give him a chance of bringing in a tarpon or sailfish if he is lucky enough to hook into one. 27. a b c d

EXERCISE 4

28. Many seeds are water-travelers, for those that are lighter than water are able to float. 28. a b c d
29. Birds, tempted by pleasantly flavored fruit, feast and then drop and scatter the seeds. 29. a b c d
30. Many seeds have wings that cause them to be carried by the wind. 30. a b c d
31. In the tumbleweeds, the whole plant breaks off from the roots when it stops growing. 31. a b c d
32. Nature's means of seed dispersal are many and varied. 32. a b c d
33. Dandelion seeds sail long distances, wafted by the breeze on delicate parachutes composed of a crown of silky hairs. 33. a b c d
34. Although the dust-like seeds of the orchids have no

special flying equipment, because of their small size, they are carried great distances by even gentle breezes.   34. a b c d
35. Coconuts can float many miles before the seed is landed on a distant shore.   35. a b c d
36. Fruits of the arrowhead have air-chambers that help them on their voyage and enable the seeds to settle far from the parent plant.   36. a b c d
37. For many seeds, birds serve as the means of transportation.   37. a b c d

TEST 10   *Suggested Time: 20 Minutes*

In each of the following exercises, the sentences form the sentence outline for a theme or composition. The sentences are out of their proper order. By circling the appropriate letter in the answer column, mark:

(*a*) if the sentence contains the central idea of the theme

(*b*) if the sentence contains a main supporting idea that points directly to the central idea

(*c*) if the sentence contains an example or illustrative fact that acts as proof

(*d*) if the sentence contains a statement that is unrelated to the central idea

EXERCISE 1

1. Over 8,000,000 men died in battle or of wounds sustained in battle.   1. a b c d
2. Many cities and villages were destroyed completely.   2. a b c d
3. The loss in human life far exceeded that caused in all previous wars combined.   3. a b c d
4. The immediate effects of World War I were almost unbelievable in their magnitude.   4. a b c d
5. Material losses can be estimated only in billions of dollars.   5. a b c d
6. Over 22,000,000 soldiers were wounded.   6. a b c d
7. Economic nationalism cut down world trade in a futile effort to rebuild destroyed manufacturing centers.   7. a b c d
8. Almost 20,000,000 civilians died because of the famine, disease, and the direct destructive forces of war.   8. a b c d
9. Trade and manufacturing as well as farming ceased in large areas.   9. a b c d

EXERCISE 2

10. At one time sponges were considered as worm houses built by worms much as bees build honeycombs.   10. a b c d
11. The skeleton, when the animal is alive, contains many tiny cells.   11. a b c d
12. The sponge is an intricate structure that once was regarded as one of nature's puzzles.   12. a b c d
13. There are many mistaken beliefs about the sponge.   13. a b c d
14. The dry material that we buy is really a skeleton.   14. a b c d
15. One ancient writer asserted that sponges were from the foam of the sea.   15. a b c d
16. A stream of water carries food and oxygen around the cells.   16. a b c d
17. Actually the sponge is an animal.   17. a b c d
18. Some even consider the sponge a type of seaweed.   18. a b c d
19. The sponges are of many different colors.   19. a b c d

EXERCISE 3

20. Foreign governments could not deal with a government lacking this function.   20. a b c d
21. Any predatory group could attempt to seize power and run the government.   21. a b c d
22. The individual would be without protection for his personal liberties.   22. a b c d
23. The property of foreigners could not be protected, nor would their businessmen be able to deal with ours lest just debts be ignored by gangster groups.   23. a b c d
24. Criminal elements could seize from the weaker citizens their wealth and property.   24. a b c d
25. Policing is one of the chief functions of government.   25. a b c d
26. Anarchy is the type of social structure in which there are no governmental structures or restrictions.   26. a b c d
27. Organized group activities would be at a standstill if governments did not have this primary of policing.   27. a b c d

EXERCISE 4

28. The glands connected to the fang in the harmless snake look like those of the deadly snakes; yet they produce nothing to hurt anyone.   28. a b c d
29. The amount of poison is slight, but the venom of many of our poisonous snakes is among the most deadly of all poisons.   29. a b c d
30. The fang in the harmless snakes lacks the hollow slit.   30. a b c d
31. The snake's fang is an eye or canine tooth, corresponding to the sharp-pointed tooth that humans have between the front teeth and the back teeth.   31. a b c d
32. Those who fear snakes should learn to recognize the harmless ones that are beneficial to man.   32. a b c d
33. In poisonous snakes the fang has a hollow channel running through it.   33. a b c d
34. The fang in a poisonous snake has one significant difference from that found in the non-poisonous snakes.   34. a b c d
35. When the snake bites, drops of poison are forced through the channel and into the victim's body.   35. a b c d

WRITING THE ESSAY

ANSWER KEY: PRACTICE IN ORGANIZATION

TEST 1 (Page 155)

				17. (N)	22. (N)	27. (N)	32. (N)
1. (d)	5. (a)	9. (e)	13. (c)	18. (b)	23. (a)	28. (e)	33. (d)
2. (e)	6. (b)	10. (a)	14. (e)	19. (b)	24. (c)	29. (a)	34. (a)
3. (c)	7. (b)	11. (c)	15. (d)	20. (e)	25. (d)	30. (b)	35. (c)
4. (N)	8. (N)	12. (d)	16. (a)	21. (d)	26. (c)	31. (b)	

TEST 2 (Page 156)

1. (b)	4. (N)	7. (c)	10. (a)	13. (e)	16. (a)	19. (b)	22. (a)
2. (e)	5. (a)	8. (e)	11. (N)	14. (b)	17. (N)	20. (N)	23. (c)
3. (d)	6. (c)	9. (d)	12. (b)	15. (d)	18. (c)	21. (e)	24. (d)

TEST 3 (Page 157)

1. (b)	6. (c)	11. (a)	16. (a)	21. (e)	25. (b)	29. (e)	33. (e)
2. (e)	7. (d)	12. (b)	17. (N)	22. (N)	26. (N)	30. (c)	34. (N)
3. (d)	8. (c)	13. (b)	18. (c)	23. (b)	27. (d)	31. (d)	35. (b)
4. (N)	9. (N)	14. (d)	19. (a)	24. (c)	28. (a)	32. (c)	36. (a)
5. (a)	10. (e)	15. (e)	20. (d)				

TEST 4 (Page 158)

1. (c)	4. (a)	7. (b)	10. (e)	13. (b)	16. (N)	19. (c)	22. (a)
2. (d)	5. (b)	8. (c)	11. (a)	14. (c)	17. (a)	20. (d)	23. (e)
3. (e)	6. (N)	9. (d)	12. (N)	15. (e)	18. (d)	21. (N)	24. (b)

TEST 5 (Page 159)

1. (c)	4. (d)	7. (c)	10. (a)	13. (c)	16. (e)	19. (d)	22. (e)
2. (e)	5. (a)	8. (d)	11. (b)	14. (b)	17. (N)	20. (c)	23. (a)
3. (N)	6. (b)	9. (e)	12. (N)	15. (d)	18. (a)	21. (N)	24. (b)

TEST 6 (Page 160)

Exercise 1		Exercise 2		Exercise 3		Exercise 4	
1. (c)	5. (a)	9. (c)	13. (c)	17. (b)	21. (d)	25. (b)	29. (a)
2. (b)	6. (d)	10. (c)	14. (a)	18. (c)	22. (a)	26. (c)	30. (c)
3. (c)	7. (c)	11. (b)	15. (d)	19. (c)	23. (c)	27. (c)	31. (d)
4. (c)	8. (b)	12. (c)	16. (b)	20. (b)	24. (c)	28. (b)	

TEST 7 (Page 161)

Exercise 1		Exercise 2		Exercise 3		Exercise 4	
1. (c)	6. (c)	10. (b)	15. (c)	19. (c)	24. (b)	28. (b)	33. (b)
2. (c)	7. (b)	11. (d)	16. (c)	20. (b)	25. (c)	29. (d)	34. (c)
3. (b)	8. (d)	12. (c)	17. (b)	21. (c)	26. (d)	30. (a)	35. (c)
4. (c)	9. (c)	13. (c)	18. (c)	22. (c)	27. (c)	31. (c)	36. (c)
5. (a)		14. (a)		23. (a)		32. (c)	37. (c)

TEST 8 (Page 162)

Exercise 1		Exercise 2		Exercise 3		Exercise 4	
1. (c)	5. (c)	8. (b)	12. (b)	15. (c)	19. (b)	22. (b)	26. (c)
2. (b)	6. (c)	9. (d)	13. (c)	16. (b)	20. (d)	23. (c)	27. (b)
3. (d)	7. (a)	10. (c)	14. (c)	17. (a)	21. (c)	24. (c)	28. (d)
4. (b)		11. (a)		18. (c)		25. (a)	

TEST 9 (Page 163)

Exercise 1
1. (c)
2. (b)
3. (a)
4. (c)
5. (c)
6. (b)
7. (d)
8. (c)
9. (c)

Exercise 2
10. (c)
11. (d)
12. (a)
13. (c)
14. (c)
15. (b)
16. (c)
17. (c)
18. (b)

Exercise 3
19. (b)
20. (c)
21. (a)
22. (b)
23. (b)
24. (c)
25. (b)
26. (d)
27. (c)

Exercise 4
28. (b)
29. (c)
30. (b)
31. (d)
32. (a)
33. (c)
34. (b)
35. (c)
36. (c)
37. (b)

TEST 10 (Page 164)

Exercise 1
1. (c)
2. (c)
3. (b)
4. (a)
5. (b)
6. (c)
7. (d)
8. (c)
9. (c)

Exercise 2
10. (c)
11. (b)
12. (a)
13. (b)
14. (b)
15. (c)
16. (c)
17. (b)
18. (c)
19. (d)

Exercise 3
20. (b)
21. (c)
22. (b)
23. (b)
24. (c)
25. (a)
26. (d)
27. (b)

Exercise 4
28. (c)
29. (c)
30. (b)
31. (a)
32. (d)
33. (c)
34. (b)
35. (c)

3. Steps in Planning Your Essay

1. Read the question carefully.
2. Use the question as the basis of your organization.
3. Plan your central idea first. Know what your conclusion will be, and then you can plan the rest of your theme. You must know your summary sentence before you begin.
4. You need not use a formal outline, but plan what you are going to say in your introduction, body, and conclusion.

The Introduction

Avoid elaborate flourishes. The introduction should point to the reader the direction of your theme. It may contain (a) a definition (b) an example (c) a statement of the problem (d) a statement of the present situation (e) a quotation (f) a dramatization of the problem.

The transition from the introduction to the body can very well be a rhetorical question based on the topic being discussed. If you are discussing heroes of today, then the transitional sentence may be, "Is it true then, that there is no hero in our world of today?" The section of the theme that follows will be your answer to the question.

The Development

Don't attempt to list reasons. This is not a test of your memory. It is a test of your ability to discuss a serious topic. The key to a mature development lies in your stressing the word *because*. You should support your statements by giving references from your own experience or from the world of literature.

The Conclusion

The Conclusion should not contain any new ideas. It should serve as a summary of what you had said before. It should end on a strong emotional note—if such a note is appropriate.

The Tone of Your Essay

1. Avoid the trite, the forced, the superfluous.
2. Be simple and direct.
3. Strive to be accurate, clear, emphatic.
4. Be modest, unassuming, and temperate.
5. Do not strive to be funny.
6. Be positive. Cynicism is to be avoided.
7. Try to achieve appropriate mood and manner.

SOME QUESTIONS AND ANSWERS

How much time should I spend in planning?

You are allowed 20 minutes for the essay. How much of this time should you spend on each step? Of course there is no pat answer to this question. *But*, if you can glance through the booklet in the first few minutes of the examination to discover whether there will be an essay to write and what the general topic is, then you can let your inner computer go to work during the first 40 minutes. Glance at the topic and then go to the other tasks at the beginning of the examination. Your mind will do the rest—without your assistance!

However, you should know generally how much time you need to plan, to write, and then to proofread a one-page theme. The only way that you can find out is by timing yourself under practice examination conditions. The topics that follow will allow you to do just that so that you can discover how much of your time should be spent in becoming familiar with the directions, how much time you need to plan the paragraph by paragraph development of your ideas, how much time you need for the actual writing, and equally important, how much time you will need for checking spelling, choice of words, punctuation, sentence structure, usage slips and how

WRITING THE ESSAY

much time you will need for doublechecking for errors of omission and carelessness.

Shall I plan a rough draft and then a finished copy?

In the 20 minutes allotted to you, you will not be able to write and then re-write. Not only will you not have time, but you will not be given the paper to do such writing. If, however, you plan in advance the content of each paragraph or section, then you will not find the need for writing a rough draft.

Shall I write a formal outline, using the Harvard Outline System?

Your outline will not be rated. You will be given one special answer sheet. Your notes will have to be made in the examination booklet. Therefore, the outline or rough draft that you think through must be just that. If you are more comfortable in planning with a formal outline, then of course do so. If you have no preference, then you should train yourself to plan just what you want to say in each paragraph and then begin to write the essay.

Should I plan a title?

This item is usually not called for. Do not waste your time in trying to think of a title—unless the question requires you to plan one.

HOW CAN I DO MY BEST?

You cannot change yourself or your outlook for the moments of examination taking. Plan to express your own thoughts with honesty and sincerity. Do not try to guess what the markers would want you to say. You do *not* know what their opinions are. They are looking primarily for the method that you use to express your ideas, and for the basis of such ideas.

The material in the review sections of this book will familiarize you with the errors in usage that you should avoid, the errors in diction that could lower their evaluation of your work. The exercises in this section will increase your ability to organize your ideas and to plan your paragraphs.

The ideal preparation takes time. The more time you can spend on each section of this book, the more effectively you will be able to express yourself. Do not waste time, however, in drilling yourself on the items you already know. Check for those that you do not have under control, and then review these until you know them thoroughly.

What shall I do if I make an error?

You will not be able to erase. Changes must be made by lining out and substituting. Do *not* block out or cross out. One line through the material to be omitted and then a neat interlinear change placed above will lead to no penalties.

Do handwriting and neatness count?

Usually, they are not taken into consideration; however, the reader will be inclined more favorably to a paper that is easier to read than he will be toward one that requires much time to decipher.

You cannot expect to change your handwriting overnight; yet, if you are careful, you can change a scrawl into a legible script. The following are some of the precautionary measures to be taken by those whose handwriting tends to be less than clear.

Letter formation
1. Dot your *i*'s and keep your *e*'s open.
   Illegible: *receive*
   Improved: *receive*
2. Close *a, d, b, q, o,* and *s*
   Confusing: *about*
   Improved: *about*
3. Close your *k* so that it is not confused with *h*.
   Confusing: *kick*
   Improved: *kick*
4. The *r* should not resemble *i*, nor should *m* look like *n*
   Confusing: *merry*
   Improved: *merry*
5. The letters like *l, b, f, h* and *y* should be looped while *t* should be closed.
   Confusing: *laughter*
   Improved: *laughter*
6. The letters *g, q, f, y* should contain bottom loops.
   Confusing: *getting ready*
   Improved: *getting ready*
7. Letters like *m, n, u,* and *w* should be rounded, not pointed.
   Confusing: *in a minute*
   Improved: *minute*

Additional fundamentals
1. Keep your letters on the line; do not write uphill or downhill.
   Confusing: *up and down*
   Improved: *up and down*
2. Avoid flourishes at the beginning or end of words.
   Confusing: *erase*
   Improved: *erase*
3. The space between letters and the spaces between words should be kept uniform.
   Confusing: *working together*
   Improved: *working together*

Must I fill the entire page?

Some people can say much in little; others can never find enough words to express themselves. It is more important that you state clearly and forcefully what you have to say than that you completely fill the page. Only through practice will you be able to develop the skills necessary to encompass the beginning, development, and conclusion of an idea in the limits of one page.

Is it better to agree or disagree with the topic?

It is not your point of view that is being rated. The essay is planned to show how well you can express your thoughts. The subject of the essay is usually one that you can explore on the basis of your personal experience, observation, or reading. The specific details that you use to support your point of view are much more important than whether to agree or disagree.

If a quotation is included, shall I copy it?

Do not waste valuable space in copying verbatim.

SAMPLES OF STUDENT ESSAYS

Read each of the following portions of essays, typical of those submitted by college applicants. In the space below each, write your analysis of the strengths and weaknesses found in each. Confine your criticism to errors in content and organization.

1. TITLE: United States as a World Leader
   Portion of Essay: Introduction only

   During these troubled times, America has a role to play. The countries of the world are torn by fears and doubts. They do not know which way to turn. In either direction, the devastation of the atom or hydrogen bomb threatens them with destruction. What should be the part that America should play?

   ANALYSIS ....
   ....
   ....

2. TITLE: United States as a World Leader
   Portion of Essay: Introduction

   I think that this topic is one of the most important in the world today. What can be more important than a topic that centers around our futures? The planners of this Writing Sample are to be congratulated in selecting this topic. If more themes were written on this and similar topics, then the world would not be in the mess that it is. We would be forced to look for solutions of the problems that face us and the rest of the nations of the world. Yes, I am pleased to be able to write about the United States as a world leader.

   ANALYSIS ....
   ....
   ....

Try to reach your discussion as quickly as possible. If you need to quote from the question, try to limit this material.

May I both agree and disagree with the topic?

Here too, you are not being rated on your point of view. The clarity of your expression and the forcefulness of your statements are what count. Therefore, if you find that there are some aspects to agree with and some aspects to disagree with, good!

How many points should I make?

Remember, you are not being asked to write a book! You do not have time to explore all aspects of the topic. Choose a limited part; stick with what you think is most important—and then explain that clearly.

Shall I skip lines between paragraphs?

Since the amount of space offered you is limited to one page, do not skip lines. Begin to write on the first line and keep your margins very narrow.

3. TITLE: Does America Have Spiritual Values
   Complete Essay

   Our country has been able to prove its boast that we have the highest standard of living in the world today. The rest of the world looks to us for the latest comforts that can make the lives of each individual pleasanter. Name any of the luxuries that you find in other countries, and the chances are that it either has a label, "Made in the United States of America" or it is an imitation of something that we export.

   The farmer can sit on his tractor, thanks to us, and do in one day what would have taken him weeks to do. Our seeds guarantee him the best return per acre of planting. The seeds are treated to fight off the diseases that years ago would have wiped out his crops.

   The city dweller also finds his life easier to live because of our efforts. His work in the factory is no longer back-breaking and muscle-pulling. Our machines have made his labor more productive and less tiring.

   Throughout the world the United States has helped all. We have not only raised our own standard of living but have helped to raise that of the other inhabitants of our globe.

   ANALYSIS ....
   ....
   ....

4. TITLE: Cowardice, Asset or Liability
   Complete Essay

   The moment of decision had come. If Harold stood his ground, he would most certainly be crushed under the merciless tracks of the oncoming tank. If he ran away, he could live to fight another day.

WRITING THE ESSAY 169

Would cowardice be an asset or liability to him?

Commonsense and foolhardiness must not be confused. When a person rushes into a situation in which he has no chance of ever winning, he is not being a coward or a hero; he is just being foolhardy. If that person were to retreat so that he could fight another time, then I do not think that that is cowardice.

Cowardice can be mental or physical. The person who does not answer the bully and allows the bully to talk against his country is just as much a coward as the person who cringes and cries enough when the bully attacks him.

Cowardice is an emotional state rather than an overt reaction. The coward does not do the right thing because he is afraid. If we could measure a person's fear, then we could tell whether he is a coward or not. Of course, a brave man feels fear too. We all feel fear in the face of danger, but the brave man labels his emotions as fear and does not allow it to become more important than the issues involved in the situation.

ANALYSIS ....
....
....

5. TITLE: Moral Standards in America
   Portion of Essay: Conclusion

In conclusion, let me summarize what I have said earlier. Big things can come in small packages, and great ideas can be summarized in a few words. Regardless of how many words are used in the statement, if there is truth to it, then you should accept it. Therefore, I repeat what I have said before. America has moral standards that are as good as those of any other nation. Now that you know this, you must react properly. Remember, the eyes of the world are on you. Do not let us down.

ANALYSIS ....
....
....

6. TITLE: Socialized Medicine?
   Portion of Essay: Introduction

I feel that the best way to decide whether we have socialized medicine or not is to analyze what it would do for the country.

ANALYSIS ....
....
....

7. TITLE: Heroes
   Portion of Essay: Introduction

Heroes, although they do not ride white chargers and wear armor, are still around today. They do not go around saving damsels in distress, but their mental courage is in evidence everywhere you turn. President Kennedy is one of these men. His decision to resume nuclear testing in the atmosphere, in order to catch up with Russia, took as much courage to announce as would a declaration of war. Franklin Roosevelt was another bold president. During his three terms in office, he led the country through war and depression. For his courage and foresight, he has won an everlasting place in the hearts of his countrymen.

ANALYSIS ....
....
....

8. TITLE: Fame
   Portion of Essay: Introduction

Many people spend their lives searching for fame. Fame is an ambiguous word. What is fame to one may not be fame to another. Fame depends too much on luck. Inner peace is better than fame to many. Fame can flare up and die out overnight. Fame is much different from greatness.

ANALYSIS ....
....
....

9. TITLE: Freedom of the Press
   Portion of Essay: Introduction

"Where the press is free, and every man able to read, all is safe." This statement runs the risk of all facile generalizations. There is much truth to it. Liberties are safeguarded when the people can get the facts readily. However, without additional avenues available to the people, freedom of the press can not be the sole guardian of their rights.

ANALYSIS ....
....
....

10. TITLE: Moral Standards of Youth
    Portion of Essay: Introduction

The headlines of our newspapers prominently display stories about scandals involving the youth in colleges throughout the world. Basketball scandals centering on corruption among our scholastic athletes rock the athletic world. Rioting youth destroy needlessly in the capitals in Europe, Asia, America. It is time to evaluate honestly the moral standards of youth. Are the moral standards of youth sinking?

ANALYSIS ....
....
....

ANALYSES ANSWER KEY: ESSAY SAMPLES / Pages 168-169

1. The student has not wandered off the topic. He did end his introduction with a sentence that points to the discussion that follows. However, the introductory phrase "During these troubled times" is trite and overdone. He spoke only in general terms. He could have improved this introduction by avoiding in *these troubled*

times and by giving a specific instance to act as anchor for his generalizations.

2. This student never reached the topic. He spoke around it, about it, but he never came to grips with the ideas involved in the topic.

3. This theme is well-organized. Each paragraph develops a single idea. The ideas in the three paragraphs unify into one central idea. BUT the idea of the composition is not that which is implied in the title. This could not be a theme that is rated satisfactory because the student spoke of how America helped to raise the standard of living of others; it does not deal with spiritual values.

4. This theme contains many good ideas, but they are just listed one after the other. The student began well by attempting to dramatize the problem. He pointed toward the development with his question ending the introduction. However, once he reached the development, he went from one idea to another, not attempting to connect them. He failed to include a conclusion.

5. The student showed a realization that the conclusion should summarize what he had previously said. He realized that the concluding sentence should be novel, if possible. However, he suddenly became involved in justifying his entire theme in a most self-conscious manner. He weakened his entire theme with his repetitious rantings.

6. Such an introduction might do on an examination, but it is totally inadequate for a theme. One sentence, except for dramatic effect or in dialog, should not constitute a paragraph. The student omitted the entire background involved in the problem.

7. The student reveals a sense of the dramatic and a felicity of phrase. However, the organization is chaotic. He rushed into the development with his examples before he had pointed the way to his conclusion. His examples are disconnected and not joined directly to the title of heroes. Each of the examples deserves a separate paragraph and a statement tying the men directly to the word *hero*.

8. This theme reveals an ability to think and to express ideas in words. However, there is a lack of organizational ability. There is a lack of skill in composing. The student began to write before deciding just what his purpose in writing was. He did not know what his conclusion would be *before* he began to write. The result is a series of disconnected statements, none of which is explained or proved. He just listed the ideas as they came to him.

9. The student makes an awkward use of the quotation given in the assignment. It could have been more skillfully woven into his introduction. However, the organization is excellent. He defines the pattern that his development will follow. He defines the point of view that he will attempt to prove.

10. The writer reveals an analytical mind, a willingness to weigh and consider on the basis of facts. There is no originality of phrasing or felicity of expression, but the organization is excellent. This student has thought through what he wants to say and is saying it clearly and more than adequately. This is a superior introduction.

4. Practice Essay Assignments

WRITING TIME: *20 minutes from the time you read the question until the time you have completed your essay.*

Write an essay of about 1½ pages of 8½ by 11 paper, the usual size of theme paper. Discuss the idea contained in the quotation. Be specific; you should support your point of view with illustrations from your own experience or by references taken from your observations or readings. You should plan to express your best thoughts in your best natural manner; quality rather than quantity will count.

1. The best way to do good to ourselves is to do it to others; the right way to gather is to scatter.

2. He who is only just is cruel—Who on earth could live were all judged justly?

3. Some will always be above others—Destroy the inequality today, and it will appear again tomorrow.

4. Wise men argue causes; fools decide them.

5. Where the press is free, and every man able to read, all is safe.

6. Liberty has restraints but no frontiers.

7. A map of the world that does not include Utopia is not worth glancing at.

8. White lies are but ushers to black ones.

9. Shallow men believe in luck; wise and strong men believe in cause and effect.

10. More firm and sure the hand of courage strikes when it obeys the watchful eye of caution.

11. Master books, but do not let them master you. —Read to live, not live to read.

12. Maxims are to the intellect what laws are to actions: they do not enlighten, but guide and direct, and though themselves blind, are protecting.

13. Prejudices are rarely overcome by argument; not being founded in reason, they cannot be destroyed by logic.

14. The fire of anger that you kindle for your enemy often burns you more than him.

15. Men have made a virtue of moderation to limit the ambition of the great, and to console people of mediocrity for their want of fortune and of merit.

16. I am weary of hearing of the tremendous power of money. I will say to the contrary that for a genuine man it is no evil to be poor.

17. A man's personal defects will commonly have, with the rest of the world, precisely that importance which they have to himself. If he makes light of them, so will other men.

18. It would be folly to argue that the people in a democracy cannot make political mistakes. They can and do make grave mistakes. They know it; they pay the penalty; but compared with the mistakes which have been made by every kind of totalitarianism, they are unimportant.

19. Books are good enough in their own way, but they are a mighty bloodless substitute for life.

20. Boredom is a vital problem for the moralist, since at least half the sins of mankind are caused by the fear of it.

21. Opinions alter, manners change, creeds rise and fall, but the moral law is written on the tablet of eternity. For every false word or unrighteous deed, for cruelty and oppression, for lust or vanity, the price has to be paid at last, not always by the chief offenders, but paid by some one.

22. Most people judge men only by success or by fortune.

23. Men's arguments often prove nothing but their wishes.

24. Men are valued, not for what they are, but for what they seem to be.

25. We have no time to make allowances; and the graduation of punishment by the scale of guilt is a mere impossibility. A thief is a thief in the law's eye even though he has been trained from his cradle in a den of thieves; and definite penalties must be attached to definite acts.

The Literature Test

Section FOUR : Improving Your Ability to Read Critically

1. *The Nature of the Achievement Test in Literature*

2. *Taste and Sensitivity in Poetry*

3. *Terms of Literary Analysis*

1. *The Nature of the Achievement Test in Literature*

There are two Achievement Tests in English, the English Composition Test and the Literature Test. Some colleges require both, others one or the other. Before attempting to master the material in this part of the practice book, make certain that the college or colleges of your choice request that you take the Literature Examination.

The information, examination tehniques, practice exercises, and practice tests that follow will sharpen your ability to interpret works of literature, a skill invaluable for entering college freshmen. These pages, however, will do little toward acquainting you with the skills required for doing your best on the English Composition Examination. Turn to the practice material for that test and see the difference!

Each examination has different emphases; practice for one is unrelated to the practice required for the other. Be positive that you are studying for the required examination.

If you are in doubt, check with the office of admissions. If the choice is yours, then spend some time examining each section and take one of the Practice Examinations in each. This procedure will help you to discover objectively which examination will center on your greater strengths—writing or reading critically. If you have to take both, then study separately for each examination for best results.

Form of the Literature Test

The test consists of several reading passages followed by multiple choice questions. The passages selected may be

- complete poems
- portions of poems
- excerpts from the dialogue in short stories or novels
- brief thoughts in paragraph form, usually taken from essays
- page-length selections from plays, novels, stories, essays

The principal sources are American and British literature of today and yesterday.

Types of Questions

Some of the questions will be similar to those found on the Verbal Examination, the morning College Boards. These will test your comprehension of

- parts of the passage
- meaning of the entire passage
- implications found in the passage
- the author's point of view

However, there will be many other types of questions on this test. These will cover your ability to recognize

- literary forms and structure
- literary devices and terms
- rhetorical devices
- allusions
- elements of style, mood

The passages selected for the Verbal Examination come from many subject areas. The selections for the Literature Examination are limited to passages from literary works. The range of questions attempts to evaluate the skills and sensitivities you have developed in your study of literature.

How This Book Can Help You

Control of literary terms and the ability to meet the range of literature come from reading regularly and widely over a period of years. This book cannot be a substitute for such experiencing. However, it will help you to review the technical terms and concepts you should know and then give you the practice that will lead you to maximum results in reading for comprehension and appreciation.

So that you can concentrate your efforts more ef-

IMPROVING YOUR ABILITY TO READ CRITICALLY

fectively, the review material has been divided into poetry and prose. Each unit begins with a review of the terms and concepts that are basic to critical understanding. These are followed by practice exercises to help you evaluate your control of these terms and concepts. The section ends with ten combined Practice Examinations to help you reach your maximum level of speed and accuracy.

2. Taste and Sensitivity in Poetry

Candidates taking the Literature Test must have a developed realization of the appropriateness of sound and sense not only in prose but also in poetry. The material in this section will review for you the terms and concepts involved in achieving an understanding of the tonal values of poetry. However, once again, unless you have experienced poetry, unless you are willing to accustom yourself through exposure to poetry, learning the terms that follow will not give you the maturity of approach being sought in the questions in this area. Once you have mastered the concepts involved, you must put to use the skills developed. You must read sufficiently to be able to agree that poetry is the best that man has thought and said, presented in condensed form.

BASIC CHARACTERISTICS OF THE BEST IN POETRY

1. Recurrent rhythms: Although the rhythm of a poem will vary from the mechanical beat of its meter, there is always a recurring beat that unifies the poem and makes it one. This rhythm is in harmony with the thought. Sadness and contemplation, for example, demand a slower beat.

> Break, break, break,
> On thy cold gray stones, O Sea!

Happiness and swiftness on the other hand demand rapid movement.

> The road was a ribbon of moonlight over the purple moor,
> And the highwayman came riding—

2. Imaginative use of language: Prose is used basically to communicate ideas and facts. Poetry stirs our feelings and imaginations. It shows us relationships that we had never dreamed existed. It puts into words that which we have often felt but have never before expressed.

> I never saw a moor,
> I never saw the sea;
> Yet know I how the heather looks,
> And what a wave must be.
>
> I never spoke with God,
> Nor visited in Heaven;
> Yet certain am I of the spot
> As if the chart were given.

3. Poetic machinery: The poet takes full advantage of the less subtle aspects of poetry such as rhymes, figures of speech and stanzaic patterns to emphasize his imagery, pinpoint the emotional reactions sought, and increase the pleasure of the reader.

4. Condensed utterance: The poet will express his thoughts in a minimum of words. He requires concentration on the part of the reader, a willingness to re-read and re-read until the full import of the words is realized. He makes each word carry a much heavier load of meaning than can be expected of the same word in prose. He expects a word or phrase to evoke a vivid mental image or specific emotional reaction.

After the reader has read the best in poetry, he feels that he has grown mentally and emotionally. He feels that he has met man and understood.

BASIC CHARACTERISTICS OF VERSE AND POOR POETRY

1. Obvious meter: Instead of the rhythms subtly harmonizing with the thought pattern, the meter in these poems drowns all else out and the regular beat of the lines comes through without variation.

> And now I see the end of all I sought
> Oh why, Oh why should it have come to nought!

2. Sentimentality: A poem should contain sentiment, true feeling, but when the poet pulls at our heart strings and brings forth sorrow or sympathy beyond that called for by the situation, the poem suffers —as does the reader.

> Stay awhile and shed two dozen tears
> For this poor thief o'ercome with fears
> That any one of a number of ills
> Could rob him so quickly of his skills.

3. Sermonizing: A poem should help to make the reader a better person through leading him to a more sensitive understanding of men and ideals. The moment the poet, however, delivers a lethal blow and then makes certain that the reader understands by drawing the obvious moral, the poet has killed the suggestiveness that must be part of a poem for it to be good.

> Therefore dear reader now you know
> A truth that has ever been so—
> The hopes of those that practice sin
> Must ever be found among the might have been.

4. False images: The poet can convey much through the pictures he evokes in the minds of his reader. These images, however, must harmonize with the thought, the mood, the sentiment. Unless the poet is deliberately planning to evoke laughter, he can easily cause a reader to smile instead of feel sad by bringing forth the wrong type of imagery.

Like poor fish turning brown in the frying pan
Jerry allowed the sun to turn his pallor to tan.

5. Prosy lines: Instead of the lines singing as in great poetry or even following a too regular beat as in limericks or verse, too often the lines in poor poetry will lose all meter and sound like prose.

Therefore dear reader I know what I say
Allan fought much too hard on that Monday

THE DEVICES OF POETRY
Figures of Speech

The figures of speech are those forms of expression that are different from the ordinary modes in order to emphasize or make the meaning more effective. In the hands of a skilled craftsman these devices can enhance the value of the written material. When misused these devices can destroy the worth of the material. The following are the figures of speech most frequently used in poetry.

1. The simile: A directly expressed comparison. It usually contains the words *like* or *as*. The successful simile can evoke an ever-expanding, vivid image in the mind of the reader. An effective simile must have an element of surprise in it; it must be appropriate; it should realize the emotional reaction anticipated by the poet.

as idle as "a painted ship upon a painted ocean"
Similes, however may be misused.
Trite (Commonplace) Simile: red as a rose innocent as a child
Exaggerated Simile: as powerful as ten men
Inappropriate Simile: As silently as a ghoul, my love glided into my heart
  Her hair drooped round her pallid cheeks, like seaweed on a clam

2. The metaphor: A comparison which is implied rather than stated. It does not contain the words *like* or *as*.

Trite Metaphor: pearly teeth, icy stare, clammy hands
Exaggerated Metaphor: one who is *the right-hand of justice*
Appropriate Metaphor: The Lord is my shepherd
a spring of love gushes from his heart
Mixed Metaphor: The bitter taste of her remarks acted as a fuse that set off my anger
  This is a big step forward in our jet-propelled push forward
  He will take a backseat in our eyes if he remains forever self-centered
  You will have to learn to steer a steady course as the sands of time fly by

thought is just as obvious. He must learn to use very sparingly
love—above moon—June day—say might—right

7. Wordiness: The essence of poetry is its economy of words. If the poet uses too many words to express an idea, if he repeats himself needlessly, or if he adds words to fill out a line, he is not writing at the highest levels.

6. Trite rhymes: Even in his use of words to be rhymed, the poet must be fully aware of the lift that his lines must give the reader's spirit. If he uses too many obvious rhymes, the reader soon feels that the

3. Personification: The figure of speech in which we give human qualities to inhuman things or objects

The wind sings a varied song

This intensifier must be used with caution by the poet. Too often it can lead to sentimentalism rather than heightened reality.

Inappropriate Personification: Nature cried in torrents when I failed the test

4. Hyperbole: Intentional exaggeration. In the hands of a skilled humorist, this can be a most powerful device. Used occasionally, it can involve the reader very quickly in the author's ideas.

My thoughts threaten to shake down the goodness that is left in the world and leave all to evil and ruin.

5. Apostrophe: The figure of speech in which the absent are addressed as though they were present, the living as well as the dead, objects as well as humans. Again, this can be a device highly charged with emotion.

Blow, blow thou winter wind
Thou art not so unkind
As man's ingratitude

This device can be so easily abused, leading to overcharged words that do not arouse the reader's imagination.

Come forth, all former graduates of Lafayette High . . .
Kindness, fill her heart with goodness, not fear

6. Inversion: The figure of speech in which words are presented out of their natural or expected order

Of arms and a man I sing

This device is frowned upon by most modern serious poets. However it is a crutch that is much overused by the beginner and those who are striving for effects that are beyond the words and thoughts that they are using.

7. Onomatopoeia: Formation of words to repre-

IMPROVING YOUR ABILITY TO READ CRITICALLY

sent natural sounds. A most effective device in appealing to the sense of sound

> *shrill* bugles *buzzing* of the bees *whirring* wings

As with the other figures of speech, this device can be effective or most inappropriate.

> Inappropriate: The buzzing of the babies in their cribs

8. Alliteration: Repetition of initial consonant sounds, rhyming of initial consonants

> furrow followed free

Alliteration gives a sense of continuity. It is one of the oldest devices in the language and one that is most effective if it is not over-used.

9. Assonance: Repetition of vowel sounds, the pairing of the same vowel sounds without regard for consonants

> and *screen* from *seeing* and *leave* in sight

This is a device used to give tonal values to lines. It is difficult to introduce and not easily sensed by the reader.

10. Rhyme: The word reserved for rhymes occurring at the end of lines

> To the seas and the *streams*
> In their noonday *dreams*

Masculine Rhyme: The rhyme ends with accented syllables

> She tried and tried in *vain*
> To bring that ease from *pain* . . .

Feminine Rhyme: A rhyme in two syllables, the first of which is accented

> sweater—letter

Rhymes add music to the lines and are a source of pleasure for the reader if the poet does not resort to misuse. The major fault is found in hackneyed rhymes, ones that have been much overused

> bright—light   flower—hour   gold—old

11. Poetic language: The fashion has long since come and gone, but many writers don't seem to be aware of this change in styles. They still insist on using old-fashioned words that were once considered elegant and poetic. Some such words are

> *ope* for open   *oft* for often   *yclept* (called)

Sometimes some of the choices offered as the fourth line in the English Achievements can be eliminated because they rely on these words while the other three lines use the more modern direct word.

THE RHYTHMS OF POETRY

The basis of poetic rhythm is in the repetition of accented syllables. These syllables are followed by unaccented ones in an ordered fashion to create the tempo of the lines. For the sake of identification, a line of poetry has been arbitrarily said to consist of a number of feet.

Feet of Two Syllables

1. The iambus: The iambic foot contains an unaccented first syllable and an accented second syllable.

> de taiĺ   con fér

2. The Trochee: The trochaic foot contains an accented first syllable and an unaccented second syllable.

> spéll ing   más ter

Feet of Three Syllables

1. The dactyl: The dactylic foot begins with an accented syllable which is followed by two unaccented syllables.

> fá mi ly   tech ni cal

2. The anapest: The anapestic foot begins with two unaccented syllables which are followed by the accented syllable.

> un re fórmed   non be lief́

THE LINES OF POETRY

Poetic lines are named according to the number of feet they contain. The most common ones follow.

Dimeter   A line of two feet
> Raise her | gently |

Trimeter   A line of three feet
> On high | our flag | is flown |

Tetrameter   A line of four feet
> Of all | the men | I e'er | have known |

Pentameter   A line of five feet
   When I | consi | der how | my light | is spent |

Hexameter   A line of six feet
   When I | have felt | the weight | of days | and years | pushing |

The lines of poetry are usually named after the type of foot that is found most frequently in it. Therefore we speak of an iambic pentameter or a trochaic trimeter. The most common line in the English language is the iambic pentameter. The dactylic hexameter, while much used in Latin and French, has proved too long for English.

You should be able to identify lines in this fashion since very often on the English Achievements, you are asked to choose a fourth line of poetry and one or more of those suggested may be defective, lacking a foot or using a different type of foot.

THE PATTERNS OF POETRY

Free Verse

The rhythm is determined by the subject matter. The lines do not follow a regular meter but vary from thought to thought. Rhyme is usually not used.

   Pile the bodies high at Austerlitz and Waterloo.
   Shovel them under and let me work—
      I am the grass; I cover all.

Walt Whitman and Carl Sandburg have helped to establish this as a staple in the repertory of the modern poet. Free verse is a modern form and therefore the images and the language used by the poet tend to be modern.

Blank Verse

Each line contains ten syllables. The predominant beat is iambic. The lines are unrhymed. Blank verse is written in unrhymed iambic pentameter. This has been most popular among the best and the poorest technicians. If each line is a complete thought, then it is *end stop*. If the ideas flow from one line to the next, then it is *enjambed*. The pause within the line is called the *caesura*.

   Here we may reign secure, and in my choice
   When I was young and thought I knew all truths

Heroic Couplet

Two lines of rhymed iambic pentameter.

   Know then thy self, presume not God to scan;
   The proper study of mankind is man.

Quatrain

Any four-line stanza. The best known of the quatrains is in the old English ballads. The most frequent ballad quatrain consisted of alternating iambic tetrameter and iambic trimeter lines rhyming *xaya*; that is, the second and fourth lines only would usually rhyme.

   The king sits in Dumferling town,
      Drinking the blood-red wine:
   "Oh where will I get a good sailor,
      To sail this ship of mine."

Sonnet

A 14 line stanza usually in iambic pentameter. The Italian sonnet has a thought division. The first eight lines, the octave, will present an idea or state a thesis; the last six lines, the sestet, will apply the idea or give the example that proves the truth in the thesis. The Italian sonnet is also called the Petrarchan or the Miltonic after the Italian master who originated the form and the great English writer who used it as the vehicle for some of his greatest poetic realizations. The Shakespearean sonnet consists of three quatrains and a concluding, summarizing couplet.

TEST OF MASTERY

I. Below is a series of paired alternatives. In the space to the left, place a check before the better alternative.

1. (a) .... How like a winter has my absence been
   (b) .... I know I've been away for a week or so
2. (a) .... She's a doll as all can see
   (b) .... How sweet and fair she seems to be
3. (a) .... The balding trees will soon be bare
   (b) .... The trees are in their autumn beauty
4. (a) .... Drive my dead thoughts over the universe,
   (b) .... Send my televised message abroad
5. (a) .... I'll fight no more like cat and dog with you
   (b) .... Since there's no help, come let us kiss and part—
6. (a) .... As silent as death the city is at night
   (b) .... Dear God! The very houses seem asleep
7. (a) .... Time cannot take one drop of your

IMPROVING YOUR ABILITY TO READ CRITICALLY

beauty from me
   (b) .... To me, fair friend, you can never be old
8. (a) .... Thus conscience does make cowards of us all
   (b) .... Because we feel we therefore fear
9. (a) .... Oft is the iris born in lands unknown
   (b) .... Full many a flower is born to blush unseen
10. (a) .... Thy soul was like a star, and dwelt apart:
   (b) .... How like a star in a comet-filled sky thou art

II. In the space to the left write *Yes* if the line contains five feet; write *No* if it is not a pentameter line.
.... 11. He walked as one who is done with fear
.... 12. To strive, to seek, to find, and not to yield
.... 13. The King sits in Dumferling Town
.... 14. The drooping of the daylight in the West
.... 15. No longer mourn for me when I am dead
.... 16. The lone and level sands stretch far away
.... 17. Gather ye rosebuds while ye may,
.... 18. And down the path they roamed with hand in hand forever more
.... 19. A Sonnet is a moment's monument
.... 20. Memorial from the Soul's eternity

III. In the space provided to the left, write *No* if the line is not one that has a poetic beat; write *Yes* if it is predominantly poetic.
.... 21. In me thou seest the glowing of such fire
.... 22. Friend, thou are not ready to partake of this meal
.... 23. The lights began to twinkle from the rocks
.... 24. Before you could say "Jack Robinson," the lawyer had trapped the defendant
.... 25. The buzz-saw snarled and rattled in the yard
.... 26. My clumsiest dear, whose hands shipwreck vases
.... 27. The trapped weasel snarled at us even though its leg was broken.
.... 28. I met an old man near a darkened house
.... 29. I am part of all that I have met
.... 30. We must share and share alike when the profits come in

IV. In the space provided to the left, write the name of a figure of speech found in each of the following.
.... 31. All the world's a stage
.... 32. How dull it is to pause, to make an end, To rust unburnished, not to shine with use!
.... 33. There is no frigate like a book To take us lands away
.... 34. The moon was a ghostly galleon tossed upon cloudy seas
.... 35. Then felt I like some watcher of the skies.
.... 36. Go forth—and Virtue, ever in your sight, Shall be your guide....
.... 37. Look how the pale Queen of the silent night Doth cause the ocean to attend upon her
.... 38. Oh God! that food should be so dear and life so cheap!
.... 39. Daughters of Time, the hypocritic Days
.... 40. For skies of couple-color as a brindled cow

V. One line in each of the following selections has been omitted. Below are four choices to complete the selection. In the space to the left, label the line
  Correct if the line is appropriate
  Rhythm if the line is inappropriate because of rhythm or meter
  Tone if the line is inappropriate because of tone or style
  Meaning if it is inappropriate because of ideas or content

A.   My candle burns at both ends;
    It will not last the night;
  But ah, my foes, and oh, my friends—
.... 41. No one knows just where it tends
.... 42. Thou canst not miss its sight
.... 43. Doctor Frank says it's too bright
.... 44. It gives a lovely light

B.   As a rule, man is a fool,
  When it's hot, he wants it cool;
  When it's cool, he wants it hot,
.... 45. Whether it's cool or can't be got.
.... 46. Always wanting what is not.
.... 47. He just can't make his mind up.
.... 48. I say it's all a lot of tommyrot!

C.   There was a faith-healer in Deal
  Who said, "Although pain isn't real,
    If I sit on a pin
    And it punctures my skin,
.... 49. I dislike what I fancy I feel."
.... 50. My epidermis is like that of a seal.
.... 51. I miss the pain that I feel.
.... 52. The pain of ache is my spiel.

D.   Yes, I'm in love, I feel it now,
    And Celia has undone me;
  And yet I'll swear I can't tell how
.... 53. She was able to bewitch me.
.... 54. The fears of death and woe are on my brow.
.... 55. The pleasing plague stole on me.
.... 56. Why my enemies do not shun me.

E.   To Mercy, Pity, Peace, and Love
  All pray in their distress;
  And to these virtues of delight
.... 57. Their eternal thanks impress.
.... 58. Return their thankfulness.
.... 59. In the hours of night their truth express.
.... 60. Conmen and yeggs their fears express.

ANSWER KEY: TEST OF MASTERY / Page 176

I. The better lines are
1. (a) 4. (a) 7. (b) 9. (b)
2. (b) 5. (b) 8. (a) 10. (a)
3. (b) 6. (b)

II.
11. No   14. Yes 17. No   19. Yes
12. Yes 15. Yes 18. No   20. Yes
13. No   16. Yes

III.
21. Yes 24. No   27. No   29. Yes
22. No   25. Yes 28. Yes 30. No
23. Yes 26. Yes

IV.
31. metaphor   36. personification   39. personification
32. metaphor   40. simile
33. simile   37. personification
34. metaphor
35. simile   38. apostrophe

V.
41. meaning   48. tone   55. correct
42. tone   49. correct   56. meaning
43. rhythm   50. rhythm   57. meaning
44. correct   51. meaning   58. correct
45. meaning   52. tone   59. rhythm
46. correct   53. rhythm   60. tone
47. rhythm   54. tone

ADDITIONAL MASTERY TESTS

PRACTICE TEST 1 *Suggested Time: 20 Minutes*

Each of the following selections contains a missing line. Beneath each are four lines which could complete the passage. Only one of the four is entirely satisfactory. The others all have a definite deficiency.

By circling the letters provided to the right, for each of the four lines, mark

(a) if the line is acceptable
(b) if the line is not satisfactory because of defect in rhythm or meter
(c) if the line is not acceptable because of style or tone
(d) if the line is inappropriate in meaning

Trochee trips from long to short
From long to long in solemn sort
Slow Spondee stalks; strong foot! yet ill able
Ever to come up with Dactyl trisyllable
....
With a leap and a bound the swift Anapests throng.

1. To be or not to be is iam's song but not for long   1. a b c d
2. In the book from each page come the iam's strong   2. a b c d
3. Iambics march from short to long.   3. a b c d
4. Then do indite iams in running song   4. a b c d

Charge once more, then, and be dumb!
Let the victors, when they come,
When the forts of folly fall,
....

5. Shout with triumph through thy hall.   5. a b c d
6. Find thy body by the wall.   6. a b c d
7. Give you credit in the ledger for the sum. 7. a b c d
8. Shout aloud, "Don't stall!"   8. a b c d

To me, fair friend, you never can be old;
For as you were when first your eye I eyed,
Such seems your beauty still. Three Winters cold
....

9. Have been our keepsake with you by my side;   9. a b c d
10. Have from the forests shook three Summers' pride; 10. a b c d
11. In the flight of our time for your love has vied   11. a b c d
12. Doth with thy love within my heart for e'er abide. 12. a b c d

My pictures blacken in their frames
 As night comes on,
And youthful maids and wrinkled dames
....

13. Sit in tearfilled silence.   13. a b c d
14. Steal away in mocking thoughts.   14. a b c d
15. Understandeth the frightening dark.   15. a b c d
16. Are now all one.   16. a b c d

Ask me no more where Jove bestows,
 When June is past, the fading rose;
For in your beauty's orient deep
....

17. Man will ever find eternal sleep.   17. a b c d
18. Roses stay in radiant heap.   18. a b c d
19. These flowers, as in their causes, sleep. 19. a b c d
20. With the light of true beauty they sleep. 20. a b c d

The breezy call of incense-bearing morn,
 The swallow twittering from the straw-built shed,
The cock's shrill clarion, or the echoing horn,
....

21. No more shall rouse them from their lowly bed.   21. a b c d
22. Will find them slightly withered in their stead. 22. a b c d
23. Blow the bugle; cattle must be fed.   23. a b c d
24. Do chide, 'tis time to arise from bed.   24. a b c d

In every cry of every man,

 In every voice; in every ban,
 The mind-forged manacles I hear.

25. When every boy is filled with fear,   25. a b c d

IMPROVING YOUR ABILITY TO READ CRITICALLY

26. That freedom's coming near, 26. a b c d
27. In every infant's cry of fear, 27. a b c d
28. O ye gods on high, please hear 28. a b c d

> In the world's broad field of battle,
> In the bivouac of Life,
> Be not like dumb, driven cattle!
> ....

29. Be a hero in the strife! 29. a b c d
30. Let us marry, be my wife! 30. a b c d
31. Dance a down-beat to the fife 31. a b c d
32. Let us drive and push and win the strife! 32. a b c d

PRACTICE TEST 2 *Suggested Time: 15 Minutes*

The stanzas of the poem that follows are in scrambled order. Read the poem first and then decide which would be the best order. If you number the stanzas in correct order, you will find it easier to answer the questions that follow. In answering the questions (e) stands for nothing follows.

A] Small is the worth
    Of beauty from the light retired:
        Bid her come forth
    Suffer her self to be desired,
    And not blush so to be admired.

B] Tell her that's young,
    And shuns to have her graces spied,
        That hadst thou sprung
    In deserts where no men abide,
    Thou must have uncommended died.

C] Then die, that she
    The common fate of all things rare
        May read in thee,
    How small a part of time they share,
    That are so wondrous sweet and fair.

D] Go, lovely Rose,
    Tell her that wastes her time and me,
        That now she knows,
    When I resemble her to thee,
    How sweet and fair she seems to be.

1. Which stanza did you put first? 1. a b c d e
2. Which stanza did you put after [A]? 2. a b c d e
3. Which stanza did you put after [B]? 3. a b c d e
4. Which stanza did you put after [C]? 4. a b c d e
5. Which stanza did you put after [D]? 5. a b c d e

A] My horse moved on; hoof after hoof
    He raised, and never stopped:
    When down behind the cottage roof,
    At once the bright moon dropped.

B] Strange fits of passion have I known:
    And I will dare to tell,
    But in a lover's ear alone,
    What once to me befell.

C] What fond and wayward thoughts will slide
    Into a lover's head!
    "O mercy!" to myself I cried,
    "If Lucy should be dead!"

D] When she I loved looked every day
    Fresh as a rose in June,
    I to her cottage bent my way,
    Beneath an evening-moon.

6. Which stanza did you put first? 6. a b c d e
7. Which stanza did you put after [A]? 7. a b c d e
8. Which stanza did you put after [B]? 8. a b c d e
9. Which stanza did you put after [C]? 9. a b c d e
10. Which stanza did you put after [D]? 10. a b c d e

A] Shake hands for ever! Cancel all our vows!
    And when we meet at any time again,
    Be it not seen in either of our brows
    That we one jot of former love retain.

B] Now, if thou would'st, when all have given him over,
    From death to life thou might'st him yet recover!

C] Now at the last gasp of Love's latest breath,
    When his pulse failing, Passion speechless lies,
    When Faith is kneeling by his bed of death,
    And Innocence is closing up his eyes—

D] Since there's no help, come let us kiss and part.
    Nay, I have done, you get no more of me!
    And I am glad, yea, glad with all my heart,
    That thus so cleanly I myself can free.

11. Which stanza did you put first? 11. a b c d e
12. Which stanza did you put after [A]? 12. a b c d e
13. Which stanza did you put after [B]? 13. a b c d e
14. Which stanza did you put after [C]? 14. a b c d e
15. Which stanza did you put after [D]? 15. a b c d e

A] I walked, with other souls in pain,
        Within another ring.
    And was wondering if the man had done
        A great or little thing.
    When a voice behind me whispered low,
        "That fellow's got to swing."

B] He did not wear his scarlet coat,
        For blood and wine are red,
    And blood and wine were on his hands
        When they found him with the dead.
    The poor dead woman whom he loved,
        And murdered in her bed.

C] I only knew what hunted thought
        Quickened his step, and why
    He looked upon the garish day
        With such a wistful eye:
    The man had killed the thing he loved,
        And so he had to die.

D] He walked amongst the Trial Men
        In a suit of shabby gray:
    A cricket cap was on his head,
        And his step seemed light and gay;
    But I never saw a man who looked
        So wistfully at the day.

16. Which stanza did you put first? 16. a b c d e
17. Which stanza did you put after [A]? 17. a b c d e
18. Which stanza did you put after [B]? 18. a b c d e
19. Which stanza did you put after [C]? 19. a b c d e
20. Which stanza did you put after [D]? 20. a b c d e

A] She's creeping slowly up past Quarantine,
    A shameless, shaggy rover of the sea;
  A commercial vagrant, dirty and serene,
    A salty chevalier of beggary.

B] No silken gowns sweep o'er her painted boards,
    She comes or goes and no one seems to care;
  A little fuel and grub are her rewards,
    She'll leave at any time for anywhere.

C] The stuff her better sisters couldn't take,
    Unsavory bits that lost the regular run;
  She fetched 'em 'cross the world for she must make
    A little profit when the year is done.

D] She'll bluster till her anchor clatters out—
    She'll fidget, yank and grumble with the tide;
  Yet she grins a little 'neath her battered snout,
    Proud because there's cargo in her hide.

21. Which stanza did you put first? 21. a b c d e
22. Which stanza did you put after [A]? 22. a b c d e
23. Which stanza did you put after [B]? 23. a b c d e
24. Which stanza did you put after [C]? 24. a b c d e
25. Which stanza did you put after [D]? 25. a b c d e

A] How much more praise deserved thy beauty's us.
If thou couldst answer "This fair child of mine
Shall sum my count and make my old excuse,"
Proving his beauty by succession thine!

B] When forty winters shall besiege thy brow
And dig deep trenches in they beauty's field,
Thy youth's proud livery, so gazed on now,
Will be tattered weed, of small worth held:

C] This were to be new made when thou art old,
And see thy blood warm when thou feel'st it cold.

D] Then being asked where all thy beauty lies,
Where all the treasure of thy lusty days,
To say, within thine own deep-sunken eyes,
Were an ill-eating shame and thriftless praise.

26. Which stanza did you put first? 26. a b c d e
27. Which stanza did you put after [A]? 27. a b c d e
28. Which stanza did you put after [B]? 28. a b c d e
29. Which stanza did you put after [C]? 29. a b c d e
30. Which stanza did you put after [D]? 30. a b c d e

PRACTICE TEST 3 *Suggested Time: 20 Minutes*

Each of the following selections contains a missing line. Beneath each are four lines which could complete the passage. Only one of the four is entirely satisfactory. The others all have a definite deficiency. By circling the letters provided to the right, for each of the four lines, mark

(*a*) if the line is acceptable
(*b*) if the line is not satisfactory because of defect in rhythm or meter
(*c*) if the line is not acceptable because of style or tone
(*d*) if the line is inappropriate in meaning

    Life has loveliness to sell,
      Music like a curve of gold,
    Scent of pine trees in the rain,
      Eyes that love you, arms that hold,
    And for your spirit's still delight,
      . . . .

1. Ships of the air with the speed of light. 1. a b c d
2. Holy thoughts that star the night. 2. a b c d
3. Great thoughts the minds of yore endite. 3. a b c d
4. The best wishes of all your friends in sight. 4. a b c d

Since brass, nor stone, nor earth, nor boundless sea,
But sad mortality o'er sways their power,
How with this rage shall beauty hold a plea,
. . . .

5. When it is so fragile, like a flower? 5. a b c d
6. When o'er its head the face of hope doth glower? 6. a b c d
7. Whose action is no stronger than a flower? 7. a b c d
8. Who cannot make the game go any slower! 8. a b c d

    I walked a mile with Sorrow
      And ne'er a word said she;
    But, oh, the things I learned from her
      . . . .

9. When Sorrow walked with me. 9. a b c d
10. As Error rained on me. 10. a b c d
11. Which circumstance should have uncovered for me. 11. a b c d
12. When Sorrow gave to me my misery. 12. a b c d

    Because I could not stop for death,
      He kindly stopped for me:
    The carriage held but just ourselves
      . . . .

13. And none whom I could see. 13. a b c d
14. Proud and private, for all to see. 14. a b c d
15. The cabbie and little old me. 15. a b c d
16. And immortality. 16. a b c d

    Not enjoyment, and not sorrow,
      Is our destined end or way;
    But to act, that each tomorrow
      . . . .

17. Finds us with enough energy 17. a b c d

IMPROVING YOUR ABILITY TO READ CRITICALLY

for the day.
18. Revives to live another day.   18. a b c d
19. Finds us farther than today.   19. a b c d
20. Leadeth thee on thy true way.   20. a b c d

My mind to me a kingdom is,
  Such present joys therein I find,
....
  That world affords or grows by kind.
Though much I want which most would have,
Yet still my mind forbids to crave.

21. You too cannot afford to miss.   21. a b c d
22. Content and fed by no bliss.   22. a b c d
23. That it excels all other bliss. 23. a b c d
24. Ah Joys! Beyond all other bliss 24. a b c d

  See, the day begins to break,
  And the light shoots like a streak
  Of subtle fire; the wind blows cold,
..............................;
25. Whilst the morning doth unfold; 25. a b c d
26. And the rising sun doth unfold; 26. a b c d
27. It's time to get up and be bold; 27. a b c d
28. Rise and shine, ye beggars bold; 28. a b c d

  There are a number of us creep
  Into this world to eat and sleep,
  And know no reasons why they're born
  But merely to consume the corn,
  Devour the cattle, fowl, and fish,
....
29. And waste away with every wish. 29. a b c d
30. Without even having an ambitious wish. 30. a b c d
31. No love! No hate! No joy! No wish! 31. a b c d
32. And leave behind an empty dish. 32. a b c d

PRACTICE TEST 4 *Suggested Time: 20 Minutes*
Each of the following selections contains a missing line. Beneath each are four lines which could complete the passage. Only one of the four is entirely satisfactory. The others all have a definite deficiency. By circling the letters provided to the right, for each of the four lines, mark
(*a*) if the line is acceptable
(*b*) if the line is not satisfactory because of defect in rhythm or meter
(*c*) if the line is not acceptable because of style or tone
(*d*) if the line is inappropriate in meaning

  He clasps the crag with crooked hands;
  Close to the sun in lonely lands,
  Ringed with the azure world, he stands.
  The wrinkled sea beneath him crawls;
  He watches from his mountain walls,
....
1. Swiftly down he swoops; in vain the victim calls. 1. a b c d
2. And like a thunderbolt he falls.   2. a b c d
3. As night within his shadow falls. 3. a b c d
4. O Eagle! Mightiest bird of all!   4. a b c d

  Yes; quaint and curious war is!
    You shoot a fellow down
    You'd treat if met where any bar is,
....
5. Or help to halfa-crown.   5. a b c d
6. O Mighty War, with cruelty ever strown! 6. a b c d
7. And at him you would never frown. 7. a b c d
8. And never throw him out of town.   8. a b c d

  The written word
  Should be clean as bone,
  Clear as light,
....
  Two words are not
  As good as one
9. Sheer in tone.   9. a b c d
10. Like unto brass that shone.   10. a b c d
11. Firm as stone.   11. a b c d
12. Containing sweetness of tone.   12. a b c d

These I have loved:
  White plates and cups, clean-gleaming,
  Ringed with blue lines; and feathery, faery dust;
  Wet roofs, beneath the lamp-light; the strong crust
  Of friendly bread; and many-tasting food;
....
13. Courage, justice and the kindly work of the good; 13. a b c d
14. I must not forget to mention old wood; 14. a b c d
15. Rainbows; and the blue bitter smoke of wood; 15. a b c d
16. Finally, I also enjoy the smell of burning wood; 16. a b c d

  Death stands above me, whispering low
    I know not what into my ear;
  Of his strange language all I know
....
17. I argue vehemently my time is near. 17. a b c d
18. 'Tis love alone I've learned to fear 18. a b c d
19. The fee he asks is much too dear.   19. a b c d
20. Is, there is not a word of fear.   20. a b c d

  I was angry with my friend:
  I told my wrath, my wrath did end.
  I was angry with my foe:
....
21. I told it not, my wrath did grow.   21. a b c d
22. He was nothing but a so and so.   22. a b c d
23. In his heart I let it grow.   23. a b c d
24. Silent, fearful, I let it grow.   24. a b c d

I made you many and many a song
    Yet never one told all you are—
It was as though a net of words
....

25. Tried real hard to catch a star.   25. a b c d
26. Flexed up to catch a star.   26. a b c d
27. Were flung to catch a star.   27. a b c d
28. Far flung tried in vain to catch a star.   28. a b c d

No longer mourn for me when I am dead
Then you shall hear the surly sullen bell
....
From this vile world, with vilest worms to dwell.

29. The church bell shrill to all that I am fled   29. a b c d
30. Give warning to the world that I am fled   30. a b c d
31. With glee so gay announce that I am fled   31. a b c d
32. In the light of the day that I am fled   32. a b c d

PRACTICE TEST 5   *Suggested Time: 20 Minutes*

Each of the following selections contains a missing line. Beneath each are four lines which could complete the passage. Only one of the four is entirely satisfactory. The other all have a definite deficiency.

By circling the letters provided to the right, for each of the four lines, mark

(a) if the line is acceptable
(b) if the line is not satisfactory because of defect in rhythm or meter
(c) if the line is not acceptable because of style or tone
(d) if the line is inappropriate in meaning

    Mock on, mock on, Voltaire, Rousseau:
    Mock on, mock on: 'tis all in vain!
    You throw the sand against the wind,
....

1. And back it flies to you with power amain   1. a b c d
2. And the wind wafts it back again.   2. a b c d
3. And the wind blows it back again.   3. a b c d
4. Once more its full force to regain.   4. a b c d

    I traveled among unknown men,
      In lands beyond the sea;
    Nor, England! did I know till then
....

5. The affinity you had for me.   5. a b c d
6. The depths of every lea.   6. a b c d
7. Fully your significant worth to me.   7. a b c d
8. What love I bore to thee.   8. a b c d

    I strove with none, for none was worth my strife.
    Nature I loved and next to Nature, Art:
...........................;
    It sinks, and I am ready to depart.

9. I warmed both hands before the fire of life;   9. a b c d
10. Fired with struggle and woe,   10. a b c d
the beacon of my life;
11. Unto each and every one comes the fire of life;   11. a b c d
12. Cursed ones! Now see the fire of my life;   12. a b c d

    I could think in the withered grass
    Spring's budding wreaths we might discern;
    The violet's eye might shyly flash
....

13. And wintry ice to come be seen.   13. a b c d
14. And young leaves shoot among the fern.   14. a b c d
15. And green chlorophyl among the fern.   15. a b c d
16. Renewal and a rebirth in this Spring's return.   16. a b c d

    I dare not ask a kiss,
    I dare not beg a smile,
    Lest having that or this,
....

17. I could then be developing a new style.   17. a b c d
18. The worms with death could then revile.   18. a b c d
19. I might grow proud the while.   19. a b c d
20. Thou couldst me then revile.   20. a b c d

    Sound, sound the clarion, fill the fife!
    To all the sensual world proclaim,
....
    Is worth an age without a name.

21. A day or an hour devoted to glorious life   21. a b c d
22. One glorious hour without my wife   22. a b c d
23. Years devoid of unwonted strife   23. a b c d
24. One crowded hour of glorious life   24. a b c d

    Come, read to me some poem
      Some simple and heartfelt lay,
    That shall soothe this restless feeling,
....

25. And toss right out the fears of day.   25. a b c d
26. And banish the thoughts of day.   26. a b c d
27. And leave me with nothing to say.   27. a b c d
28. And turn my labor into light play.   28. a b c d

    O world, thou choosest not the better part!
    It is not wisdom to be only wise,
    And on the inward vision close the eyes,
....

29. But it is wisdom to believe the heart.   29. a b c d
30. And never let that inner motor start.   30. a b c d
31. But it is best to settle in the heart.   31. a b c d
32. To your ideals and humanity's cries.   32. a b c d

IMPROVING YOUR ABILITY TO READ CRITICALLY

ANSWER KEY: ADDITIONAL MASTERY TESTS

PRACTICE TEST 1 *(Page 178)*

1. (d)	9. (d)	17. (d)	25. (b)
2. (b)	10. (a)	18. (c)	26. (d)
3. (a)	11. (b)	19. (a)	27. (a)
4. (c)	12. (c)	20. (b)	28. (c)
5. (d)	13. (b)	21. (a)	29. (a)
6. (a)	14. (d)	22. (d)	30. (d)
7. (b)	15. (c)	23. (b)	31. (c)
8. (c)	16. (a)	24. (c)	32. (b)

PRACTICE TEST 2 *(Page 179)*

1. (d)	9. (e)	17. (c)	25. (c)
2. (c)	10. (a)	18. (d)	26. (b)
3. (a)	11. (d)	19. (e)	27. (c)
4. (e)	12. (c)	20. (a)	28. (d)
5. (b)	13. (e)	21. (a)	29. (e)
6. (b)	14. (b)	22. (d)	30. (a)
7. (c)	15. (a)	23. (e)	
8. (d)	16. (b)	24. (b)	

PRACTICE TEST 3 *(Page 180)*

1. (d)	9. (a)	17. (b)	25. (a)
2. (a)	10. (d)	18. (d)	26. (d)
3. (c)	11. (b)	19. (a)	27. (b)
4. (b)	12. (c)	20. (c)	28. (c)
5. (b)	13. (d)	21. (d)	29. (d)
6. (d)	14. (b)	22. (b)	30. (b)
7. (a)	15. (c)	23. (a)	31. (c)
8. (c)	16. (a)	24. (c)	32. (a)

PRACTICE TEST 4 *(Page 181)*

1. (b)	9. (d)	17. (b)	25. (c)
2. (a)	10. (c)	18. (d)	26. (d)
3. (d)	11. (a)	19. (c)	27. (a)
4. (c)	12. (b)	20. (a)	28. (b)
5. (a)	13. (d)	21. (a)	29. (c)
6. (c)	14. (c)	22. (c)	30. (a)
7. (b)	15. (a)	23. (d)	31. (d)
8. (d)	16. (b)	24. (b)	32. (b)

PRACTICE TEST 5 *(Page 182)*

1. (b)	9. (a)	17. (b)	25. (c)
2. (c)	10. (d)	18. (d)	26. (a)
3. (a)	11. (b)	19. (a)	27. (d)
4. (d)	12. (c)	20. (c)	28. (b)
5. (c)	13. (d)	21. (b)	29. (a)
6. (d)	14. (a)	22. (d)	30. (c)
7. (b)	15. (c)	23. (c)	31. (d)
8. (a)	16. (b)	24. (a)	32. (b)

3. Terms of Literary Analysis

GLOSSARY

abstract idea A general statement about a quality or state, about a class of persons, objects, ideas. It is opposed to a specific fact or concrete statement.

> abstract: Wealth corrupts the soul.
> concrete: I read *Tom Jones*.

abstract noun Refers to a quality or state. It is opposed to a concrete noun that refers to a specific object or person.

> abstract nouns: *love, honor, courtesy*
> concrete nouns: *house, dog, person*

adage A proverb, or familiar wise saying.

> Early to bed, early to rise
> Makes a man healthy, wealthy
> And wise.

allegory A literary form in which some or all of the characters are embodiments of abstract ideas. It is a story which carries a second meaning along with its surface story: Bunyan's *Pilgrim's Progress*.

alliteration Repetition of the initial sound in words. This device, while effective in poetry and polyphonic prose can be obtrusive in ordinary writing.

> To sit in solemn silence

allusion A casual reference to some character, person, fact, idea, or event. The reader is expected to see the application of the allusion to the thought being expressed.

> He sees himself as another confident Hercules assigned to clean out the rubbish of the centuries.

ambiguity When used as a derogatory term, refers to the lack of clarity that beclouds meaning when more than one interpretation is highly possible.

> He didn't know, she said, he was to go.
> (Who commanded him to go?)

Ambiguity may also be used to describe the richness in poetry that "gives room for alternative reactions to the same piece of poetry." William Epsom referred with praise to the seven types of this kind of ambiguity.

anachronism A device describing something placed in an inappropriate period of time. It may be an unintentional error, or it may be used deliberately for effect.

> Daniel Boone leveled his tommygun at the mass of attacking renegades.

analogy A comparison of two things alike in certain aspects.

Analogies are always dangerous because we tend to assume that since two people or things are similar in one or more respects, they should necessarily be similar in others.

Since we both come from the same hometown, we should have similar ambitions.

anecdote A brief, pointed or humorous story sometimes included in a larger whole. It lacks the complicated plot of a short story. It is an effective device for beginning a speech or driving home a realization.

antagonist The main character opposed to the author's principal character.

The antagonist need not be a villain. In a story dealing with Satan, the protecting angel could be the antagonist.

anthology A collection of prose or poetry selections. Many of the textbooks used in English courses in literature are anthologies.

anticlimax The arrangement of details in such an order that the unimportant suddenly appears at the point where the critical or serious detail should be found. Anticlimax is a flaw in a story in which the hero has an unpredicted allergy attack just when he is to lead his troops into battle. It can be an effective device in humorous material.

We talked boldly of daring raids to come on the enemy supply lines. We boasted of bloody deeds we would accomplish; and fell asleep over the emptied glasses of beer.

antithesis A rhetorical device in which contrasted words, clauses, or ideas are balanced.

Love and hate, desire and fulfillment gave his life purpose and robbed him of peace of mind.

Antithesis must be used sparingly; too many sentences containing this dramatic approach gives the material a heavy, artificial tone.

antonomasia The use of a proper noun as a common name. It is a type of allusion in which the reader must see the relationship between the man referred to and the present subject.

Beware of him! He is another Hitler!

aphorism A short, pithy statement of a principle or precept.

Life is short; art is long.

apostrophe A rhetorical device in which the author addresses a personified abstraction or a person not present.

Poverty touch not his hopes!

This device is restricted in its use in prose because of the intensity it generates.

archaism A word or phrase no longer used in actual speech.

quoth eftsoon methinks

This is a facile, too facile often, device for dating a speech or work.

argument Refers, as a literary term, to the summary of the plot placed at the beginning of a section or chapter. *Paradise Lost* contains an argument summarizing the main lines of action at the beginning of each Book.

assonance The similarity in sound of vowels following different consonants, usually in stressed syllables.

Like a d*i*amond in the sk*y*

With rhymes, the consonants following the vowel must be the same: fat, bat.

In assonance the consonants are different: f*a*ct b*a*d. Assonance is a device that can effectively lead to euphony, pleasant sounding word combinations, if used sparingly in prose.

atmosphere The tone and mood established by the totality of a literary work. The atmosphere of a comedy is light while that of a tragedy tends to be somber.

autobiography A literary work in which the author describes major events in his past. A *diary* emphasizes inner rather than outward manifestations. *Memoirs* stress reactions, impressions, people met. A *journal* is more private and more episodic.

balanced sentence A sentence in which words, phrases, or clauses are set off against each other in position so as to emphasize contrast or similarity in meaning.

You may eat to live, but he lives to eat.

The balanced sentence is not favored in present-day writing because the cleverness of the writing tends to obscure the meaning behind the words.

bathos Another term for anticlimax, a sudden descent from the ladder leading to greater significance, a going from the sublime to the ridiculous, from the heights of the important to the level of trivia. Bathos can be evidenced in action or words.

Advance the fringed curtains of thy eyes
And tell me what comes yonder.

bibliography A list of books, articles, publications on a particular subject. Scholarly works follow formalized procedures in handling bibliographies.

biography The account of the life of a person.

blurb A description of the contents of a book, included on its cover or dust jacket to entice prospective purchasers.

bombast Grandiloquent, ranting, insincere, extravagant language.

From the depths of sincerity and honesty, we decry with all the emphatic force at our command, the scurrilous, unfounded accusations brought forth as so obvious an attempt to obfuscate the truth in our just and modest claims.

Bombast is a derogatory term, describing an emotionalized letting go of all controls in writing.

brevity A complimentary term implying the use of only those words needed to express an idea—and no more. Brevity is essential to forceful expression. In the telegraphic style found in some headlines and in the dialogue of popular television detective tales, brevity has been carried too far: "Saw the oncoming car. Tried to swerve. Went into skid. Three occupants of other car died. Horribly." Such stylizing is not acceptable in general writing.

burlesque The type of humorous writing which satirizes and imitates a literary convention, style, or attitude. *Don Quixote* was written as a burlesque of the medieval romance so popular in Cervantes' Spain.

cacophony Harsh combinations of sound.

blue spurt of a lighted match

The experienced writer may use cacophony as a device to emphasize action related to his dialogue, but in expository writing, he will avoid having the sound of his words interfere with the flow of meaning. Cacophony is the opposite of *euphony*.

caricature A character or action exaggerated for satiric or humorous effect. A limited number of personal qualities is usually selected for such an exaggeration.

circumlocution A round-about expression, one that avoids a direct label.

"He is a man who avoids telling or revealing in direct terms any item that may put him in a bad light, despite the needs of the listener!"

"Simply then, he's a liar!"

clarity "Absolute accordance of expression to idea." To achieve clarity, the accurate word should be specific and concrete.

classic (1) A literary work which has achieved a recognized position for its superior qualities: Shakespeare's *Hamlet*.
(2) A literary work that helped set the pattern in a previous period and therefore has historical importance: Eliot's *Silas Marner*.

cliché An expression which the author or reader feels has been so overused that it has lost its forcefulness.

as smart as a whip   as quiet as mice

Note that the cliché-label may be in the mind of the reader or the writer. What may be a cliche to one may be new and exciting to the other!

climax (1) An arrangement in which the chief point of interest is reached at the end.
(2) The moment in the plot at which a crisis reaches its highest intensity and is resolved. Narrative and expository material benefit from being planned toward reaching a climax.

coherence A work has coherence when the relationship of one part to another is clear and intelligible. Words, phrases, clauses, sentences, paragraphs, and chapters are the units which show coherence through progressive and logical arrangement. Illogical arrangement results in lack of coherence.

colloquial The level of speech in everyday conversation. Words and expressions must be appropriate to the level of the material. Expressions labeled as belonging to the colloquial level are avoided in Standard and Formal Levels of writing. Since the level of usage planned for the Achievement Tests is the Standard, the colloquial level can be marked wrong even though it is acceptable in everyday conversation.

comedy Any literary work which has a happy ending. The action is less serious than that found in a tragedy. The element of humor is irrelevant in this definition. A typical television spy or detective tale is classified as a comedy according to this definition, despite the killings and beatings that belong to the genre.

comic relief A humorous scene inserted in a serious or tragic work to relieve tension and so heighten the tragic emotion by contrast. The porter scene in Macbeth following the slaying of the king, is the classic example of comic relief at its most effective level.

conceit A complex or far-fetched comparison.

Her eyes are suns that blind

Because of the time they take for analysis such comparisons had long fallen into disrepute. However, many modern writers attempting to reach the complexities of present-day living have revived the conceit. When the comparison is startling and appropriate, the effect is commendable; when the comparison confuses the reader or leads to too great an overrefinement, then it is worthy of condemnation.

concrete noun Stresses the tangible, that which can be seen, heard, felt. It is close to the specific, the particular. The concrete has actual existence and can be experienced: The stone before me is *concrete*. Concrete terms are the converse of abstract nouns: *Honesty* is an abstract term. Effective writing tends to be concrete. Vague, unclear writing tends toward the abstract.

confidant A character to whom another reveals his most intimate feelings and intentions. *Confidante* is the feminine form. Hamlet's trusted friend, Horatio, was his *confidant*.

conflict The struggle which grows out of the interplay of opposing forces in a plot.

connotation The implications or suggestions evoked by a word. Connotation is distinguished from denotion which refers to the objective values only. Scientific writing stresses denotative values. The scientist avoids using terms that have differing connotations for his readers. The literary artists uses connotation to add emotionality.

convention Any generally accepted literary device or form. The soliloquy in which a character expresses his innermost thoughts and feelings to the audience was an Elizabethan convention.

denotation A word's most literal and limited meaning, the person, thing, or idea to which a word refers exclusive of attitudes or feelings which the writer or speaker may have. The denotation of *cow* is its dictionary definition of the four-legged ruminant. When *cow* is used to describe a human being, then the connotative values of the word are being used. The propagandist specializes in milking a word of its full connotation: *coward, national pride, one-hundred percent* patriot!

dénouement The events following the final climax of a story, the final unraveling and setting straight, the solution of the mystery, the explanation of all misunderstandings.

deus ex machina Coming from the Latin, means literally *god from the machine*. In Greek drama one of the conventions allowed a god to be lowered onto the stage to rescue one of the characters. The term today is a derogatory one, referring to any artificial device for resolving difficulties. Serious writers avoid such a device since the resolution of difficulties should grow from the action itself. The story line is weakened and the reader's credulity is strained when an unexpected and improbable happening is employed to make things turn out "right."

diction The choice and arrangement of words. The kind of diction used must be appropriate to the literary form, the subject, and the style of the period. Formal diction is inappropriate in a play set in a crude farm or in a city slum. Slang and regional expressions are inappropriate when interspersed in writing that calls for standard or formal usage.

didactic A label applied to a literary work when its principal aim is to give guidance in moral, ethical, or religious matters. Didactic is a neutral term when applied by those who accept teaching as the purpose of the material. Didactic becomes a derogatory term when the reader feels that the writer overemphasizes moral values and distorted events to achieve these aims.

digression Unrelated material inserted in a discussion. It is a violation of unity in formal essays. It is a standard device in the personal essay; it is that which puts an audience to sleep in college lectures and lowers grades on themes.

dramatic irony When the words or acts of a character carry a meaning unperceived by him but understood by the audience or reader. The irony lies in the contrast between the speaker's intended meaning and the realization of the others: the character who unknown to himself is dying makes elaborate plans for his future with his bride-to-have-been.

dynamic character One who changes as the result of the plot action. Usually the protagonist is dynamic and his growth and development as a reaction to circumstance creates the central interest in the story line. Macbeth and Lady Macbeth are dynamic in that they change. Dynamic characters are contrasted with static, stereotyped characters who remain dominated by a single quality throughout the story. The televison detective who remains unchanged in his approach to the challenges of his job is static.

economy of expression A term of praise, implying the use of the minimum number of words necessary for clarity and emphasis.

empathy The feeling of identity that a reader has when he becomes so involved with a character in a play or novel that he experiences the emotionality that he thinks the character is going through. With *sympathy* we feel for the other; with *empathy* we feel as we think the other feels.

emphasis The planning of elements so that the important items, ideas, facts, personalities are stressed.

epigram A witty, pointed, terse saying

"Life consists of sobs, sniffles, and smiles, with sniffles predominating."

epilogue (1) A concluding statement at the end of a speech or play.
(2) An appendix added after the conclusion of a play or story. An epilogue may be the conclusion of a speech, the final remarks of an actor addressed to the audience, or a scene added after the main action of a drama has ended. An epilogue is the opposite of a prologue.

epithet A word or group of words used to characterize a person.

Jude *the Obscure*   Harold *the Brave*   *wily* Ulysses

essay A short prose work stressing the author's opinion on one topic. The personal essay stresses revelation of personal reactions. The formal essay develops an idea or expresses a point of view.

euphemism A rhetorical device for conveying a harsh or unpleasant concept pleasantly or gently

pass away   in place of die

euphony The juxtaposition of words and sounds that blend together pleasantly. Writers use assonance, phrase rhythms, and alliteration as the principal rhetorical devices to achieve euphony. When used to excess such devices can result in bombast or a tone of insincerity.

exposition The type of writing in which explanations are stressed. Narrative writing tells a story; descriptive writing has as its purpose description of a scene, person, or process; in argumentation, the writer either attacks or defends a point of view. Expository writing tells how something is done or how something works.

fable (1) A short moral tale usually having animals as its characters: the stories of Aesop, La Fontaine.
(2) A story or anecdote that is labeled as untrue.

farce A humorous play depending on exaggerated, improbable situation. The humor is based on horseplay, coarse wit, gross incongruities: the typical Three Stooges' television movie.

fiction A narrative writing based on the author's free use of experience and imagination rather than on history or fact. Novels and short stories are examples of fiction.

figurative language Writing that includes one or more of the various figures of speech: simile, metaphor, apostrophe. The literal meaning of the words is avoided in favor of the connotative values. Figurative language is the basis of poetry; overuse of this type of writing makes prose vague and difficult to understand.

figures of speech Those forms of expression that are different from the ordinary modes in order to emphasize or make the meaning more effective. (See Devices of Poetry on Page 85.) These devices are most effective when used sparingly in prose; otherwise the reader's attention is caught by the device rather than the meaning.

flashback A device whereby the reader or audience views scenes or incidents that occurred prior to the opening scene: A man is walking toward the gallows. The next scene is a flashback to his childhood and the action that led to his present plight.

foreshadowing A device in which the author drops hints or prepares the reader for an event that will come later.

formal essay An essay written to explain an idea or to persuade the reader to adapt a point of view. It is serious, dignified, logically organized.

fustian Bombastic or pompously ornate language.

The heavens will cease holding a protective canopy over our earthly endeavors ere I consent to being associated in such unspeakable knavery!

genre A literary type classified by form and technique: domestic novel, formal essay, etc.

generalization A statement that applies to a group or a series. It is opposed to a fact which deals with one instance. Writers must beware of the emptiness that results from the overuse of generalizations. The more a generalization is restricted by qualifications, the more effective it becomes: *All generalizations are false, including this one* is the one generalization that I accept as valid.

hero (heroine) One capable of brave, courageous deeds. Because *hero* has connotations that confuse, the preferred term for the main character in a story is protagonist. In a tale in which the main character is villainous, *protagonist* is more appropriate than *hero* as the labeling term.

historic present The present tense used to describe past events. In some narratives, the writer will switch from the past tense to the present when attempting to dramatize a scene. This device is not in favor among modern writers.

homily A literary term used to describe a work which lectures its readers and urges them to adhere to high moral standards: a typical Sunday sermon.

hyperbole A rhetorical term for conscious exaggeration.

There were millions of people packed into that subway train!

interior monologue A recording of the thoughts and emotional experiencings of a character on one or more levels of consciousness. It is the technique employed by James Joyce in Ulysses. In a *soliloquy*, the revelations are limited to one level of consciousness, to one thought process.

inversion A rhetorical device used for emphasis, consisting of the transposing of words out of their usual order.

A man filled with fears and doubts I saw.

irony The expression of the opposite of what is intended.

You are truly kind to me!

Irony is more restrained and less bitter than sarcasm, its close relative.

irrelevant The label attached to material that does not continue the development of a thread of thought or action, something added which begins another idea. Irrelevant material or irrelevant details cause a significant lowering of grades in college themes.

journalese The term used to characterize the style patterns of the headlines and sports columnists of the daily press—clipped sentences, neologisms, slang, euphemisms. Most of the news items of today, copied from the releases of the press agencies, are written in Standard English.

King's English The term used for an expression that is fully accepted on the Standard Written English level of usage.

levels of usage The speech, pronunciation, diction, and structure of the language as means of communication with differing groups and differing purposes. The levels of usage are similar to the levels of diction:

(1) Formal   The level employed in doctoral theses, presidential messages, state documents, international communications, textbooks.
(2) Standard   The level expected in newspaper editorials, student writing, television discussions, lectures. It is the level tested for in the College Board Achievement Tests.
(3) Colloquial   The level of informal conversations, telephone discussions.
(4) Nonstandard   The level of usage limited to regional groups and slang. Such usage is correct—in its appropriate place, but not on college and college entrance themes.

literal   Accurate to the letter. A *literal* translation is one that follows the exact meaning of the original. A *literal* interpretation avoids figurative connotations. *Rosy cheeks* taken literally creates a frightening image!

litotes   The denial of the opposite to achieve intensity and emphasis. Litotes is a form of understatement: She is *not stupid*. This answer is *not wrong*.

loose sentence   A sentence in which the ideas follow their logical order, subject followed by predicate, main clause followed by adverbial clauses. It is the basic pattern in conversation and informal writing.

He reconstructed the fallen building block by block with infinite patience and with a complete disregard of time and cost.

malapropism   An error in diction caused by the substitution of one word for another similar in sound but different in meaning.

I would by no means wish that a daughter of mine be a *progeny* of learning.

Malapropisms result from the misuse of big words intended to impress.

maxim   A short, concise statement based on experience and giving some practical advice.

If you cannot beat them, join them!

Maxims are often used as the topic sentence or summary sentence in expository writing.

melodrama   A play based on a sensational, romantic plot with emphasis on emotional jolts for the audience. The typical melodrama has a happy ending achieved over a course of improbable events in which the good are rewarded and the wicked ones punished. Soap operas and typical television drama are prime examples of this genre.

mise en scene   The stage setting of a play: scenery, costumes, properties of a theatrical production.

mood   The tone of a literary work: *thoughtful, light, somber.*

negative criticism   Fault-finding without the presentation of steps for correction.

non-fiction   Literature based on actual occurrences, on facts. It is the term associated with histories, biographies, textbooks.

nonstandard   The level of slang, dialectal variations, regionalisms. College students are supposed to be able to recognize this level and avoid mingling it with the standard use and diction required for work in required and elective courses.

novel   A long story, extended fictional prose narrative. It is a representation of life in fictional narrative.

omniscient author   An author who shifts from the objective exterior world into the subjective interior world of a number of characters. He feels free to comment at any time on the significance of events or reactions.

oxymoron   The figure of speech describing seemingly contradictory terms used to create a paradox: *sad optimist, hardworking idler, conspicuous by his absence.*

parable   A short, simple story containing a moral lesson. The parable of the Prodigal Son is one of the best known examples of this genre.

paradox   A seemingly contradictory or absurd statement which may actually contain a basic truth. It is a rhetorical device used for emphasis.

"We need a man who can climb to the top and remain on the level."

parallelism   The balancing of similar items: word against word, clause against clause, sentence against sentence. It is the device that leads to balanced sentences.

It is not what he has, or even what he does which expresses the worth of a man, but what he is.

Parallelism is another effective device for achieving sentence variety and for increasing intensity of audience reaction. However, this one too must be used sparingly; its overuse leads to cluttering and rhetoric, airy thoughts without substance.

paraphrase   A restatement in different words. The paraphrase, unlike a precis or summary, may be as long as the original.

parody   A satirical imitation of a poem or other writing. The devices employed by Poe in his poems are so theatrical that his style has led to the many parodies that have been published in imitation of his most famous works.

pathetic fallacy   A projection in which human characteristics are attributed to inanimate objects.

The heavens weep with you in your sorrow.

pedantry A derogatory term used to label a display of learning for its own sake. It is applied to a style in which the author uses an excess of sequipedalianisms, quotations, foreign phrases, allusions, name-dropping.

periodic sentence A sentence in which the meaning is suspended until the end of the sentence, in which the main clause appears last.

By not arriving on time and by deliberately misinterpreting the directive, thus revealing his rejection of our suggestion, Harold brought our plan to a halt.

The periodic sentence when used exclusively gives a heavy tone to writing. It is best employed when interspersed among loose sentences to gain variety.

personal essay A prose work in which the author expresses an intimate reaction or indulges in self-revelation. The theme in which you reminisce about the advantages that have accrued to you from being the only child is a *personal essay*; when you seriously and objectively write about the main advantages and disadvantages in being an only child, then it becomes a *formal essay*.

personification The device in which inanimate objects and abstraction are referred to as having life or personality.

Good Fortune, come and be my companion, if only for a brief interlude!

Personification has fallen into disfavor in modern prose writing.

platitude An overused generalization uttered as though it were fresh and original. Polonius' advice to Laertes is the classic example: *Neither a borrower nor lender be.*

pleonasm The label applied when more words than necessary are used to convey an idea: *write it down, spell the word out, walk on foot, hear it with my own ears.*

poetic justice The good are rewarded and the evil punished. Poetic justice becomes a derogatory term when the author applies its principles with a heavy brush to the action in a plot.

poetic license The privilege claimed by authors to depart from the expected—normal order, diction, rhyme, pronunciation, grammar.

positive criticism Fault-finding, but with remedies being suggested. In the rational world of colleges, student themes must contain positive criticism to achieve maximum grades in most instances.

precis A summary or abstract. A precis usually contains less than half the number of words found in the original.

prologue A preface or introduction, usually to a play.

prose All forms of written and oral communication that lacks the regular rhythmic pattern of verse. It consists of connected ideas, not listings.

prose rhythms A constant flow of accent that is not recurrent in a regular pattern as in verse. Prose rhythm is an element of style.

protagonist The main character around whom the plot evolves. The protagonist is not necessarily a *hero* or *villain*. He may be the thief or the protecting officer of the law, depending upon the emphasis of the author.

provincial Narrow in point of view or approach. A derogatory term when applied to a writer who sees universal problems only in terms of himself and his immediate surroundings.

pseudonym A fictitious name assumed by a writer: *Mark Twain* (Samuel Clemens).

purple patch (passage) A selection in which the author seems to overstrain for effect, relying heavily on rhetorical devices and emotional tones. A purple patch is usually more rhythmic than most prose. It contains a strongly emotional tone marked by figures of speech and poetic diction. *Purple patch* is a derogatory term when used in modern criticism.

redundancy Needless repetition: repeat it *again*; descend *down*.

relevant appropriate; on the topic; fitting. Relevant materal and relevant arguments are effective additions to a theme.

rhetorical figure A specific arrangement of words for emphasis: *inversions, rhetorical question, apostrophes.* Rhetorical figures do not alter the meaning of the words employed as do figures of speech (similes, metaphors).

rhetorical question A question that is asked, not to elicit information, but to achieve a stylistic effect. It is often used by a speaker to add dramatic emphasis at the beginning of a thought unit.

Why don't our opponents accept our challenge? Let me tell you why! . . .

sarcasm A statement of the opposite of what is meant, a bitter, derisive statement of disapproval.

I am so glad to see that you are well enough to interfere with my plans!

Sarcasm is caustic, intended to hurt.

satire A type of writing which ridicules or denounces human vices and frailties. Horatian satire stresses a sophisticated, amused comment on vice or folly. Juvenalian satire is bitter, vehement, unamused in its denunciation.

setting The time and place in which the action of the plot occurs.

slang A nonstandard level of diction and usage. Slang consists of newly coined words and phrases and familiar words and phrases with meanings that have not been accepted on the colloquial or standard levels.

Cool it! It's *a gas*! He's *hip*.

slapsitck Comedy characterized by physical action such as the throwing of pies, falling into the swimming pool in formal clothing, etc.

stereotype The expected, the customary, a generalized pattern applied in a specific instance. A *stereotyped character* or *stereotype* is a stock character—the hard-boiled detective, the sweet, self-sacrificing and graying pre-Freudian mother. A *stereotyped solution* is one that is found in most stories in a specific pattern. A *stereotyped plot* is one that contains no surprises for the audience. A *stereotyped idea* is a facile generalization. *Stereotype* and *stereotyped* are usually terms of derogation.

static character A character centering about a single quality, one that does not grow or change during the action of the plot. Such characters usually surround the more complex, dynamic characters around whom the plot evolves. Hamlet is dynamic; Polonius is static.

stock character Stereotype that appears regularly in certain literary forms: the drunkard, the villain, the hero, and the heroine of the "cowboy stories," the private eye of most detective tales.

stock situation A frequently recurring incident or series of incidents found in the plot in a specific genre. Pick any incident or series of incidents in the typical "western" as your example.

style (1) The verbal pattern that characterizes a writer or writings.
Carl Sandburg's style is easily imitated.
(2) Excellence
He has style!

subjective Personal, limited to one person's standards, reactions, feelings, impressions, evaluations. *Subjective* is opposed to *objective* which stresses external, verifiable by others, followed accepted standards. The personal essay is subjective; the formal essay tends to be objective. One's impressions of an experience are subjective; an evaluation of the advantages and disadvantages of city living in statistical terms would be objective. The best college themes give the objective evidence followed by subjective reactions.

suspension The basic device in the periodic sentence in which the meaning is suspended until the end of the sentence.
Block by block, with infinite patience and with complete disregard of time and cost, he reconstructed the fallen building.

synopsis A summary, a condensation of a work. The synopsis should contain fewer words than the original.

tall tale A story of extravagant occurrences told for humorous effects. The element of belief or plausibility is in evidence in only some of the details of the story. The exploits of Paul Bunyan are typical tall tales.

theme (1) Student themes are papers written on one topic. They may center around personal reactions or evaluations of readings.
(2) The theme of a literary work is its central idea.

thesis (1) A formal essay, longer than a theme and resulting from research.
(2) A proposition to be defended or proved formally: The thesis of the author is that intelligence is mainly the result of environmental factors.

tirade A long uninterrupted speech usually condemnatory.
I am so tired of his long *tirades* on how much more responsible youth was in his day.

tone A quality of a work of art revealed in the attitude of the writer toward his material or his readers: *formal, ironic, condescending, etc.*

tragedy (1) An unfortunate occurrence.
(2) A plot that follows the classic or Aristotelian definition: disaster in the life of a ruler brought about inevitably as a result of a flaw in his character.
(3) A plot that follows the contemporary definition: an important series of related events in the life of a person significant to the audience, such events leading to an unhappy ending. The protagonist may be the victim of a flaw in his own character, forces in society, or forces in nature. The tone is one of great dignity and seriousness.

tragic flaw The defect in the protagonist which leads to his downfall.

variety Evasion of monotony in choice of words, structure of sentences, repetition of rhetorical devices, approaches to climaxes. The need for variety can be carried to extreme through the use of doubtful synonyms and inappropriate rhetorical devices.

verisimilitude The quality of reality possessed by plot, episode, setting or character. The reader is willing to accept as representation of truth those elements that possess verisimilitude.

villain An evil character opposing the forces of good found in the hero. The villain, however may be the protagonist, the main character in a story. In *Don Juan*, the main character is the villain of the action.

unity One-ness. Each element and each larger part of a work should be about one thing or tend to produce one effect. All the parts should be so related that the work is an organic whole. The introduction of an irrelevant detail destroys unity.

universality The ability of a work to appeal to a wide segment of the reading public generation after generation.

IMPROVING YOUR ABILITY TO READ CRITICALLY

TESTS OF MASTERY

I. Read each of the following sentences carefully. Then encircle the appropriate letter in the answer column
   A. if the sentence contains irony;
   B. if the sentence contains a hyperbole;
   C. if the sentence contains litotes;
   D. if the sentence contains parallelism;
   E. if the sentence contains none of these devices.

1. Such faith can move mountains.
   1. A B C D E
2. To see and hear but not to judge and evaluate are our present goals.
   2. A B C D E
3. This decision was not a foolish one.
   3. A B C D E
4. So you think you made a wise choice!
   4. A B C D E
5. It was a night that I shall long remember.
   5. A B C D E
6. Rhetoric is the art of ruling the minds of men.
   6. A B C D E
7. Hitch your wagon to a star.
   7. A B C D E
8. The spirit is willing, but the flesh is weak.
   8. A B C D E
9. The enemy is not stupid!
   9. A B C D E
10. The eyes of the tortured were pools filled with the darkness of the Hell fires.
    10. A B C D E

II. Read each of the following passages carefully. Then encircle the appropriate letter in the answer column
   A. if what is described is a parody;
   B. if what is described is a fable;
   C. if what is described is a novel;
   D. if what is described is a tall tale;
   E. if what is described is none of the above.

11. Hamlet meets a more sophisticated Ophelia who breaks his guard down by accusing him of lacking a sense of humor. She convinces him to visit her psychiatrist who gives him a tranquillizer that cures him of his anxieties.
    11. A B C D E
12. The bees decide that the moon is responsible for the lowered production in their hives. Upon consultation with the learned Queen Ant, they learn that if they avoid contact with red clover, they will destroy the moon. The Inner Party, headed by the drones, rejects the suggestion because it is unscientific. The Outer Party then declares war on the others and an incendiary destroys the hive and all in it.
    12. A B C D E
13. In a long rambling story, the author contrasts the growing years of three girls who had attended the same grade school.
    13. A B C D E
14. The author reveals how he had felt during the years he had been a member of the President's Cabinet.
    14. A B C D E
15. Henry felt that he would like to test some of the basic beliefs in our present society. He thought that he could prove that intelligence was a product of environment only and that it could be improved indefinitely. He decided to experiment with beagles. In order to reach significant results he decided to speed up the rate of learning of his subjects by tripling the speed of life around them. Humans spoke, walked, reacted three times faster than usual when in the laboratory. The beagles were forced to eat and react three times faster than the non-experimental group.
    The results were astounding. The beagles were soon doing problems in elementary algebra and studying the principles of physical anthropology. The experiment came to an unexpected ending when the beagles died of old age at the chronological age of two; the speed up had caused them to age nine times faster!
    15. A B C D E
16. The water droplets and dust particles in the air revolt against the inexorable forces of law that force them into cloud formations.
    16. A B C D E
17. A fictitious character recalls the main events that changed him from being a self-centered adolescent into a responsible adult.
    17. A B C D E
18. Tired of back-alley shenanigans, a handsome tomcat learns to type and persuades an agent to have his memoirs published. The moral that it pays to reform is stressed in this success story.
    18. A B C D E
19. The owner of a race horse discovers that the racer loves fast music. The faster the music, the greater the speed. A subminiature tape recorder is placed in the horse's ear, and he wins race after race with incredible speed. The scheme comes to an abrupt end when the horse learns that he can listen to the music—and not run; in fact he seems to derive greater enjoyment by standing still.
    19. A B C D E
20. A teenage activist, after reading the sonnet "How Do I Love Thee?", is inspired to write a poem addressed to the world, "How Do I Hate Thee/ Let Me Count the Ways."
    20. A B C D E

III. Read each of the following sentences. Then encircle the appropriate letter in the answer column

A. if the underlined portion contains alliteration;
B. if the underlined portion contains an allusion;
C. if the underlined portion contains an analogy;
D. If the underlined portion contains an epithet;
E. if the underlined portion contains oxymoron.

21. The philanthropist was merciless in his kindness.   21. A B C D E
22. The daily drudgery drowned his ambition in its sameness.   22. A B C D E
23. The wily politician allowed us to speak at length without committing himself.
    23. A B C D E
24. This could so easily be his Waterloo!
    24. A B C D E
25. I don't see how you can disagree since I like the plan!   25. A B C D E
26. Who can have kind words for a gentle executioner!   26. A B C D E
27. I read the report on Alexander the Great.
    27. A B C D E
28. His other plan was successful; this one too should succeed.   28. A B C D E
29. The common man has need for a Roosevelt in this time of crisis!   29. A B C D E
30. What swimmer could survive in such wild waters!   30. A B C D E

IV. Read each of the following carefully. Then encircle letter of the pair of words that would best complete each statement.

31. An abstract statement is a general statement. It is opposed to a .... fact or .... statement.
    A. vague .... specific
    B. general .... indefinite
    C. specific .... concrete
    D. definite .... false

32. A loose sentence is the basic pattern in .... and .... writing.
    A. arguments .... letter
    B. debates .... informal
    C. books .... informal
    D. conversation .... informal

33. Satire .... human frailties .... satire stresses sophisticated, amused comment.
    A. praises .... American
    B. exposes .... modern
    C. ridicules .... Horatian
    D. ridicules .... Juvenalian

34. Tragic flaws are .... in the .... which inevitably lead to disaster.
    A. plants .... plot
    B. devices .... action
    C. defects .... protagonist
    D. characters .... story

35. The reader is willing to accept as a representation of .... those elements that possess ....
    A. truth .... verisimilitude
    B. life .... vitality
    C. evil .... tragedy
    D. action .... plot

36. A literary form in which all or some of the characters are the embodiment of .... ideas is called a(n) ....
    A. novel .... novel
    B. abstract .... allegory
    C. modern .... journal
    D. imaginative .... allegory

37. A(n) .... lacks the .... plot of a short story although they resemble each other in other respects.
    A. anecdote .... complicated
    B. adage .... novel
    C. maxim .... involved
    D. paradox .... simple

38. Dramatic irony occurs when the words or acts of a character carry a meaning .... him but .... the audience.
    A. clear to .... not understood by
    B. developed by .... perceived by
    C. avoided by .... known to
    D. unperceived by .... understood by

39. Economy of expression results from the use of .... number of words necessary for ....
    A. necessary .... expression
    B. minimum .... clarity
    C. realistic .... emphasis
    D. given .... delivery

40. .... and .... are examples of fiction.
    A. biographies .... memoirs
    B. essays .... lyrics
    C. short stories .... novels
    D. novels .... essays

41. A sentence in which the ideas follow their .... order is called a .... sentence.
    A. inverted .... loose
    B. logical .... loose
    C. psychological .... periodic
    D. inverted .... dramatic

42. The device in which .... is referred to as having personality is called ....
    A. contraction .... metonomy
    B. a person .... drama
    C. an animal .... irony
    D. an abstraction .... personification

IMPROVING YOUR ABILITY TO READ CRITICALLY

43. A(n) .... generalization uttered as though it were original is a(n) ....
    A. logical .... principle
    B. overused .... realization
    C. trite .... cliche
    D. novel .... ideal

44. Criticism becomes .... when .... are suggested.
    A. negative .... remedies
    B. positive .... remedies
    C. valid .... results
    D. carping .... faults

45. The .... character around whom the plot evolves is called the ....
    A. static .... hero
    B. dynamic .... villain
    C. minor .... prologue
    D. main .... protagonist

46. .... repetition is called ....
    A. Unintentional .... humor
    B. Intentional .... style
    C. Needless .... redundancy
    D. Humorous .... needless

47. A question for which a(n) .... is not anticipated is a(n) .... question.
    A. answer .... rhetorical
    B. reaction .... doublebarreled
    C. discussion .... legal
    D. reply .... dramatic

48. A(n) .... of a work is called a(n) ....
    A. interpretation .... thesis
    B. condensation .... synopsis
    C. criticism .... precis
    D. reproduction .... essay

49. A .... of prose selections is called a(n) ....
    A. criticism .... critique
    B. summary .... aphorism
    C. reproduction .... classic
    D. collection .... anthology

50. A(n) .... is a .... description of a book.
    A. blurb .... complimentary
    B. circumlocution .... vague
    C. confidant .... secret
    D. inversion .... critical

V. In the space provided, write T if the statement is true; F if the statement is not true.

.... 51. A familiar wise saying is called an allegory.
.... 52. A word that is no longer in use is called an archaism.
.... 53. The account of a person's life as told by his brother is an autobiography.
.... 54. Harsh combinations of sounds are examples of cacophony.
.... 55. A caricature is a well-rounded, realistic presentation of a character.
.... 56. A cliche is a type of rhetorical question.
.... 57. A clown may be used to supply comic relief.
.... 58. A conceit is an exaggerated impression of one's own importance.
.... 59. Conflict and climax are synonyms.
.... 60. Homily and sermon are synonymous terms.
.... 61. Similes cannot be taken literally.
.... 62. Oxymoron is the denial of the opposite.
.... 63. An aphorism is similar to a maxim.
.... 64. Scenery is basic to mise en scene.
.... 65. Paradox contains antithesis.
.... 66. Pathetic fallacies are based on parables.
.... 67. A paraphrase is closer to a synopsis than to a precis.
.... 68. Pleonasm is a type of personification.
.... 69. A platitude is closer to cliche than to aphorism.
.... 70. Both prose and poetry contain rhythms.
.... 71. Stock characters are usually dynamic.
.... 72. Suspension is the basic device of the loose sentence.
.... 73. The protagonist cannot be villainous.
.... 74. A tirade is a work of praise.
.... 75. Abstractions play important roles in allegories.

VI. Encircle the letter of the word or phrase that best completes each of the following statements.

76. When more than one interpretation is possible, the result is ....
    A. analogy
    B. circumlocution
    C. ambiguity
    D. conflict

77. The .... is the main character opposed to the author's principal character.
    A. protagonist
    B. antagonist
    C. villain
    D. setting

78. The author who has Delilah awaken Samson to the ringing of an alarm clock has used the device of ....
    A. anachronism
    B. oxymoron
    C. digression
    D. epigram

79. Calling another a Solomon is using the device called ....
    A. aphorism
    B. assonance
    C. antonomasia
    D. confidant

80. An author's choice and arrangement of words reveals his level of ....
    A. diction

B. digression
C. mood
D. prose
81. A literary work whose principal aim is teach moral values is . . . .
    A. figurative
    B. ironic
    C. relevant
    D. didactic
82. The author who interrupts the action of the play to insert a scene of a previous time is employing a(n) . . . .
    A. anachronism
    B. flashback
    C. prologue
    D. epilogue
83. The writer who has traveled little and concentrates on describing only what he has actually experienced tends to be . . . .
    A. precis
    B. irrelevant
    C. provincial
    D. universal
84. George Eliot is an example of a(n) . . . .
    A. pseudonym
    B. inversion
    C. antonomasia
    D. apostrophe
85. *What was good for your father should be good for you* is an example of . . . .
    A. an anecdote
    B. an analogy
    C. anticlimax
    D. universality
86. The phrase *to see, to feel, to know, but not to judge, to favor or condemn* is an example of . . . .
    A. anticlimax
    B. atmosphere
    C. assonance
    D. antithesis
87. An emotionalized letting go of all controls in writing is called . . . .
    A. bombast
    B. bathos
    C. brevity
    D. burlesque
88. *Love* and *patriotism* are examples of . . . .
    A. concrete terms
    B. parallelism
    C. abstract terms
    D. comic relief
89. A confidant could not be the . . . .
    A. heroine
    B. villain
    C. protagonist
    D. antagonist
90. *Mother, helping hand, understanding attitude* have a pleasant . . . . for most people.
    A. denotation
    B. connotation
    C. verisimilitude
    D. analogy
91. The white hat and white horse of the hero in a western tale are accepted . . . . of that genre.
    A. digressions
    B. epigrams
    C. epithets
    D. conventions
92. How the hero and heroine will live happily ever after is usually developed in the
    A. prologue
    B. climax
    C. denouement
    D. setting
93. The reader who exclaims, "I know exactly how the main character felt at that moment" has experienced . . . .
    A. empathy
    B. exposition
    C. interior monologue
    D. inversion
94. Narrative writing based on imagination rather than fact could *not* be . . . .
    A. a novel
    B. a short story
    C. a poem
    D. a biography
95. Fustian is similar to . . . .
    A. exposition
    B. bombast
    C. interior monologue
    D. subjectivity
96. When an author digresses, the material is usually labeled as . . . .
    A. irrelevant
    B. relevant
    C. journalese
    D. litotes
97. A malapropism is similar to a(n) . . . .
    A. maxim
    B. slang expression
    C. pun
    D. homily
98. The author who tells a story strictly from the point of view of the protagonist's younger brother is not . . . .
    A. subjective
    B. paradoxical
    C. sarcastic
    D. omniscient
99. The author who reveals his insecurity by making excess use of quotations from authorities is in danger of being labeled
    A. objective
    B. provincial
    C. pedantic
    D. universal
100. Pleonasm is to redundancy as maxim is to . . . .
    A. precept
    B. short story

C. essay
D. homily
101. Slapstick would not be found during the climax of . . . .

A. farce
B. comedy
C. a novel
D. a tragedy

ANSWER KEY: TEST OF MASTERY   Page 191

I.
1. B   4. A   7. B   9. C
2. D   5. E   8. D   10. B
3. C   6. E

II.
11. A   14. E   17. C   19. D
12. B   15. D   18. B   20. A
13. C   16. B

III.
21. E   24. B   27. D   29. B
22. A   25. C   28. C   30. A
23. D   26. E

IV.
31. C   36. B   41. B   46. C
32. D   37. A   42. D   47. A
33. C   38. D   43. C   48. B
34. C   39. B   44. B   49. D
35. A   40. C   45. D   50. A

V.
51. F   58. F   64. T   70. T
52. T   59. F   65. T   71. F
53. F   60. T   66. F   72. F
54. T   61. T   67. F   73. F
55. F   62. F   68. F   74. F
56. F   63. T   69. T   75. T
57. T

VI.
76. C   83. C   89. B   95. B
77. B   84. A   90. B   96. A
78. A   85. B   91. D   97. C
79. C   86. D   92. C   98. D
80. A   87. A   93. A   99. C
81. D   88. C   94. D   100. A
82. B   101. D

The Literature Test

Section FIVE : Practice Examinations in Literature

1. *Ten Practice Examinations*

2. *Answers to Practice Examinations*

TO DO YOUR BEST

1. This is a test of your ability to read literary passages. Therefore you should read the passage first; do not endanger your understanding by looking at the questions first.

2. The first reading should be a rapid one. From it you should be able to gather what the general topic is.

3. Your second reading should be sentence by sentence. The test of comprehension at this point is your being able to follow the thought sequence from sentence to sentence. Try to pick out the topic sentence in this process.

4. Remember, you are *not* being marked on how many times you read the selection. Credit is given for the accuracy of your answers. Therefore, reread the passage sentence by sentence again if necessary. And then again!

5. If you still find the passage unyielding, then you can consider going on to the next and then coming back to this one. The time lapse will help; you will be pleased at the way the selection suddenly comes into focus during this second visit.

6. Follow the questions in order. This procedure helps since the answer to one question is often dependent on what had gone before.

7. Do not forget that you are being tested on your ability to do critical reading. Before answering a question on a portion of the passage, reread the section; do not depend on your memory!

8. In questions of content, find your answers in the selection. Do not rely on your previous knowledge. This is a test of reading, not memory.

9. Use the process of elimination to select the answer. Even if you identify the "correct" answer at first glance, eliminate the others, and thus eliminate the possibility of careless acceptance of the second best.

10. Since there is a penalty for guessing, do *not* submit an answer for a pure guess. If you can eliminate 3 of the 5 choices, then the odds are in your favor if you guess. If you can eliminate only 2 or 1 of the 5 choices, then it is better not to guess. If you cannot eliminate any of the choices, then let that answer be blank!

11. Do not dawdle or worry yourself into tension over a question or selection. If you find it very difficult, then go on to the next. If you have time, then you can return later. The passages and questions are varied; some you will find more difficult than others. The next one may be one that you can answer quickly, and then when you have finished, you can go back.

12. Pace yourself to answer as many questions as possible. However do not feel discouraged if you do not finish before the time is up, or if you have not had time to return to the questions you skipped. The form of the test that you are taking may be one that very few if any students are expected to finish.

13. Read in order!
FIRST THE DIRECTIONS: you have to know what is expected before you can give correct answers!
THEN THE SELECTION: this is a test of reading.
FINALLY, THE QUESTIONS IN ORDER: there is no short cut!

TIME LIMITS

The test that you will take will be an hour long, with fifteen additional minutes for preparation. The practice tests that follow will enable you to assess the speed with which you can work under examination conditions. However, do not strive for speed at first. Be as thorough and as accurate as you can be without dawdling when you take the initial practice tests; speed will come. It little profits to finish first —with errors of omission and careless haste!

PRACTICE EXAMINATION ONE

Total Time: One Hour
Time begun ..... Time ended ..... Time used .....
DIRECTIONS: This test consists of selections from works of literature. Read each passage carefully, and then answer the questions that follow. Refer to the passage as many times as necessary before you choose your answers.

Questions 1–8

A true classic, as I should like to hear it defined, is an author who has enriched the human mind, increased its treasure and caused it to advance a step; who has discovered some moral and not equivocal truth, or revealed some eternal passion in that heart where all seemed known and discovered; who has expressed his thought, observation, or invention, in no matter what form, only provided it be broad and great, refined and sensible, sane and beautiful in itself; who has spoken to all in his own peculiar style, a style which is found to be also that of the whole world, a style new without neologism, new and old, easily contemporary with all time.

Such a classic may for a moment have been revolutionary; it may at least have seemed so, but it is not; it only lashed and subverted whatever prevented the restoration of the balance of order and beauty.

1. The tone of the passage is best defined as
   (A) joyful
   (B) cynical
   (C) confused
   (D) didactic
   (E) scornful
2. A true classic need not
   (A) contain moral values
   (B) expose the weakness in older ways
   (C) deal with emotional values
   (D) reveal man's self to man
   (E) employ new techniques of writing
3. The test of a true classic is that
   (A) it revealed truth to one generation
   (B) it made the world a better place to live in
   (C) it has historical significance
   (D) it fills with pride the hearts of the countrymen of the author
   (E) it continues to be read throughout the world
4. A true class is revolutionary because
   (A) it clears away styles and ideas that confused men
   (B) it brings new techniques into fields of expression
   (C) it contains moral values
   (D) it is understood by so many people
   (E) it defies time
5. The author of this selection proves his points by
   (A) giving examples
   (B) citing authorities
   (C) developing his ideas logically
   (D) disproving false ideas
   (E) stating his opinions
6. An author who reveals "some eternal passion in that heart where all seemed known and discovered"
   (A) must develop a new vocabulary
   (B) distorts accepted reality
   (C) reveals new insights into man's reasons for behavior
   (D) develops a style of his own
   (E) puts old ideas into new forms
7. The diction and style of this passage are best defined as
   (A) emotional and allegorical
   (B) poetic and oratorical
   (C) abstract and philosophical
   (D) direct and moralistic
   (E) oratorical and prophetic
8. A treasure of the human mind
   (A) reveals moral truth
   (B) reveals truth, order, and beauty
   (C) contains universal passion, moral values, and mental worth
   (D) is based on observation, invention, and insights
   (E) is based on enrichment, advancement, and discovery

Questions 9–13

It is not only what we have inherited from our fathers that exists again in us, but all sorts of old, dead ideas and all kinds of old dead beliefs, and things of that kind. They are not actually alive in us; but they are there, dormant all the same, and we can never be rid of them. Whenever I take up a newspaper and read it, I fancy I see ghosts creeping between the lines. There must be ghosts all over the world.

9. The author is suspicious of
   (A) our inheritance
   (B) old ideas
   (C) whatever is not new
   (D) ideas that are not fully accepted
   (E) ways of life based on dated traditions
10. The author condemns men who
    (A) are uncritical
    (B) are cruel and merciless
    (C) condemn others for acts that they themselves have done
    (D) judge others by their inheritances
    (E) read newspapers carelessly
11. The tone of the passage is best termed
    (A) hopeful
    (B) pessimistic
    (C) romantic
    (D) cynical
    (E) didactic
12. The last sentence must be taken
    (A) literally
    (B) philosophically
    (C) figuratively
    (D) argumentatively
    (E) prophetically
13. Emphasis is achieved in this selection through
    (A) logical piling up of details
    (B) imagery and oxymoron
    (C) repetition of single words
    (D) rhetorical questions
    (E) argumentation and exposition

Questions 14–26

See, Winter comes to rule the varied year
Sullen and sad, with all his rising train—
Vapors, and clouds, and storms. Be these
   my theme,
These that exalt the soul to solemn thought

5 And heavenly musing. Welcome, kindred
                                    Glooms!
   Congenial Horrors, hail! With frequent
                                    foot,
   Pleased have I, in my cheerful morn of life,
   When nursed by careless Solitude I lived
   And sung of Nature with unceasing joy,
10 Pleased have I wandered through your
                                    rough domain;
   Trod the pure virgin-snows, myself as pure;
   Heard the winds roar, and the big torrent
                                    burst;
   Or seen the deep-fermenting tempest
                                    brewed
   In the grim evening sky. Thus passed the
                                    time,
15 Till through the lucid chambers of the
                                    south
   Looked out the joyous Spring, looked out
                                    and smiled.

14. ____ The underlying subject of the passage is
    (A) the terrors of winter
    (B) the promise of spring that follows winter
    (C) the passage of time
    (D) man's ability to find joy in winter
    (E) the pleasures associated with winter
15. ____ This selection
    (A) is complete in itself
    (B) is the opening section of a longer poem
    (C) is the concluding section of a longer poem
    (D) is the dedication of a novel
    (E) is the epilogue of a play
16. ____ The fifth line contains an example of
    (A) personification
    (B) litotes
    (C) condensation
    (D) exposition
    (E) expansion
17. ____ The last sentence is
    (A) compound
    (B) simple
    (C) loose
    (D) inverted
    (E) exclamatory
18. ____ The author was as pure as the snow because
    (A) of his profession
    (B) of his training
    (C) of his prayers
    (D) of the effect of the snow
    (E) of the coming of spring
19. ____ The mood of the selection is one of
    (A) ecstasy and wonder
    (B) fear and rebellion
    (C) resignation and suffering
    (D) questioning and doubt
    (E) acceptance and thoughtfulness
20. ____ The poet's companion has been
    (A) his closest friend
    (B) an undisclosed person
    (C) his own reactions
    (D) the animals of the woods
    (E) the fury of the tempest
21. ____ These impressions of nature are those of
    (A) a childless couple
    (B) an old man
    (C) an infant
    (D) a dying man
    (E) a young boy
22. ____ *Congenial Horrors* is an example of
    (A) simile
    (B) conceit
    (C) hyperbole
    (D) oxymoron
    (E) malapropism
23. ____ *Joyous Spring* contains an example of the use of a(n)
    (A) alliteration
    (B) allusion
    (C) epithet
    (D) archaism
    (E) euphemism
24. ____ The train mentioned in line two
    (A) rides through the sky
    (B) covers much territory
    (C) puffs its way through mountains and plains
    (D) is filled with his thoughts
    (E) is seen in the evening
25. ____ Which of the following best explain the poet's use of compound adjectives, nouns, and clauses in this poem?
    (A) The piling up of examples clarifies the poet's purposes.
    (B) It allows him to include many more images.
    (C) It gives the poem the proper tone of heaviness.
    (D) It allows the reader to anticipate the coming of spring.
    (E) It adds speed to emphasize how varied the year really is.
26. ____ This poem is written in
    (A) irregular quatrains
    (B) sonnet form
    (C) free verse
    (D) heroic couplets
    (E) blank verse

Questions 27–33

   A time there was, ere England's griefs
                                    began,
   When every rood of ground maintained
                                    its man;
   For him light labor spread her wholesome
                                    store,
   Just gave what life required, but gave no
                                    more:
5 His best companions, innocence and
                                    health;
   And his best riches, ignorance of wealth.
   But times are altered; trade's unfeeling
                                    train
   Usurp the land, and dispossess the swain;

Along the lawn, where scattered hamlets rose,
10 Unwieldy wealth and cumbrous pomp repose;
And every want to luxury allied,
And every pang that folly pays to pride.
Those gentle hours that plenty bade to bloom,
Those calm desires that asked but little room,
15 Those healthful sports that graced the peaceful scene,
Lived in each look, and brightened all the green;
These, far departing, seek a kinder shore,
And rural mirth and manners are no more.

27. This poem describes the time when
    (A) English seapower was being established
    (B) the English were developing their colonial empire
    (C) the Napoleonic wars were being fought
    (D) when small farms were absorbed into large tracts in England
    (E) the American colonies were in rebellion
28. This poem is written in
    (A) blank verse
    (B) sonnet form
    (C) ballad form
    (D) heroic couplets
    (E) free verse
29. The mood of the poet is one of
    (A) nostalgia
    (B) mirth
    (C) fear
    (D) jealousy
    (E) annoyance
30. The underlying subject of the passage is
    (A) the growth of happiness in England
    (B) the advantages of living in the country
    (C) the end of the good simple life in rural England
    (D) the disadvantages of industrialization
    (E) the growth of the cities
31. The first five lines contain
    (A) a realistic picture of the farm life that disappeared
    (B) a sentimentalized picture of past days on the farm
    (C) a picture of a rural cemetery of the times
    (D) a condemnation of farm life
    (E) a plea for the simple life
32. Line five contains an example of
    (A) a simile
    (B) a metaphor
    (C) litotes
    (D) a conceit
    (E) personification
33. Which of the following best describes the style of the passage?
    (A) allegorical and didactic
    (B) emotional and metaphoric
    (C) abstract and oratorical
    (D) generalized and simple
    (E) zealous and provocative

PRACTICE EXAMINATION TWO

Total Time: One Hour
Time begun . . . . . Time ended . . . . . Time used . . . . .

DIRECTIONS: This test consists of selections from works of literature. Read each passage carefully, and then answer the questions that follow. The questions are on their content, form, and style. Refer to the passage as many times as necessary before you choose your answers.

Questions 1–7

All the philanthropists in the world, and all the legislators, meeting to advocate and decree the total abolition of corporal punishment, will never persuade me to the contrary! There is something even more disgraceful than what I have just mentioned. Often enough you may see a carter walking along the street, quite alone, without any horses, and still cracking away incessantly; so accustomed has the wretch become to it in consequence of the unwarrantable toleration of this practice. A man's body and the needs of his body are now everywhere treated with a tender indulgence. Is the thinking mind then, to be the only thing that is never to obtain the slightest measure of consideration or protection, to say nothing of respect? Carters, porters, messengers—these are the beasts of burden amongst mankind; by all means let them be treated justly, fairly, indulgently, and with forethought; but they must not be permitted to stand in the way of the higher endeavors of humanity by wantonly making a noise. How many great and splendid thoughts, I should like to know, have been lost to the world by the crack of a whip? If I had the upper hand, I should soon produce in the heads of these people an indissoluble association of ideas between cracking a whip and getting a whipping.

1. The underlying subject of this selection is that
    (A) man is fundamentally bad and must be punished in order to know right from wrong
    (B) poetic justice can never operate in the world of carters, porters, and messengers
    (C) philanthropy can often commit grave errors in helping wrong group sections of society
    (D) brute force rather than reason is the effective control in society
    (E) no man can escape the social consequences of his acts

2. The writer of this article can best be characterized as
   (A) democratic in his desire to see that all segments of society have equal privileges when in the streets
   (B) autocratic because of his concern over the few rather than the many
   (C) democratic because he is willing to discuss calmly in this selection an injustice in our society
   (D) autocratic because of his condescending attitude toward people engaged in the service trades
   (E) totalitarian because of his advocacy of corporal punishment and desire for noise abatement

3. Which of the following best express the reaction of a modern reader?
   (A) Because of its stress on something so trivial, there must be some hidden meaning.
   (B) The article deals with a social problem and admirably suggests a positive solution.
   (C) While his solution may be practical, the problem dealt with is too insignificant.
   (D) Stratification of society has its merits; it allows some men to improve the manners of others through threats or fear of threats.
   (E) The carters, porters, and messengers appreciated the writer's willingness to help them realize faults.

4. The first sentence is an example of
   (A) epithet
   (B) alliteration
   (C) generalization
   (D) litotes
   (E) oxymoron   4. A B C D E

5. The author does not explain
   (A) why corporal punishment should not be abolished
   (B) why the thinking minds must be protected against noise
   (C) why the carters crack their whips when walking down the streets
   (D) why whipping these men would be effective
   (E) why the writer advocates corporal punishment
                                             5.

6. The author's main objection to the cracking of the whip was
   (A) it was a cruel way to treat animals
   (B) the noise brutalized the city atmosphere
   (C) the men might hurt a passerby
   (D) the whip is a symbol of oppression
   (E) the noise bothered him

7. The diction and style of this passage are best defined as
   (A) abstract and philosophical
   (B) legal and argumentative
   (C) emotional and figurative
   (D) ordinary and serious
   (E) allegorical and didactic

Questions 8–12

> I met a seer.
> He held a book in his hands,
> The book of wisdom.
> "Sir," I addressed him,
> "Let me read."
> "Child-" he began.
> "Sir," I said,
> "Think not that I am a child,
> For already I know much
> Of that which you hold;
> Aye, much."
> He smiled.
> Then he opened the book
> And held it before me.
> Strange that I should have grown
>   so suddenly blind.

8. The author's purpose in this poem was to
   (A) expose the cruelty of old age
   (B) warn youth not to be adventurous
   (C) explore man's inhumanity to man
   (D) expose ignorance
   (E) reveal a psychological truth

9. The shortness of the lines
   (A) deprives the reader of values
   (B) adds to the simpleness of tone
   (C) develops a sense of awe
   (D) gives the child a chance to act
   (E) emphasizes the wisdom of the seer

10. Which of the following best states the effect of the last sentence?
    (A) It is an anticlimax which repeats a realization already clear to the reader
    (B) It provides a philosophical conclusion that the narrator had much to atone for
    (C) It provides the ironic conclusion that we must pay for knowledge
    (D) It brings into focus the contrast between the narrative style and the variety of interpretations possible
    (E) It sharpens the reader's sense of horror at the impulsiveness of man

11. This poem does not contain
    (A) similes
    (B) imagery
    (C) generalization
    (D) literal meaning
    (E) assertion

12. This poem is written in
    (A) ballad stanzas
    (B) free verse
    (C) cadenced prose
    (D) blank verse
    (E) iambic tetrameters

Questions 13–17

A house without books is like a room without windows. No man has a right to bring up his children without surrounding them with books, if he has the means to buy them. It is wrong to his family. Children learn to read by being in the presence of books. The love of knowledge comes with reading and grows upon it. And the love of knowledge, in a young mind, is almost a warrant against the inferior excitement of passions and vices.

13. The author reveals a fear of
    (A) knowledge learned from books
    (B) emotions
    (C) authority
    (D) people's ability to obey laws and regulations
    (E) education
14. The first sentence contains
    (A) an allegory
    (B) a simile
    (C) a metaphor
    (D) oxymoron
    (E) contrast
15. The author attempts to convince the reader through
    (A) citing examples
    (B) reductio ad absurdam
    (C) appealing to the reader's sentiment
    (D) logical development of an idea
    (E) generalization
16. The author stresses the importance of . . . in the learning process
    (A) ability of the instructor
    (B) the type of textbook being used
    (C) the educational level of one's friends and relatives
    (D) atmosphere
    (E) the intelligence level of the children
17. According to the author the best that a parent can give his child must include
    (A) sensitivity to the rights of others
    (B) understanding of self
    (C) willingness to follow worthwhile ideals
    (D) fear of propaganda
    (E) love of knowledge for its own sake

Questions 18–23

Yet notwithstanding this weight of authority, and the universal practice of former ages, a new species of dramatic composition has been introduced under the name of *sentimental* comedy, in which the virtues of private life are exhibited, rather than the vices exposed; and the distresses rather than the faults of mankind make our interest in the piece. These comedies have had of late great success, perhaps from their novelty, and also from their flattering every man in his favorite foible. In these plays almost all the characters are good, and exceedingly generous; they are lavish enough of their *tin* money on the stage; and, though they want humor, have abundance of sentiment and feeling. If they happen to have faults or foibles, the spectator is taught not only to pardon, but to applaud them, in consideration of the goodness of their hearts; so that folly, instead of being ridiculed, is commended, and the comedy aims at touching our passions without the power of being truly pathetic. In this manner we are likely to lose one great source of entertainment on the stage; for while the comic poet is invading the province of the tragic muse, he leaves her lovely sister quite neglected. Of this, however, he is no way solicitous, as he measures his fame by his profits.

18. The purpose of the writer is to
    (A) condemn sentimental comedy
    (B) praise sentimental comedy
    (C) turn the reader away from this type of play
    (D) evaluate sentimental comedy
    (E) interest the general public in this type of comedy
19. The purpose of the playwright who is responsible for these comedies is
    (A) to make money by giving the audience what it wants
    (B) to improve the moral standards of the audience
    (C) to expose human vices to the audience
    (D) to discuss the moral and political issues of the day
    (E) to entertain the audience and help them forget the evils of the day
20. The characters in these plays lack
    (A) a sense of right and wrong
    (B) ability to live lavishly
    (C) deep feelings
    (D) human weaknesses
    (E) a sense of the ridiculous
21. The author feels that sentimental comedy
    (A) will be just a passing style
    (B) is one of the great contributions of his age
    (C) deals with superficial aspects of life
    (D) enhances the audience's appreciation of suffering
    (E) sets beneficial examples for the audience to follow
22. The writers of previous generations would condemn sentimental comedy because
    (A) it distorts the audience's view of life
    (B) it stresses emotions rather than thought
    (C) it makes the audience smug and complacent
    (D) it confuses dramatic forms
    (E) it proves the worth of ordinary men
23. A trait not possessed by the characters in these plays is
    (A) generosity
    (B) ability to react emotionally
    (C) a deepened sense of virtue
    (D) self-centeredness
    (E) sensitivity to the social issues of the day

Questions 24–30

Gracefullest leaper, the dappled fox-cub
Curves over brambles with berries and
                          buds,
Light as a bubble that flies from the tub,
Whisked by the laundry-wife out of her
                          suds.
5 Wavy he comes, wooly, all at his ease,
Elegant, fashioned to foot with the deuce;
Nature's own prince of the dance: then
                        he sees
Me, and retires as if making excuse.
Never closed minuet courtlier! Soon
10 Cub-hunting troops were abroad, and a yelp
Told of sure scent: ere the stroke upon
                        noon
Reynard the younger lay far beyond help.

Wild, my poor friend, has the fate to be
                                   chased;
Civil will conquer: were it other 'twere
                                   worse;
15 Fair, by the flushed early morning
                                   embraced,
Haply you live a day longer in verse.

24. By using the combination found in the opening two words, the poet
   (A) summarized the action in the poem
   (B) revealed the innocence of the fox
   (C) attempted to catch the movement of the fox
   (D) emphasized the speed of the fox
   (E) emphasized the innocence of the dogs

25. The simile in lines three and four
   (A) is inappropriate because of the image of the laundry tub
   (B) is appropriate because it emphasizes the naive, comic quality of the cub
   (C) is inappropriate because it brings another character into the narrative
   (D) is appropriate because it reveals the feelings of the cub
   (E) is appropriate because it reveals the poet's concern

26. Line five contains an example of
   (A) metaphor
   (B) apostrophe
   (C) oxymoron
   (D) assonance
   (E) alliteration

27. By leaving the way he did, the cub revealed his
   (A) fear
   (B) savagery
   (C) inexperience
   (D) love of man
   (E) hunger

28. Which of the following best describes the style of the passage?
   (A) It uses objectivity and lack of sentimentalism to develop the underlying idea.
   (B) It builds up to a climax by coming to the point at the very beginning.
   (C) It brings in many irrelevant details in order to develop the surprise ending.
   (D) It extols nature so that the reader will sympathize with wild animals.
   (E) It piles up image after image to make certain that the reader is following the action.

29. The last four lines contain an example of
   (A) melodrama
   (B) allegory
   (C) apostrophe
   (D) litotes
   (E) homily

30. The attitude of the author is one of
   (A) sorrow at the ways of man and beast
   (B) sentimental joy at the fact that the cub had enjoyed the morning of life
   (C) bitterness at the cruelty of the hunters
   (D) approval of the ways of the world
   (E) acceptance of the ways of both man and animals

PRACTICE EXAMINATION THREE

Total Time: One Hour
Time begun ..... Time ended ..... Time used .....

DIRECTIONS: This test consists of selections from works of literature. Read each passage carefully, and then answer the questions that follow. The questions are based on their content, form, and style. Refer to the passage as many times as necessary before you choose your answers.

Questions 1–6

The value of philosophy is to be sought largely in its very uncertainty. He who has no tincture of philosophy goes through life imprisoned in the prejudices derived from common sense, from the habitual beliefs of his age or his nation, and from convictions which have grown up in his mind without the cooperation or consent of his deliberate reason. As soon as we begin to philosophize, on the contrary, we find that even the most everyday things lead to problems to which only very incomplete answers can be given. Philosophy, though unable to tell us with certainty what is the true answer to the doubts which it raises, is able to suggest many possibilities which enlarge our thoughts and free them from the tyranny of custom.

1. This paragraph is organized primarily according to the principle of
   (A) partition in that the author begins with a large idea and then explains its subdivisions
   (B) cause and effect in that the author describes an effect and then relates it to its causes
   (C) chronology in that the author presents events in the order in which they occurred
   (D) explication in that he begins with a large idea and then explains it through expansion
   (E) exemplification in that he gives examples to clarify his main idea

2. A person who does not allow philosophy to help shape his life lacks
   (A) convictions based on prejudices
   (B) ability to think about the social issues of his time
   (C) beliefs of his age as reflected in the principles of his nation
   (D) knowledge of the rights of man
   (E) opinions arrived at by his independent thinking

3. Philosophy allows us to
   (A) question our doubts in the terms of our certainties

(B) become leaders of the age
(C) examine man's efforts through the ages
(D) follow the true thinking of our leaders
(E) have faith in our own ability to think

4. This selection lacks
   (A) generalizations
   (B) abstract terms
   (C) specific examples
   (D) a topic sentence
   (E) a summarizing sentence

5. The first sentence is an example of
   (A) an adage
   (B) an ambiguity
   (C) an analogy
   (D) a paradox
   (E) parallelism

6. The tone of the passage is best termed
   (A) scornful
   (B) amused
   (C) meditative
   (D) impassioned
   (E) judgmental

Questions 7–11

Bright be the place of thy soul!
  No lovelier spirit than thine
E'er burst from its mortal control,
  In the orbs of the blessed to shine.
On earth thou wert all but divine,
  As thy soul shall immortally be;
And our sorrow may cease to repine
  When we know that thy God is with thee.
Light be the turf of thy tomb!
  May its verdure like emeralds be!
There should not be the shadow of gloom
  In aught that reminds us of thee.
Young flowers and an evergreen tree
  May spring from the spot of thy rest:
But nor cypress nor yew let us see;
  For why should we mourn for the blest?

7. This poem does not contain
   (A) traditional expressions of sorrow
   (B) belief in immortality of the soul
   (C) personal sorrow
   (D) religious faith
   (E) religous resignation

8. This poem is written in
   (A) rhymed couplets
   (B) rhymed quatrains
   (C) iambic pentameters
   (D) free verse
   (E) alexandrines

9. The entire poem is
   (A) an apostrophe
   (B) a conceit
   (C) an extended metaphor
   (D) an allegory
   (E) a fable

10. Cypress should be absent from the spot because
    (A) it is a symbol of joy
    (B) it would destroy the beauty of the place
    (C) it would compete with the beauty of the place
    (D) it is too symmetrical
    (E) it is a symbol of sorrow

11. A critical evaluation of this poem must take into consideration
    (A) its frequent cacophony
    (B) its weak rhymes
    (C) its faltering rhythms
    (D) its lack of similes
    (E) its frequent cliches

Questions 12–21

Thus we feed on genius, and refresh ourselves from too much conversation with our mates, and exult in the depth of nature in that direction in which he leads us. What indemnification is one great man for populations of pigmies! Every mother wishes one son a genius, though all the rest should be mediocre. But a new danger appears in the excess of influence of the great man. His attractions warp us from our place. We have become underlings and intellectual suicides. Ah! yonder in the horizon is our help; other great men, new qualities, counterweights and checks on each other. We cloy of the honey of each peculiar greatness. Every hero becomes a bore at last. Perhaps Voltaire was not bad-hearted, yet he said of the good Jesus, even, "I pray you, let me never hear that man's name again." They cry up the virtues of George Washington—"Damn George Washington!" is the poor Jacobin's whole speech and confutation. But it is human nature's indispensable defence. The centripetence augments the centrifugence. We balance one man with his opposite, and the health of the state depends on the see-saw.

There is however a speedy limit to the use of heroes. Every genius is defended from approach by quantities of unavailableness. They are very attractive, and seem at a distance our own: but we are hindered on all sides from approach. The more we are drawn, the more we are repelled. There is something not solid in the good that is done for us. The best discovery the discoverer makes for himself. It has something unreal for his companion until he too has substantiated it. It seems as if the Deity dressed each soul which he sends into nature in certain virtues and powers not communicable to other men, and sending it to perform one more turn through the circle of beings, wrote *"Not transferable"* and *"Good for this trip only,"* on these garments of the soul. There is something deceptive about the intercourse of minds. The boundaries are invisible, but they are never crossed. There is such good will to impart, and such good will to receive, that each threatens to become the other; but the law of individuality collects its secret strength: you are you, and I am I, so we remain.

12. The selection is organized primarily according to the principle of
    (A) saturation that is the author develops an idea, gives an example and then attacks and defends it throughout the rest of the selection
    (B) ambiguity that is the author hints at an idea through the development of a topic sentence and then avoids specific examples and concrete terms so that the writer is compelled to think in and around his idea
    (C) insightfulness, that is the author suggests one facet of an unprovable truth and then goes to an-

other without attempting to link his concepts into a meaningful unit
(D) spatiality in that the author moves from the narrowest confines of an idea out to its most daring implications
(E) counterbalance each facet of his thesis is presented in the order of idea followed by its counter-effect

13. The author equates genius with
(A) mediocrities
(B) heroes
(C) underlings
(D) counterbalances
(E) pigmies

14. Which of the following defines the relationship of the last sentence in paragraph one to the rest of the paragraph?
(A) It contains an example to prove the preceding sentence.
(B) It summarizes the meaning of the entire paragraph.
(C) It serves as a transition to the next paragraph.
(D) It raises the problem that is discussed further in the next paragraph.
(E) It presents the counter-arguments to strengthen the authors thesis.

15. In his evaluation of the influence of geniuses, the author claims
(A) the genius could convert us into automatons, without minds of our own
(B) the geniuses can destroy progress
(C) mediocre people do not admire geniuses
(D) geniuses are a threat to the democratic processes
(E) the genius is power hungry

16. The author tries to convince us that
(A) we should be suspicious of geniuses
(B) we should be suspicious of our own intuitions
(C) geniuses cause waste and destruction in this world
(D) counterforces prevent geniuses from carrying mankind to excesses
(E) certain rights are not transferable

17. In our contacts with other people we should
(A) select our leaders carefully
(B) trust our leaders completely
(C) be glad to follow our leaders
(D) be suspicious of people who attack our leaders
(E) look for direction from everyone

18. We should not fear being misled by our leaders because
(A) they are all men of good will
(B) our intuitions will warn us in time
(C) they are essentially bores
(D) we shall tire of them quickly
(E) their mistakes become known quickly

19. "Every hero becomes a bore at last" is an example a(n)
(A) truism
(B) epigram
(C) blurb
(D) caricature
(E) conceit

20. The tone of the passage is best termed
(A) cynical
(B) amused
(C) detached
(D) scornful
(E) optimistic

21. Through the use of *Thus* as his introductory word, the author
(A) connects the selection with the previous paragraphs
(B) points toward the sentences that follow
(C) summarizes what has preceded this selection
(D) states his conclusion and reasons for it
(E) convinces the reader of the importance of the topic

Questions 22–29

    To fight aloud is very brave,
    But gallanter, I know,
    Who charge within the bosom,
    The cavalry of woe.
5   Who win, and nations do not see,
    Who fall, and none observe,
    Whose dying eyes no country
    Regards with patriot love.
    We trust, in plumed procession,
10   For such the angels go,
    Rank after rank, with even feet
    And uniforms of snow.

22. Which of the following best expresses the main idea of the selection?
(A) The angels are on the side of the brave.
(B) Life for the unknowns requires more courage than life does for the leaders.
(C) Angels set the example for us in our lives.
(D) Heroes' medals are always deserved.
(E) Misfortunes will always beset the common man.

23. *Charge* in line three contains the image of
(A) the debits and credits of a business account
(B) the accusations made by a lawyer for the defense
(C) payments due for an installment account
(D) the rush to enter into battle with an enemy
(E) the accusation one has to face in court in the presence of a judge

24. The second stanza forwards the poet's ideas by
(A) giving examples of the cavalry of woe
(B) showing those who can and do fight aloud
(C) explaining what is meant by patriotic love
(D) explaining why these people are angels
(E) giving examples of those referred to in lines two and three

25. "Uniforms of snow" in the last line is an example of
(A) a metaphor
(B) literal use
(C) litotes
(D) irony
(E) epigram

26. Which of the following is not implied in the final comparison
(A) God's will is in evidence even in the actions of the ordinary people in their moments of trial.

(B) The universality of suffering among men is symbolized by the multitudes of angels.
(C) The suffering we all face in life should not fill us with feelings of guilt.
(D) As men suffer so do the angels.
(E) We must take comfort from the very fact that we are suffering.

27. The tone of the poem is best termed
    (A) joyful
    (B) pessimistic
    (C) resentful
    (D) complacent
    (E) understanding

28. The diction of this passage is best defined as
    (A) oratorical and dogmatic
    (B) philosophical and abstract
    (C) charged and metaphoric
    (D) allegorical and figurative
    (E) simple and ordinary

29. The sentence structure and flow of ideas of this passage are best defined as
    (A) inverted
    (B) direct and simple
    (C) complex and abstruse
    (D) complicated but natural
    (E) dramatic and direct

Questions 30–35

    He that loves a rosy cheek,
      Or a coral lip admires,
    Or from star-like eyes doth seek
      Fuel to maintain his fires:
5 As old Time makes these decay,
    So his flames must waste away.
    But a smooth and steadfast mind,
      Gentle thought and calm desires,
    Hearts with equal love combined,
10   Kindle never-dying fires.
    Where these are not, I despise
    Lovely cheeks or lips or eyes.

30. The underlying subject of the passage is
    (A) beauty is skin deep
    (B) mental stability is the basis of true love
    (C) mental and psychological compatibility are the true basis of love
    (D) physical attraction is not the basis of love
    (E) time conquers all regardless of whether physical or mental or emotional compatibility is present

31. Which of the following best explains the function of the versification of the poem?
    (A) The regularity of the rhythms emphasizes the truth in the conclusion.
    (B) The regularity of the rhymes emphasizes the flow of ideas.
    (C) The rhyming of the last two lines in each stanza serves to help these lines serve as summaries of the thought.
    (D) The lack of variations in rhythm tends to dullen the reader's attention.
    (E) The simplicity of the rhymed pairs are in contrast to the complexity of the author's message.

32. Line five contains an example of
    (A) allusion
    (B) alliteration
    (C) oxymoron
    (D) conceit
    (E) personification

33. The effect of the style is best explained as one that
    (A) reveals how certain the poet was that he was right
    (B) reinforces the complexity of his thought pattern
    (C) reveals how uncertain he was
    (D) proves how deep his distrust for beauty was
    (E) how much he exalted intelligence

34. The third line contains
    (A) a metaphor
    (B) a simile
    (C) comic relief
    (D) a malapropism
    (E) a maxim

35. The first line contains
    (A) dramatic irony
    (B) an epitaph
    (C) a euphemism
    (D) irony
    (E) a cliche

36. The mood of the poet is best interpreted as one of
    (A) awe
    (B) doubt
    (C) excitement
    (D) conviction
    (E) horror

PRACTICE EXAMINATION FOUR

Total Time: One Hour
Time begun . . . . . Time ended . . . . . Time used . . . . .

DIRECTIONS: This test consists of selections from works of literature. Read each passage carefully, and then answer the questions that follow. The questions are based on their content, form, and style. Refer to the passage as many times as necessary before you choose your answers.

Questions 1–8

Among all the famous sayings of antiquity, there is none that does greater honor to the author, or affords greater pleasure to the reader (at least if he be a person of a generous and benevolent heart), than that of the philosopher, who, being asked what "countryman he was," replied, that he was, "a citizen of the world."—How few are there to be found in modern times who can say the same, or whose conduct is consistent with such a profession!—We are now become so much Englishmen, Frenchmen, Dutchmen, Spaniards, or Germans, that we are no longer citizens of the world; so much the natives of one particular spot, or members of one petty society, that we no longer consider ourselves as the general inhabitants of the globe, or members of that grand society which comprehends the whole human kind.

Did these prejudices prevail only among the meanest and lowest of the people, perhaps they might be excused, as they have few, if any, opportunities of correcting them by reading, traveling, or conversing with foreigners; but the misfortune is, that they infect the minds, and influence the conduct, even of our gentlemen; of those, I mean, who have every title to this appellation but an exemption from prejudice, which however, in my opinion, ought to be regarded as the characteristical mark of a gentleman; for let a man's birth be ever so high, his station ever so exalted, or his fortune ever so large, yet if he is not free from national and other prejudices, I should make bold to tell him, that he had a low and vulgar mind, and had no just claim to the character of a gentleman. And in fact, you will always find that those are most apt to boast of national merit, who have little or no merit of their own to depend on; than which, to be sure, nothing is more natural: the slender vine twists around the sturdy oak, for no other reason in the world but because it has not strength sufficient to support itself.

1. All of the sentences in the first paragraph
   (A) are loose sentences
   (B) contain homilies
   (C) are negative in their approach
   (D) are periodic sentences
   (E) contain generalizations

2. The tone of the passage is best termed
   (A) smug
   (B) joyful
   (C) scornful
   (D) elegiac
   (E) exhortative

3. The last sentence contains an example of
   (A) a conceit
   (B) a stereotype
   (C) a maxim
   (D) ambiguity
   (E) an analogy

4. The very last clause contains an example of
   (A) metaphor
   (B) alliteration
   (C) simile
   (D) antonomasia
   (E) anticlimax

5. The first sentence is an example of
   (A) a periodic sentence
   (B) a loose sentence
   (C) oxymoron
   (D) fustian
   (E) irony

6. The author developed the first paragraph through
   (A) the use of specific examples
   (B) logical presentation of counter arguments
   (C) balancing of ideas
   (D) application of the topic sentence to the present
   (E) use of contrast in the effects of the topic sentence

7. The second paragraph supports the main thesis through
   (A) mustering of relevant facts
   (B) disproving basic arguments of the opposition
   (C) statement of specific examples
   (D) citing authority
   (E) relying on namecalling

8. The author does not explain
   (A) what he means by a citzen of the world
   (B) what is wrong with nationalism
   (C) what he means by being a gentleman
   (D) what he means as a basic characteristic of a low and vulgar mind
   (E) how people can develop into being citizens of the world

Questions 9–15

    Do not weep, maiden, for war is kind.
    Because your lover threw wild hands
                          toward the sky
    And the affrighted steed ran on alone,
    Do not weep.
5   War is kind.

    Hoarse, booming drums of the regiment,
    Little souls who thirst for fight,
    These men were born to drill and die.
    The unexplained glory flies above them,
10 Great is the battle-god, great, and his
                          kingdom—
    A field where a thousand corpses lie.

    Do not weep, babe, for war is kind.
    Because your father tumbled in the yellow
                          trenches,
    Raged at his breast, gulped and died,
15 Do not weep.
    War is kind.

    Swift blazing flag of the regiment,
    Eagle with crest of red and gold,
    These men were born to drill and die.
20 Point for them the virtue of slaughter,
    Make plain to them the excellence of
                          killing
    And a field where a thousand corpses lie.

    Mother whose heart hung humble as a
                          button
    On the bright splendid shroud of your son,
25 Do not weep.
    War is kind.

9. Which of the following best expresses the effect of the repetition of the last lines of the first stanza?
   (A) It summarizes the action in the poem.
   (B) It shows the speaker's moral shock.
   (C) It helps place the blame where it should be.

(D) It lessens the tension brought about by the horrors described.
(E) It makes the poem seem unreal.

10. Which of the following is not a device used in stanzas 1, 3, 5 to increase reader reaction?
    (A) irony
    (B) dramatic example
    (C) apostrophe
    (D) simile
    (E) alliteration
11. In the second stanza the poet does not state that
    (A) insignificant men become soldiers
    (B) soldiers are born to be trained and die on the battlefield
    (C) the god of battle increases his kingdom with each battle
    (D) the drums beat a desire to fight into the spirits of the soldiers
    (E) what the men will gain by fighting
12. Line 18 contains
    (A) an allusion
    (B) an epithet
    (C) a euphemism
    (D) fustian
    (E) a flashback
13. Which of the following best explains the effect of the poet's use of cliches throughout the entire poem?
    (A) The cliches weaken the poet's message and destroy its effectiveness.
    (B) The cliches go unnoticed by the reader.
    (C) Because so many of the cliches are deliberately repeated, there is an intensifying of the feeling of horror.
    (D) The cliches allow the poet to express a complex thought simply.
    (E) The reader laughs at the poet's ineptness, because the poem assumes the tone of a folk ballad.
14. The ironic theme of the poem is best stated as
    (A) war must be considered inevitable
    (B) war is really kind in that it provides such an exciting spectacle on the battlefield
    (C) war is kind to the rulers and generals of the world
    (D) children can grow up well in this atmosphere
    (E) people should not weep for soldiers merely because they died
15. Line 23 does not contain an example of
    (A) alliteration
    (B) a metaphor
    (C) a simile
    (D) assonance
    (E) bathetic comparison

Questions 16-22

To those puny objectors against cards, as nurturing the bad passions, she would retort, that man is a gaming animal. He must be always trying to get the better in something or other:—that this passion can scarcely be more safely expended than upon a game at cards: that cards are a temporary illusion; in truth, a mere drama; for we do but *play* at being mightily concerned, where a few idle shillings are at stake, yet, during the illusion, we *are* as mightily concerned as those whose stake is crowns and kingdoms. They are a sort of dream-fighting; much ado; great battling, and little blood shed; mighty means for disproportioned ends; quite as diverting, and a great deal more innocuous, than many of those more serious *games* of life, which men play, without esteeming them to be such.—

With great deference to the old lady's judgment on these matters, I think I have experienced some moments in my life, when playing at cards *for nothing* has even been very agreeable. When I am in sickness, or not in the best spirits, I sometimes call for the cards, and play a game at piquet *for love* with my cousin Bridget—Bridget Elia.

16. Which of the following express the writer's attitude toward the old lady?
    (A) He was thoroughly convinced by her arguments.
    (B) He disagreed with her and told her so.
    (C) When she was in command, he followed her and obeyed, but he let her know that she was morally wrong.
    (D) He never argued with her, but he could also see reasons for disagreeing with her.
    (E) She was a quarrelsome old woman, and he did not want to argue with her.
17. The old woman favored playing cards for money because
    (A) other people did it
    (B) it imitated real life but without damaging penalties
    (C) it gave her a chance to be with people
    (D) the excitement was good for her
    (E) it gave her a chance to analyze people and their motives
18. The first sentence is an example of
    (A) inversion
    (B) a loose sentence
    (C) antithesis
    (D) allusion
    (E) a paraphrase
19. The mood of the writer is best interpreted as one of
    (A) anger
    (B) doubt
    (C) understanding
    (D) surprise
    (E) awe
20. Which of the following best describes the style of the passage?
    (A) It uses simple, direct statements to give clarity to the passage.
    (B) It builds up to climax by placing subordinate clauses first.
    (C) It is telegraphic in that subjects and occasionally predicates are omitted.
    (D) It uses a piling up of clauses to give speed to the direction of the paragraphs.
    (E) It imitates conversation by using italics and parenthetical elements.
21. The effect of the style is best explained as one that
    (A) shows that the sophisticated reader can enjoy this material
    (B) makes the author seem to be an intimate friend of the reader

(C) antagonizes the less sophisticated reader
(D) shows the author as unable to make up his mind
(E) shows that the succeeding generations cannot accept the values of their predecessors

22. A reason for playing cards, acceptable to the author but not mentioned by the old lady was
(A) it is a good way to spend time that is heavy and may become profitable
(B) it can lead to the lessening of tension between relatives and friends
(C) it is good mental exercise
(D) it can help another
(E) it can teach us to get along in polite society

Questions 23–29

    To him who in the love of nature holds
    Communion with her visible forms, she speaks
    A various language; for his gayer hours
    She has a voice of gladness, and a smile
5   And eloquence of beauty, and she glides
    Into his darker musings, with a mild
    And healing sympathy, that steals away
    Their sharpness, ere he is aware. When thoughts
    Of the last bitter hour come like a blight
10 Over thy spirit, and sad images
    Of the stern agony, and shroud, and pall,
    And breathless darkness, and the narrow house,
    Make thee to shudder and grow sick at heart;—
    Go forth, under the open sky, and list
15 To Nature's teachings, while from all around—
    Earth and her waters, and the depths of air—
    Comes a still voice:—

23. The "still voice" that is heard is that of
(A) man speaking to man
(B) conscience speaking to those who can listen
(C) death that comes to all
(D) nature that surrounds us
(E) earth, the mother of us all

24. The underlying subject of the passage is
(A) man's ability to conquer all except personal death
(B) love's ability to help us to live better
(C) man's inhumanity to man
(D) the eternal struggle between the forces of good and of evil
(E) achieving oneness with nature

25. The mood of the selection is best interpreted as one of
(A) excitement
(B) doubt
(C) bravery
(D) agony
(E) sincerity

26. The diction and style of this passage are best defined as
(A) emotional and oratorical
(B) abstract and didactic
(C) oratorical and didactic
(D) ordinary and didactic
(E) abstract and oratorical

27. This poem is written in
(A) trimeters
(B) tetrameters
(C) pentameters
(D) quatrains
(E) couplets

28. Lines 8–10 contain
(A) a metaphor
(B) a simile
(C) a conceit
(D) dramatic irony
(E) an epithet

29. The phrase, "the last bitter hour" is best characterized as a(n)
(A) cliche
(B) euphony
(C) fustian
(D) maxim
(E) malapropism

PRACTICE EXAMINATION FIVE

Total Time: One Hour
Time begun ..... Time ended ..... Time used .....

DIRECTIONS: This test consists of selections from works of literature. Read each passage carefully, and then answer the questions that follow. The questions are based on their content, form, and style. Refer to the passage as many times as necessary before you choose your answers.

Questions 1–8

Our eyes can see nothing behind us. A hundred times a day we laugh at ourselves when we laugh at our neighbors; and we detest in others the faults which are much more glaring in ourselves, and with marvelous impudence and thoughtlessness we express our astonishment at them. Only yesterday I had the opportunity to hear a man, an intelligent and well-mannered person, ridiculing with as much humor as aptness, the fatuity of another who pesters everybody with his pedigrees and his alliances, which are more than half imaginary (for they are most ready to pounce upon this silly subject whose quality is most doubtful and least certain). And this man, if he had retired within himself, would have seen that he was hardly less extravagant and tedious in publishing and extolling his wife's family prerogatives. Oh, the meddlesome presumption with which the wife sees herself armed by the hands of her own husband!

> As if she were not mad enough already,
> You now provoke her to greater madness.
> (Terence)

I do not mean that no man should judge unless he himself be spotless, for then no man could judge; not even if he were free from the same kind of blemish. But I do mean that our judgment, when laying blame on another who is in question, should not save us from self-judgment. It is a charitable office in one who cannot rid himself of a fault to endeavor none the less to rid another of it, in whom it may have taken less deep and stubborn root.

1. The first sentence contains an example of
   (A) a simile
   (B) a pun
   (C) a conceit
   (D) a hyperbole
   (E) a metaphor

2. The tone of the passage is best termed
   (A) naive
   (B) oratorical
   (C) condemnatory
   (D) urbane
   (E) solemn

3. The author's thesis is that
   (A) husbands are no different from all other men
   (B) man is very simple to understand
   (C) we judge others always in terms of ourselves
   (D) man can, when he wants to, be very objective
   (E) we are such poor judges of ourselves

4. The *you* referred to in the quotation applies to
   (A) Terence
   (B) the wife
   (C) the reader
   (D) the well-mannered man
   (E) her husband

5. Which of the following best describes the purpose of the quotation in the selection?
   (A) It serves to prove the preceding sentence by showing how thoughtless wives can be in their criticizing their husbands.
   (B) It serves to prove the second sentence by showing that wives can be provoked into misjudgments by their husbands' laughter.
   (C) It serves to prove the truth in the sentence that follows the quotation by proving that only those without fault can judge others.
   (D) It is a serious indictment of marriage.
   (E) It serves to prove the truth in the preceding sentence that husbands' are responsible for the distorted views expressed by their wives.

6. Which of the following best expresses the thought development in the selection?
   (A) The author presented his thesis early in the selection and then proceeded to prove it through logic and example, ending with a final summary that brings the reader back to the major premise.
   (B) Through the use of initial definition of terms and examples, the author leads us to a logical acceptance of his thesis in the final sentences.
   (C) He quickly presented an insight that he wanted to impart to the reader, followed it by examples, and then explored kindred aspects through statements and example.
   (D) He took the general topic of laughter and tried to explain it through example and quotation.
   (E) He took the general topic of self-criticism and then wrote in random fashion on whatever thoughts came to him, in a psychological rather than logical fashion.

7. The last sentence is an example of
   (A) an aphorism
   (B) inversion
   (C) a conceit
   (D) conflict
   (E) comic relief

8. The author's attitude toward the reader is best expressed in which of the following statements?
   (A) In his superior wisdom the author attempts to correct the weaknesses of the reader.
   (B) He accepts the reader as an equal who will stand beside him on the sidelines and laugh at his fellowmen.
   (C) He is a master teacher helping his reader find wisdom before he makes mistakes.
   (D) The social evils of the world will be corrected by the reader if the author can make him aware of these evils.
   (E) He sets high standards for the reader and expects him to reach them for the betterment of society.

Questions 9–18

> Skimming lightly, wheeling still,
>   The swallows fly low
> Over the field in clouded days,
>   The forest-field of Shiloh—
> 5 Over the field where April rain
> Solaced the parched one stretched in pain
>   Through the pause of night
> That followed the Sunday fight
>   Around the church of Shiloh—
> 10 The church so lone, the log-built one,
> That echoed to many a parting groan
>   And natural prayer
> Of dying foemen mingled there—
> Foemen at morn, but friends at eve—
> 15   Fame or country least their care:
> (What like a bullet can undeceive!)
>   But now they lie low,
> While over them the swallows skim,
> 20   And all is hushed at Shiloh.

9. Which of the following best explains the function of the images in the poem?
   (A) All of the images are generalized except for the church so that becomes the central image of the poem.
   (B) The images pile up one after the other to emphasize the vastness of the silence that covers the countryside.
   (C) Detail after detail is added to each image so that the image carries the thought content of the poem.

(D) The images are all presented vaguely and simply so that they will not interfere with the message of the poem.
(E) The images logically connect one with the other, one building on the other to bring into focus the last new image presented in the lines 16–20.

10. Line 6 continues examples of
    (A) dramatic irony
    (B) alliteration
    (C) internal rhyme
    (D) denouement
    (E) litotes
11. Line 14 contains an example of
    (A) assonance
    (B) malapropism
    (C) conceit
    (D) paradox
    (E) parable
12. Which of the following best expresses the author's purpose?
    (A) He used expansion of images to clarify the reader's thinking about man and nature.
    (B) He contrasted a series of objective images to show how insignificant man is.
    (C) He contrasted image and style in order to intensify the reader's sense of horror.
    (D) He blended sights and sounds to intensify the idyllic landscape.
    (E) He used peaceful images to lull the reader into an acceptance of his message.
13. Line 16 contains an example of
    (A) a loose sentence
    (B) allegory
    (C) a cliche
    (D) a metaphor
    (E) an analogy
14. A poetic device not used in this selection is
    (A) rhyme
    (B) epithet
    (C) inversion
    (D) apostrophe
    (E) understatement
15. Which of the following expresses the theme of this selection?
    (A) the beauties of the natural scene
    (B) the indestructability of nature
    (C) man's insignificance
    (D) the vastness of nature
    (E) war is wrong
16. The fact that the fighting took place on Sunday is taken advantage of by the poet
    (A) to develop dramatic irony
    (B) to enhance the image of the forest-fields
    (C) to develop the primitiveness of the church
    (D) to set the scene for the battle
    (E) to give the men a chance to pray
17. This selection can be classified as
    (A) dramatic monologue
    (B) soliloquy
    (C) stream of conscience
    (D) a lyric
    (E) none of the above
18. The dominant poetic structure is that of
    (A) blank verse
    (B) free verse
    (C) irregular ballad stanzas
    (D) sonnet form
    (E) polyphonic prose

Questions 19–26

If nature be regarded as the teacher and we poor human beings as her pupils, the human race presents a very curious picture. We all sit together at a lecture and possess the necessary principle for understanding it, yet we always pay more attention to the chatter of our fellow students than to the lecturer's discourse. Or, if our neighbor copies something, we sneak it from him, stealing what he may himself have heard imperfectly, and add to it our own errors of spelling and opinion.

19. Which of the following best explains the structure of this selection?
    (A) Through expansion and example, the author developed his thoughts, leading to his final topic sentence.
    (B) He began with a topic sentence and through examples explained it.
    (C) He began with his topic sentence and through contrast expanded it.
    (D) He presented his thesis and then used logical devlopment to convince the reader.
    (E) He began with his thesis and then used the weight of authority and insight to prove it.
20. Which of the following best expresses the author's contention?
    (A) We are all poor imitators.
    (B) Nature is the best teacher.
    (C) Man is a slow learner.
    (D) Man is a curious animal.
    (E) We should see things for ourselves.
21. The first sentence is an example of
    (A) a loose sentence
    (B) dramatic contrast
    (C) a periodic sentence
    (D) a simple sentence
    (E) climax
22. The lecturer referred to is
    (A) humanity
    (B) the expert
    (C) our neighbor
    (D) time
    (E) nature
23. All three sentences contain
    (A) climax
    (B) anticlimax
    (C) allusion
    (D) generalization
    (E) analogy
24. We human beings are "poor" because
    (A) we are economically deprived
    (B) we have so little in comparison to what nature has
    (C) we have such little understanding
    (D) we have so little strength to cope with the forces of nature
    (E) we are always so envious of others in our fight for survival

25. The tone of this selection can best be described as
    (A) cynical
    (B) joyful
    (C) indignant
    (D) philosophical
    (E) solemn
26. The approach of the author is
    (A) destructive
    (B) positive
    (C) negative
    (D) neutral
    (E) non-judgmental

Questions 27–40

```
     I had been hungry all the years;
     My noon had come, to dine;
     I, trembling, drew the table near,
 4   And touched the curious wine.

     'Twas this on tables I had seen,
     When turning, hungry, lone,
     I looked in windows, for the wealth
 8   I could not hope to own.

     I did not know the ample bread,
     'Twas so unlike the crumb
     The birds and I had often shared
12   In Nature's dining-room.

     The plenty hurt me, 'twas so new,—
     Myself felt ill and odd,
     As berry of a mountain bush
16   Transplanted to the road.

     Nor was I hungry; so I found
     That hunger was a way
     Of persons outside windows,
20   The entering takes away.
```

27. The poet's main idea may best be expressed as
    (A) Ambition can drive us along many strange paths.
    (B) Often we desire most that which we really do not want.
    (C) We soon learn that our ideals have feet of clay.
    (D) The striving for is more rewarding than accomplishment.
    (E) The striving is more satisfying than the reward itself.
28. The bread and wine mentioned in this poem were
    (A) the symbols of a religious service
    (B) things she needed for survival
    (C) the beauties of nature
    (D) the goals she had sought
    (E) the material aspects of life
29. The poem is organized primarily according to the principle of
    (A) chronology in that it presents each of the events in the order in which it occurred
    (B) cause and effect in that it shows what the poet did to bring about each of the results
    (C) derivation in that she presents a concrete situation and then evolves a principle to explain it
    (D) exemplification in that the poet presented a statement and then proceded to prove it through example
    (E) classification in that she attempted to sort out the different attitudes man and nature would have under these circumstances
30. The mood in lines 8–11 is one of
    (A) hope
    (B) envy
    (C) joy
    (D) despair
    (E) love
31. Line 16 contains an example of
    (A) conceit
    (B) metaphor
    (C) poetic license
    (D) litotes
    (E) simile
32. The first line must be taken
    (A) figuratively
    (B) literally
    (C) joyfully
    (D) ironically
    (E) philosophically
33. Line ten contains an example of
    (A) analogy
    (B) allusion
    (C) dramatic irony
    (D) apostrophe
    (E) adage
34. Line 13 contains an example of
    (A) simile
    (B) allegory
    (C) poetic license
    (D) circumlocution
    (E) caricature
35. Line 2 implies that
    (A) success had come to her slowly
    (B) she had despaired of ever being successful
    (C) success had come to her too late in life
    (D) success had come to her suddenly
    (E) success had come to her after striving for it
36. The comparison between the poet and birds in lines 11–12 is
    (A) apt because it makes the reader sense the poet's closeness to nature
    (B) is awkward since the reader is given a ludicrous image
    (C) is striking because of the implied comparison between nature's vastness and man's unlimited potential
    (D) is effective because it shows how puny the poet and birds are
    (E) is ineffective because it does not help to develop the ideas of the poem
37. The comparison between the poet and the berry of a mountain bush in the fourth stanza
    (A) emphasizes the difficulties she had gone through
    (B) deemphasizes the role she has been playing
    (C) stresses the duration of the apprenticeship period
    (D) emphasizes the insignificance of success and her feeling of inadequacy
    (E) emphasizes the change in circumstances

38. The diction of the selection is best defined as mainly
    (A) formal and emotional
    (B) symbolic and dialectal
    (C) colloquial and florid
    (D) nonstandard and abstract
    (E) colloquial and philosophical

39. A poetic device not used in this selection is
    (A) inversion
    (B) metaphor
    (C) dramatic irony
    (D) cliche
    (E) condensation

40. The poet's purpose was to
    (A) present a social problem and convince the reader to take sides
    (B) show the beauty of nature so that all can enjoy
    (C) express a deep felt emotional reaction to be shared with the reader
    (D) share an insight with the reader
    (E) delight the reader through the presentation of a pleasing realization

PRACTICE EXAMINATION SIX

Total Time: One Hour
Time begun ..... Time ended ..... Time used .....

DIRECTIONS: This test consists of selections from works of literature. Read each passage carefully, and then answer the questions that follow. The questions are based on their content, form, and style. Refer to the passage as many times as necessary before you choose your answers.

Questions 1–11

The great variety of taste, as well as of opinion, which prevails in the world is too obvious not to have fallen under everyone's observation. Men of the most confined knowledge are able to remark a difference of taste in the narrow circle of their acquaintance, even where the persons have been educated under the same government, and have early imbibed the same prejudices. But those who can enlarge their view to contemplate distant nations and remote ages are still more surprised at the great inconsistence and contrariety. We are apt to call *barbarous* whatever departs widely from our own taste and apprehension, but soon find the epithet of reproach retorted on us. And the highest arrogance and self-conceit is at last startled on observing an equal assurance on all sides, and scruples, amidst such a contest of sentiment, to pronounce positively in its own favor.

As this variety of taste is obvious to the most careless enquirer, so will it be found, on examination, to be still greater in reality than in appearance. The sentiments of men often differ with regard to beauty and deformity of all kinds, even while their general discourse is the same. There are certain terms in every language which import blame, and other praise; and all men who use the same tongue must agree in their application of them. Every voice is united in applauding elegance, propriety, simplicity, spirit in writing; and in blaming fustian, affectation, coldness, and a false brilliancy. But when critics come to particulars, this seeming unanimity vanishes; and it is found that they had affixed a very different meaning to their expressions. In all matters of opinion and science, the case is opposite: the difference among men is there oftener found to lie in generals than in particulars, and to be less in reality than in appearance. An explanation of the terms commonly ends the controversy, and the disputants are surprised to find that they had been quarreling, while at bottom they agreed in their judgment.

1. The general topic discussed in this selection is
   (A) the causes for the differences in taste among men
   (B) variety is the spice of life
   (C) analyzing men and their ideas
   (D) tastes and opinions
   (E) beauty and deformity in opinions

2. The author's thesis is that
   (A) There is a great variety in taste and opinion
   (B) There is a greater variety in taste than in opinion
   (C) There is a greater variety in opinion than taste
   (D) We cannot quarrel with others in terms of taste
   (E) Everything is relative

3. In his discussion of the word *barbarous*, the author points out
   (A) that *barbarous* is a non-judgmental term
   (B) that barbarous people disagree with us
   (C) that *unfamiliar* and *barbarous* are often synonymous
   (D) that we ourselves are *barbarous*
   (E) that *barbarous* endangers world understanding

4. Which of the following is a characteristic of *taste* that is not mentioned in the selection?
   (A) There is difference of taste even among those brought up in the most isolated, small village.
   (B) Each thinks himself the correct one in matters of taste.
   (C) Even the terms used to describe evaluations in taste do not have common definitions.
   (D) We tend to condemn that which is unfamiliar.
   (E) Modern means of communication have been lessening the taste gap.

5. The first sentence of the second paragraph is an example of
   (A) a periodic sentence
   (B) a loose sentence
   (C) coherence

(D) cacophony
(E) cliche
6. A term that is not labeled as condemnatory in this selection is
   (A) fustian
   (B) prejudice
   (C) self-conceit
   (D) elegance
   (E) assurance
7. A term that the author considers neutral is
   (A) deformity
   (B) propriety
   (C) inconsistence
   (D) fustian
   (E) simplicity
8. According to the author, people who find that they have differing opinions should
   (A) avoid trying to convince the other of his error
   (B) begin to define the words basic to the contention
   (C) enlarge their views to contemplate larger issues
   (D) cite their proofs objectively
   (E) look for an authority upon whom both sides can agree
9. The attitude of the author can best be characterized as
   (A) cynical
   (B) smug
   (C) uncertain
   (D) awed
   (E) optimistic
10. A device *not* used in this selection is
    (A) generalization
    (B) illustrations
    (C) topic sentences
    (D) rhetorical questions
    (E) judgments
11. According to the author, taste differs from opinion in that
    (A) taste is not personalized while opinion is
    (B) opinion depends upon where we were born and taste depends on our likes and dislikes
    (C) variety in taste is much more obvious than variety in opinion
    (D) opinion can be changed through discussion while taste can be changed through experiencing
    (E) the terms of opinion are more subjective than are the terms of taste

Questions 12–20

   For while the tired waves, vainly breaking
      Seem here no painful inch to gain,
   Far back, through creeks and inlets making,
4   Comes silent, flooding in, the main
   And not by eastern windows only,
      When daylight comes, comes in the light,
   In front the sun climbs slow, how slowly,
8   But westward, look, the land is bright.

12. The mood of this selection is one of
    (A) doubt
    (B) hesitation
    (C) optimism
    (D) awe
    (E) surprise

13. Line 2 contains an example of
    (A) litotes
    (B) metaphor
    (C) alliteration
    (D) cliche
    (E) irony
14. Literally the *main* is
    (A) the masses of humanity
    (B) the ocean
    (C) the principles of life
    (D) sunlight
    (E) land mass
15. Which of the following best expresses the main idea of the selection?
    (A) Man cannot live by fear and anxiety.
    (B) We should not concern ourselves over details.
    (C) Nature is our ally.
    (D) Progress is a slow process.
    (E) In our concern over what we see, we miss the greater significances.
16. Line 1 does not contain an example of
    (A) alliteration
    (B) assonance
    (C) epithet
    (D) rhymed word
    (E) simile
17. The thought content in each stanza is developed through
    (A) inversion and contrast
    (B) parallelism and figurative language
    (C) repetition of image and detail
    (D) detail and adjectival emphasis
    (E) rhyme and movement
18. Which of the following best explains the versification of the poem?
    (A) Its increasing regularity imitates the natural phenomena described.
    (B) The metrical differences from line to line show the movement of masses of humanity from event to event.
    (C) The alternation of line length suggests the alternation of events in life itself.
    (D) Its variations in rhythm echo the flow of emotion of the people involved.
    (E) The metrical differences from line to line interfere with the communication of thought from the poem to the reader.
19. Which of the following statements best characterizes an aspect of line 7?
    (A) The sudden introduction of the sun changes the thought development.
    (B) The majestic description of the rising sun illuminates the author's message.
    (C) The use of alliteration causes the line to imitate the speed of the sun.
    (D) The use of inversion adds awe and power to the sight of the rising sun.
    (E) The sun is brought into sharp contrast to the tired waves.
20. Which of the following statements best characterizes line 8?
    (A) Through contrast with the image in line 4, the author adds detail to his imagery.
    (B) Through repetition of inversion, the poet defines his terms.

(C) Through imitation of natural movement, he clarifies his purpose.
(D) Through parallelism with the image in line 4, the poet widens the implications in the selection.
(E) Through alliteration the poet shows the narrowing spotlight of reality.

Questions 21–30

Thoreau had no humor, and this implies that he was a sorry logician. Himself an artist in rhetoric, he confounds thought with style when he undertakes to speak of the latter. He was forever talking of getting away from the world, but he must be always near enough to it, nay, to the Concord corner of it, to feel the impression he makes there. He verifies the shrewd remark of Sainte-Beuve, "On touche encore à son temps et trèsfort, même quand on le repousse."[1] This egotism of his is a Stylites pillar after all, a seclusion which keeps him in the public eye. The dignity of man is an excellent thing, but therefore to hold one's self too sacred and precious is the reverse of excellent. There is something delightfully absurd in six volumes addressed to a world of such "vulgar fellows" as Thoreau affirmed his fellowmen to be. I once had a glimpse of a genuine solitary who spent his winters one hundred and fifty miles beyond all human communication, and there dwelt with his rifle as his only confidant. Compared with this, the shanty on Walden Pond has something the air, it must be confessed, of the Hermitage of La Chevrette. I do not believe that the way to a true cosmopolitanism carries one into the woods or the society of musquashes. Perhaps the narrowest provincialism is that of Self; that of Kleinwinkel is nothing to it. The natural man, like the singing birds, comes out of the forest as inevitably as the natural bear and the wildcat stick there. To seek to be natural implies a consciousness that forbids all naturalness forever. It is as easy—and no easier—to be natural in a *salon* as in a swamp, if one does not aim at it, for what we call unnaturalness always has its spring in a man's thinking too much about himself. "It is impossible," said Turgot, "for a vulgar man to be simple."

21. Which of the following best expresses the development of the thought content of the selection?
    (A) Through causality, the author associates cause and effect to develop his thesis.
    (B) Through concretization, he delivers generalization followed by example to prove his thesis.
    (C) Through explication, he cites authority and example to explain his topic sentence.
    (D) Through partition, he divides each aspect of the discussion into small aspects and then cites authority to prove his contention.
    (E) Through assimilation, he begins with specific examples, quotations, and generalizations to reach his climactic conclusion.

22. The attitude of the writer toward Thoreau is best characterized by which of the following?
    (A) admiring
    (B) caustic
    (C) genial
    (D) confused
    (E) objective

23. The writer characterizes Thoreau as
    (A) a solitary genius
    (B) a natural man
    (C) a misunderstood mystic
    (D) a sophisticated cosmopolite
    (E) a confused thinker

24. The basic contradiction in Thoreau according to this critic lies in
    (A) Thoreau's living one hundred and fifty miles away from all human communication.
    (B) Thoreau's having a rifle as his only companion.
    (C) Thoreau's coming out of the forest
    (D) Thoreau's selection of Walden
    (E) Thoreau's writing about his experiences

25. To support his contentions, the writer of this selection did not resort to
    (A) authority
    (B) allusions
    (C) ridicule
    (D) using Thoreau's writing to prove his point
    (E) defining his terms

26. The writer is not critical of Thoreau's
    (A) way of life
    (B) expressed philosophy
    (C) style of dress
    (D) subject matter
    (E) appeal to his readers

27. An ironic aspect of this selection is that
    (A) Thoreau did not have a chance to answer the critic
    (B) the critic goes out of his way to prove that he himself has a sense of humor
    (C) Walden has survived this criticism
    (D) the natural man can live in the city as well as the country
    (E) logic is of little concern to a writer

28. According to this critic
    (A) provincialism is unrelated to solitariness
    (B) cosmopolitanism depends upon cities
    (C) egotism develops in the public eye
    (D) naturalism does not depend on provincialism or cosmopolitanism
    (E) naturalism develops from self-consciousness

29. The critic implies that the Hermitage of La Chevrette was
    (A) anything but popular
    (B) anything but natural
    (C) anything but provincial
    (D) anything but cosmopolitan
    (E) anything but solitary

30. The author deduces that Thoreau could not be a hermit because
    (A) Thoreau really did not want to be one
    (B) society admired Thoreau too much
    (C) New Englanders of the time were dependent on each other
    (D) Thoreau did not know what he wanted to be
    (E) he had too many companions

[1] We are still very much a part of our time, even when we reject it.

PRACTICE EXAMINATION SEVEN

Total Time: One Hour
Time begun ..... Time ended ..... Time used .....

DIRECTIONS: This test consists of selections from works of literature. Read each passage carefully, and then answer the questions that follow. The questions are based on their content, form, and style. Refer to the passage as many times as necessary before you choose your answers.

Questions 1–15

"Suddenly, just as it reached me, Sam, perhaps frightened by the noise and wanting to get to me, dashed in front of it. The hoof of one of the horses knocked him over; I saw him roll, somersault, get up and fall again amid the forest of legs; the whole bus gave two great bumps and I saw behind it something writhing in the dust. He was almost severed in two; his belly was torn open and his entrails were hanging out, spouting blood. He tried to get up and walk, but he could only move his fore legs, which scrabbled at the ground; his hind quarters were already dead. And he was howling pitiably, mad with pain.

"In a minute or two he was dead. I cannot describe my feelings and how much I was affected. I could not leave my room for a month.

"One evening my father, who was furious with me for making such a fuss over such a little thing, cried: 'What will you do when you have a real sorrow, if you lose a wife or children?'

"In a flash I began to understand myself. I realized why little everyday troubles assumed catastrophic proportions in my eyes; I saw that I was so constituted that I felt everything over-keenly and was hyper-susceptible to painful impressions, which were intensified by my abnormal sensitiveness; and a paralysing fear of life gripped me.

"I was without physical desires or ambition; so I decided to sacrifice the possibility of happiness to the certainty of suffering. 'Life is short; I will devote myself to the service of others; I will soothe their sorrows and rejoice in their happiness,' I said to myself. 'As I shall not feel either myself directly, I shall experience these emotions only with diminished intensity.'

"And if you only knew how suffering still tortures me and wrings my heart! But what would have been intolerable agony in my own case has been sublimated into sympathy and pity.

"I could never have endured the sorrow with which I come into contact every day had it been my own. I could not have seen a child of my own die without dying myself. And, in spite of everything I still have such an undefined, subconscious fear of something happening, that the sight of the postman coming to my door sends a shiver down my spine, though now I have nothing to fear."

The Abbé Mauduit fell silent. He was looking into the fire in the great fireplace, as if seeking to read there all the mysteries and secrets of the life he might have lived, if he had faced suffering more bravely. He went on in a lower voice:

"I was right; I am not made to live in this world."

The Comtesse said nothing; at last, after a long silence, she commented:

"As for me, if I had not got my grandchildren, I don't think I should have the courage to go on living."

The Curé got up without another word.

As the servants in the kitchen were asleep, she took him herself to the door into the garden and watched his tall, slow-moving shadow in the light of his lantern plunge into the darkness.

Then she went back and sat down by the fire, and thought of many things that do not occur to the young.

1. Sam was the speaker's
   (A) brother
   (B) companion
   (C) father
   (D) dog
   (E) horse

2. Sam was killed by
   (A) a passing truck
   (B) a passing coach
   (C) a team of wild horses
   (D) a pack of horses
   (E) men on horseback

3. The accident had most likely taken place
   (A) in the woods
   (B) on a farm
   (C) in a big city
   (D) along a country road
   (E) near the school house

4. The author included all of the gory details
   (A) to arouse reader sympathy for Sam
   (B) to arouse reader sympathy for the Curé
   (C) to disgust the reader
   (D) to prepare the reader for the Curé's revelations
   (E) to arouse the reader's curiosity

5. The Curé had become a priest in order
   (A) to feel the sufferings of others
   (B) to avoid being involved in the lives of others
   (C) to avoid the responsibility of bringing up his own family
   (D) to find financial security
   (E) to be an onlooker rather than a participant

6. The writer characterized the Curé as a man
   (A) who was extremely selfish
   (B) with great ambition
   (C) with great sensitivity
   (D) with unusual intelligence
   (E) incapable of realizing his dreams

7. The reader is not alienated from the Curé because
   (A) the Curé is so frank in his revelation of his self-centeredness

(B) the Curé meant no harm to others during his career
(C) the Curé is such a weak character
(D) the Curé does not ask for our sympathy
(E) the Curé did devote his life to helping others

8. The Curé's father had wanted him to
(A) be more outgoing in his relations with others
(B) be more considerate of the feelings of his parents
(C) stop feeling guilty about an unfortunate coincidence
(D) harden himself to the misfortunes that are part of living
(E) have the sense of proportion that adults have

9. The author did not have the Curé's companion interrupt his revelations
(A) because she really did not have anything to say
(B) because she was shocked by his statements
(C) because the author wanted to catch the reader unawares when she begins to talk
(D) because he was more sympathetic to the Curé than to the Comtesse
(E) because he thought the Curé more important

10. The Curé is an example of a
(A) dynamic character
(B) stereotype
(C) antagonist
(D) stock character
(E) static character

11. The Curé and the Comtesse
(A) had many of life's struggles in common
(B) were both elderly
(C) had great respect for each other
(D) had met after many years of separation
(E) disliked each other

12. The climax of the story is reached when
(A) the Comtesse speaks
(B) the Curé leaves
(C) the Comtesse went back to the fireplace
(D) Sam died
(E) the Curé looks into her face

13. The Curé's concluding statement shows that
(A) he regrets never having married
(B) he is really in love with the Comtesse
(C) he still mourned for Sam
(D) he regrets his having run away from living his own life
(E) he would have made the same choice a second time

14. The Comtesse's single sentence was planned to
(A) prove how wrong the Curé had been
(B) prove how right the Comtesse had been
(C) contrast her way of life with his
(D) show how much she resented his attitude
(E) draw a moral for the reader

15. This incident most likely occurred
(A) when the Curé visited the Comtesse to comfort her on a loss
(B) when the Curé and the Comtesse had dined together
(C) when the couple met accidentally at a health spa
(D) when the Curé had returned to his native village
(E) when the Curé had come to the Comtesse for a contribution

Questions 16–20

The men and women who make the best boon companions seem to have given up hope of doing something else. They have, perhaps, tried to be poets and painters; they have tried to be actors, scientists, and musicians. But some defect of talent or opportunity has cut them off from their pet ambitions and thus left them with leisure to take an interest in the lives of others. Your ambitious man is selfish. No matter how secret his ambition may be, it makes him keep his thoughts at home. But the heartbroken people—if I may use the word in a mild benevolent sense—the people whose wills are subdued to fate, give us consolation, recognition, and welcome.

16. The best companions, according to this selection are
(A) people who still have their pride and their ambitions
(B) those who are benevolent
(C) those who have succeeded in the arts
(D) those who have secret ambitions
(E) those who recognize their own failures

17. The tone of the passage is best termed
(A) joyful
(B) sincere
(C) solemn
(D) scornful
(E) argumentative

18. For those who would question the meaning of *boon*, the author explains the words in terms of
(A) poets and painter
(B) pet ambitions
(C) consolation, recognition, and welcome
(D) ambitious man
(E) defect of talent or opportunity

19. The first sentence is an example of
(A) an allegory
(B) a maxim
(C) an epitaph
(D) a proverb
(E) an epigram

20. A boon companion must be
(A) trustworthy
(B) secretive
(C) interesting
(D) open
(E) lively

Questions 21–26

I have not told my garden yet,
Lest that should conquer me;
I have not quite the strength now
4   To break it to the bee.
I will not name it in the street,
For shops would stare, that I,

```
             So shy, so very ignorant,
  8          Should have the face to die.
             The hillsides must not know it,
             Where I have rambled so,
             Nor tell the loving forests
 12          The day that I shall go,
             Nor lisp it at the table,
             Nor heedless by the way
             Hint that within the riddle
 16          One will walk to-day!
```

21. The poem deals with
    (A) love
    (B) eternity
    (C) nature
    (D) death
    (E) joy

22. The thought of the poem is revealed
    (A) in line one
    (B) in line 16
    (C) in the first stanza
    (D) not until the last stanza
    (E) in lines 6–8

23. The attribution of human qualities to the non-human stresses
    (A) the poet's interests in the world around her
    (B) nature's love of all human beings
    (C) the folly of man's efforts to control nature
    (D) that man alone knows the inevitability of death
    (E) that nature is not concerned about man

24. Line 16 contains
    (A) a euphemism
    (B) a simile
    (C) a conceit
    (D) an allegory
    (E) oxymoron

25. The mood of the poet is one of
    (A) acceptance
    (B) rebellion
    (C) expectancy
    (D) desire
    (E) anguish

26. The diction and tone of this selection are best characterized as
    (A) simple and intimate
    (B) studied and ornate
    (C) didactic and philosophical
    (D) purposive and moralistic
    (E) indirect and studied

Questions 27–33

Subjects are apt to be as arbitrary in their censure as the most assuming kings can be in their power. If there might be matter for objections, there is not less reason for excuses; the defects laid to his charge are such as may claim indulgence from mankind.

Should nobody throw a stone at his faults but those who are free from them, there would be but a slender shower.

What private man will throw stones at him because he loved, or what prince because he dissembled?

If he either trusted, or forgave his enemies, or in some cases neglected his friends, more than could be in strictness be allowed, let not those errors be so arraigned as to take away the privilege that seemeth to be due to princely frailties. If princes are under the misfortune of being accused to govern ill, their subjects have the less right to fall hard upon them, since they generally do so little to be governed well.

The truth is, the calling of a king, with all its glittering, hath such an unreasonable weight upon it that they may rather expect to be lamented than to be envied for being set upon a pinnacle, where they are exposed to censure if they do not do more to answer men's expectations than corrupted nature will allow.

It is but justice therefore to this Prince to give all due softenings to the less shining part of his life; to offer flowers and leaves to hide, instead of using aggravations to expose them.

Let his royal ashes then lie soft upon him, and cover him from harsh and unkind censures; which though they should not be unjust, can never clear themselves from being unfitting.

27. The selection comes from a larger work that
    (A) evaluates the role of subjects and kings
    (B) evaluates a specific king
    (C) praises the power of the people to choose kings
    (D) laments the weaknesses in kings
    (E) shows the advantage of democracy over monarchy

28. This king did not
    (A) place his trust in the wrong people
    (B) show ingratitude to his friends
    (C) rise above pettiness
    (D) make errors that angered his subjects
    (E) expose his weaknesses to his subjects

29. The writer asks that a king be excused because
    (A) he is a human being
    (B) he tried his best
    (C) he was not worthy of the office
    (D) he did not seek this high office
    (E) his enemies were too numerous

30. This selection was most likely part of
    (A) a novel
    (B) a eulogy
    (C) a soliloquy
    (D) an epigram
    (E) an allegory

31. The diction and style of the passage are best defined as
    (A) emotional and metaphorical
    (B) detached and judgmental
    (C) solemn and formal
    (D) oratorical and funereal
    (E) abstract and philosophical

32. Which of the following best expresses the thought sequence of the selection?
    (A) The topic sentence is followed by amplification and explication.
    (B) A series of provable statements are tied into acceptable generalizations
    (C) A topic sentence is followed by a series of generalization that the writer hopes will prove the topic sentence and the conclusion and summary of action that should result.

(D) Through the use of contrast and amplification, the author proves the thesis developed in the topic sentence and repeated in conclusion.

(E) Through inference and example, the author leads the reader to the topic sentence contained in the final paragraph.

33. The sentence beginning with "What private man will throw stones . . ." is an example of
    (A) dramatic irony
    (B) a rhetorical question
    (C) poetic license
    (D) an apostrophe
    (E) a cliche

PRACTICE EXAMINATION EIGHT

Total Time: One Hour
Time begun ..... Time ended ..... Time used .....

DIRECTIONS: This test consists of selections from works of literature. Read each passage carefully, and then answer the questions that follow. The questions are based on their content, form, and style. Refer to the passage as many times as necessary before you choose your answers.

Let us spend one day as deliberately as Nature, and not be thrown off the track by every nutshell and mosquito's wing that falls on the rails. Let us rise early and fast, or break fast, gently and without perturbation; let company come and let company go, let the bells ring and the children cry,—determined to make a day of it. Why should we knock under and go with the stream? Let us not be upset and overwhelmed in that terrible rapid and whirlpool called a dinner, situated in the meridian shallows. Weather this danger and you are safe, for the rest of the way is down hill. With unrelaxed nerves, with morning vigor, sail by it, looking another way, tied to the mast like Ulysses. If the engine whistles, let it whistle till it is hoarse for its pains. If the bell rings, why should we run? We will consider what kind of music they are like. Let us settle ourselves, and work and wedge our feet downward through the mud and slush of opinion, and prejudice, and tradition, and delusion, and appearance, that alluvion which covers the globe, through Paris and London, through New York and Boston and Concord, through church and state, through poetry and philosophy and religion, till we come to a hard bottom and rocks in place, which we can call *reality*, and say, This is, and no mistake; and then begin, having a *point d'appui*, below freshet and frost and fire, a place where you might found a wall or a state, or set a lamp-post safely, or perhaps a gauge, not a Nilometer, but a Realometer, that future ages might know how deep a freshet of shams and appearances had gathered from time to time. If you stand right fronting and face to face to a fact, you will see the sun glimmer on both its surfaces, as if it were a scimitar, and feel its sweet edge dividing you through the heart and marrow, and so you will happily conclude your mortal career. Be it life or death, we crave only reality. If we are really dying, let us hear the rattle in our throats and feel cold in the extremities; if we are alive, let us go about our business.

Time is but the stream I go a-fishing in. I drink at it; but while I drink I see the sandy bottom and detect how shallow it is. Its thin current slides away, but eternity remains. I would drink deeper; fish in the sky, whose bottom is pebbly with stars. I cannot count one. I know not the first letter of the alphabet. I have always been regretting that I was not as wise as the day I was born. The intellect is a cleaver; it discerns and rifts its way into the secret of things. I do not wish to be any more busy with my hands than is necessary. My head is hands and feet. I feel all my best faculties concentrated in it. My instinct tells me that my head is an organ for burrowing, as some creatures use their snout and fore-paws, and with it I would mine and burrow my way through these hills. I think that the richest vein is somewhere hereabouts; so by the divining rod and thin rising vapors I judge; and here I will begin to mine.

1. According to this selection our major goal as human beings is to
    (A) avoid the responsibilities placed on us
    (B) fill our thoughts with nature
    (C) find out from others what they think is best
    (D) wander around the countryside
    (E) be aware ever of the passing time

2. He feels that he was wiser the day he was born than he is today because
    (A) he was fully protected from the evils of society then
    (B) his mind had not been corrupted by society
    (C) he was a feeling and not thinking creature
    (D) he had people who loved him
    (E) he had much time to his credit

3. An act that he would not consider "going with the stream" would be
    (A) rushing off to work
    (B) preparing a formal dinner
    (C) making a shopping list
    (D) watching a robin feed its young
    (E) reading the morning newspaper

4. According to the writer, we can find *reality* through
    (A) reading and thinking
    (B) relaxing and feeling
    (C) experiencing
    (D) thinking and feeling
    (E) avoiding our fellow men

5. The last sentence is meant to be taken
    (A) literally
    (B) figuratively
    (C) humorously
    (D) cynically
    (E) whimsically

6. The diction and style of this passage are best defined as
   (A) allegorical and didactic
   (B) emotional and florid
   (C) oratorical and pretentious
   (D) abstract and philosophical
   (E) concrete and didactic

7. The rails mentioned in the first sentence contains the image of
   (A) a subway train chugging into a station
   (B) a locomotive pulling the freight trains
   (C) one of the supports of a picket fence
   (D) a path through the woods
   (E) the road of living

8. Which of the following best explains the author's method of development?
   (A) He begins with a concrete example and then applies it with an overlay of abstractions or metaphorical analogies.
   (B) He condemns what we do and then shows us what we should be doing by proving that our procedure is wrong.
   (C) He begins with a fact and then uses reasoning to show us how to apply it to our daily living.
   (D) He involves himself with feelings and ideals and conveys them to us in directives.
   (E) He negatively attacks without showing us how to overcome the evils he has exposed.

9. The tone achieved by the author is deliberately developed through
   (A) detached observations
   (B) startling generalizations
   (C) distorted values
   (D) sophisticated judgments
   (E) revelation of partial truths

10. The first sentence of the second paragraph is an example of
    (A) a maxim
    (B) an analogy
    (C) metaphorical language
    (D) deliberate exaggeration
    (E) studied affectation

11. The author fears most
    (A) contact with his fellow men
    (B) being filled with superstitions
    (C) dying
    (D) living routinely
    (E) what others will think of him

12. Which of the following best explains the relationship of the second paragraph to the first?
    (A) The second paragraph contains the application of principles listed in the first.
    (B) The second paragraph contains the proof needed to show the truths contained in the first.
    (C) The second paragraph is merely a repetition of the ideas in the first paragraph and adds nothing to the reader's understanding of the first.
    (D) The second paragraph contains the philosophical base upon which the first is based.
    (E) The second paragraph acts as a transition to the new idea that is to be developed in the next paragraph.

Questions 13–20

You are not to consider that every new and personal beauty in art abrogates past achievement as an Act of Parliament does preceding ones, or that it is hostile to the past. You are to consider these beauties, these innovations, as enrichments, as variations, as additions to an existing family. How barbarous you would seem if you were unable to bestow your admiration and affection on a fascinating child in the nursery without at once finding yourselves compelled to rush downstairs and cut its mother's throat, and stifle its grandmother. These ladies may still have their uses.

13. Which of the following best explains the organization pattern of the selection?
    (A) selectivity, that is the author stresses one detail in the first sentence and then develops and enhances that detail in the remaining sentences
    (B) application, that is the author states a basic principle in the initial sentence and then applies it to prove its worth
    (C) *reductio ad absurdam*, that is the author presents an idea and then proves it worthless by citing inapplicable extremes
    (D) universality, that is the author presents a fact as a premise and then shows its lasting truth through examples
    (E) explication, that is the author presents a statement in the first sentence and then proceeds to explain and illustrate that one idea

14. The first sentence contains an example of
    (A) analogy
    (B) condensation
    (C) dramatic irony
    (D) climax
    (E) cliche

15. The third sentence contains an example of
    (A) hyperbole
    (B) *reductio ad absurdam*
    (C) irony
    (D) journalese
    (E) homily

16. Which of the following statements best states the thesis of this selection?
    (A) Artists rebel against the traditions of the preceding generations.
    (B) Beauty in art is a changeable concept.
    (C) Art has values that transcend all movements.
    (D) The artist consciously avoids imitation.
    (E) The progress of art is a continuum.

17. The author mentions *Act of Parliament* to develop his idea through
    (A) example
    (B) confrontation
    (C) explication
    (D) contrast
    (E) expansion

18. Which of the following best expresses the effect of the last sentence?
    (A) It adds to the intense horror in the example.
    (B) It assures the sophisticated reaction to the example by the reader.
    (C) It adds humor to intensify the effect of the preceding sentence.

(D) It adds a final example to further prove the validity of the author's premise.
(E) It adds the necessary fact to prove what precautions are necessary.

19. The child in the nursery is compared to
(A) an Act of Parliament
(B) the artist
(C) the work of young artists
(D) personal beauty
(E) past achievement

20. Which of the following best describes the comparison in the third sentence?
(A) inappropriate and in bad taste
(B) accurate and harmonious
(C) startling but appropriate
(D) absurd and nauseating
(E) confused and vulgar

Questions 21–28

Whether on earth, in air or main,
Sure everything alive is vain!
   Does not the hawk all fowls survey
As destined only for his prey?
5 And do not tyrants, prouder things,
Think men were born for slaves to kings?
   When the crab views the pearly strands,[1]
Or Tagus[2] bright with golden sands,
Or crawls beside the coral grove
10 And hears the ocean roll above,
"Nature is too profuse," says he,
"Who gave all these to pleasure me!"
   When bordering pinks and roses bloom
And every garden breathes perfume,
15 When peaches glow with sunny dyes,
Like Laura's cheek when blushes rise,
When with huge figs the branches bend,
When clusters from the vine depend,
The snail looks round on flower and tree
20 And cries, "All these were made for me!"

21. The meaning implied by the author's use of *vain* is
(A) foolish
(B) self-centered
(C) useless
(D) autocratic
(E) haughty

22. Which of the following best describes the development of the thought in this selection?
(A) digression, that is the author presents a thesis and then wanders off into various byways suggested by the thesis
(B) analogy, that is the author attempts to prove his thesis by showing comparable situations in which it works
(C) classification, that is the poet neatly puts many things into a group that proves his contention.
(D) chronology, that is he presents each event in order of its occurrence
(E) exemplification, that is he presents a premise and then proceeds to prove it by piling up examples

[1] Oyster beds.
[2] River in Spain and Portugal, renowned for gold dust in its waters.

23. Lines 11–12 contain an example of
(A) a climax
(B) a cliche
(C) an apostrophe
(D) personification
(E) irony

24. This poem is written in
(A) alexandrines
(B) blank verse
(C) heroic verse
(D) sonnet form
(E) free verse

25. This poem can be classified as
(A) a dramatic monologue
(B) a lyric
(C) a threnody
(D) a soliloquy
(E) none of the above

26. Line 15 contains an example of
(A) a conceit
(B) an abstract noun
(C) allusion
(D) inversion
(E) sarcasm

27. Line 16 does not contain an example of
(A) a simile
(B) alliteration
(C) cliche
(D) assonance
(E) rhyme

28. The image generated in the last two lines is
(A) awkward and confused
(B) appropriate and in good taste
(C) dramatic and of questionable taste
(D) absurd and illogical
(E) inaccurate and pointless

Questions 29–34

I saw a man pursuing the horizon;
Round and round they sped.
I was disturbed at this;
I accosted the man.
"It is futile," I said,
"You can never—"
"You lie," he cried,
and ran on.

29. Which of the following best expresses the poet's thesis?
(A) Men spend their lives in trying to obtain the impossible.
(B) Some men try in vain to achieve the impossible.
(C) Some men try in vain to help their fellows.
(D) Only the foolish try to correct others.
(E) It is difficult to make men see the futility in dreams.

30. A device used by the poet in this poem is
(A) simile
(B) dramatization
(C) personification
(D) metaphor
(E) litotes

31. This poem is written in

(A) blank verse
(B) polyphonic prose
(C) free verse
(D) heroic couplets
(E) none of the above forms

32. What is the function of the last line?
(A) to suggest the wisdom in the poet's suggestion
(B) to reemphasize the image in the first line
(C) to help the reader see the poem as an adage
(D) to emphasize the stubborn qualities in man
(E) to show that the central experience in the selection has universality   32. _____

33. The one word that may be selected as the one to disturb the harmony of diction is
(A) horizon
(B) futile
(C) pursuing
(D) accosted
(E) cried

34. The style of this passage is best defined as
(A) oratorical
(B) declamatory
(C) philosophical
(D) simplistic
(E) bombastic

PRACTICE EXAMINATION NINE

Total Time: One Hour
Time begun ..... Time ended ..... Time used .....

DIRECTIONS: This test consists of selections from works of literature. Read each passage carefully, and then answer the questions that follow. The questions are based on their content, form, and style. Refer to the passage as many times as necessary before you choose your answers.

Questions 1–12

"It's not the two thousand I regret," answered the lady, and a big tear rolled down her cheek. "It's the fact itself that revolts me! I cannot put up with thieves in my house. I don't regret it—I regret nothing; but to steal from me is such ingratitude! That's how they repay me for my kindness. . . ."

They all looked into their plates, but Mashenka fancied after the lady's words that every one was looking at her. A lump rose in her throat; she began crying and put her handkerchief to her lips.

"*Pardon*," she muttered. "I can't help it. My head aches. I'll go away."

And she got up from the table, scraping her chair awkwardly, and went out quickly, still more overcome with confusion.

"It's beyond everything!" said Nikolay Sergeitch, frowning. "What need was there to search her room? How out of place it was!"

"I don't say she took the brooch," said Fedosya Vassilyevna, "but can you answer for her? To tell the truth, I haven't much confidence in these learned paupers."

"It really was unsuitable, Fenya. . . . Excuse me, Fenya, but you've no kind of legal right to make a search."

"I know nothing about your laws. All I know is that I've lost my brooch. And I will find the brooch!" She brought her fork down on the plate with a clatter, and her eyes flashed angrily. "And you eat your dinner, and don't interfere in what doesn't concern you!"

Nikolay Sergeitch dropped his eyes mildly and sighed. Meanwhile Mashenka, reaching her room, flung herself on her bed. She felt now neither alarm nor shame, but she felt an intense longing to go slap the cheeks of this hard, arrogant, dull-witted, prosperous woman.

Lying on her bed she breathed into her pillow and dreamed of how nice it would be to go and buy the most expensive brooch and fling it into the face of this bullying woman. If only it were God's will that Fedosya Vassilyevna should come to ruin and wander about begging, and should taste all the horrors of poverty and dependence, and that Mashenka, whom she had insulted, might give her alms! Oh, if only she could come in for a big fortune, could buy a carriage, and could drive noisily past the windows so as to be envied by that woman!

1. Which of the following describes an event that had not taken place before the initial dialogue?
(A) A valuable brooch had disappeared mysteriously.
(B) The mistress of the house had searched the rooms of her employees.
(C) One of the employees had been openly accused of taking the valuable piece of jewelry.
(D) The mistress of the house was greatly distressed by the loss.
(E) The mistress of the house feels that the thief had to be one of her employees.

2. The author characterizes the mistress of the house by the following appellations
(A) lady, Nikolay, Mashenka
(B) Fedosya Vassilyevna, Fenya, Nikolay Sergeitch
(C) Mashenka, Fenya, lady
(D) Fenya, lady, Fedosya Vassilyevna
(E) Nikolay, Fenya, Mashenka

3. Fenya is a
(A) first name
(B) familiar form, a shortened form
(C) formal class name like Miss
(D) last name
(E) middle name

4. The term *learned paupers* implies that Mashenka is
(A) the lady of the house
(B) a poor relative
(C) the husband's secretary
(D) the governess
(E) one of the servants

5. Which of the following best expresses the approach used by the author?

(A) He is an omniscient author who feels free to wander into the thoughts of each of his characters and to comment on them.
(B) He is an objective author who reveals actions and scrupulously avoids taking sides.
(C) He is an expressionistic author who describes all outward action through the consciousness of one of his characters.
(D) He is a realistic author who describes actions objectively but shares the inner feelings of his protagonist without passing judgment.
(E) He is an impressionistic author who describes everything in terms of the effect outer action has on his protagonist.

6. Mashenka's daydream reveals her to be
   (A) jealous of the riches of Fedosya Vassilyevna
   (B) envious of the wealth displayed by others around her
   (C) an old, disillusioned woman
   (D) sensitive to the rights of others
   (E) feeling rejected and degraded

7. Nikolay Sergeitch sees injustice in what had been done to Mashenka and
   (A) demands that such actions be apologized for
   (B) insists that such actions not be repeated
   (C) approves of the harsh measures
   (D) tells the authorities
   (E) sidesteps a confrontation

8. The author's basic means of characterization is
   (A) foreshadowing
   (B) action and dialogue
   (C) use of descriptive adjectives and evaluative statements
   (D) soliloquies
   (E) dramatic irony

9. At this point in the story the main characters are
   (A) static
   (B) dynamic
   (C) stereotypes
   (D) unrealistic
   (E) multi-faceted

10. The word that checks our sympathy from going completely to the lady in the first paragraph is
    (A) thousand
    (B) regret
    (C) thieves
    (D) revolts
    (E) ingratitude

11. The character who will require further refinement of characterization is
    (A) Fenya
    (B) Mashenka
    (C) Nikolay Sergeitch
    (D) Fedosya Vassilyevna
    (E) Sergeitch

12. Dramatic contrast is achieved by
    (A) juxtaposing Mashenka's agitation and politeness with the lady's aggressive insinuations
    (B) Nikolay's telling what was done and what should have been done
    (C) Mashenka's crying in bed when filled with agitation
    (D) the lady's remaining at the table while Mashenka leaves
    (E) juxtaposing the remarks of Fedosya Vassilyevna and those of Nikolay Sergeitch

Questions 13–21

No man's defects sought they to know;
So never made themselves a foe.
No man's good deeds did they commend;
So never raised themselves a friend.
5 Nor cherished they relations poor,
That might decrease their present store;
Nor barn nor house did they repair,
That might oblige their future heir.
     They neither added nor confounded;
10 They neither wanted nor abounded.
Each Christmas they accounts did clear
And wound their skeins round the year.
Nor tear nor smile did they employ
At news of public grief or joy.
15 When bells were rung, and bonfires made,
If asked, they ne'er denied their aid:
Their jug was to the ringers carried,
Whoever either died or married.
Their dry log at the fire was found,
20 Whoever was deposed or crowned.
     Nor good, nor bad, or fools, nor wise;
They would not learn, nor could advise:
Without love, hatred, joy, or fear,
They led—a kind of—as it were:
25 Nor wished, nor cared, nor laughed, nor cried;
And so they lived; and so they died.

13. The couple described in this selection can best be described as
    (A) autocratic
    (B) benevolent
    (C) despotic
    (D) self-centered
    (E) conceited

14. The couple lacked
    (A) ambition
    (B) money
    (C) sense of duty
    (D) relatives
    (E) neighbors

15. Which of the following best expresses the effect of the last line?
    (A) It shows the world's reaction to the couple.
    (B) It makes the poem seem unreal.
    (C) It is anticlimactic.
    (D) It is an ironic afterthought.
    (E) It is a surprising summary.

16. This selection is written in
    (A) free verse
    (B) sonnet form
    (C) rhymed iambic tetrameters
    (D) heroic couplets
    (E) anapestic trimeters

17. The log in line 19 is characterized by *dry* to show
    (A) their selfishness
    (B) their desire to do the right thing
    (C) their lack of concern for others

(D) their extravagance
(E) their stinginess
18. A device not used in this selection is
    (A) simile
    (B) contrast
    (C) rhyme
    (D) alliteration
    (E) assonance
19. According to the poet we become nonentities when we
    (A) praise others for their deeds
    (B) object to the conduct of others
    (C) try to learn from others
    (D) do only the expected
    (E) help others to raise their sights in life
20. The tone of this selection is best termed
    (A) joyful
    (B) amused
    (C) scornful
    (D) solemn
    (E) optimistic
21. This poem could serve as an example of
    (A) a soliloquy
    (B) an allegory
    (C) a dramatic monologue
    (D) a lyric
    (E) a eulogy

Questions 22–27

I feel that you are justified in looking into the future with true assurance, because you have a mode of living in which we find the joy of life and the joy of work harmoniously combined. Added to this is the spirit of ambition which pervades your very being, and seems to make the day's work like a happy child at play.

22. The author's use of *I, you, we* serves to
    (A) show his approval of the actions of the other
    (B) confuse the reader
    (C) show his disapproval of the actions of the other
    (D) show how carefully he has evaluated the deeds of the other
    (E) reveals the double standards under which the author operates
23. Happiness, according to this author, is based on
    (A) ambition
    (B) self-confidence
    (C) zest
    (D) choice of vocation
    (E) leisure time activities
24. The tone of the passage is best termed
    (A) cynical
    (B) amused
    (C) scornful
    (D) dogmatic
    (E) pessimistic
25. The second sentence does not contain
    (A) a cliche
    (B) a simile
    (C) inversion
    (D) apostrophe
    (E) generalization
26. The author develops his thesis through
    (A) example
    (B) data
    (C) digression
    (D) amplification
    (E) none of the above
27. In this selection the author fails to
    (A) be positive
    (B) define his terms
    (C) show the advantages of his idea
    (D) persuade his reader to evaluate his own life aims
    (E) present a model to be followed

Questions 28–33

Everything that is new or uncommon raises a pleasure in the imagination, and because it fills the soul with an agreeable surprise, gratifies its curiosity, and gives it an idea of which it was not before possessed. We are indeed so often conversant with one set of objects and tired out with so many repeated shows of the same things, and whatever is new or uncommon contributes a little to vary human life, and to divert our minds, for a while, with the strangeness of its appearance: it serves us for a kind of refreshment, and takes off that satiety we are apt to complain of in our usual and ordinary entertainments. It is this that bestows charms on a monster, and makes even the imperfections of nature please us. It is this that recommends variety, and where the mind is every instant called off to something new, and the attention not suffered to dwell too long, and waste itself on any particular object. It is this, likewise, that improves what is great or beautiful, and makes it afford the mind a double entertainment. Groves, fields, and meadows are at any season of the year pleasant to look upon but never so much as in the opening of the spring, when they are all new and fresh, with their first gloss upon them, and not yet too much accustomed and familiar to the eye. For this reason there is nothing that more enlivens a prospect than rivers, sprays of water from ornamental fountains, or waterfalls, where the scene is perpetually shifting and entertaining the sight every moment with something that is new. We are quickly tired with looking upon hills and valleys, where everything continues fixed and settled in the same place and posture, but find our thoughts a little agitated and relieved at the sight of such objects as are ever in motion and sliding away from beneath the eye of the beholder.

28. Which of the following contains the principal idea of the selection?
    (A) Whatever is new or novel is more worthwhile than that which is old and worn.
    (B) Newness makes a thing interesting.
    (C) We must beware of changing the old for the new just to achieve variety.
    (D) There is nothing new under the sun but change makes it so.
    (E) We cannot evaluate the worth of an item until it has grown out of its newness.

29. Which of the following describes the development of the ideas in this passage.
    (A) The thought moves by association, from one aspect to another as the author sees some connection between the parts, a connection not obvious to the reader.

(B) The thought moves from a generalization to an application of the generalization to a final summation of the thought.
(C) The thought moves from a generalization to a series of insights called forth to prove the generalization which is further refined in the final sentence.
(D) The thought moves from specific to specific example until the author has evolved enough proof to carry his final generalization.
(E) The thought moves in chronological order from event to event in a time sequence until all is summarized in the final sentence.

30. The tone of this passage is
    (A) argumentative
    (B) hopeful
    (C) humorous
    (D) scornful
    (E) dogmatic

31. Which of the following best expresses the purpose of the third sentence, beginning with "It is this that bestows. . . ."
    (A) It is the sentence that begins the second series of ideas in the selection.
    (B) It offers an example to prove the truth in the author's thesis.
    (C) It offers an insight to prove the truth of the preceding statements.
    (D) It is a generalization that further refines the author's thesis.
    (E) It is a logical thought-sequence in the steps leading to a full development of the author's thesis.

32. The author's implied purpose in this selection was to
    (A) entertain the reader
    (B) improve the reader's sense of right and wrong
    (C) prevent the reader from making mistakes
    (D) convince the reader to follow a cause
    (E) to reveal an insight

33. We find fountains fascinating because
    (A) of the symmetry of the waterfall
    (B) of the symmetry of the pedestal
    (C) of the symmetry of water and monument combined into a unit
    (D) of the movement of the water
    (E) of the beauty of nature

PRACTICE EXAMINATION TEN

Total Time: One Hour
Time begun . . . . . Time ended . . . . . Time used . . . . .

DIRECTIONS: This test consists of selections from works of literature. Read each passage carefully, and then answer the questions that follow. The questions are based on their content, form, and style. Refer to the passage as many times as necessary before you choose your answers.

Questions 1–8

> There is a pleasure in the pathless woods,
> There is a rapture on the lonely shore,
> There is society, where none intrudes,
> 4   By the deep Sea, and music in its roar:
> I love not Man the less, but Nature more,
> From these our interviews, in which I steal
> From all I may be, or have been before,
> 8   To mingle with the Universe, and feel
> What I can ne'er express, yet cannot all
>   conceal.

1. The interviews discussed are
   (A) with his fellow man
   (B) with the sea
   (C) with the woods
   (D) with society
   (E) with nature

2. Which of the following expresses the poet's principal thought?
   (A) Contact with man corrupts the soul.
   (B) Joys of nature can be absorbed by man.
   (C) Contact with nature brings us close to a oneness with the Universe.
   (D) Only by expressing his feelings in words can the poet communicate with his fellow men
   (E) Man can better his position in society through contacts with nature.

3. Line 1 contains an example of
   (A) poetic license
   (B) fustian
   (C) allegory
   (D) alliteration
   (E) cliche

4. Which of the following best defines the function of the repetition in the first three lines?
   (A) It sets a note of sincerity for the reader.
   (B) It clarifies the author's purpose.
   (C) It slows down the flow of images in the poem.
   (D) It adds a note of cacophony to attract the attention of the reader.
   (E) It adds a note of simplicity to a complex idea.

5. Line 3 contains an example of
   (A) inner rhyme
   (B) oxymoron
   (C) simile
   (D) sarcasm
   (E) verisimilitude

6. The poem is written in
   (A) heroic couplets
   (B) ballad quatrains
   (C) blank verse
   (D) sonnet form
   (E) none of the above

7. The tone of this selection is
   (A) mystical
   (B) ironic
   (C) humorous
   (D) skeptical
   (E) destructive

8. Line 5 does not contain
   (A) contrast
   (B) balance
   (C) generalization
   (D) metaphor
   (E) alliteration

Questions 9–15

Yet let us ponder boldly—'tis a base
Abandonment of reason to resign
Our right of thought—our last and only place
4   Of refuge; this, at least, shall still be mine:
Though from our birth the faculty divine
Is chain'd and tortured—cabin'd, cribb'd, confined,
And bred in darkness, lest the truth should shine
8   Too brightly on the unprepared mind,
The beam pours in, for time and skill will couch the blind.

9. This poem is written in
   (A) free verse
   (B) Petrarchan sonnet form
   (C) heroic couplets
   (D) ballad quatrains
   (E) blank verse
10. Which of the following best expresses the poet's main idea?
    (A) Education leads us to intellectual freedom.
    (B) Thinking without goals to aim at is a sterile accomplishment.
    (C) Thinking alone can free man.
    (D) Divine faculties are lost when we are imprisoned.
    (E) We must seek refuge from base abandonment.
11. Which of the following best expresses the thought development found in the selection?
    (A) The poet uses negative proofs to support his initial premise and final conclusion.
    (B) The author follows the topic sentence with specific examples to prove that and his final summation.
    (C) The poet connects cause and effect in several instances to prove the truth in his final statement.
    (D) The poet begins with an insight and follows that with several generalizations to prove its truth.
    (E) A chronological sequence of events are summarized until the climax of the thought pattern is reached in the last line.
12. The poet makes use of repetition in line 6 to
    (A) emphasize the power of the mind
    (B) emphasize the powers of evil
    (C) to slow down the flow of his thoughts
    (D) to pile up image after image to clarify his concepts
    (E) give as large a scope to the enumeration of the forces of ignorance
13. The poet contends that
    (A) society should protect the young from mature thoughts
    (B) there is no danger in planning boldly
    (C) society cripples our ability to think during the educational process
    (D) thinking cannot cause any permanent damage to the thinker
    (E) thoughts can be dangerous
14. A synonym for the word *base* in the first line is
    (A) fundamental
    (B) correct
    (C) evil
    (D) righteous
    (E) erroneous
15. Line 6 contains
    (A) onomatapoeia
    (B) paradox
    (C) litotes
    (D) cliche
    (E) alliteration

Questions 16–20

It is natural for man to indulge in the illusions of hope. We are apt to shut our eyes against a painful truth, and listen to the song of the siren till she transforms us into beasts. Is this the part of wise men, engaged in a great and arduous struggle for liberty? Are we disposed to be of the number of those who having eyes see not, and having ears hear not the things which so nearly concern their temporal salvation?

For my part, whatever anguish of spirit it may cost, I will to know the whole truth—to know the worst and to provide for it.

16. The writer equates the "illusions of hope" with
    (A) the search for truth
    (B) temporal salvation
    (C) anguish of spirit
    (D) painful truth
    (E) false interpretations
17. If we are to have liberty, we must
    (A) have anguish of spirit
    (B) have illusions
    (C) have hope
    (D) know the facts
    (E) have courage
18. The third sentence does not contain an example of
    (A) oxymoron
    (B) rhetorical question
    (C) parallelism
    (D) cliche
    (E) generalization
19. The advantage in knowing the truth is that
    (A) we can then struggle for liberty
    (B) we can disregard hope
    (C) we can provide for all possibilities
    (D) we can overcome the worst
    (E) we will not be beasts
20. Which of the following statements describes the pattern of thought in this selection?
    (A) The author uses logic to combine the flow of thought from one sentence to the next, equating hope and truth in terms of liberty.
    (B) The author uses examples to prove the contention in his initial sentence.
    (C) The author contrasts liberty with truth and

hope to arrive at the conclusion found in his last sentence.
(D) The author develops the thought content by going off into digressions that are not related to the topic sentence.
(E) The author uses analogy to go from example to final generalization.

Questions 21–28

The division of Europe into a number of independent states, connected, however, with each other, by the general resemblance of religion, language, and manners, is productive of the most beneficial consequences to the liberty of mankind. A modern tyrant, who should find no resistance either in his own breast, or in his people, would soon experience a gentle restraint from the example of his equals, the dread of present censure, the advice of his allies, and the apprehension of his enemies. The object of his displeasure, escaping from the narrow limits of his dominions, would easily obtain, in a happier climate, a secure refuge, a new fortune adequate to his merit, the freedom of complaint, and perhaps the means of revenge. But the empire of the Romans filled the world, and when that empire fell into the hands of a single person, the world became a safe and dreary prison for his enemies. The slave of Imperial despotism, whether he was condemned to drag his gilded chain in Rome and the senate, or to wear out a life of exile on the barren rock of Seriphus, or the frozen banks of the Danube, expected his fate in silent despair. To resist was fatal, and it was impossible to fly. On every side he was encompassed with a vast extent of sea and land, which he could never hope to traverse without being discovered, seized, and restored to his irritated master. Beyond the frontiers, his anxious view could discover nothing, except the ocean, inhospitable deserts, hostile tribes of barbarians, of fierce manners and unknown language, or dependent kings, who would gladly purchase the emperor's protection by the sacrifice of an obnoxious fugitive. "Wherever you are," said Cicero to the exiled Marcellus, "remember that you are equally within the power of the conqueror."

21. Which of the following contains the principal idea of this selection?
    (A) Europe of today is better than the Europe of Rome because of the many different states.
    (B) Liberty survives better in a world of many nations than in a world empire.
    (C) Emperors can punish more relentlessly than kings.
    (D) The slaves of Roman despotism could not escape punishment.
    (E) The Romans were less humane than are the citizens of modern Europe.

22. Which of the following expresses the purpose of the final sentence?
    (A) The author used authority to prove the cruelty of Roman rulers.
    (B) The author brings in an irrelevance to show his scholarship.
    (C) The author cites an authority to prove how all controlling Rome was.
    (D) The author uses the quotation to summarize his thesis.
    (E) The author uses contrast to prove his initial statement.

23. A device used in the first sentence is
    (A) balance
    (B) litotes
    (C) dramatic irony
    (D) rhetorical question
    (E) cliche

24. The independent states protect liberty better than could Rome because
    (A) one country could declare war on another
    (B) a refugee could be extradited
    (C) one country could overcome another
    (D) an escaped rebel could set up forces for liberation in the safety of another country
    (E) the tyrant could have a treaty that would cause the other countries to drive out his enemies

25. There was no hope for rebellion against Rome because
    (A) the rulers were ruthless
    (B) there was no place to flee
    (C) the people were too loyal
    (D) the nations feared Rome too much
    (E) the known world was too small

26. Which of the following expresses the thought pattern followed by the author of this selection?
    (A) He set up two premises, one dealing with modern Europe and the other with ancient Rome and then gave examples to prove his contentions.
    (B) He developed a chronological sequence to tie events together, leading to the climax in his final sentence.
    (C) He used amplification, stating a premise in his first sentence and then explaining the premise in other words in each of the following sentences.
    (D) He connected cause and effect, balancing one sentence with the next to build to his final premise.
    (E) He logically builds on facts stated in his first sentence and avoiding facts and examples uses logical proof to derive the thought presented in his final sentence.

27. The tone of the passage is best termed
    (A) joyous
    (B) cynical
    (C) destructive
    (D) solemn
    (E) scornful

28. The diction and style of this passage are best defined as
    (A) allegorical and stately
    (B) emotional and judgmental
    (C) studied and scholarly
    (D) floridly oratorical
    (E) abstract and philosophical

Questions 29–34

Never love unless you can
Bear with all the faults of man!
Men sometimes will jealous be,
Though but little cause they see,
And hang the head in discontent,
6   And speak what straight they will repent.

Men that but one saint adore,
Make a show of love to more;
Beauty must be scorned in none,
Though but truly served in one:
For what is courtship but disguise?
12 True hearts may have dissembling eyes.
Men, when their affairs require,
Must awhile themselves retire;
Sometimes hunt, and sometimes hawk,
And not ever sit and talk:—
If these and such-like you can bear,
18 Then like, and love, and never fear!

29. One fault of man not mentioned in the selection is
    (A) men often tell untruths to their beloved
    (B) men are sometimes jealous of their beloved
    (C) men will sometimes pay attention to another while still thinking themselves loyal to their beloved
    (D) men tend to be too truthful when asked a direct question
    (E) men cannot long be idle in talk, but must have games and sports

30. This selection does not contain at least one line that can be classified as
    (A) trimeter
    (B) tetrameter
    (C) pentameter
    (D) unrhymed
    (E) containing one iambic foot

31. The diction in this selection can best be defined as
    (A) floridly oratorical
    (B) studiedly colloquial
    (C) didactic and exhortative
    (D) abstract and philosophical
    (E) argumentative and emotional

32. The tone of the selection can best be interpreted as
    (A) sophisticated
    (B) scornful
    (C) naive
    (D) cynical
    (E) optimistic

33. The poet in this poem assumes
    (A) that not all men react in the same fashion
    (B) that all men resemble courtiers in courting
    (C) all courtship contains elements of cheating
    (D) love is an irresistible force
    (E) men are inconsistent

34. A premise upon which the poet based his advice is that
    (A) the beloved is a saintly person
    (B) no woman can love a man who is jealous
    (C) women prefer men who hunt and fish
    (D) women normally do not know the faults of their beloved
    (E) love does not have its base in ordinary emotions and routines of life

ANSWERS TO PRACTICE EXAMINATIONS

ANSWER KEY: PRACTICE EXAMINATION ONE / Page 196

1. (D)	6. (C)	11. (B)	16. (A)	21. (E)	26. (E)	31. (B)
2. (E)	7. (D)	12. (C)	17. (D)	22. (D)	27. (D)	32. (E)
3. (E)	8. (B)	13. (C)	18. (D)	23. (C)	28. (D)	33. (D)
4. (A)	9. (E)	14. (E)	19. (A)	24. (A)	29. (A)	
5. (E)	10. (A)	15. (B)	20. (C)	25. (E)	30. (C)	

Summary of Results

Number Correct _____

Number Wrong _____

Number Omitted _____

Self-appraisal Chart

Total Correct	Percentile
31–33	99
28	90
15	50
12	25

Conversion Chart

The total number correct on the Literature Test is converted to a scaled score ranging from 20 to 80. This conversion enables you to compare your results with those of all other candidates who have taken the test. Half of the scores fall above 50, half fall below. Two-thirds of the candidates score between 40 and 69. The more competitive schools usually prefer candidates who achieve 65 or above.

The following conversion chart can give you a rough approximation of what your Literature score would be for this practice exam.

Number Correct	Test Score	Number Correct	Test Score	Number Correct	Test Score	Number Correct	Test Score	Number Correct	Test Score
33	80	29	73	25	64	22	69	19	57
32	79	28	70	24	63	21	59	18	53
31	77	27	68	23	61	20	58	17	51
30	75	26	67						

ANSWER KEY: PRACTICE EXAMINATION TWO / Page 199

1. (E)	6. (E)	11. (A)	15. (E)	19. (A)	23. (E)	27. (C)
2. (D)	7. (D)	12. (B)	16. (D)	20. (E)	24. (C)	28. (A)
3. (A)	8. (E)	13. (B)	17. (E)	21. (C)	25. (B)	29. (C)
4. (C)	9. (B)	14. (B)	18. (D)	22. (D)	26. (E)	30. (E)
5. (D)	10. (D)					

Summary of Results

Number Correct _____

Number Wrong _____

Number Omitted _____

Self-appraisal Chart

Total Correct	Percentile
29–30	99
25	90
16	50
10	10

Conversion Chart

The total number correct on the Literature Test is converted to a scaled score ranging from 20 to 80. This conversion enables you to compare your results with those of all other candidates who have taken the test. Half of the scores fall above 50, half fall below. Two-thirds of the candidates score between 40 and 69. The more competitive schools usually prefer candidates who achieve 65 or above.

The following conversion chart can give you a rough approximation of what your Literature score would be for this practice exam.

Number Correct	Test Score	Number Correct	Test Score	Number Correct	Test Score	Number Correct	Test Score	Number Correct	Test Score
30	80	27	74	24	67	21	60	19	54
29	79	26	73	23	64	20	57	18	51
28	77	25	70	22	63				

PRACTICE EXAMINATIONS IN LITERATURE

ANSWER KEY: PRACTICE EXAMINATION THREE / Page 202

1. (D)	7. (C)	12. (E)	17. (C)	22. (B)	27. (E)	32. (E)
2. (E)	8. (A)	13. (B)	18. (B)	23. (D)	28. (E)	33. (A)
3. (E)	9. (A)	14. (A)	19. (B)	24. (E)	29. (A)	34. (B)
4. (C)	10. (E)	15. (D)	20. (E)	25. (A)	30. (C)	35. (E)
5. (D)	11. (E)	16. (D)	21. (B)	26. (D)	31. (C)	36. (D)
6. (C)						

Summary of Results

Number Correct _____

Number Wrong _____

Number Omitted _____

Self-appraisal Chart

Total Correct	Percentile
33–36	99
30	90
17	50
10	25

Conversion Chart

The total number correct on the Literature Test is converted to a scaled score ranging from 20 to 80. This conversion enables you to compare your results with those of all other candidates who have taken the test. Half of the scores fall above 50, half fall below. Two-thirds of the candidates score between 40 and 69. The more competitive schools usually prefer candidates who achieve 65 or above.

The following conversion chart can give you a rough approximation of what your Literature score would be for this practice exam.

Number Correct	Test Score	Number Correct	Test Score	Number Correct	Test Score	Number Correct	Test Score	Number Correct	Test Score
36	80	32	75	28	63	25	57	22	54
35	79	31	73	27	60	24	56	21	53
34	79	30	70	26	59	23	55	20	51
33	78	29	67						

ANSWER KEY: PRACTICE EXAMINATION FOUR / Page 205

1. (A)	6. (A)	10. (D)	14. (C)	18. (A)	22. (D)	26. (D)
2. (D)	7. (E)	11. (E)	15. (B)	19. (C)	23. (D)	27. (C)
3. (E)	8. (B)	12. (C)	16. (D)	20. (E)	24. (E)	28. (B)
4. (B)	9. (B)	13. (C)	17. (B)	21. (B)	25. (E)	29. (A)
5. (E)						

Summary of Results

Number Correct _____

Number Wrong _____

Number Omitted _____

Self-appraisal Chart

Total Correct	Percentile
28–29	99
24	90
16	50
10	10

Conversion Chart

The total number correct on the Literature Test is converted to a scaled score ranging from 20 to 80. This conversion enables you to compare your results with those of all other candidates who have taken the test. Half of the scores fall above 50, half fall below. Two-thirds of the candidates score between 40 and 69. The more competitive schools usually prefer candidates who achieve 65 or above.

The following conversion chart can give you a rough approximation of what your Literature score would be for this practice exam.

Number Correct	Test Score	Number Correct	Test Score	Number Correct	Test Score	Number Correct	Test Score	Number Correct	Test Score
29	80	26	75	23	67	21	60	19	53
28	79	25	73	22	63	20	57	18	49
27	76	24	70						

ANSWER KEY: PRACTICE EXAMINATION FIVE / Page 208

1. (B)	7. (A)	13. (E)	19. (B)	25. (D)	31. (E)	36. (C)
2. (D)	8. (B)	14. (D)	20. (E)	26. (C)	32. (B)	37. (E)
3. (C)	9. (A)	15. (E)	21. (C)	27. (D)	33. (A)	38. (E)
4. (E)	10. (B)	16. (A)	22. (E)	28. (D)	34. (C)	39. (D)
5. (E)	11. (D)	17. (E)	23. (D)	29. (C)	35. (E)	40. (D)
6. (C)	12. (C)	18. (C)	24. (B)	30. (B)		

Summary of Results

Number Correct _____

Number Wrong _____

Number Omitted _____

Self-appraisal Chart

Total Correct	Percentile
37–40	99
34	90
24	50
17	10

Conversion Chart

The total number correct on the Literature Test is converted to a scaled score ranging from 20 to 80. This conversion enables you to compare your results with those of all other candidates who have taken the test. Half of the scores fall above 50, half fall below. Two-thirds of the candidates score between 40 and 69. The more competitive schools usually prefer candidates who achieve 65 or above.

The following conversion chart can give you a rough approximation of what your Literature score would be for this practice exam.

Number Correct	Test Score	Number Correct	Test Score	Number Correct	Test Score	Number Correct	Test Score	Number Correct	Test Score
40	80	37	78	34	70	31	64	28	54
39	79	36	76	33	68	30	61	27	51
38	78	35	73	32	67	29	58		

ANSWER KEY: PRACTICE EXAMINATION SIX / Page 212

1. (D)	6. (D)	11. (D)	15. (E)	19. (C)	23. (E)	27. (B)
2. (B)	7. (C)	12. (C)	16. (E)	20. (D)	24. (D)	28. (D)
3. (C)	8. (B)	13. (A)	17. (A)	21. (C)	25. (E)	29. (E)
4. (E)	9. (B)	14. (B)	18. (A)	22. (B)	26. (C)	30. (C)
5. (A)	10. (D)					

Summary of Results

Number Correct _____

Number Wrong _____

Number Omitted _____

Self-appraisal Chart

Total Correct	Percentile
28–30	99
26	90
17	50
11	25

Conversion Chart

The total number correct on the Literature Test is converted to a scaled score ranging from 20 to 80. This conversion enables you to compare your results with those of all other candidates who have taken the test. Half of the scores fall above 50, half fall below. Two-thirds of the candidates score between 40 and 69. The more competitive schools usually prefer candidates who achieve 65 or above.

The following conversion chart can give you a rough approximation of what your Literature score would be for this practice exam.

Number Correct	Test Score	Number Correct	Test Score	Number Correct	Test Score	Number Correct	Test Score	Number Correct	Test Score
30	80	27	74	24	65	22	59	20	53
29	79	26	70	23	63	21	56	19	50
28	78	25	67						

PRACTICE EXAMINATIONS IN LITERATURE

ANSWER KEY: PRACTICE EXAMINATION SEVEN / Page 215

1. (D)	6. (C)	11. (B)	16. (E)	21. (D)	26. (A)	30. (B)
2. (B)	7. (E)	12. (A)	17. (B)	22. (E)	27. (B)	31. (C)
3. (D)	8. (E)	13. (E)	18. (C)	23. (D)	28. (C)	32. (C)
4. (A)	9. (C)	14. (C)	19. (E)	24. (A)	29. (A)	33. (B)
5. (E)	10. (E)	15. (B)	20. (D)	25. (E)		

Summary of Results

Number Correct _____

Number Wrong _____

Number Omitted _____

Self-appraisal Chart

Total Correct	Percentile
32–33	99
28	90
16	50
11	25

Conversion Chart

The total number correct on the Literature Test is converted to a scaled score ranging from 20 to 80. This conversion enables you to compare your results with those of all other candidates who have taken the test. Half of the scores fall above 50, half fall below. Two-thirds of the candidates score between 40 and 69. The more competitive schools usually prefer candidates who achieve 65 or above.

The following conversion chart can give you a rough approximation of what your Literature score would be for this practice exam.

Number Correct	Test Score	Number Correct	Test Score	Number Correct	Test Score	Number Correct	Test Score	Number Correct	Test Score
33	80	29	72	26	68	23	62	20	57
32	79	28	70	25	66	22	60	19	54
31	78	27	69	24	65	21	60	18	50
30	75								

ANSWER KEY: PRACTICE EXAMINATION EIGHT / Page 218

1. (D)	6. (E)	11. (D)	16. (E)	21. (B)	26. (A)	31. (C)
2. (B)	7. (E)	12. (A)	17. (D)	22. (E)	27. (C)	32. (B)
3. (D)	8. (A)	13. (E)	18. (B)	23. (C)	28. (C)	33. (D)
4. (D)	9. (B)	14. (A)	19. (C)	24. (E)	29. (E)	34. (D)
5. (B)	10. (C)	15. (B)	20. (C)	25. (E)	30. (B)	

Summary of Results

Number Correct _____

Number Wrong _____

Number Omitted _____

Self-appraisal Chart

Total Correct	Percentile
31–34	99
27	90
16	50
12	25

Conversion Chart

The total number correct on the Literature Test is converted to a scaled score ranging from 20 to 80. This conversion enables you to compare your results with those of all other candidates who have taken the test. Half of the scores fall above 50, half fall below. Two-thirds of the candidates score between 40 and 69. The more competitive schools usually prefer candidates who achieve 65 or above.

The following conversion chart can give you a rough approximation of what your Literature score would be for this practice exam.

Number Correct	Test Score	Number Correct	Test Score	Number Correct	Test Score	Number Correct	Test Score	Number Correct	Test Score
34	80	31	78	28	72	25	65	22	57
33	79	30	75	27	70	24	63	21	54
32	79	29	74	26	68	23	60	20	51

ANSWER KEY: PRACTICE EXAMINATION NINE / Page 221

1. (C)   6. (E)   11. (D)   16. (C)   21. (E)   26. (E)   30. (E)
2. (D)   7. (E)   12. (A)   17. (B)   22. (A)   27. (B)   31. (C)
3. (B)   8. (B)   13. (D)   18. (A)   23. (E)   28. (B)   32. (E)
4. (D)   9. (B)   14. (A)   19. (D)   24. (D)   29. (C)   33. (D)
5. (E) 10. (E)   15. (E)   20. (C)   25. (D)

Summary of Results

Number Correct _____
Number Wrong _____
Number Omitted _____

Self-appraisal Chart

Total Correct	Percentile
33	99
27	90
16	50
12	25

Conversion Chart

The total number correct on the Literature Test is converted to a scaled score ranging from 20 to 80. This conversion enables you to compare your results with those of all other candidates who have taken the test. Half of the scores fall above 50, half fall below. Two-thirds of the candidates score between 40 and 69. The more competitive schools usually prefer candidates who achieve 65 or above.

The following conversion chart can give you a rough approximation of what your Literature score would be for this practice exam.

Number Correct	Test Score	Number Correct	Test Score	Number Correct	Test Score	Number Correct	Test Score	Number Correct	Test Score
33	80	29	74	26	68	23	58	20	53
32	78	28	73	25	64	22	56	19	52
31	75	27	70	24	61	21	55	18	52
30	74								

ANSWER KEY: PRACTICE EXAMINATION TEN / Page 224

1. (E)   6. (E)   11. (A)   16. (E)   21. (B)   26. (A)   31. (B)
2. (C)   7. (A)   12. (E)   17. (D)   22. (C)   27. (D)   32. (A)
3. (D)   8. (D)   13. (D)   18. (D)   23. (A)   28. (C)   33. (B)
4. (A)   9. (C)   14. (C)   19. (C)   24. (D)   29. (D)   34. (A)
5. (B) 10. (C)   15. (E)   20. (A)   25. (B)   30. (C)

Summary of Results

Number Correct _____
Number Wrong _____
Number Omitted _____

Self-appraisal chart

Total Correct	Percentile
32–34	99
28	90
17	50
13	25

Conversion Chart

The total number correct on the Literature Test is converted to a scaled score ranging from 20 to 80. This conversion enables you to compare your results with those of all other candidates who have taken the test. Half of the scores fall above 50, half fall below. Two-thirds of the candidates score between 40 and 69. The more competitive schools usually prefer candidates who achieve 65 or above.

The following conversion chart can give you a rough approximation of what your Literature score would be for this practice exam.

Number Correct	Test Score	Number Correct	Test Score	Number Correct	Test Score	Number Correct	Test Score	Number Correct	Test Score
34	80	31	75	28	70	25	63	22	55
33	79	30	74	27	68	24	59	21	54
32	78	29	73	26	65	23	58	20	51

The leading SAT Study Guide

Revised Tenth Edition
Samuel C. Brownstein and Mitchel Weiner
672 pp. $5.95 pa. $15.00 cl.
Complete preparation for the SAT,
PSAT/NMSQT, ACT, and College Board
Achievement Tests

6 Model Examinations: Practice your skills and preview your results. With sample questions that help you discover your weak spots and develop your strengths.
Includes: VERBAL APTITUDE TEST
MATHEMATICAL APTITUDE TEST
TEST OF STANDARD WRITTEN ENGLISH

Self-Instructional Study Plans: Specially designed study programs for the three parts of the examination. These are systematic methods of reviewing and improving your score.

Math Review: 950 practice questions on arithmetic, fractions, decimals, percent, geometry, coordinate geometry

Verbal Review: 1000 questions on vocabulary /
125 sentence completion drills;
100 word relationship practice items/
175 reading comprehension questions

Grammar Refresher: The fundamentals of basic English, as required by most colleges. With practice exercises that strengthen skills in grammar and usage.

Also: With typical CEEB Achievement Tests in the following subjects:
English Composition
(including the new Essay Portion),
Math Level 1, Biology, Physics, Chemistry,
French, German, Spanish

Also available:

**HOW TO PREPARE FOR
COLLEGE ENTRANCE EXAMS
(SAT) POCKET EDITION**

Brownstein & Weiner; pa., $2.50
Brief preparatory course for the SAT with a model test; answers explained.

At your local bookseller or order direct adding 10% postage plus applicable sales tax.
BARRON'S EDUCATIONAL SERIES, INC.,
113 Crossways Park Drive, Woodbury, N.Y. 11797

BARRON'S GUIDES TO COLLEGES, BETTER GRADES, HIGHER SCORES

☐ **PROFILES OF AMERICAN COLLEGES, Volume One: Descriptions of the Colleges.** In-depth descriptions of over 1400 fully accredited four-year colleges, including facts on costs, programs of study, admissions requirements, student life, and campus atmosphere. America's most complete college guide. $9.95

☐ **PROFILES OF AMERICAN COLLEGES, Volume Two: Index to Major Areas of Study.** How to locate the colleges with the courses you want to take. Easy-to-use chart format shows the programs offered at over 1400 colleges. $8.95

☐ **THE MIDWEST:** Illinois, Indiana, Iowa, Kansas, Michigan, Minnesota, Missouri, Nebraska, North Dakota, Ohio, South Dakota, Wisconsin. $5.75

☐ **THE NORTHEAST:** Connecticut, Delaware, District of Columbia, Maine, Maryland, Massachusetts, New Jersey, New Hampshire, New York, Pennsylvania, Rhode Island, Vermont. $5.75

☐ **THE SOUTH:** Alabama, Arkansas, Florida, Georgia, Kentucky, Louisiana, Mississippi, North Carolina, Oklahoma, Puerto Rico, South Carolina, Tennessee, Texas, Virginia, West Virginia. $5.75

☐ **THE WEST:** Alaska, Arizona, California, Colorado, Hawaii, Idaho, Montana, Nevada, New Mexico, Oregon, Utah, Washington. $5.75

☐ **GUIDE TO THE TWO-YEAR COLLEGES, Volume 1.** Descriptions of over 1200 two-year colleges. Requiremnts, costs, enrollment, programs. $6.95

☐ **GUIDE TO THE TWO-YEAR COLLEGES, Volume 2.** Occupational Program Selector. Listings of majors available at the nation's two-year colleges. In chart form for easy use. $4.50

☐ **HANDBOOK OF AMERICAN COLLEGE FINANCIAL AID,** by Proia and DiGaspari. Data on financial aid at over 1400 four-year colleges, including grants, scholarships, and loans. $8.50

☐ **HANDBOOK OF JUNIOR AND COMMUNITY COLLEGE FINANCIAL AID,** by Proia and DiGaspari. Financial aid information for over 1200 two-year colleges. $8.50

☐ **HOW TO PREPARE FOR THE MEDICAL COLLEGE ADMISSIONS TEST (MCAT)** by Cibes, Guyer, Hannum, and Seibel. Extensive practice and review offered in all aspects of the test. Six full-length model tests. $6.50

☐ **GETTING INTO MEDICAL SCHOOL,** by Brown. Provides the inside story on the medical school admission process, as well as a directory of American medical schools. Features data on admissions for minorities and women. $3.95

☐ **HOW TO PREPARE FOR THE AMERICAN COLLEGE TESTING PROGRAM (ACT),** edited by Shapiro. Covers all four ACT subject areas—English, Math, Social Studies, and Natural Science—with complete review and practice tests. $5.50

☐ **MATHEMATICS WORKBOOK FOR COLLEGE ENTRANCE EXAMINATIONS** by Brownstein. Provides intensive drill, practice exercises, problems, quantitative comparison. 10 model exams. $5.95

☐ **METRIC CONVERSION TABLES.** A convenient book of tables for quick and efficient conversion from the customary to metric system. For students, business people, consumers, travelers. $4.50 pa.

☐ **BETTER GRADES IN COLLEGE WITH LESS EFFORT,** by Kenneth A. Green. How to survive in college without killing yourself. Practical, legitimate tips and shortcuts to better grades with less hassle. $2.95

☐ **HANDBOOK OF COLLEGE TRANSFER INFORMATION** by Proia. Admissions data for over 1300 colleges accepting transfer students—degree requirements, deadlines, costs, housing. $5.50

☐ **VERBAL APTITUDE WORKBOOK FOR COLLEGE ENTRANCE EXAMINATIONS** by Weiner. Preparation for college boards and all admission, placement, and scholarship exams where word usage and understanding are tested. $3.75

☐ **STUDY TIPS: How to Study Effectively and Get Better Grades** by Armstrong. Organize study time and develop good learning skills; read faster with understanding; achieve a good writing style. $2.50

☐ **HOW TO PREPARE FOR LAW SCHOOL ADMISSION TEST (LSAT),** by Epstein, Horvath, Shostak, and Troy. A review of all aspects of the test for the prospective law student. Three sample exams, all with answers explained and complete descriptions of more than 140 approved law schools. $6.95

☐ **GUIDE TO MEDICAL, DENTAL AND ALLIED HEALTH SCIENCE CAREERS,** by Wischnitzer. Descriptions of AMA-accredited schools with data on admissions, curriculum offerings, and facilities. With a model MCAT. Also includes data on dental schools, sample DAT questions; careers in health. $6.50

☐ **WRITING THE HISTORY PAPER: THE STUDENT'S RESEARCH GUIDE,** by David Sanderlin. Clearly explains the goals of historical research, how to organize a topical paper, and how to express one's thoughts on paper. With detailed appendices which offer the sources for research. $2.50

HOW TO PREPARE FOR COLLEGE BOARD ACHIEVEMENT TEST series. This series can be used to supplement textbooks, clear up difficult areas, and diagnose your weak spots and test your progress. Each volume includes model exams with answers.

☐ **BIOLOGY,** $5.75
☐ **CHEMISTRY,** $5.50
☐ **ENGLISH,** $3.95
☐ **EUROPEAN HISTORY AND WORLD CULTURES,** $6.95
☐ **FRENCH,** $3.
☐ **GERMAN,** $4.50
☐ **LATIN,** $3.95
☐ **MATH LEVEL I,** $5.50
☐ **MATH LEVEL II,** $5.95
☐ **PHYSICS,** $5.95
☐ **SOCIAL STUDIES/AMERICAN HISTORY,** $5.95
☐ **SPANISH,** $4.50

Barron's Educational Series, Inc.
113 Crossways Pk. Dr., Woodbury, N.Y. 11797

Please send me the books checked above.

Name _____
Address _____
City _____
State _____ Zip Code _____

All prices subject to change without notice. Please enclose check or money order with order for books. Add applicable sales tax. Also add 10% transportation charges.